Prisoner of the Vatican

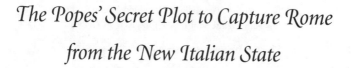

The Popes' Secret Plot to Capture Rome from the New Italian State

David I. Kertzer

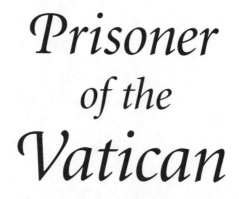

HOUGHTON MIFFLIN COMPANY

BOSTON · NEW YORK

2004

To little Sammy Bear

with hopes for the next generation

For information about permission to reproduce selections from
this book, write to Permissions, Houghton Mifflin Company,
215 Park Avenue South, New York, New York 10003.

Visit our Web site: www.houghtonmifflinbooks.com.

Library of Congress Cataloging-in-Publication Data
Kertzer, David I., date.
Prisoner of the Vatican : the popes' secret plot to capture
Rome from the new Italian state / David I. Kertzer.
p.   cm.
Includes bibliographical references (p.) and index.
ISBN 0-618-22442-4
1. Pius IX, Pope, 1792–1878. 2. Leo XIII, Pope, 1810–1903. 3. Garibaldi,
Giuseppe, 1807–1882. 4. Roman question. 5. Popes—Temporal
power. 6. Church and state—Italy. 7. Rome (Italy)—Annexation
to Italy, 1870. 8. Rome (Italy)—History—1870–1945. I. Title.
DG798.7.K47 2005 945'.63084—dc22 2004054097

Printed in the United States of America

BOOK DESIGN BY ROBERT OVERHOLTZER

MAPS BY JACQUES CHAZAUD

QUM 10 9 8 7 6 5 4 3 2 1

Contents

Maps and Illustrations

Prologue

THE PRIME MINISTER could no longer deny the obvious: a political disaster was taking place in the streets of Rome. The small, private funeral procession carrying Pius IX's mortal remains to their final resting place was turning out to be neither small nor private. As midnight approached, he learned that 100,000 people had converged on St. Peter's Square, spilling into the surrounding streets. Agostino Depretis, who had come to power five years earlier in the historic victory of the left, had agreed to the late time, thinking that a procession at that hour would attract less public attention. He now saw how wrong he had been. How could he not have realized the potential for pandemonium in the dark? Outside the great basilica of St. Peter's, in the flickering light cast by their torches, stood the massive crowd of rosary-carrying, prayer-chanting devotees of the last pope-king. The prospect that thousands of loyal partisans of Rome's deposed pontifical ruler were about to try to march through the heart of the city made the elderly Depretis shudder.

For years now, the government had banned all Church processions in the Holy City, deeming them a threat to public order, a dangerous provocation to patriotic Italians. Yet, as the midnight bells rang, the coffin containing the pope's body emerged from St. Peter's, leading a procession such as Italy would never see again.

Scores of police surrounded the four official horse-drawn carriages as they began to move out. Two hundred carriages of the wealthiest Catholic faithful formed a line behind them, followed by three thousand candle-bearing marchers chanting Latin and Italian prayers and reciting the rosary. But the solemn mood did not last long. Scores of anticlerics—some screaming angrily, some playfully if maliciously—set upon the marchers and tried to drown out their prayers. Angered by the effrontery of the scabrous anticlerical songs and enraged by the cries of "Long Live the King!," "Long Live Garibaldi!," and "Long Live the Army!," some of the faithful, unable to restrain themselves, took up the defiant cry "Long live the pope!"

As the procession approached the Sant'Angelo bridge, which links Rome's right bank, home of the Vatican, to the main part of the city, on the left, policemen struggled haplessly to keep the anticlerics away from the processioners. Ominously, as the pontiff's body neared the ancient bridge, shouts of "Into the river with the pope!" and "Toss him in the river!" rose from the anticlerical ranks. "It was only through God's extraordinary protection," Turin's Catholic newspaper would later report, "that those venerated bones were not thrown into the Tiber."

The procession moved toward the heart of Rome, where windows displaying glowing lanterns in honor of the defunct pope were smashed by well-aimed stones. Squads of soldiers, held in reserve for just such an eventuality, found themselves unable to make their way to the scenes of violence because the narrow streets were so packed with the devout, the irreverent, and the simply curious. Before long, the anticlericals' rocks began to hit their first human targets, one finding a particularly exalted mark in the face of the nephew of Pius IX's successor, Leo XIII.

For the faithful, the sacrilege could hardly have been greater, and accounts of the outrages en route would fuel Catholics' anger worldwide. This was, after all, a funeral procession for the beloved pope who had reigned longer than any of his predecessors, longer than even St. Peter himself. The stories were horrifying: "Among the assailants," we learn from a typical Catholic report, "was one who, to add some sort of bizarre bravado to their cruel deeds, tore a torch from a pious citizen without warning and then rammed it into the face of a noble maiden who was so engrossed in reciting her prayers that she had been oblivious to the outside world."[1]

With the violence mounting and multitudinous missiles now raining down on the wagon bearing the pope's body and on the ecclesiastical escort in the carriages behind, the police begged the lead carriages to abandon their funereal pace. Speeding up to a half trot, they finally succeeded in outpacing their assailants and, at 3 A.M., reached their destination, the Church of San Lorenzo. The prayer-chanting processioners, some bloodied, all enraged, were left long behind in streets swarming with police, soldiers, and assorted troublemakers.

It was the morning of June 13, 1881, three years after Pius IX's death and almost eleven years after he had become a prisoner of the Vatican.

Introduction:
Italy's Birth and Near Demise

*M*ODERN ITALY, it could be said, was founded over the dead body of Pope Pius IX. Although Italy had been a geographical label since Roman times, the idea that a distinctive Italian people inhabited the boot-shaped peninsula and its islands was more recent, and the notion that they should have an independent state of their own more recent still. Only with the French Revolution's attack on the principles of absolutism and divinely ordained hierarchy could such an idea gain ground, and only with the rise of nationalism as the political creed of the nineteenth century could "Italy for the Italians" become the new watchword. But creating a sense of common Italian identity among the people of the peninsula was no easy matter. Not only were they not accustomed to being part of the same country, few of them spoke Italian, 97 percent speaking a kaleidoscope of dialects and languages that were in good part mutually unintelligible.

In the aftermath of Napoleon's defeat in 1814, the Italian nationalist movement faced a peninsula that was divided into a patchwork of states and duchies propped up by foreign forces, the Austrian empire foremost among them. But the nationalists were not entirely discouraged, for they knew that autocratic mini-states were vulnerable to the wrath of their subjects from within and to armies from without. Assorted dukes and kings had painfully learned the latter lesson when Napoleon's armies had, not many years earlier, swept through the peninsula and deposed them all. For Italy's nationalists, then, the most daunting obstacle was not the Austrian occupation of northeastern Italy, nor the tottering Bourbon monarchy that ruled all of the South and Sicily, nor the assorted dukes and their duchies. No, there was a far greater power, a far more imposing foe, one that cut the peninsula in two, blocking North from South, its capital the legendary city of Romulus and Remus, the symbol of Italy's ancient greatness.

For more than a thousand years the popes had ruled over these Papal States, a swath of territory that extended from Rome northward through Umbria and the Marches to Ferrara and Bologna. Deposing the duke of Modena or the grandduke of Tuscany, or even driving the Austrians out of Lombardy and Veneto, was one thing. Deposing the pope from his thousand-year earthly reign was something very different, for the pope, though having little in the way of military might, had weapons that no other ruler could ever hope to wield.

What the pope had was the belief — enshrined in official Church dogma and pronounced by parish priests throughout the land — that he ruled over a divinely ordained kingdom as God's representative on earth. The creation of a unified Italian state, the pope insisted — and in this he had centuries of Church teachings to back him up — was contrary to God's wishes. It could only be accomplished by force, and anyone taking part in such an assault would be throwing in his lot with the Devil himself. There could be no place in the Church, or in Heaven above, for such agents of evil.

In some ways, the task that the pope faced in battling the Italian nationalists was nothing new. True, modern nationalism was a recent development. But ever since popes became kings in the early Middle Ages, they had to fend off challenges from civil rulers who sought to reduce their authority, if not to seize their land. In such cases, the pontiffs inevitably cast their battle as a struggle pitting the forces of God against those of the Devil, the forces of darkness against those of light. But rarely did they limit themselves to such otherworldly arguments, recognizing the benefits of marshaling more terrestrial forces to their side as well. If the popes held on to their Italian lands over centuries in which other regimes and other states rose and fell and other borders shifted, it was also because they became masters of playing on the rivalries of Europe's secular rulers.

And here we get to one of the embarrassing facts of Italian unification: it first came about, in 1859–1860, only through the assistance of a foreign army, the French, who helped drive the Austrians from the peninsula. It was completed, with the taking of Rome in 1870, only when Pope Pius IX's former foreign protectors — Europe's two major Catholic powers, the French and the Austrians — decided, for different reasons, to abandon him to his fate. But still the newly unified Italy was a tenuous creature, born not of a mass nationalist movement — for relatively few Italians were involved, or even seemed to care[1] — but of a fortunate coincidence of a small nationalist elite, an opportunistic Savoyard monarchy based in Turin in the northwest of the peninsula, a microscopic ragtag army under the command of a popular hero deeply distrusted by the emerging Italian government, and a series of European rivalries that prevented any of the continent's powers from heeding the pope's desperate pleas.

Italians — but also others who learn about Italian history today — are led to believe that the nation was securely established once Rome was taken in 1870. But it is an illusion, the product of a natural tendency to view history backward. In fact, in the first two decades of Rome's new position as capital of Italy, there was no certainty that the end of the Papal States was any less fleeting than it had been several decades earlier, when, in the course of ten years, Napoleon deposed two popes and chased them from Rome. Nor did Catholics have to look back even that far to find grounds for hope; little more than two decades earlier, in 1848, popular revolts had driven Pius IX, then in the first years of his papacy, into exile. Then, too, the usurpers had triumphantly pronounced the permanent end of papal rule. Yet, once again, the pope had shown how fleeting were the victories of the Church's enemies, returning to power behind the French and Austrian armies. Why, loyal Catholics asked, should God's cause not triumph once more? Was He not still on the pope's side?

When, on September 20, 1870, Italian troops finally broke through Rome's walls and claimed the city as part of the new Italian state, Pius proclaimed himself a "prisoner of the Vatican." Denouncing the "usurper" state, he retreated into the Vatican complex and, spurning the government's entreaties, refused to come out. Confident that God would not long abandon His Church, Pius did all he could to help the divine cause, from excommunicating Italy's founders — the king, his ministers, and his generals — to calling on Europe's Catholic rulers to come once again to his aid. Following the pope's lead, the Catholic press assured its readers that Rome's sacrilegious conquerors would, like their predecessors, soon meet an ignominious end. The Papal States would return.

A dramatic battle unfolded, the drama punctuated by the death of its two protagonists — Pius IX and Victor Emmanuel II — within a month of each other in 1878. Yet, even with a new pope, Leo XIII, and a new king, Umberto I, both dramatically different from their predecessors, the battle continued, the stakes high, the outcome uncertain.

This is the story told in the pages that follow, a story of outrageous accusations, mutual denunciations, terrible fears, and raucous public demonstrations, a chronicle of frenetic diplomacy and secret dealings. While the struggle was partly fought through symbols, ritual, and rhetoric, rocks were hurled along with epithets. War throughout Europe was prophesied, at the end of which, many in the Vatican hoped and believed, Italy would once again be carved up by foreign powers into a series of weak, dependent states and the pope returned to power in Rome. This battle — almost entirely unknown today outside scholarly circles — still leaves a deep mark on the Italian soul. Without understanding this history, there is no way to understand the peculiarities of Italy today.

The protagonists of this fateful conflict live on in statues of granite and marble that dot town squares from Venice and Turin to Naples and Palermo, in elaborate tombs, famous paintings, and obscure popular art. Rome itself is filled with outsized monuments, statues big and small, and a panoply of plaques commemorating the battles of unification. But, oddly, the story that they tell, together with the sanitized accounts found in the textbooks of every Italian schoolchild, has rather little to do with what happened. The actual history is, today, too dangerous, too embarrassing, still too raw for public view. The most basic fact of the creation of modern Italy — that its greatest foe was the pope himself — is one that cannot easily be mentioned, and certainly not to children, whose understanding of how their country was founded contains a hole at its center. The Italian or the foreigner visiting Rome today can scarcely grasp what the battles for Italian unification were about.

It is too bad, because the true story of the birth of modern Italy, involving the demise of the Papal States and the pope's efforts to undo Italian unification, offers a gripping tale of intrigue and pathos filled with outsized characters and high drama. It features an Italian king,

Victor Emmanuel II, whose greatest passion in life was hunting and who viewed his government ministers with disdain, but who somehow rose to the challenge of unifying Italy. Although he had little love for the Church or the clergy, the king never stopped dreaming of the day that the pope would deign to receive him. It was a day that he would never live to see.

For his part, Pius IX was without doubt the most important pontiff in modern history. While deeply religious, he was politically inept. Remarkably gregarious, he loved nothing more than hosting audiences and, before Rome was taken, strolling through Rome's streets and chuckling at people's startled reactions to the white-robed pope-king in their midst. Yet, if he was a man of great charm and warmth, a man with a famous smile, he also had a fearful temper and a short fuse. And, as if from the cast of a twopenny melodrama, ever at the goodly pope's side was the dark figure of Giacomo Antonelli, long his secretary of state, his right-hand man, who compensated for the pope's lack of political sophistication with his own diplomatic savvy. A cardinal without ever having been ordained a priest, Antonelli fit the popular stereotype of the goodly pope's evil adviser, an image promulgated in this case not only by Italy's anticlericals and nationalists but by many of the Curia's cardinals as well, jealous of the stranglehold Antonelli seemed to have over Pius.

Rounding out the cast of characters at the center of this dramatic history as it began to unfold, and whose true role in the rise of modern Italy is today obscured from popular view, is Giuseppe Garibaldi, a man for whom "colorful" seems too weak a term. Condemned to death as a young man for taking part in a nationalist uprising in Genoa, he spent most of his early adult and middle-age years in exile as a sailor, adventurer, and frequent participant in popular uprisings, including a series of wars in South America, where he had taken refuge. When, in the face of a popular revolt, Pius IX fled Rome in 1848 and the end of papal rule was proclaimed, Garibaldi returned to Italy to lead the makeshift army that defended the new Roman Republic. Yet when the French responded to the pope's plea and sent their troops to retake Rome, Garibaldi, despite all his heroic efforts, could not long hold them back and was forced into exile once again. Almost single-handedly responsible for the fact that the new Italian state that took shape in 1860 included Sicily and the entire Italian South — not a part of the peninsula in which Victor Emmanuel or his ministers had any interest — Garibaldi lacked all political artifice. Yet he did have one unshakable belief: he was convinced that the priests were a parasitic scourge on the Italian nation, the papacy a cancer that had to be excised.

And then there were all the foreign rulers and diplomats whose decisions would determine whether the pope would one day return to power, whether Italy would remain united or soon crumble. There was the massive, mustachioed Otto von Bismarck, the German chancellor who presided over what by late 1870 had emerged as the continent's leading power. Bismarck's six-foot, four-inch frame and considerable bulk would cast a large shadow over Europe in these years, inspiring a mixture of respect, anger, and fear. With a huge head, a shrinking fringe of whitening hair, a drooping mustache, bushy eyebrows, and large protruding eyes, Bismarck carried himself with military bearing and, indeed, always wore a white military uniform in Berlin as befitted a member of the Prussian gentry who held the rank of major general. Also, befitting his origins, he despised urban life, retreating as much as possible to his rural estates. Known to sit down for a meal and eat what would normally feed three men and to drink one or two bottles of champagne at his midday meal alone, he was apt to smoke his way through eight or ten Havana cigars a day and cap off his dinner with a bottle or two of brandy.

Disdaining any crass appeal for popularity, in his nearly three decades in power Bismarck confined his speeches almost entirely to parliament. His voice came as a surprise to those who had never heard him, for the big man spoke in something of a thin falsetto. Yet, when he was spotted ordering a mug of beer from a parliamentary aide — a sure sign that he was getting ready to mount the podium — word spread quickly, and the deputies rushed in from the halls to hear him. Bismarck's speeches were typically witty, sardonic, sarcastic, and — although he rarely used a prepared text — filled with rarefied literary allusions. Of his subordinates he expected information but not advice, still less criticism. If Pius IX's angry outbursts were entirely spontaneous and fleeting, Bismarck's were more calculated. "It's useful for the entire mechanism if I get angry at times," he said. "It puts stronger steam in the engine." Although he would soon lead Germany's own campaign against the Catholic Church, Bismarck — himself, like the

German emperor, a Protestant — was above all a political opportunist. As we shall see, at one point he even toyed with the idea of providing a German refuge for the pope and pronouncing Germany the world center of Catholicism.[2]

Then there was Napoleon III, emperor of France. Born in 1808, seven years before Bismarck, Louis Napoleon grew up in the wake of his uncle and namesake's bitter defeat. A participant in the Italian nationalist uprisings in 1831, he was arrested nine years later in France for conspiring to overthrow the monarchy there. Escaping from prison after six years, he took part in the French revolt of 1848 and by the end of that year was elected president of the new regime. Although he was a champion of nationalism who viewed the pope-king as a regrettable relic of the Middle Ages, his first priority on taking power was to solidify his rule. And so, in an effort to attract domestic Catholic support, he dispatched his army in 1849 to defeat Garibaldi and retake Rome for Pius; three years later, he orchestrated a plebiscite that pronounced him emperor of France. He was no longer Louis Napoleon but Napoleon III. Meanwhile, the French troops remained in Rome, charged with protecting the pontiff from revolt or invasion. There, but for brief periods, they remained until the historic summer of 1870, when the declaration of papal infallibility by the First Vatican Council, coinciding with the outbreak of France's war with Prussia, led Napoleon to withdraw his troops. Only then — when the coast was clear — was Victor Emmanuel willing to send in his own army and claim Rome as Italy's new capital.

We are about to enter a world that no longer exists, of a pope who was a king, of a king ashamed to share his capital with the pope who had excommunicated him, of nervous nobles, anticlericals bent on seizing the Vatican, would-be assassins, and suspicions of conspiracies everywhere. Some of its characters were eloquent, some playful, some sober, and some grim; some were witty and urbane, some abusive and inebriated. Some invoked the highest principles of Enlightenment morality, some the sacred principles of revealed truth. Still others seemed more intent on bellowing epithets as loudly as their voices would allow. The result was the mixture of contradictory traits that is the hallmark of modern Italy.

Many books deal with one aspect or another of this story, although most were written a century or more ago, when none of the Vatican archives for the period were available. Books that try to tell the whole story addressed in these pages, based on the original documents but written for a broad audience, are few indeed. None, so far as I know, are based on both the historical archives of the Vatican and the records of the Italian state. Curiously, in fact, most of the great Italian historians of national unification — reflecting their secular allegiances — felt uncomfortable even setting foot in the Vatican. To a considerable extent, this odd division of labor continues even today, with the historians of Italian unification — identified with the proponents of a secular Italy — generally avoiding research that would entail working in the Vatican archives, leaving it to Church historians, some of the most illustrious being priests themselves. Even among the latter, however, the great majority who have written on our topic lacked access to the Vatican's documents from the period following Leo XIII's ascendancy to the papacy in 1878, for most wrote before 1979, when these archives were first opened to researchers. It is, in part, the use of this rich trove of material that allows us here to shed new light on the battle waged by the pope and his Curia aimed at depriving the new Italian state of its capital.

Today, we all take for granted that the pope is forever on the move, traveling thousands of miles at a time to minister to his far-flung flock. How strange it is to be reminded that, for fifty-nine years after the taking of Rome, no pope would set foot outside the Vatican, no pope would even enter Rome's own churches nor escape Rome's summer heat by retreating to the papal villa in the nearby hills at Castel Gandolfo. To travel beyond the minuscule patch of land that remained under his control would mean acknowledging that the pope was no longer a prisoner of the Vatican. This, for almost six decades, no pope was willing to do.

1

Destroying the Papal States

*P*IUS IX had not always been such a bitter enemy of progress, of things modern. When he ascended to St. Peter's throne in 1846, among his first acts was the introduction of gas streetlights and railways to the Papal States, an implicit rebuke to his predecessor, Gregory XVI, who had viewed them as dangerous departures from the way God meant things to be. The new pope also won popular favor in these first months by freeing political prisoners and calling for the reform of the Papal States' notoriously corrupt and inefficient bureaucracy.

But, caught up in the intoxicating spirit of revolt that swept Europe with shocking speed in 1848, people soon wanted — no, demanded — more, much more. In April of that year, Pius rejected pleas that he support efforts to drive the Austrians out of the Italian peninsula. In November, amid increasing disorder, calls for a constitution, and demands for an end to the papal dictatorship, his prime minister was stabbed to death in the middle of Rome in broad daylight.

Fearing for his life and by then practically a prisoner in his Quirinal Palace in central Rome, the pope decided to escape. Dressed as a simple priest, his face partially concealed by tinted glasses, he furtively boarded the carriage of the Bavarian ambassador and, with his help, made his way south to the seaside fortress of Gaeta, north of Naples in the Kingdom of the Two Sicilies.

The pope's earthly realm was slipping from his grasp as revolts from Bologna to Rome drove out the cardinal legates and ushered in local governing committees that proudly proclaimed the end of papal rule.

In Rome, a Constituent Assembly elected by popular vote in January 1849 put power in the hands of a triumvirate that would soon include Giuseppe Mazzini, Italy's great theorist of nationalism, who was living in exile in London. Article 1 of the constitution of the new Roman Republic pronounced the pope's temporal power forever ended. The people were now free to say, think, write, and act as they liked; the Inquisition was no more. The Jews were freed from their ghettoes, and even Protestants could worship freely. From then on, the government was to be elected by the people.

The new utopia did not last long before the French and Austrian troops marched in and restored the pope to power. Any sympathies that Pius had previously felt for offering more civil liberties or a measure of democracy were now gone. As he saw it, God had intended the pope to rule over the Papal States and, indeed, only by having such temporal power could the pontiff enjoy the freedom that he needed to perform his spiritual duties. The Inquisition was restored, as was the Index of prohibited books; the Jews were forced back into their ghettoes; all newspapers and books were again heavily censored. French troops patrolled the streets of Rome, propping up papal rule.

The Kingdom of Sardinia quickly emerged as the best hope for those who sought change. Despite its name, the kingdom's capital was Turin, in the northwestern region of Piedmont, and included the neighboring region of Liguria as well as the kingdom's namesake, the island of Sardinia. Under the Savoyard dynasty it alone had preserved the reforms introduced in 1848, which had turned an authoritarian state into a constitutional, parliamentary monarchy. Church control of schools was ended, freedom of religion proclaimed, and the Jesuit order, viewed as the subversive agent of papal power abroad, banished.

By midcentury, most of the educated classes of central and northern Italy had become alienated from the Church — or at least from its center of power in Rome — and were hostile to the continued presence of foreign troops in the peninsula. Resentment in Lombardy and Veneto to the Austrians' rule kept tensions high, as did their troops, who patrolled much of the Papal States, and the French soldiers who guarded Rome.

The king of Sardinia, Victor Emmanuel II, whose penchant for military adventure — and incompetence — was notorious, began to glimpse his chance for greatness. What could be more glorious than putting himself at the head of an army that would conquer much of Italy and, in so doing, not only dramatically enlarge his realm but cast him as a great Italian patriot? Yet his advisers, Prime Minister Count Camillo Cavour chief among them, urged caution. To take on both the French and the Austrians would, he knew, be suicidal.

The king's big chance came in July 1858, when Napoleon III met secretly with Cavour in France and hatched a plan to drive the Austrians — their common enemy — from the Italian peninsula. The plan also involved removing three-quarters of the Papal States from the pope's control, leaving only Rome and the region around it for the pontiff, under French protection, a measure designed in part to placate French Catholic opinion. There was no discussion at the time of attacking the Kingdom of Naples in the South nor of unifying all of Italy under a single government. In fact, Napoleon III seems to have envisioned some kind of loose confederation of weak states taking shape in Italy, possibly under the titular presidency of the pope himself. This would have the virtue of weakening his chief rival, Austria, and creating an ally to his south in the Kingdom of Sardinia while ensuring that the fractionated Italian peninsula would never produce a state strong enough to compete with the French for European influence.

War broke out near the Piedmontese border with Lombardy in May 1859 and quickly spread to the Papal States as Italian nationalists fueled revolts that again sent the cardinal legates packing. Plebiscites demanding unification with the Kingdom of Sardinia quickly followed. Meanwhile, responding to a plea from the Sicilian proponents of unification, Garibaldi assembled a force of a thousand volunteers — wearing open-collared red shirts in place of regular uniforms — and set sail. Landing near Palermo in May 1860, these poorly trained irregulars dispatched the Bourbon army with embarrassing ease, so, after conquering Sicily, they headed north, up the Italian boot, on their way to Rome.

Alarmed yet excited, Victor Emmanuel II could no longer merely stand by. To do nothing while Garibaldi's red shirts, in the name of unifying Italy, marched into the Holy City would court disaster. Should Garibaldi succeed in taking Rome, he would put Victor Emmanuel to shame. In place of a large northern Italian state under the Savoyard monarchy, the frightening specter of all Italy unified under a revolutionary republic became all too real. And so the king sent his army south, intercepting Garibaldi north of Naples before he could attack

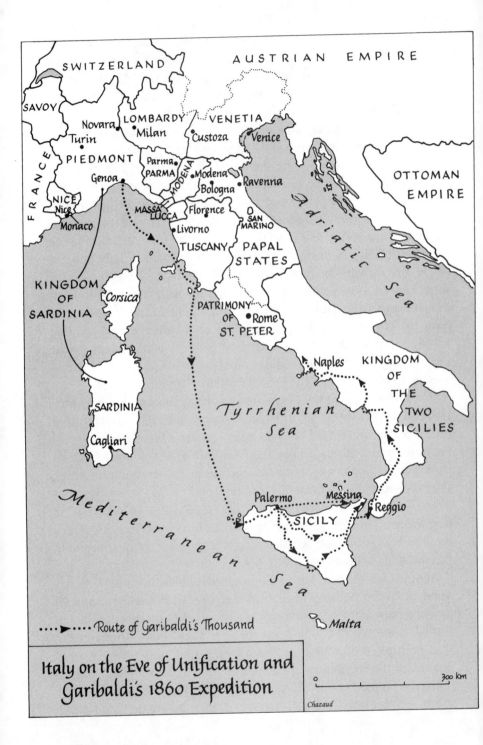

Route of Garibaldi's Thousand

Italy on the Eve of Unification and
Garibaldi's 1860 Expedition

Rome. There, a curious military ceremony took place, with Garibaldi handing over control of the newly fallen Kingdom of Naples to the Savoyard king. Rome — at least for the moment — remained in papal hands.

A year later, the new Kingdom of Italy was officially inaugurated. Technically, it was simply the continuation of the old Kingdom of Sardinia, so no new constitution was thought necessary. Although the Italian state was much larger than the king or his ministers had imagined three years earlier, when they had hatched their plot with the French emperor, two big holes remained. Rome and the region around it were still in the pope's hands and, in the Northeast, Veneto and its capital, Venice, were still under Austrian control.

Faced with the demise of most of his earthly domain, Pius IX struck back as best he could. Rebuffing Victor Emmanuel's attempts to negotiate, the pope, in an encyclical in January 1860, demanded the "pure and simple restitution" of the Papal States, excommunicated all those guilty of usurping the papal lands, and voiced his belief that God would not long allow the outrage to stand. The days of a unified Italian state, he was sure, were numbered.[1]

Yet the unification of Italy under the Savoyard king left many of Italy's most ardent nationalists unhappy. Mazzini, a principled opponent of monarchy and a committed republican, had been willing to hold his nose during the battle against the Austrians because he believed that the first priority should be driving the foreigners out of the peninsula. But the situation had changed. His already dim view of the monarchy got even dimmer when it became clear that the new government had no immediate plan to take Rome. For the nationalists, an Italian state without Rome as its capital was inconceivable.

In 1862 Garibaldi, the peripatetic Hero of Two Worlds — so called because of his exploits in South America — again tried to force the king's hand by summoning his motley army of red shirts for a march on Rome. Gathering his forces in Sicily, the scene of his triumphs two years earlier, he prepared for the march north into the Holy City, leaving the Savoyard king and his ministers in a painful quandary. They could hardly allow a private army to march across the country, nor were they prepared to turn against the French, whose troops were guarding the pope. Yet, realizing that Garibaldi was far more popular than anyone in the government — more popular than the king himself — they feared sending the army against him.

After much hand-wringing, the Italian leaders decided that they had no choice. Garibaldi had to be stopped. A contingent of Italian troops caught up with the red shirts at the edge of a mountain forest in southern Calabria, at Aspromonte. Thinking that the approaching Italian colonel had come to talk, Garibaldi told his men not to shoot. But the Italian troops opened fire. In the resulting carnage, a bullet shattered Garibaldi's foot, a wound that plagued him for the rest of his life. Some of his red shirts were killed, others injured, and not a few were seized and then summarily executed, charged with having deserted the regular army.

Aspromonte sent shock waves through the peninsula. Italy's greatest hero had been shot and crippled by the Italian army, acting on the king's orders, and all because he had had the courage to risk his life in an effort to claim Rome for Italy.

Meanwhile, in the Holy City, the pope tried hard to buck up his supporters' sagging spirits. In February 1864, Odo Russell, Britain's perceptive — if sometimes acerbic — envoy to Rome, reported that Pius was eager for the upcoming Carnival celebrations to be as successful as ever. The partisans of Italian unification responded by calling for a boycott. The *Italianissimi*, Russell wrote, "won't attend the Carnival and won't dance, whilst the *Papalini* or *neri* ["blacks"; the Roman aristocrats devoted to the pope were called the black nobility] dance frantically to show their devotion to the Pope because His Holiness told some old princesses that he wished the faithful to be gay and happy. In consequence we saw this winter at the balls given by the pious *Papalini* the oldest dowagers attempting to be frolicsome, and old Princess Borghese, who has scarcely been able to walk for the last half century, hobbled through a quadrille with Field Marshal Duke Saldanha who had not danced since the Congress of Vienna, and all this in the name of religion!"[2]

Desperate to get the French troops out of Rome — their presence in the middle of the peninsula an affront to Italian nationalist sentiment — the Italian government came up with a proposal that it hoped would take care of the problem, at least in the short run. The resulting agreement, signed on September 15, 1864, and subsequently dubbed the Convention of September, called for all the French troops to leave Rome within two years. In exchange, the Italian government made two major concessions. It agreed to transfer its capital from Turin to Florence — a move that in fact did take place the following year — thus apparently renouncing the nationalist dream of making Rome Italy's capital.[3] And it promised not only not to attack papal territory, but to prevent anyone else from threatening it. Napoleon III insisted on this pledge, for he had to convince the conservative French Catholics that, in withdrawing the French troops, he was not abandoning the pope.

The Italian government and the king clearly made the agreement in bad faith. If they could get the French troops out of Rome, they thought, they would eventually find some pretext to annex it.[4]

In all matters involving relations with other states, the pope relied heavily on his secretary of state, the powerful and controversial Giacomo Antonelli. Something of a lady's man despite being rather ugly, Antonelli was as arrogant and severe with his underlings as he was solicitous and charming with foreign diplomats and aristocratic visitors. One of Pius's biographers, Adolph Mundt, described him in typically unflattering terms: "Antonelli is a tall, thin man who wears on his dark, yellowish face, a savage expression but one that is, at the same time, demonically astute. His long head resting on his shoulders brings to mind that of a bird of prey." Antonelli's biographer, the American Frank Coppa, while painting a much more positive picture, stresses his lack of friends, his relentless self-control, and his insistence on formality, having even his parents and brothers address him as "Monsignor" and preferring them to refer to him as "His Eminence."[5]

Returning from a trip to London just after the Convention of September was signed, Odo Russell was surprised to find that Antonelli and others of the Curia remained optimistic about the future. The cardinals, wrote the British envoy, "laugh in anybody's face who mentions the departure of the French troops from Rome." When Russell reminded the prelates that they had, a few years earlier, been similarly convinced that the Austrians would never leave Lombardy, nor that Victor Emmanuel would ever dare seize any of the Papal States, they stood their ground. Napoleon III, they insisted, could never leave the pope "in a helpless condition to the Piedmontese and the tender mercies of his subjects, the Catholics of France and of the whole world will not stand it."[6]

Antonelli, it turned out, had some reason for his optimism, as Russell discovered a week later when he again met the secretary of state. As was often his custom, Antonelli took the British envoy by his arm for a walk as they chatted. The French emperor, Antonelli told him, had recently conveyed a message through the papal nuncio in Paris.

"Tell the Pope," Napoleon had said, "to be calm, to trust in me and to judge me by my deeds and not by my words."

From this conversation and from other sources in Paris, Antonelli assured Russell, "it has become evident that the Convention of 15 September has several meanings, one put upon it at Turin and the other at Paris publicly and officially, whilst a third interpretation, and the only correct one, exists in the Emperor Napoleon's mind. Much as I have thought about it, I know not what His Majesty's ultimate plans may be. . . . But one thing becomes clearer than it ever was before to my mind, namely that he does not intend Italy to unite."

Russell remained skeptical. Was it really the French emperor's intention to see the new Italian state dismantled?

Antonelli tried to explain: "First of all the Convention contains in itself the destruction of the unity of Italy, for it reserves the Temporal Power to the Pope and deprives Italy of Rome, and Italy can never be a united nation without Rome. Secondly, the Convention declares Florence to be the future capital of Italy, that is, it forms the great political center of Italy in the north. Now the North did not require any other capital than Turin while it waited for Rome. The danger to unity is in the south."[7] Had Naples been declared the capital, Antonelli explained, the South might have been placated. But by making Florence the new capital, he argued, "the Convention leaves the South free to fall off, separate and constitute a southern Kingdom." Clearly, said Antonelli, "Napoleon imposed Florence on the Italians as their capital so that Naples might be free to act for herself and Italy become a Confederation divided into three, namely a northern and southern Kingdom and the Holy See in the center." To make the plan palatable to Victor Emmanuel, Antonelli added, Napoleon was willing to allow a Savoyard prince, perhaps even one of the king's own sons, to become king of Naples.

Antonelli then surveyed the hazards ahead. Napoleon's true intentions, he admitted, could not fully be known. But whatever Napoleon had in mind, the pope would pursue the same path, for he could follow no other. He would denounce those who sought to take the papal lands from him, and he would insist on the return of the Papal States.

"In the coming struggle, we may be beaten and submerged," said Antonelli. "I am the first to admit that it is possible, nay, I will say even probable, but we will do our duty towards the Holy Church like honest men knowing that when God in his mercy allows these trials to pass His Church will rise again as she has ever done before and her enemies will be dispersed and confounded."

On his way home, Russell ran into Prince Altomonte, a former minister in the court of the deposed king of Naples. Asking the prince what he thought of the new Italian treaty with France, Russell was surprised to hear him parrot Antonelli's view. Napoleon did not want Italy to unite, he said, and the Convention, by securing the pope's temporal rule over Rome and imposing Florence, the capital of northern Italy, on the Italians, had left Naples free to secede as long as its Bourbon throne was occupied by a prince of the House of Savoy."[8]

Such optimism sprang from another source as well, for tensions in Europe were high, pitting Prussia against Austria and both against France. The one thing that all of these antagonists shared was an opposition to the rise of a strong, united Italy that could compete with them for influence. War seemed imminent, and for those in the Vatican there was reason to believe — or, at least, to hope — that the belligerents would see to it that the Italian kingdom was soon cut down to size.

In mid-January 1865, Antonelli discussed just such a prospect in a conversation with the British envoy. "Like the Pope," Russell reported in his dispatch to London, "Antonelli hopes in a European war to set matters right again in the Holy See!"[9]

Yet, by the time of Russell's New Year's audience with the pope the following year, he found the pontiff — known for his rapid mood changes — despondent and frustrated.

"How is it," Pius asked him, "that the British can hang two thousand Negroes to put down an uprising in Jamaica, and receive only universal praise for it, while I cannot hang a single man in the Papal States without provoking worldwide condemnation?"

"His Holiness," Russell recounted, "here burst out laughing and repeated his last sentence several times holding up one finger as he alluded to hanging one man, so as to render the idea still more impressive."

This and other aspects of their encounter left the British envoy uneasy. While the seventy-three-year-old pope appeared to be in excellent health, his conversation, Russell reported, "bore the unmistakable signs of the approach of second childhood." The pontiff's ministers feared his growing irritability and were loath to say anything that might upset him. And so, Russell concluded, "notwithstanding the proverbial goodness and benevolence of Pius IX, he seems to inspire them with unreasonable apprehension and inexplicable terror."[10]

A few months later the pope was in a better mood, having new reason to believe that a European war would soon lead to the restoration of the Papal States. Fighting had begun in June 1866, pitting Austrian forces against Prussia and Italy. The Italians had joined Prussia in an attempt to seize the disputed lands held by Austria on the northeast of the Italian peninsula. But the war was not going well for them, and on June 24 the Austrians pulverized the Italian army at Custoza, near Verona.

"The war absorbs every other interest," Russell reported from Rome, "and the success of the Austrians at Custoza fills the Papal party with unbounded joy."[11]

But the cardinals' delight was short-lived, for farther north the Prussians soon overwhelmed Austria's army. And, embarrassingly for the Italian king, while Italy's regular army and navy were both being routed by the Austrians, Garibaldi, again leading his own army of irregulars, was scoring a series of impressive victories against them.

On July 10 Russell chronicled the change of mood: Austria's losses, he wrote, have "destroyed the hopes entertained, but a few days ago, by the Papal Government and the Legitimists in Rome. They had prayed for and hailed the war as their only salvation and had never doubted that Austrian troops would again occupy the lost provinces of the Pope and would re-establish Francis II on the throne of Naples."

"I called again on Cardinal Antonelli this morning," Russell reported, "and found His Eminence looking painfully ill and unusually excited. 'Good God,' he exclaimed and struck his forehead with the palms of his hands, 'what is to become of us?' "[12]

With the Convention's deadline for the departure of the French troops from Rome rapidly approaching, some of Pius's advisers were urging that he escape from Rome while he could and take refuge in Austria or Spain.

This was the situation in December 1866 as the French flag was taken down from Rome's Sant'Angelo Castle and the last French soldiers boarded their ships in the papal port of Civitavecchia, bound for home.[13]

With Rome no longer protected by foreign troops, Victor Emmanuel and his ministers found themselves in an awkward position. The nationalist movement had long insisted that Italian unification would be complete only when Rome was made capital of Italy, and the lack of popular support for papal rule inside the city was well known. Yet, in signing the Convention of September, the Italian government had made itself the guarantor of papal rule in Rome, the king's honor at stake.

The trick, from the king's as well as his ministers' point of view, was to find a way to provoke a "spontaneous" revolt in Rome, which they could use as a pretext for sending in troops to restore order. To this end, they were secretly financing a number of subversive groups in the Holy City. Yet this tactic was proving to be not only frustrating but also dangerous. It was frustrating because the Romans, disgruntled though they may have been, seemed none too eager to put their lives at risk by revolting against papal rule. The pope, after all, still had thousands of his own military recruits — almost all foreigners — as well as a disreputable, and greatly feared, force of irregulars that patrolled the streets. But the government's plotting was also dangerous, for plans could easily go wrong. After all, the most likely candidates for the secret subsidies were revolutionaries who would be pleased to see the Italian monarchy fall along with the papacy.

In the government's campaign of deceit and plotting, Garibaldi came to play a central role. In some ways this was odd, for Garibaldi despised dissimulation. Undeterred by the disastrous fate of his march on Rome in 1862, he again deemed the time right for forcing the government's hand by leading his army on Rome. While careful to keep a safe public distance, the king secretly encouraged him, for such an expedition was exactly the excuse that he needed to justify sending in his own troops.

Leaving his island retreat of Caprera, off the Sardinian coast, early in 1867, wearing his trademark red shirt and embroidered cap, the sixty-year-old Garibaldi set off on a European tour to drum up support for his crusade. He put one of his sons in charge of collecting funds from wealthy donors while urging patriotic women to sew red shirts for his men.

In early September, speaking at an international conference in Geneva, Garibaldi called on the Italian state, on taking Rome, to declare the papacy "the most noxious of all sects," to end it, and to replace the Catholic priesthood — an engine of ignorance in his view — "with the priesthood of science and intelligence."[14]

Believing, with good reason, that he had the Italian government's tacit approval for his assault, Garibaldi returned to Italy and readied his forces. But early on the morning of September 24, as he was about to cross into papal territory, Italian troops seized him and escorted him back to Caprera, where he was effectively placed under house arrest. Italy's leaders wanted to use Garibaldi's capture to show other governments their good faith in upholding the treaty with France while hoping that Garibaldi's bold call for an uprising would prompt a revolt in Rome. They could then argue that, despite their best efforts, the pope was not safe in Rome and so justify sending their troops into the Holy City.

Yet Rome remained embarrassingly quiet. Its people did not revolt.

True to form, Garibaldi soon made a dramatic escape from Caprera, leaving a friend on his terrace dressed in his clothes and walking with crutches to imitate him while he ran the naval blockade of his island in a small boat, his gray beard stained black to help avoid detection. He made his way to Florence, where, given his immense popularity — only increased by his latest exploits — the government dared not arrest him again. Garibaldi prepared his army for the final attack on Rome.

But, in Paris, Napoleon could take no more. Angered by the Italians' double-dealing, he ordered French troops back into the Italian peninsula and, on November 3, 1867, they caught up with Garibaldi's irregulars at Mentana, a few miles north of Rome. There the red shirts were routed, 1,600 of them taken prisoner. Although Garibaldi escaped, he was once again arrested by Italian police. Still afraid to put him on trial, the government sent him back to Caprera, where he was kept as a virtual prisoner for the next three years.[15]

The situation was now anything but stable. French troops were again patrolling Rome's streets. They had been gone less than a year.

In early 1868, Odo Russell described the new mood in Rome. The presence of the French forces, he wrote, "tends to make of Rome a fortified city and of the Pope a military despot." According to the British envoy, "the clerical party who rejoice with great joy in their present turn of fortune and believe in their future triumph, pray devoutly that general European war may soon divide and break up Italy." The pope, Russell reported, had himself become almost giddy at the turn of events.

On March 26 the British envoy had an audience with the pope. With the return of the French troops, along with his own expanded papal army, Pius told him, he now had, in proportion to his population, the largest army in the world. He chuckled at the thought: "If the interests of the Church ever required it," Russell recalled the elderly pontiff telling him, "he would even buckle on a sword, mount a horse, and take command of his army himself like Julius II."[16]

From the pope's perspective, the situation was now looking better, much better. But Pius was by nature an optimist, a disposition that would be sorely challenged by the events to follow.

2

The Pope Becomes Infallible

*T*HE POPE HAD WATCHED helplessly in 1859–1860 as most of his states were taken from him, but he vowed to hold on to what remained. The enemy, as he saw it, were the forces of the Devil and all those who wittingly or unwittingly did his work. These were the foes of the Church, the pope, and so of God Himself. With the Church besieged, the Lord demanded that His vicar on earth stand firm.

What most drew Pius IX's ire was not the Italian king, nor his ministers, nor even the generals who led the battles against him. What most enraged him were those Catholics who thought it possible to reconcile their religion with such blasphemies of modern times as the belief that church and state should be separate or that the papacy could survive and even flourish without ruling its own land.

The principle that non-Catholics should have the same rights as Catholics was, for the pope, one of the greatest outrages of all. At an audience in 1863, a French cleric asked the pontiff how he could call on the rulers of non-Catholic countries to give Catholics equal rights when he denied such rights to non-Catholics in his own states. For Pius, the question was preposterous. How could God's vicar on earth support the right to preach error and heresy to Catholics? "The pope certainly wants liberty of conscience in Sweden, as he does in Russia, but he does not want it in principle," reported the French visitor. "He wants it as a means provided by Providence to spread the truth in these regions."[1] Early the next year, in a letter to Emperor Franz Josef in Vienna, the pope again rejected the suggestion that he offer his subjects religious freedom. "If by equality of rights for all religions," he wrote, "you mean recognizing all religions and treating them equally, this would be the greatest insult imaginable to the one true Catholic religion." The pope explained: "It contains the absurdity of confusing truth with error and light with darkness, thus encouraging the monstrous and horrid principle of religious relativism, which . . . inevitably leads to atheism."[2]

In December 1864, as part of his effort to combat liberalism, the pope issued what may well be the most controversial papal document of modern times, the encyclical *Quanta cura,* with an accompanying Syllabus of Errors. While the encyclical itself received relatively little attention, the Syllabus — listing the eighty propositions associated with modern life that no good Catholic could subscribe to — was another story. It held that no Catholic could believe in freedom of speech, freedom of the press, or freedom of religion. Catholics were forbidden to believe that the pope could live without a state of his own or that there could be a separation of church and state. The last proposition attracted the most attention, for it rejected the view that "the Roman Pontiff can and should reconcile himself to progress, liberalism, and modern civilization."

The reactionaries in the Church exulted. But for most Catholics — or at least those who cared about such matters — the Syllabus produced disorientation and dismay. The pope, it seemed, hoped for a return to the Middle Ages. While loyal Catholics were uneasy, anticlericals were ecstatic. A Piedmontese newspaper asked how long it would be until the pope, having condemned the discoveries of modern science, would ban the trains, the telegraph, steam engines, and gaslights in those lands he still ruled. In Naples and Palermo, groups of Freemasons publicly burned copies of the encyclical and the Syllabus.[3]

The pope had no intention of doing away with the trains or the telegraph, but there was no mistaking his embrace of a medieval vision for the Church. The very language used in *Quanta cura* recalled an era in which the papacy was locked in bitter struggles with a series of medieval emperors. It offered an apocalyptic vision of the forces of good arrayed against those of evil: "Our Predecessors have, with Apostolic fortitude, constantly resisted the nefarious machinations of wicked men, who, like raging waves of the sea foaming with their own deceptions, and promising freedom while they are themselves the slaves of corruption, have striven by their deceitful opinions and most pernicious writings to demolish the foundations of the Catholic religion and of civil society, to remove all virtue and justice, to corrupt all souls and all minds."[4]

The Syllabus represented the triumph of the Curia's reactionary faction, which in these years was closely identified with the Jesuits. More than any other major religious order, the Jesuits — or Society of Jesus — recruited their members from the aristocracy, whose fierce identification with the old order they typically shared.[5] By contrast, although Cardinal Antonelli had little sympathy for the liberals, he had thought the encyclical and Syllabus a bad idea. Ever the practical politician, he feared the harm that they would do to the pope's cause in Europe's capitals.[6] As he predicted, throughout Catholic Europe political leaders lost no time using the Syllabus to paint the papacy as an anachronism and a danger, urging a drastic reduction in the Church's influence in public life.

Odo Russell was among those who viewed *Quanta cura* as a disaster for a papacy. "At a moment when the Holy See stands in need of all support of the faithful," the British envoy wrote, the pope "has seen fit to condemn the honest exertions of the ablest defenders of the Church." The impact, he thought, would be enormous, for either the Catholic clergy would be forced to take part in "a vast ecclesiastical conspiracy against the principles which govern modern society" or they would refuse, thereby putting "the Catholic clergy in opposition to the vicar of Christ whom they are bound to obey." If the current path continued much longer, Russell predicted, the break between the Church and the progressive nations of Europe would become irreparable.[7]

As the forces poised to put an end to the thousand-year papal reign gathered steam outside his shrunken kingdom, Pius IX called a special Jubilee to beseech God to keep the Church's enemies at bay. In early March 1866 magnificent processions, led by eye-poppingly dressed cardinals, made their way through the streets of the Holy City, with a sea of monks and friars parading behind them, bearing sacred images aloft and holding blazing candles. Among the highlights of the celebrations were ceremonies conducted at several of Rome's historic churches, where priests piled books banned by the Index onto large braziers and, assisted by the papal police, set them on fire.[8]

The pope soon followed this gathering with a much more ambitious event, summoning all of the world's bishops and cardinals for a grand Ecumenical Council. The first such council to be held in Rome in over 350 years, it had two goals: to endorse the Syllabus and with it the pope's condemnation of the modern age, and to sanctify the principle — not previously an official part of Church doctrine — that the pope was infallible.

The goal originally envisioned for what came to be known as the First Vatican Council was nicely expressed by Bishop Félix Dupanloup, one of France's most influential Churchmen, in a letter to Antonelli in the months following Garibaldi's defeat at Mentana. The gathering of all the world's bishops would offer such a show of strength, he wrote, that it would make it impossible for France to dream of ever abandoning Rome. "The Council will at the same time be a great force against Piedmont," the bishop predicted. "Our strongest argument against *Rome capital of Italy*," he explained, "is *Rome capital of Catholicism*." In the face of the massive gathering of bishops and cardinals in Rome, "the pretensions of the Piedmontese will become not merely impossible, but the object of ridicule."[9]

Yet influential sectors of the Church looked with horror on the prospect of an enormous Vatican spectacle aimed at denouncing freedom of speech, freedom of religion, and freedom of the press, and many also opposed the idea of pronouncing the pope infallible. In a letter written in June 1869, just six months before the Council was called to order, Charles Emile Freppel, bishop of Angers, captured this mood. "The Council is being held either too soon or too late. Too late, because we are at the end of the pontificate of a tired and discouraged old man . . . who views everything through the misfortunes he has suffered. For him, everything that takes place in the modern world is, and must by necessity be, an 'abomination.'" On the other hand, the bishop continued, "It is too soon, because it is clear that the situation in Europe is not yet settled." He blamed the Jesuits for the pope's unfortunate decision to call the Council.[10]

Hostility toward the Jesuits was evident among the American prelates attending the Council as well. A few days before the Council began, Bernard McQuaid, bishop of Rochester, New York, wrote to a colleague at home: "Since coming to Europe, I have heard much of the question of the infallibility of the Pope, which with us in America was scarcely talked of. The feeling is very strong, *pro* and *con*. It seems that the Jesuits have been at the bottom of it, and have been preparing the public mind for it for the past two years. They have not made friends for themselves by the course they have followed, and if in any way the harmony of the Council is disturbed, it will be by the introduction of this most unnecessary question." He concluded, "[T]here is no telling what the Jesuits will do, and from the manner in which they are sounding out the Bishops, I am inclined to think that they will succeed in having the question forced upon us. In my humble opinion, and almost every American Bishop whose opinion I have heard agrees with me, it will be a great calamity for the Church." Or as the bishop of Pittsburgh lamented three months into the Council, speaking of the proposal of papal infallibility, "It will kill us . . . we shall have to swallow what we have vomited up." What worried him most was the Protestant anti-Catholic sentiment in the United States and the frequent charge that Catholics viewed the pope as a kind of deity. In the past, he said, we have always angrily denied such accusations, but if infallibility is pronounced, he asked, how will we be able to defend ourselves?[11]

The intellectual leader of the movement against the Council and against papal infallibility was a man who would not be in Rome for the historic gathering. The redoubtable Ignaz von Döllinger, Germany's most renowned Church historian and one of Europe's most influential Catholic theologians, was convinced that the Council would be a calamity for the Church, and he devoted the months leading up to it, and the months of the Council itself, to a frantic and doomed effort to persuade the bishops to vote against the propositions that would be put before them. In the most public of these efforts, a series of articles in the newspaper *Allgemeine Zeitung*, Döllinger, using a pseudonym, accused the Jesuits and the pope himself of preparing an "ecclesiastical revolution." A papal seizure of power was planned that, he warned, would undermine the bishops' authority and create a papal dictatorship. It was but the last step, the Church historian argued, in a centuries-long drive toward centralization that had produced "a tumor that is disfiguring the Church and causing it to suffocate."[12] Influenced in part by Döllinger, Bishop Dupanloup, who had earlier championed the calling of a Council, published a booklet that appeared a month before its opening ceremonies, setting out all the reasons why he now believed it unwise to declare the pope infallible.[13]

Yet it was not only the Jesuits who championed papal infallibility. Although never an official part of Church doctrine, the principle had been taught within the Church for centuries. Most Italian bishops, and many elsewhere, were convinced that this was exactly the right time to publicly embrace it. With the authority of the pope — and so of the Church — threatened, with much of the Papal States already in enemy hands and what little remained exposed to usurpation at any time, anything that could bolster the papacy, they believed, was to the good.[14]

Much was made of the torrential rain that drenched the crowd on the Wednesday early in December 1869, when the Council opened. Was it an omen of things to come, as many feared? St. Peter's had been packed with the curious and the devout since seven that morning; outside, carriages from the most luxurious to the merely serviceable clogged the square. Seats of honor were reserved for the recently deposed royalty who had come to pay homage. Leopold II, former grand duke of Tuscany, was there, although looking poorly — he died a few months later — along with his son Ferdinand IV. Beside them was Francis II, who was the king of Naples until Garibaldi drove him out in 1860. The former head of the Duchy of Modena was present as well. Special places were reserved for Generals Kanzler and Du Mont, whose troops guarded what remained of the Papal States. Of the thousand or so bishops, cardinals, and heads of religious orders throughout the world who were invited, 774 were there that first day. They formed a solemn — if soggy — procession to their red seats, which filled the right transept of the massive basilica. Although the great majority came from Europe — Italy with more than two hundred having by far the most — forty had made their way from the United States, nine from Canada, and another thirty from Latin America. After the bishops, cardinals, and other Church dignitaries were in place, the pope was carried to the front entrance of St. Peter's in his *sedia gestatoria*, getting out to walk the length of the nave on foot. After a mass was said, each of the fathers paid homage to the pope on his throne, the cardinals kissing his hand, the bishops his knee, and the abbots and religious superiors his foot.[15]

Among the uninvited observers who struggled to catch a glimpse of the proceedings was Ferdinand Gregorovius, the esteemed German historian then in the midst of writing his massive multivolume history of Rome. "The heat," he recalled the next day in his diary, "was unendurable. Clouds of steam rose from the wet clothes and umbrellas, from the dripping of which the marble floor was turned into a puddle." A Protestant, Gregorovius viewed the Council with deep suspicion. As with all past such councils, he wrote, here too the tension between the pope's authority and that of the bishops was evident to all. But the pope had now become, he thought, a tool in the hands of the Jesuits, who sought an ever greater concentration of power at the center. "Rome," Gregorovius wrote on December 26, "presents the spectacle of the deification, amounting to insanity, of despotism. If the movement is really carried: if the bishops, in fear and fanaticism, yield submission to the will of the pope: it is to be hoped that the unity of Germany will quickly bring to pass a second reformation."[16]

People in higher places than Gregorovius likewise warned of the disaster that would befall the Church if the plan to proclaim papal infallibility went ahead. Among those in a position to make such a prediction come true was Napoleon III, who, through the archbishop of Algiers, warned Cardinal Antonelli two months into the Council that should papal infallibility be voted in, he would have all French troops withdrawn from Rome. He would have no choice, he said, because French public opinion would, in such circumstances, demand it.

Odo Russell, in reporting this news to London, observed that the French emperor clearly had little understanding of how Pius's mind worked. "I am surprised," he wrote, "that the Emperor Napoleon and Count Daru [his foreign minister] should know so little of the character of Pio IX as to suppose that advice or threats of any kind could turn him from his path of duty. Pio IX has the faith that moves mountains and believes in his divine mission. Martyrdom at the end of his Pontificate would be the reward from heaven he has prayed for all his life." The pope, as the British envoy rightly observed, was impervious to appeals to political calculation. "His stand-point is that of a divine teacher ready to suffer and die for his faith, and he cannot yield to the advice of the temporal sovereigns of the earth to whom his life is to serve as an example." Although Pius was well aware that the French troops had restored him to his throne ten years earlier and that it was those same troops who kept him in power in Rome even today, wrote Russell, the pope in his own mind "owes them no gratitude for it, since they merely performed a sacred duty."[17]

In writing back to Russell, the British foreign minister expressed the view then common among Europe's political elite, that the drive for papal infallibility was a "monstrous assault on the reason of mankind." But he saw a silver lining in the cloud, for he believed that such a move would make "church despotism" so extreme that it would inevitably drive Catholics away from the Church. "I cannot therefore regard the prospects of papal triumph with the alarm of Gladstone," the foreign minister wrote to Russell, "who (strange to say) is almost exclusively occupied by it and thinks that Catholic governments will bitterly rue the day when they determined to be passive spectators of what they well knew was about to happen."[18]

Word of the French emperor's threat to pull his troops out of Rome spread quickly. Gregorovius, in reporting the rumor in his diary on June 7, added somewhat maliciously: "Many seriously believe that the Pope is out of his mind. He has entered with fanaticism into these things, and has acquired votes for his own deification." The German scholar predicted that "important events" would transpire before the year's end. In this, he could not have been more prescient.[19]

Anticlericals in Italy, meanwhile, were having a field day skewering the pope's claim to be the voice of God on earth. One satirical journal put the matter in verse:

> When Eve bit the apple, and told Adam he can
> Jesus, to save mankind, made himself a man;
> But the Vicar of Christ, Pius number nine
> To make man a slave, wants to make himself divine.[20]

The pope's mood, meanwhile, swung between his proverbial affability and his no less characteristic flashes of anger. That large numbers of prelates opposed the pronouncement of papal infallibility enraged him. For Pius, infallibility was less a matter of theological learning — an area in which he recognized his own inadequacies — than of faith, commitment to the Church, and loyalty to the pope. His deep dislike of Catholic liberals turned him especially against the substantial segment of the French episcopate that sided with the opposition. His comments to visitors in these months about the French prelates were anything but diplomatic; he dubbed Bishop Henri Maret a "cold soul, a snake," and Georges Darboy, archbishop of Paris — who would the next year be murdered by the revolutionaries in Paris — "bad and wrong-thinking." When carried away, the pope sometimes made statements he later regretted, as when, in the midst of the Council, he told a Jesuit confidant: "I am so committed to going ahead with this, that if the Council decides not to act, I'll send them all home and proclaim the doctrine myself."[21]

As month after month of deliberations in St. Peter's droned on, the bishops complained ever more insistently about the seemingly interminable Council. Many of the bishops were old and infirm, and even the fittest found it wearying to sit hour after hour, struggling to understand the endless speeches — all in Latin — in the vast church. The opposition was slowly being worn down as it became clear that the infallibility forces had a majority and that voting in the minority could prove hazardous to a bishop's career. The most the minority could hope for was a less sweeping version of the infallibility proposition.

Yet on June 18, in one of the more memorable speeches at the Council, Cardinal Filippo Guidi briefly gave the anti-infallibility forces something to cheer about. Guidi held the title of archbishop of Bologna but had never been able to take up his position there. Having served for a number of years as a papal emissary in Vienna, he was viewed with suspicion by the Italian government — then fresh from two wars with Austria — and so never received permission to assume his post, a necessary step in his taking charge of Church property. When he rose to speak in St. Peter's that day, he did so as the designated representative of the Dominicans. Rivals of the Jesuits, the Dominicans believed that the Church's infallibility was embodied in the bishops and cardinals as a whole, not in the pope alone.

No sooner had the cardinal finished his speech and returned to the monastery where he was staying than a messenger told him that the pope wanted to see him right away. He hastened to the pope's apartments, where Pius impatiently waited.

"I would never have thought that Your Eminence would give a talk designed to please the opposition," the pope told him. "Whose orders are you following?" he asked. "You, on whom I myself bestowed the cardinal's hat! I who brought you up from nothing! Who is it who teaches you to speak of papal infallibility in such a way?"

Cardinal Guidi tried to stand his ground, not easy with Pius IX even under the best of circumstances.

"Blessed Father, I am prepared to defend what I said, because I haven't said anything that does not conform to the doctrine of St. Thomas."

"No, no, that's not true," the pope replied. "You said, and I know you did, that the pope is obligated by binding decrees to follow the traditions of the Church. But that's an error!"

Still, the cardinal held his ground: "It's true. That is what I said. But it is not an error."

This was too much for the pontiff, who struggled unsuccessfully to contain his anger. "It is an error," he thundered, "because I, I am the tradition! I, I am the Church!"

As soon as the cardinal had gone, the pope called for his personal physician. "This friar," the pope said, "has made my blood boil." The doctor struggled to calm Pius down and took his pulse. With the pontiff still fuming, he ordered a purgative.

Cardinal Guidi had a more pleasant evening in store: all night a succession of bishops came to congratulate him for his courageous speech. So great was the press of the bishops' carriages that they overflowed the piazza outside the monastery and filled the streets nearby.[22]

For both sides the stakes could be no higher, for, as they saw it, the fate of the Church itself lay in the balance. The majority was certain that unless the papacy was strengthened, the Church's enemies would soon destroy it; the opposition feared that the Council would lose the Church the few influential political allies it still had left.[23]

The anti-infallibility forces ultimately lost their battle, but they did succeed in watering down the more potent version of papal infallibility that Pius favored. The final text limited the pope's infallibility to those occasions on which he articulated the Church's most solemn teachings, ex cathedra. Such a restricted view would not, for example, cover the pope's condemnation of the basic principles of civil liberties in the Syllabus.[24]

On July 18, in the midst of a frightening storm, with thunder booming and the skies flashing with lightning, the episcopate gathered in St. Peter's to cast a final vote. While some of the opposition — including twelve of the seventeen German bishops — stayed away, others came and dutifully cast their yes vote.[25] Of the 549 present, only two voted in opposition, in one case more likely from confusion than conviction. When the balloting was completed, at five minutes to noon, cries of "Long live the infallible pope!" went up from the spectators' gallery. The rumbling of applause signaled a mixture of excitement and relief that the six-month ordeal was over. Notably missing were the ambassadors to the Holy See from the principal Catholic countries of Europe —

France, Austria, Spain, and Portugal — an expression of their governments' displeasure.

Nor was there any sign that the people of Rome were particularly excited by the historic event. The Holy See's efforts to have the city illuminated that evening in celebration — lighting up Bernini's colonnade outside St. Peter's, placing special lights on the Jesuits' Church of Jesus and on the tower at the top of the Capitoline hill — found little echo among the population, whose dwellings remained dark. The next day, the pope found it necessary to reassure his entourage, who had nervously commented on the inauspicious weather that had greeted both the convening of the Council and the concluding vote. Did not God, Pius asked them, choose to give Moses the Tablets on Mount Sinai amid just such celestial fireworks?[26]

Throughout Europe, emperors, kings, and prime ministers voiced their anger. If the pope was now infallible, where did this leave their authority when the pope's wishes conflicted with their own? Within days of the decision, the Austrian government voted to abrogate its concordat with the Vatican; within months the Swiss government, citing the new proclamation, unleashed a campaign against the Catholic clergy. Bismarck was reported to have been delighted at the infallibility proclamation, believing that the negative popular reaction to it in Germany would undercut the pope's influence there. Odo Russell's remarks in his report to the British foreign minister, written on the very day of the vote, were typical. That the final version of infallibility was substantially toned down from the original was lost on Russell, as it was on other political leaders in Europe. "The independence of the Roman Catholic hierarchy has thus been destroyed," he wrote, "and the supreme absolutism of Rome at last been obtained."[27]

3

The Last Days of Papal Rome

O N JULY 27, 1870, saying·only that their troops were needed elsewhere, the French announced plans to remove their forces from Rome
immediately. The pope would now be on his own. After informing
Cardinal Antonelli, the French ambassador said that he would come
back later in the day to learn the pope's reaction.

"What did the Holy Father have to say when he heard the news?"
asked the French ambassador on his return.

"After he heard the telegram read," replied Antonelli, "he simply
shrugged his shoulders."

"Without saying anything?" asked the ambassador incredulously.

"He added," responded Antonelli, "that he hoped that this time the
French would never come back."[1]

The French soldiers appeared to share the pope's sentiment. Reports
coming in from Civitavecchia, the port from which the troops were
leaving, told that, as they boarded their ships, some shouted "Down
with the pope! Down with the government of the priests! Vive l'Italie!"
Embarrassed, the French commander, still in his nightclothes, had had
to run into the streets to silence them.[2]

Count Kulczycki, whose reports informed the Italian government of
these developments, described the upheaval then under way in Rome:
"News of the pullout from Pontifical territory has produced consternation in the Vatican, where up to the last minute people had deluded
themselves about what was going to happen." According to Kulczycki,
with the recollections of the French bishops' opposition at the Council

so fresh, suspicions quickly turned in their direction: "It is being said in the Vatican that it is the bishops of the minority and Monsignor Darboy in particular who, on their return from Rome, persuaded the Emperor to deliver this terrible blow."

Diplomatically, the pronouncement of papal infallibility could not have come at a worse time for the Church. With the French troops being pulled out of Rome, a war that would redefine the balance of power in Europe about to break out on the French-German border, and the Italian government under intense internal pressure to send troops into Rome, Pius had succeeded in antagonizing even his friends in foreign governments.[3]

In retrospect, the disaster that awaited the French on their decision that month to go to war against Prussia seems so predictable that the question naturally arises of how an intelligent and crafty leader like Napoleon III could have made such a fateful blunder. But the Napoleon of 1870 was only a shell of the charming, bright, competent leader of earlier years. He was enfeebled by a series of illnesses, his left arm was paralyzed, and his eyes glazed over. Able to walk only haltingly, he was in constant pain, taking an ever-increasing dosage of drugs, and his judgment was not what it used to be. In the hallowed tradition of blaming the king's advisers, historians have tended to hold the people surrounding Napoleon responsible for the decision to go to war. Of them, none has drawn more attention than his wife, the Empress Eugénie. A Spaniard, eighteen years his junior, she was consumed by hatred of the Prussians in general and of Bismarck in particular. As the French parliament was debating the war budget, she remarked that "*ma petite guerre*" — my little war — was about to begin.[4]

No sooner had Napoleon proclaimed war on Prussia than the lack of even minimal preparations for the campaign became apparent: the French generals did not even have maps of the land they were supposed to invade. As August came without a French offensive, the Germans could not believe their good luck, having ample time to move their troops by train from all over Germany to the French border. With news of the German troop movement spreading fear among the French troops, Napoleon III himself came to the front to take charge, a move that proved to be among his last as emperor. Even in the best of health he had no talent for military leadership, and he was now, in addition to his other ills, so wracked by pain from kidney stones that he was barely able to mount his horse. At the beginning of August, France's squabbling generals, unable to agree on a plan, sent the troops under their various commands on a bewildering series of uncoordinated marches. On August 6, Prussian troops defeated the disorganized French forces across a broad front, and the specter of ultimate catastrophe began to appear. Dreams of repeating France's victories under another Napoleon in 1806 gave way to the horrifying realization that France itself was about to be overrun.[5]

When war between France and Prussia first broke out, many assumed that Italy would come to France's aid, not least the French government itself. They had reason to expect such help, for Italy's king, ever ready to put himself at the helm of military adventure, continued to dream of the triumphs that had so notably eluded him in the past. Although Prussia had shown its military might four years earlier in easily defeating Austria, Victor Emmanuel was certain that the French would prevail. The previous year he had conducted secret negotiations with Napoleon III behind the back of his own prime minister, promising that the Italian army would come to France's aid in a war with Prussia in exchange for some unnamed territorial concessions.

The republicans, the left, and public opinion in general in Italy opposed siding with France, which they viewed as their enemy, for it was France that had for the past decade kept them out of Rome. By contrast, it had been Prussia that, in 1866, through its defeat of Austria, had given Italy the city of Venice and the lands around it. At rallies from Palermo to Turin, shouts of "Viva Garibaldi!" and "Viva la Prussia!" mixed with cries of "To Rome! To Rome!"[6]

On August 3, an Italian military attaché brought Napoleon a secret plan, offering Italian support in exchange for permitting the Italians to take Rome. But the French emperor rebuffed the proposal, fearing that it would enrage his Catholic supporters, who were about the only supporters he had left. The French Catholic right would, he said, rather see "the Prussians in Paris than the Italians in Rome."[7]

Amazingly, despite the first catastrophic French defeats and Napoleon's rejection of the Italians' proposal, Victor Emmanuel persisted in pressing for Italian military intervention on behalf of the French. He apparently went so far as to tell Napoleon that he would dismiss his prime minister and the entire cabinet if they refused to go along with him. Fortunately for the Italians, the king's ministers — and most notably his prime minister, Giovanni Lanza — were finally able to persuade him that siding with the French would be disastrous and likely to lead to a republican insurrection in Italy.[8]

In Rome, the pope and Church leaders watched developments with mounting alarm. Antonelli was certainly under no illusions: should the French be defeated, he knew there would be nothing to stop the Italians from seizing the Holy City.

In Antonelli's mind, the hopelessness of their position could be attributed in no small part to his own defeats in internal Church politics, including the vote for papal infallibility. What most angered him was the prospect that he would be held responsible for what was to come. "They want to have me take the blame for things that I not only didn't do, but that I opposed with all my might," said Antonelli on the day of the final infallibility vote. "You will see," he told one confidant, "that they will say that it is I who will have wrecked the papacy."[9]

With many convinced that the loss of Rome was only days or weeks away, the Holy City was filled with rumors of the pope's imminent departure. As Count Kulczycki reported, "The Jesuits and the other prelates of their party are pressing Pius IX to leave immediately . . . They are advising him to ask the English for protection and move to Malta."

At the same time, others in the Vatican were pleading with the pope to find a way to come to terms with Italy and perhaps save Rome from occupation. Among them was Cardinal Antonelli himself. He had no luck.[10]

Meanwhile, the Holy See was trying to calm the people of Rome, who found themselves locked inside the city gates. *L'Osservatore Romano*, closely identified with the pope, ran a series of articles offering French assurances that — appearances notwithstanding — the Convention of September remained fully in effect.[11]

The pressure on the king and his prime minister to seize Rome could no longer be stopped. On August 13, while attempting to pass himself off as an Englishman named John Brown, Giuseppe Mazzini was recognized on a ship in Palermo, where he had gone to promote a republican uprising against the Italian king. Seized by the Italian police, he was taken to Gaeta, the same fourteenth-century castle north of Naples where the pope had himself taken refuge from the Roman revolution of 1848. The government needed the prophet of Italian nationalism out of the way. On September 8, Lanza sent a telegram to the prefect who oversaw Gaeta: "Recommend maximum vigilance custody Mazzini. His escape at this moment would create serious embarrassment for the government."[12]

The same day Lanza sent a similar telegram to the prefect of Sassari, in Sardinia, where Garibaldi was being kept under government surveillance in Caprera, with the order to arrest him should he attempt any move to the mainland.[13] The irony could scarcely have been greater: the two heroes of the Risorgimento, its theorist, Mazzini, and its general, Garibaldi, were both under Italian police control as Rome was about to be taken.[14]

The pope, however, remained convinced that the Italians would never conquer the Holy City. For one thing, he was not yet persuaded that the French — whose Convention of September offered him a guarantee against Italian invasion — were going to lose. By August 20, when the Swiss general Hermann Kanzler, head of the papal army, went to see Pius, news of the massing of Italian troops on the border of the Roman territories had already reached them, yet the pope told him to remain calm. "The Holy Father, whom I saw this morning," Kanzler reported, "does not believe all the rumors about an imminent violation of his territory by Italian troops. He believes such an attack is only possible by revolutionary bands."[15]

The pope explained this confidence in an article that, it appears, he ordered to be written for *L'Osservatore Romano* in mid-August. It stressed the promises received from both Bismarck and the king of Prussia that the pope's territory would remain intact and also told of the assurances given by the Italians to the French diplomats that they had no intention of taking Rome by force. In another story in the newspaper, on August 16, datelined Florence, the correspondent could not have been more confident: "I repeat, this government has no intention of occupying any part of the Pontifical State."[16]

Not all shared this optimism, and Pius was growing irritated by the ever more insistent pleas he was getting from his military officers, asking what to do should the Italian troops cross into papal territory. When, on Wednesday, August 17, Monsignor Randi, the pope's police commissioner, came to see him and asked for such instructions, the pope jumped out of his seat angrily and shouted: "Can't you understand that I have formal assurances that the Italians will not set foot in Rome? How many times must I keep repeating myself?"[17]

On August 20, Italy's House of Deputies passed a motion of confidence in the government on the condition that it commit itself "to resolve the Roman question in a manner in keeping with national aspirations."[18] Alarmed by the lightly veiled threat, Cardinal Manning, the archbishop of Westminster and the leader of the Catholic Church in England, met with William Gladstone to call for British assistance in defending the pope. Within days, a British envoy informed Antonelli that the British warship *Defence* had arrived at Civitavecchia with instructions to take the pope aboard should he wish to flee.[19]

The pope can perhaps be forgiven for his misreading of the situation in these days, for he was getting very mixed signals from his diplomatic corps. On the afternoon of August 23, for example, he received a telegram from a high Church source in Vienna telling him that the Austrian emperor had just offered assurances that Italian troops would not enter papal territory.[20] Pius had also read a dispatch from the Florence correspondent of *L'Osservatore Romano* the previous day, saying that it was "impossible that the government could now be thinking of violating its treaties." The paper reprinted a story from a Florence newspaper close to the Italian government which had branded the idea of taking advantage of France's misfortunes by marching on Rome as "neither honest, nor loyal . . . a policy unworthy of a great nation."[21]

But, at the same time, the pope received a long report from his nuncio in Vienna that painted a very different picture. Prussia, he wrote, was secretly urging the Italian government to occupy all of the pontifical state, including Rome. Under the Prussian plan, an honorific position would be reserved for the pope and perhaps also a small patch of land, the Leonine city in Rome being one possibility. The Austrians, for their part, had no difficulty with this plan, the nuncio wrote, although Count Beust, the Austrian foreign minister, thought that the arrival of Italian troops in Rome might well lead the pope to abandon the city. "Should the Holy Father seek asylum," the nuncio learned, "Austria will offer him an Italian city within the Empire, either Trent, Gorizia, or Zara, or another city of Dalmatia."[22]

Although the situation looked bleak, it was not yet hopeless. Italy's ambassador to France had again assured the French foreign minister that there was to be no attack on Rome, news that the papal nuncio in Paris hastened to pass on to the Holy See. In a second long note on the same day, the nuncio described the chaotic situation in France, which, he thought, also offered some hope. The military disasters, he wrote, were sparking a widespread return to the Church. "Not only the good people but also the [religiously] indifferent have been struck by the coincidence of its being the very day that the troops were withdrawn from Rome that the French army's catastrophe on the Rhine began, and the conviction is spreading and deepening that the French government's sins toward the Holy See have provoked God's wrath on France."[23]

Despite all its public disclaimers, the Italian government was then frantically casting about for an excuse to take Rome. On August 25, Prime Minister Lanza described some of these shadowy efforts. He had met a few days earlier with a representative of a group of parliamentary conspirators who were planning to create chaos in Rome. They were funneling funds to operatives in Rome who were supposed to organize armed assaults on military barracks, aimed at provoking a popular uprising. The prime minister was skeptical. "These are all very nice and easy things to say, but impossible to put into practice in Rome," he wrote, "which lacks both courageous youths and men energetic enough to lead them."

Although Lanza thought their plan impractical, he did not want to discourage them entirely. "I gave them a little hope," he recalled, adding that he would consider helping them "when they begin to think seriously about taking direct action to push the Papal Government into complete anarchy, and so give the Italian Government a rationale for intervening to restore order and protect the Holy Father." He then described how it might best be done, supported by secret funds that he would provide. "Above all," wrote Lanza, "it is necessary to bribe the [papal] troops, and this will be done. This will produce constant, loud arguments among the soldiers, who are from different countries and so are already suspicious of one another, and then it will only take a little breeze to fan the conflagration." Other steps would follow: "With the money spent judiciously and with caution, the soldiers' brawls will then spread to the lower classes, through provocations in the taverns, on the streets, and wherever else it is possible." Should all go according to plan, Lanza wrote, "at night the city would be continuously disturbed by the sounds of gunfire. We would arrange for Italian flags to be raised, here one time, there another. In short," he pledged, he would do everything "to show the whole world that Rome was in the throes of total anarchy, and that the pope's Government could no longer control the situation with its own forces." But, the prime minister warned, the matter had to be handled with care: "See that as many disorders as you like break out in Rome, and of any kind, but not revolution, nor even assaults on the barracks. We will provide the money, and then we will see."[24]

Prime minister since the previous year, the sixty-year-old Lanza was from Piedmont, like many of Italy's major government figures of the time, having served as Cavour's minister of education in the government of the Kingdom of Sardinia in 1855 and in a series of ever more powerful posts thereafter. A bit taller than average, with a big head and large, dark brown eyes and bushy eyebrows, he had a rather severe air about him, although when he laughed, his face softened. He had a prominent, somewhat curved nose and broad cheeks, with a droopy mustache that hung over his well-trimmed beard. His voice was distinctive, robust, but somewhat nasal. Although his accent seemed to betoken an aristocratic origin, he was in fact the son of a blacksmith who had become a modest property owner.[25] Lanza had gone far, and he was about to play a central role in mediating among the king, the conservatives, and the left in guiding Italy into Rome and in making Rome the new capital.

The other major protagonist of the Italian government in 1870 was the minister of foreign affairs, Emilio Visconti Venosta. The first-born son of a noble family of vast landholdings, based in Milan, Visconti was swept up in the revolutionary movement of 1848. Nineteen years old at the time, he joined Garibaldi's forces in the battle to eject the Austrians and became enamored of Mazzini. But a few years later he repudiated the republican champion, believing that the Savoyard monarchy offered the best hope for unifying Italy. In 1863 Visconti was appointed minister of foreign affairs for the first of what would turn out to be seven times, the last of which would take him into the twentieth century.[26]

Made foreign affairs minister again in 1869, Visconti entered into a peculiar relation with Lanza. They were very different characters: Lanza was energetic, decisive, and outgoing; Visconti, brooding and cautious, carefully measuring every word. While Lanza led the effort to convince his colleagues in the government to take Rome and had no great sympathy for the papacy, Visconti was consumed by the desire to preserve good relations with the Holy See, fearful that brash action by the government might lead the pope to seek refuge abroad. The Vatican's demonization of Visconti pained him deeply, while Lanza sloughed off such attacks. Until the very day that the Italian forces rushed into Rome, Visconti nourished the hope that, despite all the pope's protests, he would in the end agree to a compromise with the Italian state.[27]

On August 29, Visconti sent a confidential dispatch to Italian ambassadors throughout Europe, arguing that the upheavals that were now unsettling Europe had rendered the Convention of September null and void. Italy sought to reconcile two fundamental aims, he told them, guaranteeing its national aspirations and the right of the Romans to determine their own future while ensuring "the pope's independence, freedom, and religious authority."

Yet, Visconti complained, the Holy See had refused to discuss any solution to the problem and had instead become "an enemy Government established as an enclave within the Kingdom, seeking in the confusions sweeping Europe to trigger new military intervention." As a result, Italy now faced a mortal threat, for, Visconti charged, "the Roman territory is the nerve center for the party that plots foreign intervention aimed at restoring another political order on the peninsula."

But still he thought military action against Rome might be avoided. All depended on the pope's willingness to listen to reason. For the past ten years, Visconti explained, in the course of negotiations among the various Catholic countries, "the possible bases of a definitive solution of the Roman question have been confidentially agreed upon." And here Visconti came to the government's secret plan, set out in an attached memo. The Italian ambassadors were to bring the plan to the attention of friendly governments in a final effort to avoid military confrontation with the pope. It is a remarkable document, and had Pius accepted the plan, the future of Rome, Italy, and the papacy might have been very different.

Titled "Notes on the Leonine City" and written, like Visconti's dispatch, in French, it begins by offering some historical background: "The Tiber divides Rome into two parts, one of which, on the right bank of the river, is commonly known as the *Leonine city,* named for Popes Leo III and Leo IV, the first having founded it, and the second seeing it through its completion in 849." The Leonine city had been surrounded on three sides by a wall, much of which still remained, extending 1,300 meters long and 700 wide, with the Tiber forming the fourth.

The solution to the Roman problem was clear: give the pope the Leonine city. Fifteen thousand people lived within its borders, and it had room for many more if its spacious gardens were cut back to allow the construction of new buildings. It already contained a large number of churches and palaces. Indeed, Visconti concluded, with "St. Peter's church, the Vatican and all its huge conglomeration of attached buildings, the tombs of the apostles and of the most famous popes, numerous religious and artistic monuments, the Leonine city is both a remarkable city and a splendid residence for the sovereign head of the Catholic religion."[28]

The pope, unmoved, dismissed the Italian offer out of hand. In the battle between God's forces and those of the Devil, he knew who would prevail. "In the Church Hierarchy," the Italian prefect based just south of Rome told Lanza, "the belief is growing that Italy, as it exists today, will not last long. . . . They predict with certainty and with growing confidence that 1871 will see Italy cut up into at least three parts: the South, the North, and the Papal lands in the middle, placed above both others." Toward this end, the prefect charged, the Holy See was conniving with foreign powers, including Prussia.[29]

The pope and his allies kept trying to convince themselves and the nervous Roman population that, notwithstanding the massing of Italian troops on their border, there was no chance of invasion. On August 30, L'Osservatore Romano admitted that the number of Italian soldiers there was growing every day but added, "It is certain that this force has no offensive aim of any kind, but is at the Roman border out of respect for the Convention of September." As evidence, the correspondent cited the soldiers' lack of a mobile telegraph and postal system. "This clearly shows," he concluded, "that these troops are intended to operate inside the kingdom [of Italy], to be ready in case of any disorders provoked by the subversive parties."[30]

And so the historic month of September 1870 began. On the first day of the month came one of the most painful military defeats in French history, the Prussian victory at Sedan, where Napoleon III himself was captured. When news of the French disaster reached Italy two days later, the nationalists were ecstatic. Lanza could wait no longer and called on the government to approve a march on Rome, disingenuously using as his pretext the likelihood that if the government did not act, the revolutionaries in Rome might take things into their own hands. Still his foreign minister, Visconti, hesitated, believing that Italy was bound by the September Convention.

Events in France finally pushed things over the edge. On September 4, with their disgraced emperor in captivity, the French proclaimed the end of the monarchy and the establishment of a new republic. The news had a dramatic effect in Florence, not least on the king himself. Victor Emmanuel had felt constrained not to invade Rome by his agreement with the French emperor, whom he regarded as a friend. Now there was no French emperor. And whatever remaining scruples he had about renouncing the treaty evaporated when he realized that if he were to stand in the way of taking Rome, he could well suffer a fate similar to Napoleon's. The Italians, like the French, might well turn against their king and proclaim a republic.

The king was also influenced by reports from Rome that the pope would never agree to a peaceful end to his remaining state. "The Vatican," Count Kulczycki wrote to the foreign ministry on September 5, "will submit only to an act of violence."

The count also described the surprising division of opinion in the Holy See about just what France's defeat meant for the future of papal rule. The pope had been stunned by the news, and Antonelli was so stricken that, uncharacteristically, he had also let his emotions show. Yet many Roman prelates reacted with glee to the news of Napoleon's captivity and fall. Kulczycki explained: "'That's the end of Italian unity!' they all cried. They are more than ever convinced that Prussia's dismantling of Italy is now near."[31]

On September 6, the king approved sending Italian troops into Rome, contingent on making one last attempt to convince the pope to accept a peaceful solution. But Victor Emmanuel, on the eve of what many would see as his great triumph, was not a happy man. In these fervid weeks he had felt constantly pressured by his ministers to do what they wanted, when it was in just such circumstances of high international drama that he felt it was he who should be making the decisions. He was particularly annoyed with Lanza, an irritation he made clear every time they met. Practically on the eve of the march into Rome, the prime minister decided that he could take no more, sending the king a letter of resignation on September 7. "The sense of lack of confidence and of unhappiness in the direction of state affairs that Your Majesty has repeatedly manifested to me," Lanza wrote, "both in our private meetings and in the presence of my colleagues, has caused me such despair that I no longer wish to remain as head of Your Majesty's government." Stung by the note and fearful of losing his talented prime minister at such a critical moment, Victor Emmanuel reluctantly urged him to stay on.[32]

The next day, Visconti sent a circular to all of Italy's foreign ambassadors, providing the official justification for Italy's decision to seize Rome. Every government, he wrote, reserves for itself the right of self-defense. The chaos overtaking Europe, leading to upheaval in the pontifical lands, had now made it impossible for Italy to remain idle. Italy could not stand by while the pope faced the rising threat posed by Rome's rebellious population, for the Italian government had pledged to ensure his safety. As a result, Italy now felt compelled to occupy the papal lands.[33]

What most worried the Italians as they prepared to invade Rome was France, which, despite its catastrophic military situation and its political chaos, remained formally pledged to protect the integrity of the pope's remaining domain. With this in mind, a little after midnight on September 7, before distributing his circular to all the ambassadors, Visconti sent a separate telegram to his ambassador in Paris. Hopeful that the new republican government might be willing to change course, Visconti advanced two arguments. First, he wrote, the French should be aware that, in seizing Rome, Italy had the tacit backing of all of the continent's other powers: Austria, Prussia, Spain, Switzerland, and Bavaria. Second, Visconti added, if the new French leadership did not oppose the Italian move, "it would help us eliminate the source of great difficulty for the future relations between Italy and France," and "everyone in our country, unanimous as they are regarding the Roman question, would feel in the French Republic's debt."[34]

On September 8, the king called on Count Ponza di San Martino, a prominent Piedmontese conservative, to deliver a final personal plea to Pius.[35] In the letter he gave to the count, the king claimed to be motivated only by a desire to protect the pontiff: together they faced growing revolutionary threats aimed against both papacy and throne. Given these dangers, wrote Victor Emmanuel, "[i]n order to ensure the security both of Italy and the Holy See, I see the inescapable necessity of sending my troops, which are already guarding the border, to occupy those positions that are necessary for Your Holiness's safety." In a phrase that likely sent the temperamental pope's blood pressure rocketing, the king added: "I trust that Your Holiness will not want to see this precautionary measure as a hostile act."

Along with the letter, the count carried a document that Lanza had prepared, setting out ten articles to serve as the basis for an agreement between Italy and the Holy See. The pope would retain the inviolability and prerogatives attaching to him as a sovereign. The Leonine city would remain "under the full jurisdiction and sovereignty of the Pontiff." The Italian state would guarantee the pope's freedom to communicate with the Catholic world, as well as diplomatic immunity both for the nuncios and envoys in foreign lands and for the foreign diplomats at the Holy See. The government would supply a permanent annual fund for the pope and the cardinals, equal to the amount currently assigned to them by the budget of the pontifical state, and would assume all papal civil servants and soldiers onto the state payroll, with full pensions, as long as they were Italian. Finally, Lanza pledged, "[t]hese provisions will be considered as a public bilateral treaty and will be the object of an agreement among all the Catholic Powers who choose to enter into it."[36]

Despite this last-minute effort, the prime minister had little reason to be optimistic that war could be avoided. On the very day that Ponza was sent to Rome, Lanza heard from Count Kulczycki. The Holy See, he reported, had already decided to respond to the king with an emphatic "*non possumus*" (we cannot). At the same time, Pius was trying to calm Rome's restive population, taking a carefree stroll the previous day down the entire length of the Corso, in the middle of the city. The Jesuits had won out, Kulczycki wrote, and the pope would take the approach he had used successfully the last time he faced losing Rome. The moment that the Italian troops entered the city, he would excommunicate the king and the members of the Italian government and then announce his impending departure. He would issue a call to all the world's Catholic faithful to come to his aid, as he had from Gaeta twenty-one years earlier.[37]

Count Ponza and his aide, the Marquis Guiccioli, traveled overnight by train from Florence to Rome on a special carriage that had been seized a decade earlier from the grandduke of Tuscany, sending word to the secretary of state on their arrival. Antonelli responded immediately, fixing an appointment with them for that very evening, the ninth, at 7 P.M., and scheduling their meeting with the pope for the following morning at ten o'clock.[38] Both Antonelli and Ponza later wrote about their encounter that evening, which lasted over two hours. Antonelli recorded the full text of the conversation, beginning with Ponza's first words:

"I come, Your Eminence, bearing a letter from King Victor Emmanuel for His Holy Father, and I am pleased to be able to carry out such a benevolent mission, aimed at giving the Italian Government's guarantee of the continued independence and prestige of the Holy See."

"Excellent. Then your Government, Signor Count, recognizes the absolute need of independence for the Head of a Religion that has interests in countries throughout the world?"

"Yes, Your Eminence, indeed, it is convinced of it."

"Ah, that comforts me, Signor Count, and I am pleased to hear that this great truth has finally been understood."

"Let's be clear, I refer to spiritual independence."

"Indeed, spiritual independence, because the Holy See above all has need of it in order to carry out its earthly mission."

"Precisely, Your Eminence, and I will be pleased to bring the King and the Government the wonderful news that the longed-for pacification has been concluded."

"Yes, but first we must discuss the details, Signor Count, and see if they truly guarantee this independence of the Pope that your Government so reasonably desires."

Here Antonelli paused in his reconstruction of the conversation to observe that Count Ponza began to employ all of his vaunted eloquence to convince him of the value of what the king was offering: a bolstering of papal prestige and authority, unlimited respect for the Holy Father and his Court, and financial support and the protection of Catholic institutions. "All this and much more the Count promised," recalled Antonelli. The cardinal then spoke:

"Very well, Signor Count, and I certainly want to believe in your loyalty, and in that of your Government. But in whose name, Signor Count, do you promise all this?"

"Why, in the name of the King's Government!"

"Well then, permit me, Signor Count, first of all, to remind you that this Government is constitutional, and as you well know, the Minister who is in power today may change tomorrow, and be replaced by someone of a very different outlook. Then there is Parliament, which claims for itself the right of emending and approving or not approving all of the promises that you have been charged by the Minister to make to the Holy See. Now, are you able to guarantee that the Parliament in the future or some Minister who might succeed the current one will support and preserve unchanged any agreement on this subject that we may conclude today?"

These remarks, Antonelli reported, seemed to unsettle the count. "Well, I hope so," Ponza replied, "and the Italians' good sense gives me good reason for such a belief."

There followed a tense exchange in which Ponza tried to convince the cardinal that should a treaty with the Holy See be signed, future parliaments would view the papacy even more positively and the threat from revolutionaries would be greatly reduced. Antonelli rejected his arguments, turning the king's attempt to join the fate of the monarchy and the pope on its head:

"Let's be frank, Signor Count. You cannot ignore the reason why it is the anarchists more than anyone else who are pushing for taking Rome. It is because they hope one day to be able to bury both the Papacy and the Monarchy here. Meanwhile, thank Heavens, in this little territory that has up to now been left to the Holy See, we find ourselves living in perfect tranquility, and in this way, I might add, the Pope's continued independence offers, at the same time, a shield for the Monarchy."

Antonelli contrasted Rome's current peace with the upheavals that buffeted the Italian government, a result of its reliance on parliamentary democracy.

"Do you really think, Signor Count, that under such circumstances the time seems right for coming here with these proposals?"

The count did what he could to hold his ground: "But, indeed, the Government hopes that the steps proposed here will offer a way out of the difficult situation in which it finds itself."

"I, on the contrary," concluded the secretary of state, "tell you that with measures like the ones that they are proposing, your Government is going to create an ever more difficult situation. And so it is useless for us to waste any more time on this topic. Let the Florence Government do what it wants. For its part, the Holy See will not and cannot agree to actions that have been planned to its detriment."[39]

When Pius himself received Ponza the following morning, according to one telling, the pope greeted him by bellowing, "What a bunch of hypocrites!" Undeterred, Ponza gave the pope both the king's letter and Lanza's list of provisions for safeguarding the Holy See.

Ponza described the pope as "grieving deeply" as he recognized the approaching end of his reign as pope-king, but the Italian envoy saw some hope in his reaction: "He will not recognize the legitimacy [of the taking of Rome]. He will protest to all the world, yet he expresses too much regret for the French and Prussian slaughter not to give me some hope that it is not a model that he would want to follow."[40]

Ponza then sent a telegram to Lanza, telling him of the pontiff's refusal of the king's offer. The die had been cast. The next day, September 11, the Italian troops crossed into the pontifical state. As they swept in, the soldiers plastered large posters addressed to the "Italians of the Roman Provinces" on the walls. Signed by Raffaele Cadorna, the head of the Italian army division in charge of the taking of Rome, they assured the populace that the army had come on a mission of peace, aimed at ensuring Italy's security and the well-being of the people of the Roman territories. "The independence of the Holy See," Cadorna pledged, "will remain inviolable, as will the freedom of the citizens, both more fully guaranteed than they ever were under the protection of foreign forces."[41]

The Italian soldiers who pasted this proclamation on the walls covered up one put up the previous day from the head of the pontifical army, General Kanzler. It painted quite a different picture: "Romans! A horrendous evil is being attempted. The Holy Father, in His peaceful possession of His Capital and of the few provinces spared from usurpation from His dominion, is threatened without any reason by the troops of a Catholic king. Rome is therefore in a state of siege." Kanzler called on the citizenry to remain in their homes. The same day, he had telegraphed the commanders of the various divisions of his troops scattered around the Roman territories with the news that Ponza's ultimatum had been rebuffed. "We may be attacked at any time. Take measures not to get cut off."[42]

As the Italian troops began their advance through the papal lands,

Pius sent Victor Emmanuel a short note: "Count Ponza di San Martino has given me a letter that Your Majesty wished to direct to me, but one that is not worthy of an Affectionate Son who claims to profess the Catholic faith." The pope told the king that he would not respond in detail to his proposals, for to do so would simply "renew the pain that my first reading caused me." But the Lord's ways were not easy for mere mortals to fathom. "I bless God," wrote the pope, "who has seen fit to allow Your Majesty to fill the last years of my life with such bitterness." He concluded, "I ask God to shed his grace on Your Majesty, protecting you from danger and dispensing his mercy on you who have such need of it."[43]

4

Conquering the Holy City

*A*S ITALIAN TROOPS marched on Rome from both north and south, the pope frantically sought help from Europe's great powers, but circumstances were against him. France was still locked in a war with Prussia, its capital circled by enemy troops, its emperor overthrown, and a new republican government not yet fully formed. Prussia was not only occupied with its war but was in the process of unifying all of Germany into a single state, while Austria, having been defeated just four years earlier by Prussia, was leery about acting on its own.

Yet, from the pope's perspective, Austria had no excuse not to come to help him. After all, for decades it had been Europe's most influential Catholic power, its soldiers more than once going in to quell revolts in the Papal States in the nineteenth century. The last burst of papal diplomatic energy before the attack on Rome was thus, not surprisingly, aimed at the Austrian emperor. Within twenty-four hours of the pope's meeting with Count Ponza, Antonelli received a coded message from his nuncio in Vienna. In response to the telegram that the secretary of state had sent him on the ninth, he had arranged an emergency meeting with the Austro-Hungarian foreign minister, Count Friedrich von Beust. "Catholic Austria's abandonment of the pope," the nuncio told Beust, "would be viewed in the Catholic world as a form of parricide." Beust replied that he would speak with Franz Josef and get back to him quickly.[1]

On the morning of the twelfth, Beust summoned the nuncio and gave him the bad news. Austria could do nothing to help, for if the emperor were to take a stand against the invasion of Rome and Italy went ahead anyway, the emperor's dignity would be grievously offended. This slight would be grounds for war against Italy, something that Austria wanted at all costs to avoid. Beust assured the nuncio that Austria remained devoted to the pope and that "all of the cities of the Empire were at his disposition" should he wish to flee Rome. The nuncio was furious. "It takes some nerve," he replied icily, "to invite me to move into your house while you do nothing to prevent me from being thrown out of my own." He begged Beust at least to announce publicly that the Imperial Government would be displeased by an Italian invasion. "But they would not even grant me this."

The nuncio had his own theory about why the pope's pleas were being repulsed. Count Beust had often written against the Vatican Council's pronouncement of papal infallibility, and "I cannot get away from the conviction that this treatment by the Austro-Hungarian cabinet regarding the Italian invasion is nothing other than a vile vendetta against the Council's decisions." It did not help that Beust was himself not only a Protestant but a Freemason as well.[2]

As the French military situation grew only worse, the pope's dwindling hopes of any help from that source were quickly evaporating. Jules Favre, the foreign minister of the new French republic, refused to publicly renounce the September Convention or to offer France's approval of the Italian march on Rome. Yet, in private conversations, he made it clear that France would do nothing to stop the assault. In a letter written on September 10 to a colleague, he explained: "You know our opinion. . . . The temporal power has been a scourge to the world, it is prostrate, we will not resurrect it. But we feel too unhappy to trample on it."

At this point the pope should have had no illusion about the prospects of getting any help from the foreign powers. Yet Pius was a man of deep faith, confident that God was on his side. As Ponza, the king's emissary, was leaving on September 10, the pope was said to have told him as he was going out the door: "I am neither a prophet nor son of prophets, but I tell you that you will not enter, or if you enter you will not remain."[3]

On September 16, the Italian forces occupied the pope's port, Civitavecchia. All that remained was the final sweep into Rome, but the government still hoped to avoid seizing the Holy City by force, all too aware of the outrage such a scene would provoke among Catholics worldwide. After taking the port, the Italian war minister, at the king's request, instructed Cadorna to send a final appeal to the papal government to end its military resistance. Cadorna wrote to General Kanzler the same day. "I have the honor of informing Your Excellency," the letter began, "that Civitavecchia surrendered this morning to royal troops. Following this fact, the futility of further bloodshed should be all the clearer, especially considering the strength of the forces involved in the attack compared to those on the defense." Under these circumstances, Cadorna pleaded, "I judge it not without utility to renew the request that you offer no resistance to the military occupation of Rome." Perhaps not helping his cause with the pope, the Italian general added: "These sentiments are those of His Majesty the King, of the government, and of all Italians, including those in the provinces that have already been occupied by royal troops, who exult in the thought of being part of a common homeland." He concluded with the warning that, should it refuse his proposal, the papal government would be responsible for the many pointless deaths that would result.

Later the same day General Kanzler sent his reply. "The taking of Civitavecchia," he wrote, "does not substantially change our situation. . . . You appeal to humanitarian sentiments, which certainly are no dearer to anyone than to those who have the pleasure of serving the Holy See. But it is not we who have in any way provoked the sacrilegious attack of which we are the victims. It is thus up to you to show that you are animated by such humanitarian sentiments, refraining from your unjust aggression." Addressing the loyalties of those living in the Roman territories, Kanzler insisted that the pope's subjects "have given indisputable proof of their attachment to the Pontifical government." Responsibility for any deaths that were to follow, then, lay clearly with Cadorna and his government, who, should they move on Rome, would assume an "immense responsibility before God and before the tribunal of history."[4]

In the face of the pope's refusal to cede Rome, Lanza needed to find a way to take the city without unduly roiling the diplomatic waters. The problem was not military, for there was no question that the heavily outnumbered papal force could not long hold off the Italians. The problem was what would happen after Rome was taken. The memory of the Roman Republic of 1849 came to mind, when the French and Austrians heeded the pope's pleas and sent their armies to take back the lands he had lost.

In mid-September, Lanza received a report from Rome offering a disheartening portrait of its population. Three classes lived there, his correspondent explained: the clerical class, the bourgeoisie (lawyers, doctors, merchants, storekeepers), and the lower class. The clergy, humiliated by the Italian conquest, would nurse their grievances and dream of the day they could take revenge on the usurper state. The bourgeoisie, on the other hand, long excluded from influence by the papal government, would dream of having their greatest ambitions fulfilled, "but because it is impossible for all of them to put their hand in the till," Lanza's informer predicted, "they will become part of the opposition and the extreme party." Meanwhile, the lower classes, the *basso popolo*, "are wild and bloody and will remain in large part devoted to the sects, the instrument of vendettas on behalf of the revolutionary parties." He would not even speak of the aristocracy, he explained, "because they are too stupid to be capable of doing either good or bad."[5]

On September 18, Italy's minister of war sent Cadorna instructions to attack, specifying that he spare the Leonine city, reserving it for the pope. The plan of attack was left entirely up to the general, with the caution that "political conditions require, more than ever, prudence and moderation." The following day Cadorna sent final orders to his officers. His instructions regarding the right bank of the Tiber were clear. The Italian troops were to leave the Leonine city alone.[6]

The pope, realizing that much of his remaining territories had already been occupied by the Piedmontese — he refused to call them Italians — went through the city to the *scala santa*, the holy steps, just across from the massive St. John in Lateran basilica. Believed to have originally been the stairway in Pilate's palace in Jerusalem and brought to Rome by the mother of Emperor Constantine in the fourth century, it had attracted pilgrims for centuries. The elderly Pius IX climbed the twenty-eight steps on his knees. At the top, before the crucifix, in a trembling voice he prayed to God to watch over his people. Those with him were brought to tears. Afterward, outside in the piazza, a general asked the pope to bless his troops. Pius then got in his large red carriage and waved to all the faithful lining the streets as he made his way back to the Vatican. Along the way he heard shouts of "Holy Father, don't abandon us!," for rumors were rife that he would leave Rome as soon as the Italian forces arrived.[7]

The pope faced a difficult decision. Greatly outnumbered and totally surrounded, protected by only a ring of ancient walls that were far

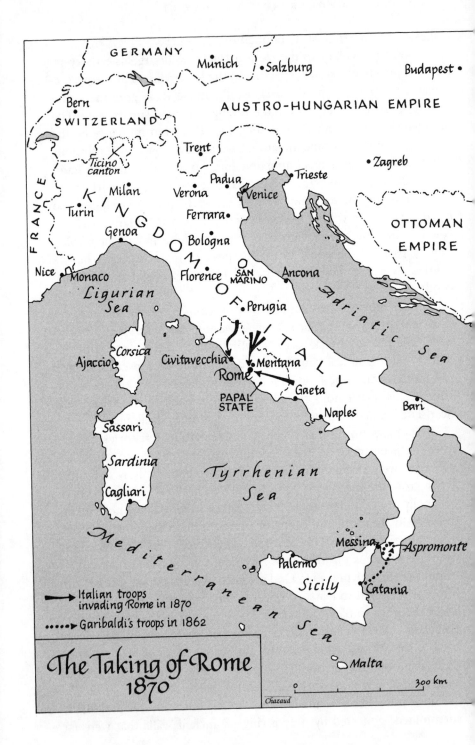

GERMANY
Munich • Salzburg
Budapest •
Bern
SWITZERLAND
AUSTRO-HUNGARIAN EMPIRE
FRANCE
Ticino canton
Trent
• Zagreb
KINGDOM
Milan
Padua
• Trieste
OTTOMAN
EMPIRE
Turin
Verona
Venice
Genoa
Ferrara •
Bologna
Nice
Monaco
Ligurian
Sea
Florence
SAN MARINO
Ancona
OF
Perugia
Adriatic Sea
Corsica
Ajaccio
Civitavecchia
Rome
Mentana
ITALY
PAPAL STATE
Gaeta
Bari
Sassari
Naples
Sardinia
Cagliari
Tyrrhenian
Sea
Messina
Aspromonte
Palermo
Sicily
Catania

Mediterranean Sea

→ Italian troops invading Rome in 1870
•••• ▸ Garibaldi's troops in 1862

Malta

The Taking of Rome
1870

300 km

Chazaud

from impregnable against modern artillery, the pope's soldiers could not possibly prevail. To order them to fight was to consign many of them to a death that would, in a military sense, have little purpose. Yet he was loath to allow the Italians to take Rome without a fight, believing that to do so might be interpreted as showing that he had given his consent. On September 7, Pius called in his three generals and said that while they should mount a clear resistance to the attack, its aim should be above all to show that the city was being taken by force. Once they had made this clear, they should surrender.[8]

The American consul in Rome, D. Maitland Armstrong, offers an enticing glimpse of what Roman life was like in the days preceding the final battle. As it happened, the consul had returned to Rome in mid-September using the same gate that the Italian troops would use to enter the city a few days later. He described the earthen barricades and deep trench outside Porta Pia and the piles of sandbags reinforcing the inner side. In these final days of papal Rome, Armstrong observed, the city "was in a state of quiet expectancy, almost, it seemed of apathy, the streets were comparatively deserted, most of the shops closed, all telegraphic and postal communication cut off, from the 12th until the 23d of September the mails were not received. On the walls were posted proclamations declaring the city in a state of siege, forbidding all people to enter or leave the city, or to assemble in any considerable numbers in the streets."[9] He described a population having little enthusiasm for continued papal rule, noting that despite the desperate attempts of the authorities to attract volunteers to defend the Holy City, only two hundred in all of Rome were willing to enlist, and "with the exception of these and the few Romans already in its service not one of the people raised a hand for the defence of the Papacy." Unsavory men who had previously served the papal authorities as spies were now given uniforms and patrolled the streets, fueling popular resentment.

At 5 A.M. on September 20 the attack began, moving along an arc that ran across a third of the city walls, with cannons booming out forty shots each minute. Armstrong gave this eyewitness account:

The old walls generally proved utterly useless against heavy artillery, in four or five hours they were in some places completely swept away, a clear breach was made near the Porta Pia fifty feet wide, and the Italian soldiers in overwhelming force flowed through it and literally filled the city, simultaneously the Porta San Giovanni was carried by assault. A white flag was hoisted over from the dome of St. Peter's. After the cannonading ceased the papal troops made but a feeble resistance, and they who a moment before ruled Rome with a rod of iron, were nearly all prisoners, or had taken refuge in the Castle of St. Angelo, or St. Peter's square.

The Italian forces avoided unnecessary damage or bloodshed, according to Armstrong, as they aimed their fire solely against the outer walls and not into the city: the only noncombatant deaths came as the result of stray shots. Indeed, a bullet had gone through the American consulate's window.

The disinclination of the papal forces to fight more fiercely, in the American consul's view, was reinforced by their realization that the people of Rome welcomed the Italians as their liberators, as "no private citizens made the least effort or demonstration in favor of the Papal Government." In all, Armstrong reported:

> it was an easy victory for the Italians, and the loss, in killed and wounded, on both sides, was not great, they were in over-whelming force, with very heavy artillery and they knew that the mass of Romans were their friends; the Zouaves [the papal troops], on the other hand, although they never could have imagined how much they were detested, must have, at heart, feared the people, and could not fight their best; they were a fine looking body of men, many of them, even the common soldiers, of superior education and refinement, some of them undoubtedly served the Pope from religious feeling, many for the sake of the romance and adventure of the thing, very few for pay, as it was ridiculously small.[10]

The consul's account was mistaken on at least one count. While the troops in the major line of assault — under Cadorna's command — limited their fire to the destruction of the walls, the troops on the other side of the city, charged with creating a distraction, did not. Under General Nino Bixio, they lobbed cannon shots perilously close to St. Peter's itself.

Bixio was a colorful, swashbuckling, but also rather troubled figure. Born in Genoa in 1821, he had been the uncontrollable son of a wealthy father, his mother having died when he was young. Not knowing what to do with the willful child, his father sent him off into the merchant marine at the age of thirteen, and while still a youth he had suffered a shipwreck and imprisonment in the West Indies. In 1847, already a devout republican, Bixio met Mazzini and joined the revolts of 1848. Fighting alongside Garibaldi, he was wounded defending the Roman Republic in 1849. Ten years later, as Garibaldi's right-hand man, he accompanied the hero through Tuscany and Romagna before being given command of one of the two ships that carried Garibaldi's "thousand" volunteers to Sicily in 1860. He was far from loved by his men, who feared his violent temper.

Cadorna had never liked Bixio, whom he saw as more suited for the role of leader of the revolutionary rabble than a proper military officer, but Bixio had been the beneficiary of the policy that brought Garibaldi's irregulars into the official Italian army a decade earlier. Addressing parliament in the 1860s, the flamboyant Bixio had proposed his own solution to the Roman question: the matter was simple, he said. Just throw the pope and all of his cardinals into the Tiber.[11]

By 6 A.M., only an hour after the first sounds of battle were heard, members of the diplomatic corps began to arrive at the Vatican to be with the pope on what they knew would be a historic day. Wearing their finest uniforms and riding in their best carriages, eleven foreign envoys made their way in, including the ambassadors of Prussia, Austria, and France. At seven-thirty the pope, as was his habit, entered his private chapel, along with Antonelli and other members of his entourage. There the diplomats had the strange experience of hearing the pope say mass to the sounds of the cannons.

The pope then assembled the diplomats in his library, where he launched into a long monologue. Those who reported on the meeting observed that the pope seemed oddly impervious to what was going on outside. After thanking them for their presence on this sad occasion, he appeared to lose himself in memories of years past, dwelling on the pleasant times he had had as a young man, in 1823, when he sailed to South America as a member of the papal diplomatic corps. In the midst of these reveries, he was interrupted by the arrival of Count Carpegna, Kanzler's chief of staff, who brought news of the opening of a breach in the walls at Porta Pia. The pope hurried out, with Antonelli at his side, as they prepared Kanzler's final orders. It took little time for the terms of the surrender to be drafted by General Cadorna and signed by Kanzler. All of Rome, excluding the Leonine city, was now ceded to the army of His Majesty the king of Italy. The defeated papal troops were escorted back to St. Peter's Square, protected from the jeering Romans by troops bearing the Italian tricolored flag.[12]

The dream of a unified Italy had come to pass. Uncensored newspapers could now appear. One of the first, on September 23, captured the delirious mood:

> After fifteen centuries of darkness, of mourning, of misery and pain, Rome, once the queen of all the world, has again become the metropolis of a great State. Today, for us Romans, is a day of indescribable joy. Today in Rome freedom of thought is no longer a crime, and free speech can be heard within its walls without fear of the Inquisition, of burnings at the stake, of the gallows. The light of civil liberty that, arising in France in 1789, has brightened all Europe now shines as well on the eternal city. For Rome it is only today that the Middle Ages are over.[13]

The mood of the pope's defenders was glum. Yet they were not without their own hopes for the future, drawing comfort from the knowledge that Rome had been overrun by invaders many times before. In each case God had made sure that the Holy City was restored to its divinely ordained owners, its enemies — His enemies — brought low.[14]

5

The Leonine City

TWO MONTHS AFTER the Holy City was taken, an Italian government envoy went to see Bishop Giovanni Simeoni, secretary of the Vatican's Congregation for the Propagation of the Faith, the body in charge of the Church's missions overseas. He wanted to sound the bishop out on ways that the government might cooperate with the Catholic missions abroad to their mutual benefit, but the bishop would hear none of it. The Holy See could not have any dealings with a government that had usurped the pope of his rightful earthly kingdom, said the bishop, and, in any case, he believed, the days of the new regime were numbered. "It is for us just a matter of time," he predicted. "When it will be, I don't know. It might be postponed a bit, but someday I will have the pleasure of writing you that the Restoration has come." Like others around the pope, Simeoni made no distinction between the restoration of the pope's rule in Rome itself and the restoration of the entire Papal States, for they were one and the same. Nor was this illusion shared only by prelates in Rome. In this sense, the letter that Archbishop Martin Spalding of Baltimore sent in early October 1870 was typical. "Our most beloved Father should be consoled," he wrote, for "such an abnormal state of affairs certainly cannot last very long. Divine providence will soon bring the needed remedy. I couldn't be more convinced of it."[1]

The leaders of the Italian government, meanwhile, had other ideas. In his early September letter to the pope, the king had specifically promised him full sovereignty over the right bank of the Tiber, intending that Rome would be forever divided between its secular left bank, over which he would preside, and the sacred domain of the Church on the right. This view is reflected in the September 23 comments of one of Italy's most prominent statesmen, Marco Minghetti, the former prime minister who was then serving as Italian ambassador to Vienna. "Italian troops will not enter the Leonine city," he wrote to Lord Acton that day.[2] What he did not realize was that the soldiers were already there.

On September 21, as General Cadorna stood at Porta San Pancrazio, south of the Leonine city, reviewing the foreign pontifical troops heading out of the country, he was surprised by the arrival of Count Harry von Arnim, the Prussian ambassador to the Holy See, who urgently sought his attention. Scuffling had broken out in the Leonine city between the papal gendarmes and the *popolani*, the lower classes, Arnim told him. The pope was upset, and those around him feared for his safety. Pius, according to Arnim, asked that Italian troops be sent in to preserve order.

Cadorna had told his troops not to enter the Leonine city, which he had defined very broadly to include not only the area within the old walls erected in the ninth century by Leo IV — containing the Vatican, the residential area between the Vatican and the Tiber (called the Borgo), and the Sant'Angelo Castle — but also the stretch of largely unoccupied land to the south going up the Gianiculum hill to the Porta San Pancrazio, where he now stood. Cadorna was not pleased by the pope's request. Certainly, he argued, Pius had sufficient forces left to maintain order, for he had Noble Guards, Palatine guards, Swiss guards, and gendarmes — only the papal army itself had been disbanded. But if, Cadorna told the Prussian ambassador, the pope still needed the Italian forces, he would have to put his request in writing and either sign it himself or have Antonelli or Kanzler do so.

While Arnim's carriage rattled over the cobblestone streets back to the Vatican, Cadorna sent orders for two of his battalions to move into position at the Sant'Angelo bridge, taking care to remain on the left bank. Arnim soon returned with a letter signed by Kanzler. "His Holiness has asked me to inform you," the general wrote, "that he wants you to take energetic and effective measures for the protection of the Vatican, for with all of his troops now dissolved, he lacks the means to prevent those who would disturb the peace — both immigrants and

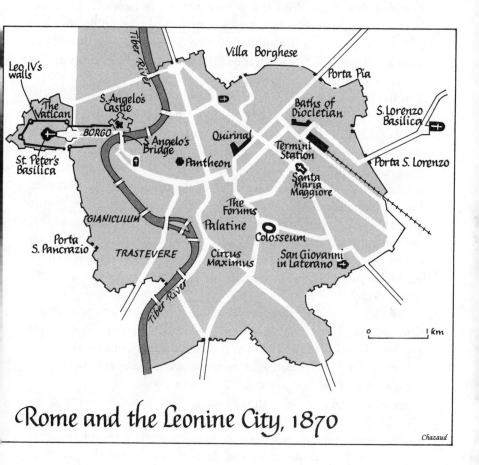

Rome and the Leonine City, 1870

Leo IV's walls

Tiber River

Villa Borghese

Porta Pia

The Vatican

S. Angelo's Castle

Baths of Diocletian

S. Lorenzo Basilica

BORGO

S. Angelo's Bridge

Quirinal

Termini Station

Porta S. Lorenzo

St. Peter's Basilica

Pantheon

Santa Maria Maggiore

GIANICULUM

The Forums

Palatine

Colosseum

Porta S. Pancrazio

TRASTEVERE

Circus Maximus

San Giovanni in Laterano

Tiber River

0   1 km

Chazaud

others — from coming to cause disturbances and disorders under his sovereign residence." With this official request in hand, Cadorna ordered the two battalions to cross the bridge and take up positions in Sant'Angelo castle, in the square outside St. Peter's, and around the Vatican. He immediately telegraphed the news to the war minister, who by return wire gave his approval.[3]

In the wake of the violent seizure of Rome, Lanza, Visconti, and Italy's other leaders desperately wanted to show the world that the Holy See could live in harmony with the enlarged Italian state. Nothing would be more valuable than some sign that the pope was willing to make peace with them. On September 22, Lanza sent instructions to Cadorna — now the military ruler of the occupied city — stressing that the pope should be treated with the utmost respect. "Look into whether a visit paying homage might not be displeasing to him, so that you can express these intentions face to face in the name of the King and his government."[4] This idea, it turned out, was too much to hope for. The pope would not receive him or any other representative of the usurper king.

For Lanza and his colleagues, the pope's refusal to accept the Leonine city was a great embarrassment. The Italian diplomatic corps had trumpeted the king's offer to governments throughout Europe as evidence that king and pope could coexist peacefully. Papal refusal raised the specter of a battle to the death for Rome.

Meanwhile, in keeping with the procedures it had followed in all the other lands annexed to the Savoyard monarchy, the government organized a popular plebiscite so that the Romans could vote on joining the Kingdom of Italy. It was crucial to show the world that the people of Rome were eager to be part of Italy.

At the time, Rome had a population of about 240,000, divided into fourteen *rioni,* or districts, and further divided into fifty-four parishes. Most Romans were illiterate and few spoke Italian, but in this respect they were no different from most Italians.[5]

As the October 2 date neared, the residents of Borgo, the *rione* in the middle of the Leonine city, were growing increasingly restive. They, too, they insisted, were part of Rome and the new Italian state, and they would never submit to a continued papal theocracy. They too wanted to cast their votes in the plebiscite, thereby posing a ticklish problem for the government. If they voted and overwhelmingly favored becoming part of Italy, how could they be left behind?

Albert Blanc, the secretary-general of the Italian Foreign Ministry, proposed a solution in a September 30 report to Visconti. The government, he urged, should expropriate all the land and buildings in Borgo, compensating their owners by using the proceeds from the sale of Church property seized elsewhere in Rome. The government should then give all of Borgo to the Holy See; any resident who preferred to live under Italian jurisdiction could move across the river. Such a plan would give the Holy See full sovereignty over a city that was large enough to accommodate 40,000 people and that could easily house all of the religious orders that were being evicted from their properties in other parts of the Roman provinces.[6]

The prime minister, eager to see this plan put into effect, telegraphed Cadorna the next day, the day before the plebiscite, with a warning: "It is important that the Government and the municipality take no action during the plebiscite that prejudices the question of the Leonine city, which must be considered as a Pontifical territory." The plebiscite, Lanza instructed, was not to be held in Borgo, and no political demonstration of any kind was to be allowed there.

Shortly before 2 A.M. on the eve of the plebiscite, Blanc telegraphed Visconti to reassure him: "All measures have been taken to prevent anything that might offend the pope. No ballot boxes will be located in the Papal City."[7]

But, apparently unknown to Blanc, earlier that same evening Cadorna had been besieged by the residents of Borgo, irate that they were to be prevented from voting. The general came up with a compromise. While, by government order, no votes could be cast in Borgo, a separate ballot box reserved for residents of the papal territory would be set up on the Campidoglio, the site of Rome's municipal government, for those who wanted to vote.

October 2 was a day of celebration in Rome. Bursting with patriotic fervor, people draped tapestries from their windows and pasted *Sì* on their hats and on the ribbons that hung from their buttonholes. At the end of the day, to the noisy delight of those congregated at the city capital for the counting of the vote, a large delegation of Borgo's residents arrived wearing hats with *Sì* on them. In their ballot box were the 1,566 Borgo votes, every one a yes.[8]

In all, the Romans that day voted 40,785 Sì, 46 No, a tally so lopsided that it offered plenty of ammunition to the pope's defenders. At the polling place, the Jesuits of *Civiltà Cattolica* reported, the man in charge offered each voter a choice between taking a card that said yes and one that said no. Those who asked for the yes ballot were greeted by the applause of the surrounding crowd. Those who dared to ask for the no faced jeers and whistles.[9] While the vote may have been far from an accurate reflection of opinion in Rome, there is no doubt that on that day the vast majority of the Roman population was truly excited, happy to be released from papal rule and eager to be part of the new Italian state.

Blanc, in reporting the results, told Visconti that he did not know how Borgo's residents could be forced to live under papal rule. "But," he added, not without some contradiction, "this does not detract from the idea that leaving the Leonine city to the Pope remains practical, advantageous, and inevitable."[10]

A few days later, Blanc formulated what became the final government proposal for trying to reconcile the apparently irreconcilable: the ceding of the Leonine city to the pope while allowing its population to be citizens of Italy. In a letter to Visconti, Blanc sketched out the new plan. The pope would have sovereignty over the Leonine city. Not only would he enjoy immunity from the Italian government, but so too would the Vatican palaces and all the headquarters of the Church hierarchy and members of the Vatican offices, the cardinals and bishops, and the central offices of the religious orders. The Holy See would have the right to expropriate any other property in the Leonine city that it deemed desirable for ecclesiastical use. The Italian government would provide a large annual subsidy to the Holy See to cover the expenses of all of its offices, in addition to the sum annually assigned to the pope himself. At the same time, the inhabitants of the Leonine city would enjoy the civil and political rights of Italian citizens — with certain exceptions in keeping with the pope's sovereignty. No newspaper, book, pamphlet, or other written material could be sold or posted without papal approval, nor would any theatrical performance, public speech, demonstration, or other such public activity be allowed without pontifical authorization. All artisans and professionals would require Vatican approval in order to conduct business there.[11]

Plans so complicated had no chance of being put into practice unless the pope was willing to negotiate. And, as Antonelli made clear in a letter he sent on October 10 to the papal nuncio in Vienna, Pius was in no mood for compromise.

"The Holy Father," Antonelli wrote, "knowing he has right on his side and resolved to withstand all hardships in order to carry out His duties and live up to the pledge that He took, will never lower himself by entering into any dealings with the usurpers and will never enter into any negotiation that is not directed at restoring the fullness of His dominions and His Sovereign rights." The whole Catholic world should know with absolute certainty, Antonelli added, "that He will not yield, regardless of what the consequences may be." Although the king of Florence — as Antonelli called Victor Emmanuel II — wanted to give the Leonine city to the Holy Father, he wrote, "such a proposal, like any other of its kind, is not going to be and will never be accepted."[12]

The likelihood that Pius could be brought around to a realistic assessment of the new political situation was never very great, and hopes in the Italian cabinet were further diminished by reports that the trauma of losing Rome had increased the pontiff's otherworldly proclivities. On October 12, Blanc sent Visconti a disturbing report: "For some time the pope has been trying to bring about a miracle, during one of those times when he has the sensation of inexhaustible vitality, which he takes to be a visitation of the Holy Spirit." The pope had recently raised his arms and commanded a cripple: "Get up and walk." When the poor man collapsed in a failed effort, the Vatican had the episode hushed up.[13]

Eager to show the other European powers its great respect for the pope, the government decided to appoint Alfonso La Marmora, an army general and former prime minister, in charge of Rome. Widely known in European diplomatic circles as a prudent and conservative man eager to bring about the conciliation of church and state, close to the king and from an aristocratic family of Turin, La Marmora was viewed with disdain by the left, who angrily protested his appointment.[14]

If Lanza had any hopes that La Marmora's reputation as a friend of the Church would open up new possibilities for accord, they were soon dashed. On his arrival in Rome, La Marmora asked to be received at the Vatican so that he could pay homage to the pontiff. Neither Pius nor Antonelli would see him. Lanza tried to console the general: "Their resentment against the King's Government is still too fresh for them to want to establish a relationship immediately with the person who represents this Government." Yet Lanza expressed the wish that as time passed Pius would bow to the new reality.[15]

La Marmora was quickly besieged by the residents of Borgo. A large, noisy delegation protested that they did not want to be separated from the rest of the city and would not remain subjects of the pope. They were to be disappointed. "As you can imagine," La Marmora reported to Lanza, "I was not moved, and rejecting their criticisms, their assertions, and their suspicions, I told them that the Government had already done more for the Romans than I had ever believed possible. As for what would happen, it was necessary to give the situation enough time and to observe the greatest prudence, otherwise we all ran the grave risk of ruining everything." La Marmora ended his letter with a plea to Lanza that a final decision on the fate of the Leonine city be made soon.[16]

The prime minister was fast losing hope. Pius, he was now convinced, would never recognize the legitimacy of the Italian state that had taken his lands. Oddly, less than two weeks after Lanza had tried to reassure the ruffled La Marmora that the pope would eventually come around, he wrote to him: "I do not believe, and I never believed in conciliation. If I were in the pope's or Antonelli's shoes, I would find it odd and personally insulting that someone who took something so large from me which I (let's leave aside whether rightly or wrongly) highly valued should come and ask me for conciliation without returning all or at least part of what he had taken from me. And so if I wanted to do to the pope what I would want done to me under similar circumstances, I would not torment him with proposals for a conciliation that is impossible."

Visconti, the cabinet's most influential champion of conciliation, had by the same time also given up hope. In a letter to his brother on October 25, he wrote that the only thing that could now be done was to impress on the foreign powers how great an effort the government was making to ensure the Holy See's independence. The people of Rome, he added, were not helping these efforts. "They are distrustful, impatient; they want to see the king come to Rome right away, the convents and monasteries abolished immediately, the capital moved there without delay."[17]

In the Vatican, the mood was dark. Gregorovius, an eyewitness, described the scene: "The cardinals never show themselves, or if they drive out, their carriages bear no marks of distinction; all their pomp and magnificence have ended in smoke. Only solitary priests slink through the streets, timid and shadowlike." Yet Gregorovius did not spare the government his barbs. When the pope on November 1 issued an order of excommunication against the usurpers of his realm, Gregorovius reported, "[T]he Government was petty-minded enough to confiscate the newspapers which printed it."[18]

As events unfolded in Rome, the rest of the world looked on, some with glee, others with horror. Disruptions caused by the Italian invasion, along with the continuing chaos in western Europe produced by the Prussian assault on Paris, meant that the initial reports about the pope's fate were slow in coming. In a letter sent on September 26, the papal nuncio in Munich complained that the only news received to date came from the Italian government, giving a one-sided account of the army's triumphal entrance into the Holy City. "Everyone is anxiously and fearfully asking," the nuncio wrote, "about the state of the Holy Father and his precious health." But they had other questions as well: "What will happen to the cardinals and the clergy?" That a Catholic king like Victor Emmanuel could have committed such an outrage was incredible, the nuncio fumed, and would "forever stain his name in infamy before the tribunal of history." Attached to this message was a petition signed by German princes, barons, counts, and lawyers denouncing the taking of Rome and the ending of Pius IX's temporal power.[19]

The papal nuncio to the Netherlands was similarly agitated. On September 27 he sent Antonelli a telegram in numeric code, reporting that the news that had reached Holland told of the Romans' joyous reaction to the arrival of the Italian troops. He was trying to do everything he could to drum up diplomatic support, but the Dutch were more concerned about the chaotic situation in France and, in any case, were inclined to accept the taking of Rome as a fait accompli. The nuncio urgently sought instructions on how best to spur the bishops and Catholic faithful to effective action.[20]

Within a few days of his retreat from the Quirinal Palace, the site of his former offices and now in the midst of a hostile Rome, Antonelli began sending a series of dispatches to his nuncios describing the pope's parlous position and soliciting the help of friendly governments. On September 26 he wrote to his nuncio in Vienna. What was most intolerable for the pope, wrote Antonelli, was that, robbed of his temporal kingdom, he could no longer fulfill his obligations as God's Vicar on earth. The government controlled all means of communication, his cardinals lived under threat, and sacrilegious books in great number were being publicly sold on the streets of Rome. Yet the pope could not protest against any of these outrages for fear that he would expose his sacred person and the clergy as a whole to threats and worse. Under these conditions, concluded Antonelli, it was crucial for the nuncio to impress on the Austrian foreign minister and on the emperor himself the need to champion the pope's course.[21]

As the telegraph and postal systems began to work again, Antonelli received a flurry of dispatches from his nuncios. They reported frenetic activity by Italy's ambassadors abroad, aimed at assuring Europe's governments that the pope and the Holy See were unharmed. On October 1, for example, Italy's ambassador in Vienna had met with Count Beust to relay, in the nuncio's words, the "sacrilegious guarantees that the Italian Government is pretending to want to give the Holy Father." The Italians were claiming, he wrote, that "the extraterritoriality that the Holy Father now enjoys guarantees him his full spiritual Sovereignty and independence." But he also reported something that was now missing from the government's promises: there was no longer any mention of papal rule over the Leonine city.[22]

Later in the month, the pope informed the Catholic world that he had no choice but to suspend the Vatican Council because the Italian occupation of the Holy City made its continued work impossible. Visconti quickly fired off a circular to Italy's ambassadors abroad. "With all due respect for the Holy Father's decision," he told them, "it is my duty to declare that nothing justifies the fears expressed in the pontifical bull. It is well known and clear to all that the Holy Father is perfectly free to resume the Council in St. Peter's or in any other basilica or church in Rome or elsewhere in Italy that it might please His Holiness to choose."[23]

Throughout Europe, Catholics were in a state of shock. Catholics in Malines, Belgium, held one of the countless protest meetings that swept Europe in these weeks. Taking up the imagery of the pope as "prisoner of the Vatican," the protesters blasted the seizure of Rome as not only a sacrilege but an act of parricide, "the crime of the most ungrateful child against the common Father of the great Christian family."[24]

Such meetings were not entirely spontaneous. Under Antonelli's direction, the nuncios coordinated an effort to persuade the Church hierarchy in each country to stir up mass protests. In trying to maximize the political and popular impact of these protests, the nuncios struggled mightily to get the bishops to work together. This feat, as the nuncios constantly complained to Antonelli, was no easy matter.

On October 20, the nuncio in Munich reported the latest developments in that heavily Catholic region of southern Germany. The archbishop of Cologne had written a long letter of protest to the Prussian king, sending copies to all of Germany's bishops. He charged that Pius "had become a prisoner in his own home, lacking the liberty and independence that are absolutely necessary for the exercise of his apostolic ministry" and implored the king to come to the pope's defense, "so that the present intolerable conditions in Rome are remedied and the necessary steps are taken to restore the absolute liberty and independence of the Papal See."

Along with a copy of this letter, the archbishop sent the bishops a confidential note calling on them to follow his example. It was not what the nuncio had wanted, for he had urged the archbishop to coordinate the efforts of all of his colleagues into a single powerful protest. But the archbishop had refused, insisting on going his own way and leaving the other bishops to act singly as well. The reason for this failure, according to the nuncio, were the rivalries that plagued the German episcopate.[25]

At the same time, the Brussels nuncio — the recipient of ten different dispatches from Antonelli over the previous two weeks — reported on developments there. His efforts to get the Belgian bishops to organize a massive popular petition campaign had failed. Instead, the bishops and the heads of the various Catholic associations had sent their own letters of commiseration to the pope. The reactions in Belgium to the pope's plight, the nuncio wrote, had frankly not met his expectations. There had been much talk but little action. True, special masses and processions had been held to express solidarity with the pope, and virtually all the bishops had directed pastoral letters to their flocks protesting the outrage. But the Belgian government, which called itself Catholic, had not lifted a finger in the pope's defense.[26]

The nuncio kept pushing the Belgian government, arguing that the rights of Catholics everywhere were being violated by the pontiff's imprisonment. But the foreign minister had rebuffed him, asking how the

Belgian government could act when "no other government was doing anything for the Holy See." The nuncio concluded his report to Antonelli on a pessimistic note: "It seems that everyone thinks that reconciliation between the Holy See and Victor Emmanuel can be arranged."[27]

Antonelli had entrusted the Belgian nuncio with the task of forwarding copies of his recent instructions to the nuncio in France, but it proved impossible, for Paris was by then under Prussian siege and no mail was getting through. It was only after the French nuncio escaped from the capital and made his way in late October to Tours, southwest of Paris, that he was finally able to reestablish contact with Rome.

Clearly, he told Antonelli, no help for the pope was to be expected anytime soon from the French, who were barely able to defend their own country. Nor did the prospect of aid from the Prussians appear likely. On his way to Tours, he had stopped in Versailles, where the Prussians had set up headquarters for their assault on Paris. There he had met King Wilhelm, as well as the king's brother, Prince Friedrich, and Count Bismarck. All voiced concern for the pope's welfare but said that their hands were full and they could not get involved in Roman affairs.[28]

Antonelli was keeping a close watch on the chaos in France. He was well aware that current circumstances made any immediate French help unlikely, but he did see some hopeful signs. In late October, *L'Osservatore Romano* quoted Adolphe Thiers, soon to become the head of the French provisional government, as saying: "If Italy loves its unity, it must renounce Rome. If it would rather stay in Rome, it must renounce its unity." The next day the paper returned to the theme, reporting that as soon as the Franco-Prussian War was over, a new French government under Thiers would help decide the future of Rome. And, the paper prophesized, "the acts of a State headed by a person who has always decisively proclaimed his opposition to the political unity and current organization of the Peninsula cannot be too favorable for Italy."[29]

In a meeting on November 9, the papal nuncio told France's provisional foreign affairs head that, as soon as the war ended, the Great Powers would have to arrange a conference aimed at reordering the states of Europe. The nuncio clearly expected France to support the restitution of the Papal States, not least because of the growing enmity in France toward the Italians. Just a few days earlier, the Italian government had again declined a French request to send 100,000 soldiers to help repel the Prussians. "Dislike for the Governors of Florence is lodged in every Minister's heart," the French foreign minister had said, and this, the nuncio concluded, "ought to be a good omen for the future."[30]

Once Antonelli was back in touch with his nuncio in France, he began sending him ammunition for the struggle ahead. The Italian government, Antonelli wrote, had the nerve to claim that they were showing the pope and the cardinals the utmost respect. Is this, he asked, what they call "the complete stripping of the august Head of the Church of all of his dominions, of all of his income, the bombardment of the capital of Catholicism, the impieties that are being spread through the population through newspapers, the violent attacks against religion and against the monastic orders, the profanation of the Catholic cult, which is being labeled superstition, the stripping of all public schools of every sacred image, which has been ordered by government authorities and already carried out, the removal of the name of Jesus from above the grand portal of the Roman College?" Nor was this all. Shouts of "Death to the Pope!" were now heard regularly outside the Vatican walls. The pope had become "morally and materially a prisoner in the strictest sense." Of this, Antonelli concluded, there could no longer be any doubt.[31]

Yet from Europe's capitals the secretary of state received, at best, only the most generic offers of support. In mid-November, for example, the Vienna nuncio told him of a recent meeting with Count Beust. Reciting the litany of the pope's woes, the nuncio told the count that the Holy See found Austria's continued indifference "a great disgrace that can be interpreted as Austrian complicity in this sacrilege." Austrian inaction was inexcusable, said the nuncio, for "I have seen you write an angry note to the government of the Danubian principalities at the first sign of an insult aimed at a couple of Jews. . . . Only the Holy Father can be robbed, injured and driven from his house while Austria remains silent and indifferent."

Count Beust tried to calm him down. In fact, he told the nuncio, the emperor was very upset, "and I promise we will do something."

"What exactly he means by this 'something,'" the nuncio observed to Antonelli, "I still do not know . . . until I see some action I have no faith." Yet, the nuncio still believed that the emperor might be moved to act, feeling pressured by all of the Catholic protests. "Let us hope to God," the nuncio concluded, "that there is some result."[32]

With the pope's decision to refuse the offer of the Leonine city now irrevocable, the battle lines were drawn. The pope was not asking foreign governments to help him strike a compromise with the Italian government. From his perspective, the only goal possible was the dismantling of Italy and, as Antonelli put it in his instructions to the papal nuncios, "the full and absolute restoration of the pope's dominions."[33]

6

The Reluctant King

BARREL-CHESTED, SPORTING a handlebar mustache and a furry patch of beard on his chin and intimidating those around him with his bluster, Victor Emmanuel II came from a lineage that was related by marriage and descent to all of the kings and dukes in Italy he had overthrown. Uninhibited and often crude, eccentric, and disorganized, the monarch was not one for diplomatic niceties. He was used to saying what he meant — and in fact likely to voice whatever came into his head — much to the discomfort of his aides. He mixed a certain joviality with the haughtiness befitting a Savoyard king. Lazy and pigheaded, he had little sense of his own limits, which were considerable. Yet behind his much vaunted military bearing lurked a basic timidness and awkwardness, an inchoate recognition of his social inadequacy. Following his family's tradition, he had been given a Spartan education heavy on discipline, so he had no problem camping out with his soldiers on their march. Above all, he enjoyed riding horseback through the countryside. Proud of his ancestry and ever eager to defend the Savoyard honor, he disdained the court and all its ceremony and pomp. Although not stupid, his intellectual background and horizons were limited. Following the tradition of the Savoyard kingdom, Italy's first king never felt comfortable speaking Italian and avoided it whenever possible, sticking with his native Piedmontese dialect or its close cousin, French. But even in French he was incapable of writing literate prose. And although he disliked public appearances, he had a certain vanity about his looks, blackening his graying hair, beard, and bushy mustache with dye. Indeed, on one occasion, while waving to the cheering crowd in Venice's San Marco Square, sweat produced rivulets of black dye that formed dark stripes on his face, much to the crowd's amazement.[1]

Victor Emmanuel had three passions in life: hunting, war, and the desire to play a critical role in national life. One of his closest aides estimated that the king had spent a third of his life hunting, killing as many as a thousand animals in a day. At each of his many estates he kept a large number of horses and dogs, attended by a small army of keepers. In the hope that it would encourage the king to spend more time in the capital, Lanza agreed to have the government purchase a thirty-thousand-acre estate for him near Rome, making sure that it was always well stocked with game.

Victor Emmanuel viewed himself as a talented military leader, which he was not. While he was not lacking in physical courage, military tactics and strategy were well beyond him, and his romantic view of war would on more than one occasion seriously threaten the kingdom over which he reigned. His disposition was less than ideal for a constitutional monarch. Although at times intimidated by his ministers' superior intelligence and political knowledge, he believed that the most important decisions were best made neither by parliament nor by his ministers but by himself. This illusion, along with a degree of jealousy, had led him into a tense relationship with the man credited with being the diplomatic brains behind Italian unification, his prime minister, Camillo Benso, Count of Cavour. Nor was it merely chance that in the eight years following Cavour's death, in 1861, there were ten different governments, the king dissolving one after another when he grew irritated with the prime minister of the moment, even when the minister remained popular in parliament. The king was also not above secretly conniving in matters of military and foreign affairs — the other elements of government, economic policy, social welfare, and the like, bored him terribly — working with a small group of advisers at court and leaving the government in the dark. Up until the time of his death he kept personal agents in other European capitals to help him work around his own foreign ministers. In the words of Filippo Mazzonis, one of the foremost historians of Italy's first king, Victor Emmanuel's "level of institutional sensitivity was close to zero."[2]

The Italian government operated under a constitution that Victor

Emmanuel's father had granted in response to the revolts of 1848 in Piedmont. It called for a House of Deputies, whose members were elected by the small portion of the population who were eligible to vote, and a Senate, whose members were chosen by the king himself. The ministers were all appointed and could be dismissed by the king at his pleasure. The king was also commander in chief of the military, the position he valued above all others.

Seeing himself as Italy's great unifier, Victor Emmanuel especially resented the public adulation that Garibaldi enjoyed both in Italy and abroad. Having been fired on and wounded by royal troops, Garibaldi was no fan of the monarch nor, for that matter, of the monarchy. The king's disposition was not helped by such outbursts as had occurred in 1865 in Turin, when crowds shouted "Long live Garibaldi!" "Death to the king!" and carriages pulling into the royal palace were showered with rotten eggs and bottles of ink.[3]

In late 1867, after the sorry spectacle of the king's secret encouragement of Garibaldi's expedition on Rome and his subsequent denial of his involvement, the British foreign secretary reported on his recent visit to Florence. Italian government ministers, he wrote, found the king to be "an intriguer whom no honest man could serve without damage to his own reputation." The picture got even worse: "There is universal agreement that Vittorio Emanuele is an imbecile; he is a dishonest man who tells lies to everyone." In return, the king had no more positive view of the political class than they did of him. Nor did he have a particularly positive view of his subjects. There were only two ways of governing Italians, he told another British visitor, "by bayonets and bribery." Italians, the king firmly believed, were totally unfit for a parliamentary system.[4]

The king's credentials as leader of the unified Italian state were tarnished, not only by his disinclination to speak Italian, but also by his antipathy toward the southern half of his new country. He was known to complain that he had never wanted southern Italy to become part of his kingdom, and he also had mixed feelings about having taken Rome; he was intoxicated by the glory of it all but uneasy about living in the pope's shadow.

Victor Emmanuel had little interest in religion and even less regard for priests. Yet, although Pius IX had excommunicated him for having seized much of the Papal States in 1859–1860, he always had a soft spot for the pope, whom he affectionately called "that poor devil of a holy father."[5] When the king fell ill in 1869, he desperately sought release from the pope's excommunication decree so that he could receive last rites. Told that this would be done only if he regularized his long-standing union with a plebian woman — his wife having died many years earlier — the king hastily arranged a wedding at his sickbed. When the pope insisted that he add a written apology for his role in despoiling the Papal States, Victor Emmanuel balked. But a compromise was hastily reached: the king apologized verbally to his confessor and pledged that if he recovered, he would never again do anything to harm the Holy See. Last rites were then administered. As fate — or God — would have it, the king soon recovered and before long sent his army to conquer what little remained of the pope's lands.

Once Rome had been taken by the royal troops, the king found himself in an uncomfortable position. The proud scion of a French-speaking Savoyard dynasty, Victor Emmanuel viewed Rome as a foreign city inextricably linked to the pope and the Curia. Although proud to be seen as the king who unified the Italian peninsula, he had no desire to spend time in Rome and would never feel at ease there. Had there been any way for him to avoid moving to Rome, he would have been relieved.

The problem was that the king's vision of Italy did not coincide with that of his subjects. Ironically, both the Catholics and the Italian nationalists were of like mind in seeing Rome as the natural capital of the peninsula. Earlier in the century, when an influential group of Catholics searched for a way to reconcile the papacy with Italian unification, they proposed creating an Italian federation of states over which the pope would, in some fashion, preside. In this vision, Rome was the natural capital of Italy; they could imagine no other city in its stead. For Mazzini and other antipapal Italian nationalists, on the other hand, Rome was the spiritual center of quite another vision of the country. Unification meant the rise of the third great Rome, after the ancient empire that had once ruled much of the world and then the Rome of the popes, the city again a center of worldwide importance. Even beyond this feeling, given the papacy's claims as the rightful ruler of Rome, the failure to make Rome Italy's capital risked ceding the Holy City to the pope, making it a foreign center at the heart of the new Italian state.[6]

Yet many of Rome's new rulers had mixed feelings about the city, which few of them knew well. Cavour, the architect of Italian unity, had never set foot in Rome. Its new governor, La Marmora, regarded the city as a political and cultural backwater overrun by priests. "Moving the seat of government to Rome," he argued, "is an error that may cost Italy dearly, for Rome is not suitable either morally or materially." Like other nationalist conservatives, La Marmora's reservations were mixed with fear at the prospect of an Italian king sharing the same city with the pope. La Marmora proposed what came to be known as the Russian solution, with Rome, like Moscow, as the holy city and Florence, like St. Petersburg, as the seat of government. His proposal did not get far.[7]

The anomaly of having the king and the pope in the same city, claimed by each as his capital, was keenly felt in other European capitals as well. Two days after the Italian troops pushed through Porta Pia and into Rome, the British ambassador to Italy advised London of the difficulty of having "a constitutional and excommunicated king by the side of an infallible pope; of a Representative Parliament by the side of an absolute authority; of a liberty of the press and freedom of discussion by the side of the Inquisition." He concluded that it would produce "a state of things which can hardly be expected to work harmoniously."[8] Foreign ministers throughout Europe likewise voiced misgivings about Italy's rush to move its capital.[9]

The conservatives in the Italian government were of two minds. To move the capital to Rome risked inflaming the conflict with the pope; not to move it risked energizing the left-wing forces and perhaps even threatening the monarchy. What was most remarkable at the moment, reported Italy's foreign minister, was the depth of popular antipathy in Rome against "the government of the priests." The Romans feared that the king's government — which they viewed as a foreign body of Piedmontese — was planning to work out a deal with the pope at their expense. They wanted the capital to be moved immediately and the monasteries and convents that dominated the city abolished at once. But what was the government to do, asked Visconti in late October, "if while the king entered by one gate the pope left by the other?" The king would certainly not be received by the pope, and the sight of the new ruler marching in triumph through the Holy City in the face of an overthrown pontiff seemed more fitting for a revolutionary rabble-rouser than for a royal sovereign. "The king feels this keenly," Visconti reported, and the prospect of going to Rome under such conditions "produces in him the greatest repugnance."[10]

Time was growing short. Among the most pressing problems was finding suitable royal quarters in Rome. The most splendid choice, and the one identified with political rule in Rome, was the Quirinal Palace, the huge complex at the top of the Quirinal hill in the center of the city. But the Quirinal was closely identified with the papacy. For the king to move into the palace would be rubbing salt into Pius's wounds.

In the early years of Christian Rome, in late antiquity, the pope had made his residence at his cathedral, the Lateran, on the left bank of the Tiber. While the Lateran continued to be the pope's seat as bishop of Rome, a new papal residence was ultimately built at the Vatican, with the more or less permanent shift coming in the twelfth century. In the second half of the sixteenth century the Quirinal Palace was constructed, its elevation offering some relief from the heat for the popes in summer. By the nineteenth century it was so central to the papacy that the conclaves selecting new popes were moved there, including the one in 1846 that elected Pius IX himself.

Despite all the worries and warnings, in late October the government decided not only that the capital should be speedily moved from Florence to Rome, but that the king's new home must be the Quirinal Palace. In sending the news to La Marmora, Lanza admitted that the decision would lead to a new volley of denunciations from the Vatican, but, he predicted, other countries would soon realize that the move was inevitable.[11] In fact, Lanza's greater immediate problem lay not with the pope but with the king. As he reported, "The king finds the idea of residing in a palace contested by the pope to be truly repugnant, and he says that, coming to Rome, he would rather bring his hunting tents with him to live in. He is joking here, but what is serious is his marked repugnance to the idea of moving into the Quirinal, especially if the pope decides to remain in Rome." The king had told Lanza to see whether there wasn't some other palace in Rome he could have, but, the prime minister observed, there was not only the practical problem of finding other quarters fit for a king but the symbolic problem, which was even greater, "for Roman opinion considers the Quirinal to be the true royal court."[12]

La Marmora urged Lanza to reconsider. True, he wrote, many Romans view the Quirinal as Rome's royal residence and would be upset if the king refused to live there. But it was also true that "not a few Romans, and many people abroad, would appreciate the king's regard for the pope's feelings" were he to decide to live elsewhere. As a compromise, La Marmora suggested at least waiting until Pius IX died before having the king move into the Quirinal. But, in his view, it would be better still if the capital were not moved at all. "In this great impatience in the Country for moving the Capital immediately to Rome," wrote the general, "I see a great deal of deception and very few serious reasons."[13]

Two days later, La Marmora met with Cardinal Di Pietro at the latter's request. The cardinal was apparently acting on behalf of Antonelli, who, along with Pius, would not receive the new governor of Rome himself. Di Pietro sought word on whether the king had decided to come to Rome, telling the general that such a move would gravely offend the pope. La Marmora tried to put the best face on the situation, telling the cardinal that he "hoped that the Holy Father recognized the fact that our Sovereign had so far resisted the chorus of demands that were coming in from all parts of the country insisting that he go to Rome, and was doing so out of personal regard for the Holy Father."[14]

Despite La Marmora's objections, the government decided to move and ordered him to take possession of the Quirinal Palace. When first asked to hand over the keys to the building, Pius is said to have responded: "Who do these thieves think they are kidding asking for the keys to open the door? Let them knock it down if they like. Bonaparte's soldiers, when they wanted to seize Pius VII, came through the window, but even they did not have the effrontery to ask for the keys."

Rebuffed by the pope, La Marmora found a locksmith, who on November 8 used a picklock to force open the massive front gates. In his account of the incident, Pius IX's biographer Bishop Pelczar noted — not without a certain satisfaction — that the locksmith was struck dead shortly thereafter.[15]

As the pope saw it, such signs of God's wrath were everywhere, although none was more powerful than the flood that devastated Rome as the new year approached. The Romans were used to periodic flooding, so when the fall proved to be exceptionally rainy, they looked at the Tiber's rising waters with some concern. By Christmas the water level was several meters above normal, and soon the lands along the river were under water, the newly liberated Jewish ghetto first among them. Mail service from northern Italy was suspended as the Tiber's rising waters flooded the railroad tracks north of the city.[16]

Ugo Pesce, an Italian visitor to Rome at the time, offers a firsthand account of what happened. He was walking home after midnight on the twenty-eighth, he recalled, when he saw the waters from the river begin to pour through Rome's main street, the via del Corso. "The reflections from the reddish lanterns held aloft by members of the national guard flickered eerily from the water, which seemed to be as black as ink." Pesce's friend told him not to worry, that flooding right along the river was common. But when Pesce awoke the next morning, the water outside his door was so deep that he could not get out of his building. Jumping from roof to roof, he finally found a place where he could reach the ground. The rains began again, and the swollen Tiber became a frightening sight, huge trees sweeping by and Rome's side streets turning into streams deep enough for large boats to navigate. On the twenty-ninth the rains finally stopped. Women leaned from their upper-story windows, yelling for the loaves of bread that the national guardsmen were handing out from their boats. Store owners could still not get into their ruined shops.[17]

For those in the Vatican, Rome's punishment showed God's hand. At the beginning of the new year, the cardinal vicar of Rome sent out a circular letter: "Such a great disaster, which in the eyes of the unbelievers seems to be nothing more than the result of random fate," he wrote, "must be recognized for what it is: the tremendous scourge of divine punishment."[18]

By the time of the flood, the issue of how to coax the king to the Holy City had become a major problem for the government. The pope had made it known that he would not receive the king, the foreign ambassadors to Rome had said that they could not pay even courtesy visits to the king in the pope's city, and the king himself would rather have done almost anything than move to Rome, where the Church's opposition to his rule was so painfully clear.

In sending the flood, God, it appeared, had not only answered the pope's prayers but the king's as well, for it gave him a way to visit the Holy City without the ostentatious display normally reserved for such a royal entry. As Visconti wrote to his brother, "I insisted that the king take advantage of the opportunity offered by the Roman flood to make the trip and to leave immediately. It is a way to avoid many difficulties — to handle the complex emotions that the trip would produce by portraying it as having a charitable purpose, and to avoid the celebrations and all the hullabaloo." The king agreed and left almost immediately, accompanied by Lanza, Visconti, and a bevy of retainers.[19]

The king's visit could hardly have been briefer, less than thirteen hours in all, during part of which he slept. Nor does it seem that he was met by great popular acclamation, although his announcement that he was giving the municipal government 200,000 lire to alleviate the suffering of the people did win him favor. According to the Dutch ambassador to Rome, the government was forced to secretly hire a hundred shills to surround the royal carriage and provide a satisfying chorus of "Long live the king." Victor Emmanuel took care to do nothing to offend the pope, staying clear of the Leonine city. His reaction when he at last set foot in his new residence, the Quirinal Palace, that day depends on whose account can be believed. According to one report, he turned to La Marmora and said, whether triumphally or simply with relief we do not know: "Finally, I'm here!" But partisans of the pope told a different story. As the king first stepped into his new palace, they said, he felt a horrifying chill. In the distance he could see St. Peter's and the Vatican. "Oh, what a shadow those buildings cast!" he is said to have moaned.[20]

During his visit, the king sent the pope a brief letter. Dated Rome, December 31, 1870, it read:

Most Blessed Father

I come to Rome at this time to aid, insofar as I can, those damaged by the extraordinary flooding. I stay only a few hours, and I seize this opportunity to offer my most obsequious respect to Your Holiness, for whom I have always had the greatest veneration and filial affection.

Your Most Devoted son,
Victor Emmanuel

On the back of the pope's copy in the Vatican archives is the note: "No reply made." In fact, although the king and the pope would subsequently live just a mile apart, the pope would never meet him.[21]

Leaving the Rome train station after his whirlwind tour, the king felt great relief. He had accomplished what was expected of him — staking a royal claim to the Holy City — in a way much easier than he could have hoped. While some remarked that the king seemed to have remarkably good fortune, always in the right place at the right time, he now mulled over a less appetizing interpretation of recent events. Could it be a coincidence that within three months of his troops' assault on the pope the Tiber had risen up and torn through the Holy City, causing cadavers to glide through the streets and houses to crumble? Superstitious by nature, the king had difficulty dismissing the thought, as he would forgetting something else, the prediction of Catholics that if he should occupy the Quirinal, he would meet an untimely death there.[22]

Meanwhile, in Florence, the Italian parliament debated the final bill authorizing the transfer of the capital. Although a few voices denounced the prospect of two sovereigns in one city, neither recognizing the legitimacy of the other, the bill was passed in January 1871 by a huge majority in the House of Deputies but, revealingly, by a much more modest margin in the Senate, whose members were closely identified with the king.

The rush to move the capital was fueled by fears of what might happen when the Franco-Prussian War ended. What, Lanza and his colleagues wondered, would France do once it recovered from the Prussian assault? A London *Times* article in early January, datelined Florence, offered a frightening prospect: "A firm persuasion is . . . gradually gaining ground day by day in this country that France will not fail to vent her resentment in a second Italian war as soon as she has sufficiently recovered her strength after peace has been signed to enable her to do so, and it will be her object this time to undo all that she did during the first war, and to restore the Papal Government."[23] As it happened, on January 28, the day after the Italian parliament voted to move the capital, Paris capitulated to the Prussian army. The siege was over, but the truly fearful bloodbath was still months away.

The leaders of the precarious new republic in France were themselves children of the Enlightenment, with little enthusiasm for restoring the pope's lands to ecclesiastical rule. Yet they were under pressure from France's Catholic right, for whom the papal cause was sacrosanct, and they were also eager to restore France's influence in European affairs after their disastrous defeat. When the pope pleaded for their help in stopping the Italians from moving their capital, he found a willing audience.

In April, the French envoy to Florence met with Visconti, urging that he stop the transfer of the capital. But Visconti would not be swayed.[24]

The French foreign minister, Jules Favre, then offered a solution that echoed the one La Marmora had earlier suggested: "If [Italy] would consent to view Florence as the seat of government, it would solve the Papal question. It would show great sense, and the political credit that it would thereby garner, as well as the honor, would offer a considerable advantage." He added: "Focus all of M. Visconti-Venosta's attention on this difficult topic. Rome, under royal rule — an integral part of the Italian nation, but remaining Holy or, better yet, the Dominant center in the domain of the faith — would lose none of its prestige and would redound to Italy's credit. And conciliation would then come about naturally, because the pope would become accustomed to seeing himself as living in his own home, not having the king around."

The French envoy presented Visconti with this proposal the day he received it. But, as he reported back to the French foreign minister, he had little luck. "To give up transferring the capital, or even to delay it," Visconti told him, "would expose Italy to a dangerous crisis for which no minister would accept the responsibility." Italy's foreign minister then asked rhetorically, "And what would the pope gain? . . . Instead of finding himself in the presence of a strong government, which has the best intentions and would maintain perfect order, he would find himself in the presence of a prefect and a municipal council that lacked sufficient authority to put down the excesses of a population irritated to see itself deprived of a capital." In any case, Visconti added, even if they kept the capital in Florence, the pope would still demand that his kingdom be restored. It would take more than this gesture, far more, to satisfy the pope.[25]

With the capital's transfer just weeks away, foreign pressures on Italy to delay the move continued to grow. On June 4, in Vienna, the Austrian foreign minister, Beust, told Marco Minghetti, the Italian ambassador, of a meeting he had just had in Munich with the Bavarian foreign minister. Why not make Rome into the Moscow of Italy? the Bavarian minister asked, again echoing La Marmora's suggestion. Rome would then technically be the capital, but it would not be the seat of government. Minghetti replied that the idea had already been much discussed in Florence but that it was impossible for two reasons. First, if Rome were not the capital, which Italian city would be? If Florence were to be the permanent capital, the people in Naples and Turin would be up in arms, feeling that they had better claims; unlike Florence, they had both had long histories hosting royal courts. Second, without the government, Rome, instead of becoming a center of conservatism, would be the center of intrigue and popular agitation of all kinds.[26]

On July 1, 1871, the Italian government moved to Rome. Victor Emmanuel came the next day. Although he had sent instructions that popular celebrations be minimized in order not to unduly offend the pope, the city was excited nonetheless. The king arrived from Naples shortly after noon in a long line of carriages filled with an assortment of government ministers and generals decked out in their most colorful uniforms. Flowers rained down from the balconies, but Gregorovius, who was there, observed that the king appeared "stiff, and gloomy and ugly." The European powers, bowing to the pleadings of the Holy See, kept their emissaries away. "Today," Gregorovius wrote in his diary, "is the close of the thousand years' dominion of the Papacy in Rome." In the shadow of the Vatican, the cannon of Sant'Angelo Castle thundered. "How the Pope's heart must have quailed at every shot!" wrote Gregorovius. "A tragedy without a parallel is being enacted here."[27]

For the faithful abroad, the king's occupation of the pope's Quirinal Palace was a horrifying sight. In early July, *Le Monde* expressed a widespread sentiment: "The simultaneous existence at Rome of two independent sovereigns is impossible." No one was more conscious of this fact than Victor Emmanuel, who would spend as little time as possible in his new capital and, indeed, could not be convinced to stay more than a day and a half after his triumphal arrival on July 2. In the years that followed, he stayed in Rome only when he had no alternative, such as for the opening ceremonies of parliament.[28]

The king explained this discomfort one day when talking to the queen of Holland: "I would really love to see the pope leave Rome, because I can't look out the window of the Quirinal without seeing the Vatican, and it seems to me that Pius IX and I are both prisoners." Or, as he was reported to have said another time: "Over there a prisoner who is free, here a free man who is a prisoner."[29]

7

Pius IX in Exile Again?

*L*ONG BEFORE THE KING ever set foot in the Holy City, the pope had already excommunicated him and all those guilty of despoiling the Papal States. The founders of the modern Italian nation were again excommunicated in *Respicientes ea omnis*, the encyclical released on November 1, 1870, which declared the Italian state's occupation of the Papal States null and void. The Holy See, the pope pronounced, would never reconcile itself with those who had stolen its lands. "Despite our advanced age," Pius wrote, "we prefer . . . with divine aid, to drink the cup to the dregs rather than accept the iniquitous proposals which have been made to us.[1]

The proposals that the pope had in mind — aside from the offer of the Leonine city — were part of the Italian government's effort to calm international opinion by enacting what came to be dubbed "the law of guarantees." Lanza and his colleagues needed to show Europe's other powers that the Italian occupation of Rome had done nothing to prevent the pope's fulfilling his spiritual role as head of the Church. Before September 20, when they were trying to convince foreign governments not to oppose their march into the Holy City, Lanza, the king, and the foreign minister pledged that once they took Rome, they would submit to an international conference aimed at crafting the protections offered to the Holy See. But once they controlled Rome, they were just as eager to prevent such a conference. These were internal Italian matters, Lanza insisted. No foreign government could tell the Italians what to do within their own borders. Yet, as Lanza was well aware, their only hope of getting other governments to go along with them was to prove that they had already provided for the pope's security and freedom.

The Italians had another aim in trumpeting their law of guarantees. They wanted to allay fears that the pope, now in some sense a subject of the king of Italy, would become a court chaplain to the monarch who had usurped him. A pope controlled by Italy — a prospect made all the more credible because all the popes for the past three hundred years had been Italian — risked turning Catholics abroad into agents of a foreign power. Ironically, from this perspective, the more loudly Pius denounced the Italian leaders the better they liked it, for it offered proof of his independence.[2]

Agreeing on just what guarantees should be offered proved to be difficult. Cavour's famous doctrine of "a free Church in a free State," implying the complete separation of church and state, was championed by some conservatives, including Lanza and Visconti. But others followed the long European tradition that viewed government oversight as necessary, not least in the appointment of bishops, a prerogative that secular rulers enjoyed elsewhere. For the many anticlerics, allowing the Church full freedom was a prescription for national suicide; the Church was the sworn enemy of the state, dedicated to its destruction. The vast network of parishes, monasteries, and schools — if left alone — would, in this view, prove to be the new state's downfall. As a result, fierce debate raged in parliament for the first months of 1871, and the final legislation, signed by the king in Turin on May 13, was full of compromises.

The law began with a pledge that the pope's person was to be considered "sacred and inviolable." Any attack on him was to be treated in the same way as an attack on the king. The Italian government would render the pope all honors due a sovereign, and he was to be paid the huge sum of 3,225,000 lire per year, free of taxation, from the public treasury to cover his own expenses and those of the Holy See. The Vatican palaces, with their museums, works of art, libraries, and surrounding gardens, as well as the Lateran Palace and Castel Gandolfo, the summer estate outside Rome, would all be reserved for the pope and considered inalienable and exempt from taxes. No public official or police would be allowed to enter any of these buildings unless explicitly invited. Foreign emissaries to the Holy See would enjoy the same rights accorded foreign diplomats to Italy, and the pope was assured of the ability to correspond freely with the Episcopate and the whole Catholic world.

The law of guarantees further specified that Italian bishops would not be required to pledge their loyalty to the king, and no government authorization would be needed for the Church to publish its own official acts. However — and here came a clause that caused much anguish in the Church — government approval would still be necessary for new appointees to be allowed to take control of Church property outside Rome. This provision thus required new bishops to receive government permission before taking up residence in their new bishopric, a requirement long followed in other Catholic countries, but it created special problems here because the Church refused to recognize the legitimacy of the state.[3]

A week after the law went into effect, Visconti sent a copy (in French) to all of his ambassadors, asking them to bring it to the attention of the governments they served.[4] The pope did not wait so long. Just two days after the king signed the law, Pius IX released an encyclical, *Ubi nos*, addressed to bishops throughout the world. "Our days," the pope lamented, "are filled with bitterness." Conditions were getting ever worse: "We are compelled to repeat the words of St. Bernard," said the pope, " 'this is the beginning of the evils; we fear worse evil.' "

Pius went on to warn of the pernicious plans of the "Piedmontese government," which, in order "to deceive Catholics and allay their anguish, has promoted certain empty immunities and privileges, commonly called 'guarantees.'" He reminded the bishops that when the guarantees were first discussed several months earlier, he had "stigmatized their absurdity, cunning, and mockery." Yet the shameless Piedmontese government had pressed ahead with its plan, a "novel and unheard-of sacrilege." There could be no compromise. "We never can and never shall allow or accept those 'guarantees' devised by the Piedmont Government, whatever their motive. Nor shall we ever accept other similar ones," the pope insisted. "Divine Providence gave the civil rule of the Holy See to the Roman Pontiff. This rule is necessary in order that the Roman Pontiff may never be subject to any ruler or civil power." Pius then turned to the foreign powers and called for their help. Voicing his belief that "the rulers of the earth do not want the usurpation which We are suffering to be established," he concluded with the prayer: "May these rulers join in a common effort to have the rights of the Holy See restored."[5]

The pope's constant calls to Catholics throughout the world to return him to power rattled the Italian government. With the conclusion of the Franco-Prussian War in view, they expected the great powers' attention to turn once again to the Italian question, or rather the Roman question. Early in March 1871, Visconti confided his worries to Italy's ambassador to Berlin. Cynically manipulated by Italy's many enemies, Visconti wrote, "the Roman question dominates our politics," introducing "an element of uncertainty in Italy's future." He added: "The Roman Curia asks and wants one thing and one thing only: war on Italy to restore temporal power by military intervention." The Jesuits, Visconti believed — a belief that was widely shared — had the pope under their spell and were working feverishly to get him to reject any compromise.[6]

Long viewed with a combination of suspicion, distaste, and grudging admiration, the Jesuits had been repeatedly expelled by secular rulers. In 1773, Pope Clement XIV, bending to such pressure, disbanded the order and had its leader locked up in Sant'Angelo Castle, where he died two years later. Resuscitated in 1814, the order continued to be controversial. Pius IX himself had not been that well disposed to the Jesuits at the beginning of his papacy, resenting their opposition to his attempted reforms and suspicious of their ambition. Yet, after the revolutions of 1848 he increasingly became dependent on them, viewing them as the most theologically and politically sophisticated advisers he had.[7]

In 1850, eager to have a publication that would defend papal powers and champion his causes, Pius turned to a group of Jesuits in Rome; they launched La Civiltà Cattolica and published it twice a month. Quickly becoming the most influential Catholic publication in the world, it offered the Vatican's views on the issues of the time. By the 1860s, the influence of Rome's Jesuits was beyond dispute: they served as key advisers in preparing both the Syllabus of Errors and the Vatican Council. As articulate and dogged champions of papal infallibility and the necessity of temporal power, constantly on the lookout for signs of liberal thinking in the Church, the Jesuits viewed the world much as the pope did.[8] As Lord Acton wrote in 1870, when he was in Rome to lobby against papal infallibility, Pius IX "made [the Jesuits] a channel of his influence, and became an instrument of their own."[9] By early 1871, cartoons were appearing in the liberal press in Rome that portrayed the pope as a Jesuit stooge. In one, titled "The Flight to Corsica" (alluding to the Jesuits' efforts to get Pius to flee Rome), Antonelli is seated on an ass behind the pope — who is pictured as the size of a child — holding a large umbrella over him. A Jesuit leads the ass with a rope.[10]

The Jesuits were scarcely more popular among their fellow priests. In November 1870, one of Lanza's confidential emissaries met secretly in the Vatican with the widely respected Father Augustin Theiner, the former head of the Vatican Secret Archives. One of the major subjects of their conversation was what the Italian government should do about the Jesuits.[11]

The report that Lanza received offered clear advice: the Italian government must immediately expel them from all of Italy, including Rome. The Jesuits, Father Theiner warned, would forever be an insuperable obstacle to concilation, not only for the present pope but for his successor. The popular demonstrations throughout the Catholic world calling for the restoration of the pope's temporal power, said Theiner, were entirely the work of the Jesuits, who were forcing unenthusiastic bishops to toe the line.

Sending them into exile, Theiner counseled, would not only be good for the government, it would also work to the Church's benefit, and members of the other religious orders would applaud the move. The "ignorance and crude fanaticism of the Italian clergy, and the imbecility of the Italian episcopate," Theiner charged, "are the sole product of Jesuit education in Italy, the absorption of the Italian Church by Jesuitism."[12]

One morning a few weeks later, Lanza's emissary had a confidential meeting with Cardinal Pietro De Silvestri, another enemy of Jesuit influence in the Vatican. The cardinal was no doubt nervous, for members of the Curia had recently been warned against having any contact with Italian officials, and those coming under suspicion were being watched.

Nothing was more important for the Vatican, said the cardinal, than showing the world that disorder reigned in Rome and that the pope would remain a prisoner until freed by foreign intervention. It was crucial, he advised, for the Italian government to prevent disorders in the vicinity of the Vatican and to guard against any disruption of religious functions elsewhere in the Holy City.

"The Jesuits," said Cardinal Silvestri, "are the soul of the Vatican, and every hostile project originates with them." Father Picirillo, the director of *Civiltà Cattolica,* he charged, had become all-powerful. "It is absolutely necessary to expel them all from Italy."[13]

Although Theiner and Silvestri may have exaggerated the Jesuits' influence, there were in fact no greater champions of the wholesale rejection of the Italian state than the Jesuits, who were constantly pressing the pope to take a hard line. Their calls in *Civiltà Cattolica* for foreign intervention to restore the Papal States led to repeated demands from the secular press to have the paper shut down.

In an article in the spring of 1871, the Jesuits counterattacked. "The unity of a state with a nation can be a good thing or a bad thing, according to the circumstances," they argued. Ethnic Germans lived in Germany, but Germans also lived in Austria, and few argued that it posed any problem. Why must a single state encompass all Italians? As for the liberals' denunciation of Catholics who sought the help of foreign armies to restore the pope to power, this was sheer hypocrisy. In 1859, didn't Victor Emmanuel and Cavour call on the French army to help them conquer northern Italy? "What right do they have to complain if others imitate their example?" Foreign intervention, the Jesuit journal observed, "is always a good thing if it comes in aid of an innocent oppressed party, and indeed, sometimes it is obligatory." In the current case, it was not even a matter of foreign intervention, for all baptized Catholics were children of the pope and viewed Rome as their own home. Consequently, the journal concluded, their intervention on behalf of the pope "is a domestic matter, not a foreign one."[14]

Even before the Italian forces had seized Rome, the pope had been besieged by advisers urging him to leave Rome and Italy behind. According to all accounts, his most trusted Jesuit advisers were among the most insistent in pressing him to leave at once.[15]

But where exactly was he to go? Over the next two decades, no destination was mentioned more often than the British island of Malta. On September 6, Lanza received a report from another source in Rome: "The Jesuit Party, which is the strongest in the Vatican, is trying to convince the Pope to escape to Malta and believes it is succeeding."[16] Three days later, another informant told him of a conversation he had had recently with a former general of a religious order, who confirmed the pope's decision to go to Malta. Antonelli, in this account, had doubts about such a course, "but the Jesuits count more than Antonelli at this moment."[17]

It would not be easy to convince Pius to leave Rome again, for he was now an old man, and a voyage into the unknown had little appeal. Yet his emotional reaction to the taking of Rome, and his tendency to change his mind rapidly on nondoctrinal matters, meant that his departure was far from impossible. Just before the attack on Rome, he is said to have told the Prussian ambassador: "There, you see all my things are packed up. I depart as soon as they enter."[18]

When the Italian troops occupied Rome, the pope could no longer put off the decision. But before making the fateful choice, he decided to ask ten cardinals to provide a written reply to the question: "Should we think of taking the difficult step of leaving Rome and if so, where to?" In the wake of the Italian invasion, it was deemed too dangerous for the cardinals to appear in their purple robes on the streets of Rome, so no meeting of the Sacred College of Cardinals was called. But what is a bit odd about the pope's survey is that, rather than ask Antonelli to coordinate the consultation, he sidestepped his secretary of state and instead asked a trusted adviser, Cardinal Costantino Patrizi, to take charge. Also curious was the selection of cardinals to be approached: while ten were asked to provide their advice, another seventeen cardinals then in Rome were not. The list was apparently prepared by the pope himself, composed of those whose judgment he most trusted. The urgent requests were sent out by Patrizi just a day after the Italian occupation of Rome, the answers dribbling back in between the twenty-fourth and the twenty-seventh of September.[19]

Although earlier there had been strong support among the cardinals for having the pope leave Rome in case of an Italian invasion, now that the city had fallen, many were having second thoughts. Of the ten, only two urged immediate departure, including the first response, from Monaco La Valletta, the cardinal vicar of Rome. "It seems to me," he wrote, "that staying here would result in much damage and no advantage, while leaving, although not succeeding in preventing a long series of damages for poor Rome, would however have the great virtue of safeguarding the liberty and dignity of the Holy See." Where the pope should go Monaco declined to say, urging only that "the Holy Father procure a safe refuge outside Italy as quickly as possible, and that the [Sacred] College [of Cardinals] follow him there."[20]

By contrast, the other cardinals were more worried about the dangers of leaving Rome. Cardinal Giuseppe Bizzarri was the first of them to respond. True, he wrote, concern for the Holy See's independence argued for leaving Rome immediately, but such a move would come at a high cost. Given the old age and increasing infirmity not only of the pope but of many of the cardinals, such a voyage would be arduous and even dangerous. And it was not difficult to predict what would then happen in Rome, for with the pope gone, the new state would feel free to bring about "the holy institutions' total destruction."

He then came to the question of where the pope might go. The places most often proposed were Malta, the Tyrol in the northeast of Italy under Austrian control, Belgium, and the Catholic provinces of southern Germany. "But would the pope even in these areas be able to freely exercise his jurisdiction and enjoy true independence?" he asked. "Malta and the provinces along the Rhine are under the authority of Protestant governments, while Tyrol is under a government that is in some ways hostile."

Cardinal Filippo de Angelis offered similar advice. The pope should not be tempted by what happened in 1848. That was a very different situation, for Rome had fallen into anarchy, the pope's palace was under siege, his life threatened, and his ability to exercise his spiritual office brought practically to an end. Rather, the proper precedents to follow were those of Pius VI and Pius VII, who, although virtually prisoners of Napoleon's army, refused to leave until they were forced to at gunpoint. And, the cardinal predicted, with the pope out of the way, no sacrilege would be spared Rome: "One might well," he warned, "see our principal churches converted into synagogues and Protestant churches."

Other cardinals were more guarded, seeing grave dangers in either staying or leaving. Such was the advice given by Cardinal Luigi Bilio, one of those closest to the pope during the recent council. Just how sure could the pope be that were he to go into exile, his calls for the restoration of his states would be heeded by Europe's powers? The cardinal also asked what would happen if, notwithstanding all the agitation of Catholics around the world, no country would take up arms on his behalf? "Where today is the Catholic power," he asked, "where is the Sovereign to whom the Holy Father can go to beg for help and aid with the *moral certainty* of being *quickly* restored to his See and to the tranquil possession of his usurped domains?"[21]

Yet Bilio recognized that other considerations argued in favor of flight. To stay risked giving the impression that the pope believed that he could continue his holy mission without his states. The longer this situation lasted, the more it would seem acceptable and even natural. Staying in Rome also risked reinforcing the stability of the Italian government and placing "obstacles in the way of or at least slowing down certain political upheavals which, in the final analysis, might work to the benefit of the Holy See's cause, preparing the way for a Restoration."

"Before being asked, on His Holiness's orders, to give my opinion on this extremely serious question," Bilio wrote, "I was convinced of the absolute necessity of leaving Rome as soon as possible. But now, considering the question more carefully," he concluded, "I find myself perplexed and unsure."

As for where the pope should go if he fled, Bilio had a different suggestion: Belgium. The population was Catholic, communication with the rest of the world would be easy, and the devotion of the royal family would assure the Holy Father an honored place and the freedom to carry out his mission. But what most recommended Belgium over Malta was something else: as soon as the Franco-Prussian War ends, thought Bilio, "the Holy Father will be able to pass easily into the neighboring French territory, and thereby with his presence stir that generous nation to avenge the injuries inflicted by Victor Emmanuel's government on the Holy Father no less than on France itself."

Lanza and Visconti followed the anguished debate in the Vatican as best they could. In the days immediately after Rome was taken, they feared nothing so much as that the pope would flee, and their diplomatic correspondence overflows with reports on the subject.[22] On September 28, Visconti received a message from Rome that the Prussian ambassador to the Holy See was involved in a plot to get the pope to take refuge in Germany. Visconti telegraphed Minghetti, Italy's ambassador in Vienna, the same day: "I fear that the Pope, giving in to the Jesuits' pressure, is going to leave Rome." He urged Minghetti to get the Austrian government to do all it could to dissuade him.[23]

The Italian foreign minister received somewhat reassuring news later in the day from his secretary general, Albert Blanc, who had just that morning met with Cardinal Antonelli. "His Eminence," Blanc reported, "assured me repeatedly that up to now the pope has not been thinking of leaving." But Antonelli had added that "nothing can be guaranteed for the future." If things got worse, the pope might well leave.[24]

Aware that Antonelli was himself fighting a battle to convince the pope to stay and that he was in danger of losing out to what Blanc characterized as the Jesuit faction, the secretary-general sent Visconti a second telegram the same day, warning that the pope might attempt to escape secretly, at night, bound for a ship on the coast.[25]

A similar warning came in a breathless telegram to Lanza sent from Rome at one o'clock that morning from a person who had just spoken with the pope's personal physician. Pius, he learned, was making secret arrangements to leave quickly, planning to take the old papal escape route along the raised passage running from the Vatican to the Sant'Angelo Castle, from there into a boat on the Tiber, and then to the coast, where a steamship awaited him.[26]

The following day Minghetti, in Vienna, reported that the Austrians, through their ambassador in Rome, were advising the pope not to leave. Although the Austrian government had earlier offered the pope a refuge, Minghetti wrote, should he actually take them up on their offer, "they would find themselves greatly embarrassed."[27] The Austrians told Minghetti that the real problem lay with the Germans, charging that Prussia's ambassador to Rome, Harry von Arnim, was secretly trying to convince the pope to come to Germany.

Suspicions of a German plot were widespread. In England, in late September, Lord John Russell, the former British prime minister, warned Archbishop Manning of reports that he, too, was getting from Rome "that Baron Arnim offered the Pope an asylum in Germany — Fulda, I think — and strongly pressed his Holiness to accept." The allegations were soon getting confirmation from Antonelli himself, who told the British envoy in Rome that Arnim had been urging him to convince the pope to leave Rome and come to Prussia. Arnim, it seems, was a magnet for conspiracy theorists and far from popular among his diplomatic colleagues. As one of them described him: "His exterior is haughty and spiteful, so that he more often repulses people rather than attracts them."[28]

Arnim denied that he was encouraging Pius to flee. Meeting with Blanc at the end of September, the Prussian ambassador claimed that, on the contrary, he was doing all he could to calm things down. The pope, he reported, "is obsessed with mystical ideas and awaits a miracle. Given the unpredictability of his nervous susceptibilities," he warned, "no one can know if he will end up staying or leaving." Yet Arnim's own superior, Bismarck, himself began to suspect that Arnim was disobeying his instructions and issuing invitations to the pope on his own authority. On October 3 he wrote, telling him emphatically, "Refrain from any utterance on the question." He added: "Now for your own information I remark that if the pope should leave Rome I do not know how to find him a satisfactory place of refuge."[29]

Among those most upset about the rumors were the Catholics of France, whose capital was then under German siege. The archbishop of Tours sent a worried note to Antonelli: "The rumor is spreading here, Eminence, that the pope is going to leave Rome, retreating to another city, under the protection of Prussia." Such stories, he hastened to add, were undoubtedly groundless, but the prospect — remote though it may be — was so upsetting that he felt compelled to write. "If you will permit me to say so, Eminence, such a decision would produce a most deplorable effect on souls here." The king of Prussia, as part of his un-quenchable ambitions, might well seek to lure the Holy Father into his territories. But the archbishop was certain that in the end Pius would come to regret such a move, for he would surely end up as a mere client of the king. Acceptance of the Prussian offer would send shock waves through France and "scandalize the entire Catholic world."

A week later Antonelli replied rather curtly: "I thank you for your communication regarding the eventual departure of the Holy Father from Rome. Your comments are most appreciated, but I can assure you that I have never entertained the thought of moving to a place such as the one that you mentioned."[30] Yet something rings false in Antonelli's language. It was odd for him to use the first person in discussing Vati-can policy. The archbishop had hit a nerve.

In fact, that fall the Vatican was engaged in secret efforts to get the Prussians to agree to host the pope. Early in November, at the Vatican's request, Archbishop Ledóchowski of Posen traveled to Versailles to meet with Bismarck. While the Prussian king remained resolute in his opposition to hosting the pope, Bismarck — who had previously op-posed it as well — had now, curiously, changed his mind. He began to think that coming to the pope's rescue might attract greater support for his government from Germany's Catholics while helping to sup-press the opposition in Prussia's Polish territories. He also thought it might hasten the end of the remaining French military resistance, with French priests finding it awkward to urge their flock to wage war against the pope's saviors. In fact, just after the Italians seized Rome a few weeks earlier, Bismarck, in ruminating over the possibility that the pope might flee, had voiced his ambivalence. "We have already been asked if we would grant him asylum," he told a companion at the time. "I do not object to Cologne or Fulda," he said, then explained: "It would be an astounding thing, but understandable, and rather advantageous for us if we appeared to the Catholics what we are in actuality, the only power at the present time that can and will give protection to the head of the Church." Having the pope outside Rome would, he thought, also have the advantage of cutting the pontiff down to human size. "People are inclined to turn Catholic," the German chancellor mused, "when they get a glimpse of the pomp and ceremony of Catholicism in Rome, especially women." By contrast, if Pius were to live in Germany, he would be viewed "as an old man seeking help, as a good old man, as one of the bishops, who like the others eats and drinks, takes a pinch of snuff, even smokes a cigar — it would be much less dangerous."[31]

A new crisis loomed in late January 1871 with the final vote of the Italian parliament to move the capital. The threat to leave Italy was the strongest card that the Vatican had to play, not only in putting pressure on the Italian government but in getting the attention of the various European powers, whose leaders feared, for good reason, that having the pope outside Italy would dangerously disrupt the balance of power. And nothing would more dramatically destabilize the new Italian state than the pope's living in exile, calling on the world's leaders to return him to his rightful home.

Although the Italians were concerned about the rumors of Prussia's encouragement of papal flight, their suspicions fell most heavily on France. Yet an examination of the French diplomatic correspondence shows that the French leaders had no interest in having the pope flee. "Tell Cardinal Antonelli," Favre instructed his ambassador to the Holy See, "that we are ready to receive him with all due respect in Corsica, or at Pau, in Algiers . . . but that we continue to believe that the reconciliation which will permit him to stay in the Vatican is still the best solution."[32] At the same time, Favre asked his ambassador in Florence to speak with Visconti. Tell him nothing of our offer of Corsica or Pau,

Favre cautioned, but urge him to redouble the government's efforts to keep the pope in Rome. "In making his continued stay impossible for him," warned Favre, "Italy is playing a dangerous game. It may set something in motion whose impact would be incalculable." What was worse, France would inevitably be dragged in. "This mess must be avoided at all costs," wrote Favre. "With a little humility and good sense, the Italian government can keep the pope and so save itself from great misfortune."[33]

A month later — from Versailles, where the French government had taken refuge following the uprising in Paris and the establishment of the Paris Commune — Favre again wrote to his ambassador in Florence. Although the world was collapsing around him, Favre had not changed his sober advice. The envoy was to persuade the Italian government to show sufficient respect for the pope so that the danger that he would flee could be avoided. Above all, the Italians should reverse their decision to move their capital to Rome, for, as the French ambassador subsequently warned Visconti, "We have reason to fear that the Pope will leave Rome the day that you effectively move the seat of government there."

What Favre most wanted to avoid was having the pope call on him to provide refuge on French soil. "In asking us for asylum," Favre wrote to his envoy, "the Holy Father will create a real embarrassment for us. We would receive him properly, but we would be unable to halt the inopportune zeal of his friends and the excesses of his enemies. We would be placing the Roman question in the thick of our national passions, to the great detriment of our internal peace and of our guest's dignity."[34]

The French envoy's efforts to convince Visconti to keep the capital in Florence got nowhere. "If we followed this advice," Visconti subsequently wrote, "we would have put everything into doubt again, reopened the Roman question domestically, and produced agitation that would be impossible to control. Offending and arousing national sentiment against the pope, considered an obstacle to the final creation of Italy, was not a means to restore calm around the Roman question." Visconti was also skeptical that the pope would actually leave Italy, not least because nowhere would he have as much freedom as he had where he was. True, "the fanatical party and the Jesuits are continuously urging him to go," Visconti told the French ambassador, but what the situation demanded was not new action by the Italians but rather French help in convincing the pope to stay.[35]

As the July 1 date for moving the capital approached, Antonelli urged the world's governments to leave their ambassadors in Florence, arguing that moving them to Rome would imply approval of the Italians' control of the Holy City. Yet he was unsuccessful. When, to his consternation, he learned that the Austrian government had approved the move of its embassy, he called in the Austrian envoy to the Holy See and again brandished the Vatican's ultimate threat: "To recognize officially the present state of affairs at Rome is to push us to the last extremity. We had decided to endure whatever we could, but I fail to see how the position of the Holy See can continue hereafter to be tenable at Rome." Before dismissing the envoy, Antonelli told him that should the pope now decide to flee Rome, the fault would not lie with Italy alone: "You, as well as the other powers that, by the official presence of their representative, recognized the Italian government, would be largely responsible."[36]

Lanza and Visconti wanted to believe those reports that dismissed the papal threats to leave Rome as the idle posturing of an ailing, elderly man who would never give up the comfort of his familiar surroundings for a frightening sea voyage and a dubious destination. Yet some of their most trusted advisers not only believed that the threats were real but were convinced that the pope was about to go. On June 11, Count Kulczycki reported that Pius was disbursing funds to the members of the Curia to enable them to buy nonclerical garb to aid in their escape. On the twenty-third, reporting on the meetings the pope had been hastily arranging to help him decide whether to go, the count concluded, "I believe that the Pope will leave."[37]

Around the same time, another of Visconti's sources of inside information on the Vatican, Prince Ruspoli, reported that it was now the pope himself — impetuous as always — who was angrily calling for an immediate departure. The pope had not believed that the Italian government would go through with its threat to move to Rome. When he realized that the king was in fact on his way, Ruspoli reported, his first reaction was that he should go immediately to Corsica, "leaving in his wake all the excommunications and all the medieval anathemas that the Roman Curia disposes of."

The prince believed that it was the cardinals in Rome who were now restraining the pope. "Enriched from public monopolies," wrote Ruspoli, "Antonelli and other of Rome's cardinals own land, palaces, and villas. It is only natural that they do not want to provoke a crisis, as they have too much to lose." Each time that upsetting news arrived, triggering the pope's anger, the cardinals found a way to distract him and calm him down. The prelates were most ingenious, the prince reported. On occasion they would improve his mood by presenting him "with a petition signed by priests, monks, and nuns." Other times, the irreverent prince reported, the cardinals brightened him up by announcing "the arrival of a foreign delegation, which was generally composed of a dozen uneducated Englishmen, along with a similar number of Germans of the same ilk and a handful of Poles." And so the harried cardinals were able to avert yet another threat: "The Pope calms down, while they get other distractions ready for the next time that he goes into one of his usual fits."[38]

8

The Papal Martyr

PIUS IX CAN BE FORGIVEN if he failed to realize that 1870 was not to be a repeat of 1848 for either him or the Church. The Catholic press reflected his certainty that, as in past invasions of Rome, this one too would soon be repulsed. Two days after Rome was taken, Milan's Catholic daily assured its readers: "That they will leave Rome is a certainty, just as the Napoleonics, the Mazzinians, and before them all the other enemies of the Church. How and when they will leave, it is not yet possible to say. Probably they will leave soon and they will leave badly." A few weeks later the paper proclaimed: "The hand of God, which in the catastrophe of Sedan [the dramatic French defeat at the hands of the Prussians] brought down the foundation of the whole Babel-like tower constructed against the papacy, will destroy the ruins that still stand. The temporal throne of the popes is destined to see other thrones fall."[1]

Deep was the pope's faith in God, and the God that he knew so well would never allow the forces of evil to triumph. He would never abandon His Church. "The storm against us will, perhaps, grow worse," Pius told a group of Austrian visitors in March 1871, "but it must eventually recede. I do not know either when or how, but there will certainly arrive the day in which the Lord will command the stormy seas to be still. For while He, in the just designs of His Providence, allows all revolutions to take place, He also fixes the point past which they cannot go."[2]

The pope continued to see France as his greatest hope, amid signs that the conservative Catholics were gaining strength and reports of France's anger at the Italians for failing to aid them in their fight with the Prussians.

On February 8, 1871, elections in France brought victory to the conservative monarchists and a defeat for the anticlerical republicans. The pope was exultant, knowing that French Catholics viewed the restoration of his kingdom as a sacred cause. When a week later Adolphe Thiers was appointed provisional head of the government, many in the Vatican were excited, remembering him as a supporter of the pope's temporal power.[3] But the pope was to be disappointed, for, given the situation in which France found itself — occupied by the Germans, its capital in turmoil — Thiers was not eager to antagonize Italy. "I am very decided," he wrote, "not to resurrect the Roman question, which we are in no position to bring to a happy solution. Infinite regard for the pope, earnest entreaties that he be spared further torments, that is our natural and honorable role; but to embroil ourselves with Italy at this moment would be an imprudence and a folly."[4]

Yet the pope would not easily relinquish his faith in the French. In March the count of Harcourt, a conservative Catholic much appreciated by the Vatican, was appointed ambassador to the Holy See. Over the next several months, Italians inside the government and liberal journalists outside speculated feverishly about Harcourt's presumed role in plotting the pope's restoration. The French foreign minister, Jules Favre, too was concerned about what the arch-Catholic Harcourt might do. He had been appointed to keep the French conservatives happy, but Favre — himself no acolyte of papal power and partly for this reason detested by the right in France — wanted to be sure he did nothing to stir up trouble. "Should the Holy Father seek to engage you in a conversation on this subject," Favre instructed Harcourt, "I want you to be struck by a respectful deafness." With Antonelli, Favre told him, he could be more explicit. His message was simple: "France is by a great majority favorable to the institution of temporal power, but it will do nothing to reestablish it."[5]

Meanwhile, Thiers and his compatriots had other problems, as did the Church, for a popular uprising had erupted in Paris. Officially pronounced on March 28, the Commune was a revolt against the conservative clerical forces that dominated the government. While its leaders called for universal suffrage and the complete separation of church and state, the rioters took special aim at the Catholic clergy. Churches and monasteries were sacked, and priests hauled off to jail. Attacked by military forces loyal to the government, the Commune finally dissolved in late May in a bloody week of fighting and chaos, in which twenty-four clerics, including the archbishop of Paris, Georges Darboy, recently returned from the Vatican Council, were put before a Communard firing squad and murdered. The forces of the right were no less brutal: twenty thousand Communards were killed in the week of fighting, and another twenty-two thousand executed at its end.

But the chaos in Paris did nothing to distract French conservatives from their campaign on the pope's behalf. To the contrary, they saw a link between the two: "Our disasters began the day we abandoned Rome," *Le Monde* told its readers on May 8. "They will not end until we resume the defense of the Holy See . . . France succumbed twice. She rose in 1814 with the restoration of Pius VII. She will rise in 1871 only after restoring Pius IX." The pope heartily agreed, telling a delegation of Frenchmen: "The atheism of the laws, religious indifferentism, and those pernicious doctrines known as Catholic-liberalism, it is these, these that are the true causes of the ruin of States, and these have brought great ruin on France."[6]

Although France's ambassador to Florence insisted that his country had no desire to take up the pope's call for action against Italy, the Italian government kept getting disturbing reports of a secret French plot aimed at restoring the Papal States. On May 10, Visconti received such news from one of his informants in Rome: in the wake of its humiliating defeat by the Prussians, he reported, "France will not be pacified until it wages an external, glorious — at least as far as their vanity is concerned — war." The only logical target for attack, he added, was Italy, and "seeing as the hatred against us is intense, such a war would be extremely popular." The French embassy to the Holy See, Visconti's informant charged, "is our sworn enemy and is doing everything it can to excite the French government and the French nation against us."[7]

By June, French bishops and their allies were organizing a huge petition drive aimed at forcing the French government to take military action. They demanded that the French ambassador to Italy be recalled and that warships be put at the disposal of a French colonel in the pope's service. Meanwhile, *L'Univers*, France's principal Catholic newspaper, whose editor, Louis Veuillot, was close to Pius, kept up a drumbeat for war on the pope's behalf. Among Veuillot's arguments was that such a war would help France in its struggle with Prussia, although his logic was less than clear. "We do not say," he wrote in early July, "that France should make war on Italy right away, but we think that . . . a war against Italy to restore the pope to his provinces would be the best road to the return of Alsace and Lorraine to France.[8]

As it turned out, the conservative Catholics' saber rattling cost them dearly, for the French population, weary of bloodshed, had little appetite for a new military adventure. With partial parliamentary elections scheduled for July 2, the republican press accused the Catholics of wanting another war, the bishops a new crusade. As a result, the Catholics suffered a major defeat, and the republicans won most of the open seats.[9]

The transfer of Italy's capital from Florence to Rome on July 1, 1871, did nothing to stanch the rumors of France's secret plans to take in the pope and thereby place itself at the head of Catholicism worldwide. There was much speculation that the French monarchists — closely linked to the Church — saw taking in the pope as a means of coming to power. Reflecting on this scenario, the liberal Roman newspaper, *Il Diritto*, concluded that the pope's flight to France would be equivalent to a French declaration of war on Italy aimed at restoring the pope's temporal power. These suspicions were fanned by the Prussian ambassador in Rome, Arnim, who as part of his campaign against France was spreading word of just such a nefarious French conspiracy.[10]

Visconti and Lanza were desperate to find out what the pope was going to do. On November 10, their chargé d'affaires in Paris told of a meeting he had just had with the new French minister of foreign affairs, Rémusat, in which France's plans to send an ambassador to the Italian government in Rome were discussed. "He told me," the envoy wrote, "that he feared that the new French ambassador's arrival in Rome might trigger the Pope's departure. Signor de Rémusat insisted on this prediction and led me to believe that he had received some kind of warning that justified it."

Advised by the Italian envoy that the pope's refuge in France would provoke deep sentiment against France in Italy, Rémusat replied that he was well aware of it and of the many other dangers that would come from having the pope on French soil. But what choice did his government have? he asked. They could hardly close the door to the pope when the French republic took in political exiles of every stripe. They had already done all they could to discourage Pius from such a course, he insisted, but the Italians should not fool themselves into thinking that it would make any difference. "From the general tone of Signor de Rémusat's remarks," the Italian chargé d'affaires concluded, "I got the impression that his predictions of the Holy Father's departure from Rome are founded on something more solid than mere supposition."[11]

Lanza and Visconti remained suspicious of French intentions.[12] Their worry that Pius might be taken into exile by the French was heightened because, ever since the Italians seized Rome, the French had stationed a warship, the *Orénoque*, in the harbor of Civitavecchia for the sole purpose of carrying the pope off at any time he chose. As month after month passed with the ship still docked in the Italian harbor, the king and prime minister tried mightily to pretend it was not there. But the liberal papers showed no such restraint, constantly warning that the presence of the ship reflected France's plans to restore the pope to power in Rome.

At the same time, in Berlin, Bismarck, who had just succeeded in unifying Germany, was becoming increasingly worried about the Vatican's influence on German affairs. Of greatest concern was the new Catholic Center party, which was pressing the government to take the pope's side in his struggle with Italy. Bismarck reacted by unleashing the fateful crusade against the Catholics that came to be called the *Kulturkampf* (literally, "struggle for culture").

These German developments in turn fed the fears of the French government about the impact of having the pope on French soil. Thiers realized the danger, as he explained in a September 1872 letter to his own foreign minister: "During the open war undertaken by Prussia against the papacy, the retreat of the pope into France would be a serious matter. Honor would not allow us to refuse, but it is not necessary to invite embarrassments."[13]

Although Thiers himself was not eager to take the pope's side, he was under great pressure from French conservatives. Events came to a head late in 1872. In both 1870 and 1871, the officers of the *Orénoque* had gone to pay homage to the pope on Christmas. While in Rome, they studiously avoided paying their respects to the king or to any other Italian official. With the Italian press denouncing the French for scheming with the Vatican and the presence of the French warship in the Italian harbor a continuing sore point, Thiers decided that a change should be made in the Christmas rites. The ships' officers were told to pay their respects to the pope on Christmas, as they had in the past, but then — in an effort to be more evenhanded — they were to offer their respects to the Italian king on New Year's.

Antonelli and Pius IX, enraged at this news, called in Count Jean François de Bourgoing, who had become the new French ambassador to the Holy See a few months earlier. Afterward Bourgoing, a staunch Catholic, handed in his resignation to protest the French slight to the Holy See. The incident became a political scandal in France, where Thiers depended on the National Assembly's conservative Catholic majority. A difficult several months followed, as Thiers struggled frantically to placate the pope.[14]

For the Italians, the affair simply served as a painful reminder of the presence of the French warship in their harbor. In mid-January 1873, Visconti wrote to his ambassador in Paris, Costantino Nigra, urging him to get the French government to withdraw the ship. "A Government has the right to send one of its ships to a port of a friendly State," Visconti pointed out, "but there are limits to the amount of time such a ship can stay there; even if these are not specified in any treaty, they are understood and appreciated."[15]

The French insisted on keeping the *Orénoque* in the Italian harbor, prompting a new drumbeat of denunciations of the French in the Italian press. A year later, Visconti again wrote to Nigra, expressing his fear that, with the upcoming opening of the 1874 session of the Italian parliament, he would be asked to explain why the government was allowing a French warship to remain so long in its harbor. Given the ease with which the French could get a ship to Civitavecchia should the pope request it, he wrote, it was difficult to see the continued presence of the *Orénoque* as anything other than a willful provocation. Finally, on October 13, the *Orénoque* sailed for France. To console the pope, the French informed him that they would keep another ship in Corsican waters, ready to come to his aid at any time.[16]

In all these years, no European monarch would visit the Italian king in his new capital for fear of antagonizing his Catholic subjects. One monarch alone visited Rome. In an ill-fated effort to bring peace between the pope and the new Italian state, Don Pedro II, the emperor of Brazil, arrived in 1871. A pious member of the Portuguese royal family, of the house of Alcantara, Pedro was the titular head of the Catholic Church in Brazil. On November 27, Pedro was ushered into the Vatican hall reserved for receiving monarchs, where the pope awaited him.

"What is it that Your Imperial Majesty desires?" asked the wary Pius IX, no doubt warned of the emperor's intentions.

"Holy Father," he replied, "please do not call me Emperor, as I come to you as the Count of Alcantara."

"Very well, then, dear Signor Count, what is it that you want of me?"

"I have come to beg Your Holiness to allow me to present the king of Italy to you."

At this, the pope rose from his chair and, staring him in the eyes, replied:

"You have come to me with such a proposal in vain, Emperor. The King of Piedmont can first bring an end to his sacrilegious acts and restore to the Church the lands he has stolen from it. Then I will permit you to present him to me. Before that, never! I would advise you against becoming his representative, for that would be beneath your dignity. Given the present state of things, he will never come here with my permission. If he wants, he can break open the doors of my palace as he knocked down the gates of Rome with his cannons, and as he forced open the door of my palace at the Quirinal. But in that case, as he enters, he will see me leaving by the opposite door."[17]

Although rapidly losing hope that any of the European rulers would come to his aid, the pope never lost his belief that God would not long allow the sorry state of affairs to continue. He now placed his faith in the power of the Catholic people. And in appealing to them for help, no image proved more potent than that of the papal prisoner of the Vatican.

The prisoner image was not new. In 1860, Count Charles de Montalembert, deeply involved in the Catholic Church in France, wrote a warning that, in the wake of the taking of Rome in 1870, *Civiltà Cattolica* and other Catholic papers began quoting regularly: "You can become the rulers of Rome as the barbarians were before you, and all the persecutors from Alarico to Napoleon. But you will never be sovereigns and never the equal of the pope. Pius IX may perhaps become your prisoner, your victim, but he will never be your accomplice. As a prisoner, he will become your cruelest embarrassment, your most horrific punishment." He further prophesied: "The spectacle of this Old Man, robbed of the patrimony of fifteen centuries, victim of the blackest treachery, wandering the globe in search of an exile . . . will raise against you and your accomplices, in everyone's hearts in all the world, a storm that will destroy you, but only after first dishonoring you forever. Take care that the Italians do not become the Jews of the Christian future. Take care that from the shores of Ireland to those of Australia, our children do not learn from the cradle to curse your name."[18]

So powerful was the image of Pius IX as the prisoner of the Vatican that in France priests and nuns began to sell, as holy relics, straw that he was made to sleep on. And so dramatically did the pope's popularity, and the cult of his martyrdom, grow, especially in France, that the historian Marcel Launay dubbed the phenomenon "*papolâtrie*" — papal idolatry.[19]

An avalanche of letters of condolence and a huge number of petitions from the Catholic faithful around the world descended on the Vatican, commiserating with the pope on his imprisonment. One of them even came, in early 1871, from a tribe of North American Indians. "Although we poor Indians don't have very clear ideas on all that is just and right," they wrote, "nonetheless we regard it as a crime seeing how they are treating you. Not even forty or fifty winters ago, when we were still far from having any civilization, would we have behaved in such a manner toward you."[20]

In late August 1871, as the day for moving the Italian government to Rome approached, and with it Victor Emmanuel's move to the Quirinal Palace, the pope decided to send a private letter to the king. It was vintage Pius IX.

"They say that this metropolis," wrote the pope, "is destined to be the capital of Italy. But while I know no Rome other than the one that belongs to the Holy See and is the capital of Catholicism worldwide, it seems to me that the work of the revolution has made of this great city, not the capital of Italy, but rather of disorder, confusion, and impiety." Monasteries and convents had been seized, and even the nuns disturbed from their sacred sanctuary. "Is it possible," he asked, "that after having usurped the last bit of temporal dominion, you also want to attack the Pope in the exercise of his spiritual power?" Such outrages would have grave consequences, he warned, unleashing "those punishments that God inflicts on his enemies." Then he added his warning to the king. The attack on the papacy was just the first step on a perilous road. "Majesty, it pains me to say it, but it is certain that after having shouted 'Death to the Pope!' they will shout 'Death to the King!' For my part, I am at peace and I place myself in God's hands. But," he added, "can Your Majesty actually say that you are equally untroubled?"[21]

Battling mounting physical ills, over the next few years the aged pope insisted on continuing to host large audiences, drawing strength from the devoted crowds. In addressing a group of Roman youth in October 1872, he used a new metaphor, but his message was unchanged: "The land that has been usurped," Pius told them, "will be like a volcano that with its flames threatens to devour all the usurpers." The following year, speaking to the heads of the religious orders, he warned that despite all the government's talk of guarantees, it in fact sought nothing other than the destruction of the Church itself. But, the pope assured the monks, the forces of evil would not succeed. "When it seemed that the Devil would triumph by means of the Aryans, and the land for a time faced the appalling prospect of being entirely infected by that heretical plague, the Church nonetheless rose up once again. And this time too it will again rise up, because there is no force that can stand against the finger of God."[22]

Although such confidence in divine intervention was widespread among the Catholic faithful, not all were so sure. Following a visit to Rome in May 1872, the priest Leonardo Murialdo, who would be made a saint a century later, described what he had found: "The priests, the bishops, and the Catholics are living a continuous and not terribly useful illusion, firmly believing that, at any moment, some miracle will take place to bring about the [Church's] triumph. And this is what is being preached from every pulpit, enraging Italian patriots and alienating the true moderates."[23]

And so the world witnessed a peculiar spectacle. Two sovereigns uneasily shared the same capital, the one — thought to be on his last legs — hurling epithets at the other, who was younger and more robust but diffident, swaggering on the battlefield but cowardly before the pope's sacred glow. Or, as the mischievous Gregorovius put it in his entry for January 12: "The Pope continues to sit like a mummy in the Vatican, while the King now and then appears, immediately to go off again on some distant shooting expedition."[24]

9

Anticlericalism in Rome

WHILE THE POPE was warning all who would listen that Italy's ultimate goal was to destroy the papacy and the Catholic Church, Lanza was trying to assure the world of the government's benevolence. But not all Italian patriots were so eager to contest the pope's charge. The anticlerical wing of the unification movement believed that destroying the Papal States was but one — albeit crucial — stage in the larger project of ending the anachronism that was the infallible pope himself. None held this view more firmly than the great hero of unification, Giuseppe Garibaldi. In one of many such tirades, he once urged his followers: "Fight against the Papacy, Italy's internal enemy, which has been a cancer on all humanity! Fight against the theocracy, erecting over the ashes of the papal throne a building that, based on morality and science, is worthy of being the temple of humanity!" Likewise, in a public appeal in 1872, Garibaldi urged the government to liberate Italy from the papacy, replacing it with "the religion of truth, religion without priests, based on reason and science."[1]

The hatred that Garibaldi and his comrades harbored toward the Catholic clergy — from the pope down to the village priest — could hardly have been more visceral or intense. As the enemies of Italian unification, dependent on foreign troops to protect them from the people's ire, the clergy represented the forces of darkness. Shortly after the taking of Rome, Garibaldi wrote his famous novel, *I Mille (The Thousand)*, a fictional account of his triumph in Sicily and march toward the Holy City in 1860. It is a story of good against evil, and most evil of all were the Catholic clergy. "The Italian priest," Garibaldi explains early in his book, "is always the traitor of his country."

"Tyrants and priests, convents and prisons, prisons and mercenaries, there is such an affinity between these scourges of humanity as not to be able to distinguish among them, to consider them the same emanation from hell," writes Garibaldi. "When I think of the power of the priests," says one of the heroes in the book, "I think of how they have reduced even the greatest of nations to the lowest level, inflicted every kind of humiliating degradation on it, having sold it out to the foreigner so many times and, above all, having trained it to the kissing of hands, the genuflections, the fear, the prostitution, and every form of outrageous brutalization, so that in the end one of the most beautiful peoples has been stunted, bent over, made morally and materially inferior to all those peoples who once sat at their feet. Thinking of the power of the priests . . . I often wonder whether these cretins . . . are nothing other than one of the many families of monkeys that I saw in the New World."[2]

But Garibaldi reserves his greatest hostility for the Society of Jesus and the Church hierarchy. "The Jesuits," he wrote, "are nothing other than hypocrites, liars, and cowards." They are "a sect whose aspiration is the idiocy and servility of all those who are not Jesuits." Italy's greatest hero pulled no punches:

> Jesuitism and tyranny represent the evil found in the human family. They are the parasitical plants that want to live and eat at others' expense, and not content to eat for one, they want to eat for a hundred. To sustain their injustice, they use every atrocious means they can to dominate the common people, who in turn call them "villain." Nor are the rest of the priests much better. Wherever they are found they form the local cell dedicated to destroying the Italian homeland and selling it out to foreigners. They preach a series of idiocies about the virginity of the mother of Christ, the supernatural content of the holy wafer, and the like whose preposterous falsehood they laugh at among themselves but peddle to the credulous. "Don't do what I do, but do what I say" is their motto.[3]

Italy's anticlerical movement comprised an odd assortment of the middle classes: doctors, lawyers, journalists, intellectuals, schoolteachers, and artisans. They were found not only in the large cities, but in small and medium-sized towns as well, and in the South as well as the North. The new religion was to be the worship of science, the new creed, a faith in progress. The Catholic religion represented the hand of medieval superstition and inequality, faith in the supernatural rather than in reason. As groups of anticlericals formed throughout the country, they held conferences celebrating science and conducted civil funerals in place of funeral masses. The better to show their disdain for the Church, on Catholic holy days they held bacchanalian balls.

In 1864, the first Democratic Society of Freethinkers was formed in Siena, with the post of honorary president given to Garibaldi. The following year, societies of freethinkers were formed in Naples and Milan, and others soon sprouted up. A barrage of publications appeared, denouncing the Church, the priesthood, and the pope. Uneasily allied with these new societies were the Freemasons. While also anticlerical, they were still weak in Italy in the 1860s and 1870s and often ridiculed by the freethinkers for their secrecy and quasi-religious rites.

In January 1871, Rome's first Society of Freethinkers was founded, holding its inaugural meeting in front of the Trevi fountain. Its goal was to establish an alternative to the Vatican in Rome, eliminating both the papacy and the Church hierarchy. Rome, so long identified with the pope, would soon symbolize the triumph of reason over superstition.

Along with the freethinkers, and partially tied to them, was the republican movement — itself divided into various factions — which similarly saw the Vatican as Italy's curse. The day after Rome was taken, the first republican daily newspaper, appropriately titled *La Capitale*, appeared. As *La Capitale* saw it, an unholy alliance between the Vatican and the Italian right was the greatest threat faced by the nation. In these first days after September 20, *La Capitale*, and other papers like it, urged the government to occupy the Leonine city, move the capital to Rome without delay, ban the Jesuits, close down the religious orders, seize Church property, and keep priests out of the public schools. In January 1871, *La Capitale* began to publish a series of unflattering biographies of popes and cardinals. Its malevolent portrait of Pius IX on the twenty-fourth of the month created such an uproar that the police seized all copies of the issue. "The papacy is dead," an anticlerical deputy exclaimed in parliament that day, "and the Italian Government need only bury a cadaver."[4]

While most of Italy's anticlerical clubs and republican organizations were either local or, at best, linked to weak national associations, two of the major sources of anticlerical agitation in Italy were parts of well-organized international networks. One was the Socialist International, founded by Marx during the early years of Italian unification, which at the time included both socialists and anarchists. By 1872 the first Italian section of the International had been organized in Rimini; another opened the following year in Bologna. The other large network, a very different kind, was the Freemasons. What united them was their belief that the papacy was a vestige of the past that had no place in modern times.

Followers of the Socialist International were champions of the working classes, and their primary targets were land and factory owners, other elites, and the government. Their view of a man like Lanza or Visconti Venosta was not much more favorable than their view of Pius IX. The Church was for them only a secondary issue. The Freemasons, on the other hand, were another matter. Heavily influenced by the republican ideals of Mazzini, they championed a secular state, worshiping at the altar of science and progress. Although they came from a wide range of social classes, their leaders were mainly professionals.

The Socialist International ultimately proved to be a much greater threat to the Church, but Pius IX and, later, Leo XIII were obsessed with the danger posed by the masons, whom, along with the socialists and freethinkers, they indiscriminately branded as members of "sects."[5] Yet at the time of Italian unification the masons were few and their organization weak. The first Masonic lodge was established in Rome in 1873, but it was only after 1879 that the few thousand members in Italy were sufficiently organized to carry out any concerted action. Not that it prevented Church publications — and, indeed, popes — from portraying them as the occult forces behind Italian unification, responsible for the taking of Rome.

The Roman police archives for these years are full of reports of violent encounters between anticlerics and loyal Catholics. The police kept the anticlerics under careful watch, and the government had little affection for them. Not only were their raucous demonstrations and sacrilegious publications a source of continuing embarrassment for the government internationally, but they were apt to direct their barbs against the government and the king as well.

On October 15, 1870, the Roman authorities wrote to the provincial government of nearby Frascati to ask about reports they had received of a hostile demonstration against a priest who had allegedly refused to baptize a baby. "They tell me," the Roman police official wrote, "that the population has even descended into violent acts against the parish priest's residence, which was pelted with stones and damaged." Two days later the head of Frascati's provincial government responded, recounting the facts. Tarquinio Balzoni had brought his newborn baby to the cathedral to be baptized, but the priest in charge "vigorously refused to administer the Baptism because the Godfather had been excommunicated both for being the Vice Secretary of the Municipal Government and for having voted in the plebiscite for the annexation of the Roman Provinces to the Kingdom of Italy." The priest's refusal provoked the ire of the citizenry, and attempts by the head of the province and the chief of the police squad to convince him to perform the baptism got nowhere. But, the provincial head hastened to add, there had been no violence and no attack on the priest's home. These were malicious rumors.[6]

On December 6, 1870, in a typical report, a Roman police official wrote that some youths were running through Rome's streets at night shouting "Long live Pius IX!" Other small groups — of a different bent — had been disturbing public tranquility by shouting "Long live the Republic!" The official assured police headquarters that he was doing all he could to discover who was behind the disorders and to prevent them in the future.[7] Meanwhile, other disturbing reports told of the Vatican's plans to use the observance of the Immaculate Conception to organize a demonstration against the Italian government. The police official in charge of the area around the Vatican, warning of these plans, relayed a bizarre rumor. Word was circulating around the Vatican, he reported, "that on the sacred day of the Conception a miracle will take place. People will wake up to find that not a single Piedmontese soldier remains in Rome!!"[8]

The Italian authorities did have reason to worry. At 4 P.M. on December 8, disorders erupted on the imposing steps of St. Peter's and beneath the columns stretching out around the square. The police report the following day found fault on both sides, blaming the violence on "the reciprocal hatred between the lower classes of Rome and those who see themselves as the most loyal supporters of the Pope's temporal power." Angry shouts and threats had led to fisticuffs and general mayhem. With the arrival of a squad of police, the rioters dispersed, and seven arrests were made.[9]

Three days later, new violence broke out in St. Peter's Square. The police had gotten word that the troublemakers were going to return to the basilica to create more mischief, so the official in charge stationed police throughout the square in front of the world's most famous church. Through the afternoon, more and more men of an anticlerical bent streamed into the piazza — at least a thousand, according to later police reports. The police struggled to get them to disperse. Around 5 P.M., as two young members of the pope's Swiss Guard left St. Peter's, one of the groups of young men approached them, accusing them of being *caccialepri,* former members of the reviled urban papal police squad. A growing crowd, in an increasingly foul mood, began to shout "Kill them! They're *caccialepri!*" The police rushed in and escorted the two young men to safety. When they arrested two of the troublemakers, hundreds of their companions began threatening the officers, demanding that they be released. Police reinforcements moved in, arresting eight men in all. In this and other such cases, what stands out is how many of those arrested were artisans: a tinsmith, a hatmaker, a blacksmith, a cabinetmaker.[10]

Violent encounters between the anticlerics and Catholics erupted with regularity around the city in these first months and years after the taking of Rome; remarkably, none resulted in serious injury. One of the more dramatic of these scenes occurred on March 10, 1871, at the Church of Jesus, the Jesuits' principal church, and so a particularly juicy target for the anticlerics. The previous day, a group of young anticlerics had confronted a group of devoted Catholics of the church. Their accounts varied. According to the Catholics, a young man named Enrico Santini, a lieutenant in the national guard, came into the church during the sermon and began to ridicule the preacher. After the service, as he was leaving with his coterie, he again raised his voice to the other churchgoers: "You don't believe all that nonsense that that monk has been spouting?" he asked. A group of angry young men confronted him, and a fight broke out.

A later government report told a different story: Santini, wearing civilian clothes, had attended mass at the Church of Jesus. At 11:30 A.M., as people were leaving, twenty former *caccialepri,* using as their pretext the charge that they had seen Santini smile disrespectfully, attacked him with fists and sticks, leaving him bleeding. It was due to this un-provoked assault, in this account, that the following day some friends of Santini's decided to gather outside the huge door of the Church of Jesus, waiting for the celebrants to come out from mass.

The anticlerical crowd grew rapidly to two thousand, spilling out be-yond the piazza and into the small streets that fed it. *Civiltà Cattolica*, in its account of the events that followed, characterized the throng as "composed in large part of filthy plebes and lowly beggars," many of whom were "either nonbelievers, or foreign Protestants in the city, or Jews." Again the chaos that ensued spawned two very different stories. In the liberal press, what precipitated events were the *caccialepri*, who strutted out of the church with a threatening swagger. "This is one of the usual lies of the liberal press," responded *Civiltà Cattolica*. "Can you imagine how a handful of young men, courageous, true, but virtu-ous and modest, as are those whom the rabble call '*caccialepri*,' would want to leave the church with a threatening expression toward such a large crowd?" What both sides admit is that the crowd showered the young Catholic men with insults, and scuffling broke out on the steps of the church. The police already stationed there were soon reinforced by two companies of infantry, who formed a defensive line in front of the church, facing the crowd. Despite repeated orders to disperse, the people would not leave, so the soldiers fixed their bayonets and began to move toward the throng. The crowd retreated from the soldiers but then reformed, continuing to hurl insults at the men filing out of the church.

Amid the mayhem, the soldiers received orders to move into the church itself. As the secular Roman newspaper *La Libertà* told the story, the police and soldiers were forced to go in to quell the violence that had broken out: "Some police agents and some soldiers entered the church where the disorder was great. Many clubs were seized, be-longing for the most part to those who were already in the church; and it was discovered that some of these had blades affixed to them. It has come to our attention that a number of knives were also seized." Again, *Civiltà Cattolica* offered a very different story. The huge doors of the church, which had been closed as soon as the disorder in the pi-azza began, were flung open violently and "a horde of *carabinieri*, na-tional guard, and policemen raced in furiously with their swords out and their daggers drawn, followed by soldiers with their rifles aimed straight ahead. It was this violent entry of armed forces in the church that was the true cause of the disorder that followed, especially because of the fright it gave the women who were inside. Many were arrested in the church, honest, upstanding young men, guilty of nothing other than having attended the sacred gathering, and among them a young priest, the son of Count Barbellini." For the Jesuit journal, the lesson was clear: "These disorders, which have by now become so frequent, are proof of the . . . impossibility of the coexistence in Rome of two Sovereigns, the one spiritual, the other temporal."[11]

Italy's minister of foreign affairs, Emilio Visconti Venosta, was so concerned by the poor impression that news of the melee was making abroad that he sent a long dispatch to his ambassadors, offering the government's account. "It is possible that the reactionary press," he wrote, "is seeking to give these incidents an importance that they are far from meriting. It would be well if you were in a position to counteract these exaggerations with the truth." In his account, the troubles had all begun with the priest, the Jesuit Father Tommasi. In a series of sermons at the Church of Jesus, the priest had angered the city's patriotic majority by his constant, and barely veiled, political diatribes. The partisans of the old regime, Visconti charged, saw attending Tommasi's fulminations as a way to flaunt their own hostility to the Italian state. Realizing the potential for an outbreak of popular anger against the champions of papal rule, the government made sure that police were outside to maintain order. Indeed, on the day in question, the crowd was well behaved until, as the worshipers began to file out, some in the crowd began to whistle at them. "A *caccialepre* surrounded by many of his comrades responded," Visconti wrote, "with various gestures and ironical remarks." This in turn led to an exchange of punches and blows with clubs on the church steps.

According to the Italian foreign minister, the police and soldiers moved in immediately, making some arrests and quelling the disorder, but at the same time they heard shouts of distress from women in the church, so they moved inside, quickly restoring order there as well. Thanks to the authorities' quick response, there had been no serious injuries. It was worth noting, Visconti pointed out, that among those arrested inside the church was a priest, Count Barbellini, caught as he was distributing clubs to the *caccialepri*.[12]

If Visconti and Lanza were eager to trumpet the Church's freedom in the new Italy and the continued respect enjoyed by the pope, anticlerics had a very different agenda. For them, the taking of Rome meant the end of centuries of clerical tyranny, the close of an era of medieval superstition, and the beginning of a bright new future of science and reason. And in showing their disdain for the central beliefs of Catholicism, they found few occasions more potent than those that marked the death of one of their heroes.

An early opportunity of this kind presented itself in April 1871 with the death of Mattia Montecchi, one of the leaders of the 1849 Roman Republic. Rome witnessed an event that would earlier have been inconceivable, a civil funeral and burial. To aggravate the Church further, the ceremonies were scheduled for Ash Wednesday. Seven thousand people strode solemnly through Rome's streets. The banners of scores of republican societies were held aloft while assorted veterans of Garibaldi's battles marched proudly. For the first time, too, Rome saw a group marching publicly under the banner of the Freemasons and, just behind them, another carrying the white banner of Rome's Society of Freethinkers. Many of Rome's municipal councilors walked behind the funeral carriage, whose cross had been removed for the day, and each guild — of goldsmiths, marble workers, hairdressers, carriage drivers, hatmakers, tailors — marched with a tricolored flag.

The significance of the sacrilegious rite was not lost on either side. The liberal newspaper, *La Capitale*, enthused: "Yesterday's demonstration was majestic, powerful, solemn. Honoring Montecchi, it affirmed, in a public fashion, a new civil faith . . . This splendid affirmation of emancipated conscience was necessary in Rome, the ancient city of the priests." In contrast, *Civiltà Cattolica*, shocked at the demonic display, downplayed the significance of the number of participants, composed, it asserted, of "not a small number of Jews and Garibaldians, who constituted the majority of that rabble."[13]

Under pressure from the anticlerical groups, Lanza and his colleagues moved quickly to combat the Church's hold over Rome's schools. The government seized the Collegio Romano, the Jesuit institution that offered the only secondary education in Rome, and created a public school in its place. Under Italian law at the time Rome was taken, religious education by priests was mandatory in the public schools. On September 29, 1870, in an attempt to placate the anticlerics, a government order made attendance at such lessons optional. Yet the clergy's influence on education was never entirely eliminated. Not only were there not enough qualified teachers for all the new public schools, but municipalities found it cheaper to hire priests than laypeople.[14]

The Vatican, predictably, was horrified by these attempts to substitute secular for Catholic education, but it was even more angered by the government's efforts to weaken the religious orders. These efforts had a long history. Back in 1848, new Piedmontese laws banned the Jesuits from the lands of the Savoyard monarchy, followed by an 1855 law suppressing other religious orders. The contemplative orders, especially, were seen as parasitic, the monks and nuns suspected of a variety of sins, from sloth to sex. The teaching and preaching orders, on the other hand, were suspected of spreading disloyalty to the government and regarded as a public threat. As the old regimes fell in the battles of unification in 1859–1860, among the first acts of the provisional governments that came to power was the suppression of monasteries and convents.

The government faced a special set of problems in moving to Rome, for over a third of the land both in the city and in the surrounding province was held by the Church. The early 1871 law on the transfer of the capital to Rome included a clause authorizing the expropriation of the buildings belonging to religious corporations on the grounds that they were needed to house government offices. Church libraries became the basis of new public libraries, Church art the foundation for new municipal museums, Church hospitals the hospitals of the new state.

Bowing to foreign pressure, the government allowed the headquarters of the general of each religious order to remain in Rome. And while the orders were technically dissolved, and many did suffer greatly, for the most part they were allowed to reconstitute themselves under the fiction of being civil corporations. While many convents and monasteries were seized — and even today many of Rome's major government buildings consist of expropriated Church property — most of the orders found ways around the new rules

As usual, the Jesuits were a particular target. Driven from the city, they found refuge elsewhere in the country and abroad. But it was not just Italy that fought them, for Austria, France, Germany, and other countries were hounding them as well. In 1880, the Italian Jesuit Francesco Altini, having taken refuge in Spain, told his sister of his travails:

"After being kicked out six times, from Verona, Padua, Rome, Tramin, Brixen, and Alleux, I am patiently awaiting the seventh."[15]

In June 1873, when the Law of Suppression of Religious Corporations went into effect, Pius responded by excommunicating Victor Emmanuel by name, including as well all his ministers and the members of parliament who had voted for the law. The next day, Italian police seized all the copies of the newspapers that carried the text of the papal decree. The Vatican's *Osservatore Romano* responded with a threat of its own: "Everyone says that we have returned to 1848 [when the pope was driven out of Rome]. We must console ourselves with the knowledge that 1848 was followed by 1849."[16]

Two years later, the pope protested yet another of the king's actions, although this time, rather than issue an excommunication, he addressed a special plea directly to Victor Emmanuel. Parliament had just passed a law extending military conscription to the clergy. With tears in his eyes, on April 13, 1875, Pius IX told a group of visitors: "Majesty, I beg you, I beseech you in the name of your illustrious ancestors, in the name of the Virgin Mary . . . in the name of God Himself and, I would add, for your own interest, do not sign yet another decree harming the Church! Stop your course . . . and go no further down the slippery slope that is leading you into the deepest abyss!" But Victor Emmanuel, unmoved, signed the bill on June 7.[17]

When, early the following year, the right — in power since the birth of the Kingdom of Italy — fell, the pope had new reason to fear for the Church. Italy's new rulers were men who had, years earlier, cast their lot with Mazzini and Garibaldi. The new prime minister, Agostino Depretis, was himself a Freemason; in choosing his cabinet, he selected men known for their hostility to the Vatican. Yet, with a trace of bravado, Milan's Catholic newspaper, *L'Unità Cattolica*, claimed to be pleased that they no longer had to deal with the hypocrites formerly in power. "The men of the Left do not pretend; they are wolves like those of the Right, but they are wolves both in words and in deeds. At least we now know whom we have before us: it is an impious, cruel, tyrannical adversary, but one that is clear about it . . . They do not want reconciliation with the Church, but its destruction."[18]

Depretis was hardly less combative. In October, *La Libertà* carried his latest thoughts on the Church: "Let us not delude ourselves. There is in Italy and in Europe a party which conceals its worldly aims and its thirst for dominion under the mantle of religion. The traditions of Gregory VII are not yet extinct within the papal Curia; the Syllabus is still its *modus agendi;* and it is a formidable power because of its new despotic constitution, its complete and perfect organization, the breadth of its ramifications, the great influence which it continues to exert over the masses." The new prime minister concluded: "I am a defender of religious liberty . . . but when religious sentiment turns against the political organization of the state, it is time to sound the alarm in order that provision might be made for the latter's defense. The war has begun, and it will be necessary to wage it *à outrance.*"[19]

The fall of the right in Italy coincided with an important transition in the Vatican as well, for on November 6, 1876, Giacomo Antonelli drew his last breath. Despised by his fellow cardinals for the power he wielded and the way he kept them from the pope, Antonelli was probably more intensely disliked in the Vatican than he was among Italy's liberals. Although jealous cardinals had long whispered to the pope about Antonelli's alleged mistresses and thirst for wealth, Pius had always viewed him as the astute judge of political realities that he himself was not.

By September, Antonelli, who had long suffered from painful episodes of gout, had to be carried on a couch into the pope's study to present his daily briefings. On November 5, told by his doctor that the end was near, he called in his Jesuit confessor. Never an ordained priest, Antonelli had not been a particularly religious person and made no pretense now of any great religiosity. Yet he remained faithful to Pius and despaired at what the unworldly pontiff would do without his sober advice.[20]

Pius's reaction to Antonelli's death was the subject of much speculation. Some in the Vatican claimed that the pontiff was relieved to be rid of his secretary of state and shed no tears for the man who for over a quarter of a century stood at his side. In one account, on hearing that Antonelli had called for his confessor, the pope exclaimed, "God be praised!" The belief that Pius was happy was further fueled by the cardinal's funeral being practically a furtive affair, held at 5 A.M. But another account reports that on hearing the news, the pope, himself in weak health, murmured, "Our separation will not be long." He then canceled all his appointments and went to his private chapel and spent the day in prayer.

Whatever the truth of these accounts, there is no doubt that the relationship between the two men had been peculiar. Despite their many years together, the pope had never developed a real friendship with Antonelli, a man so unlike himself. Nor did later events do much to burnish Antonelli's reputation. When his will was read, it was discovered that he had left relatively little of his large fortune to the Church. Then, in a case covered in sordid detail by the press, the estate was itself sued by a young woman claiming to be his illegitimate daughter.[21]

The new government's offensive against the Church began within weeks of Antonelli's death when the new minister of justice, Pasquale Mancini, viewed by the Vatican as a notorious anticleric, introduced a bill aimed at combating "the abuses of the clergy." Prison terms and large fines would be levied on any priest found to be inciting hatred of the government or encouraging disobedience of the law.

A Neapolitan lawyer famous for his oratorical powers in parliament, Mancini was deeply suspicious of the Church hierarchy. While believing that people should be free to hold any religious beliefs they liked, he thought it a matter of survival for the state to oversee the affairs of the Church to ensure that the public good was served. He had, in fact, opposed the law of guarantees.[22]

In January 1877, the House of Deputies, now dominated by the left, approved the bill on clerical abuses, 150–100. As the Senate prepared to discuss the measure, Pius once more denounced the king and called on Catholics throughout the world to come to his aid. He had never been clearer in declaring that Italian unification could not be reconciled with his own spiritual freedom and could not be allowed to stand. Church leaders abroad urged the restoration of the Papal States. In France, the bishop of Nîmes proclaimed: "Italian unity has not been consummated; Pius IX is still king; the temporal power will exist again." He added his own prophecy: "After a great crash, in which perhaps many armies and crowns will go under, the nations of the world will call out in a single voice: 'Return Rome to its former ruler; Rome belongs to the pope; Rome belongs to God!'"[23]

In March, Mancini instructed government offices on how to deal with the newspapers that were publishing the pope's new denunciation. Throughout the country, the minister of justice wrote, true Italians were learning of the papal allocution with horror, aghast at "the excessive and violent language adopted in this document against the

Kingdom of Italy and its laws and institutions." The pope, he charged, clearly aimed "to profit from every opportunity to unmake the new Italian Kingdom, if at all possible, and to bring back the papacy's temporal power." Pius IX, wrote Mancini, continued to insist "that the pope must either be the Sovereign of Rome or he can be nothing other than a prisoner" and was urging the world's bishops "to use every means in their power to set the foreign governments against Italy and its government."

What then should be done about the publication of this call to arms against the Italian state? asked Mancini. While the Vatican's publication was protected under the law of guarantees, there was no question that the reproduction of such a seditious document by anyone else was illegal. "Nonetheless," Mancini concluded, "the current Minister, deep in his faith in the unity and liberty of the fatherland, and vigilant against the machinations of the clerical party, believes this a propitious occasion for giving the world a solemn proof of forbearance, although provoked beyond all reasonable limits by those who speak, not the mild language of a religion of charity and peace, but who without any inhibition go so far as to express the political desire for the destruction of the State and its government." The simple reproduction of the papal allocution would not be prevented, he said. But newspapers that printed favorable comments about it were another matter. Their editors were to be arrested and charged with attempted subversion of the state.[24]

Two months later, the pope finally had some good news. Italy's more conservative Senate had (narrowly) voted down the clerical abuse law. This round, at least, had gone the Vatican's way.[25]

10

Two Deaths

VICTOR EMMANUEL WAS NEVER comfortable in his new home. He was plagued by the sight of the Vatican, which seemed to taunt him, and ever mindful of the prophecy that his new palace, stolen from the pope, would be his premature tomb. He also periodically suffered from malaria, a curse of the Holy City, which did nothing to encourage a positive attitude toward Rome.

He had returned to Rome from Turin just in time for the obligatory festivities greeting the new year of 1878, yet he arrived feeling somewhat ill and was eager to leave again, planning to depart after a state dinner scheduled for Sunday, January 6. But on the fifth he came down with a high fever. Sunday evening, he seemed to be getting better, but on Tuesday he took a turn for the worse, and his doctors began to be concerned, diagnosing a case of pleuri-pneumonia.[1]

News of the king's illness reached the pope on Monday. Although he had excommunicated Victor Emmanuel many times, the pontiff still had an odd affection for the wayward monarch. He feared for his soul and, at the same time, no doubt hoped that the prospect of dying outside the grace of the Church and fear of eternal damnation might finally bring him around. The pope summoned his sexton, Bishop Francesco Marinelli, and gave him the task of going to the Quirinal, gaining entry to the king's chamber, and seeing to his spiritual health. Realizing his task would not be easy, the bishop asked the pope's permission to seek the help of Father Valerio Anzino, the king's chaplain. With the pope's blessing, on Monday morning he headed for Anzino's rooms at the Church of St. Sudario and told the chaplain of his mission. Anzino assured the bishop that the king would be pleased to learn of the pope's concerns for his well-being, but, he warned, it would not be easy for the bishop to see him. Anzino, they decided, would speak with one of the royal aides and have him get word to the king, so that the king himself could issue orders allowing the bishop to enter.

Marinelli returned to the Vatican, anxiously awaiting word. He waited in vain.[2]

That same day, having heard of the king's illness, the priest at the Church of Saints Vincent and Anastasio, the parish of the Quirinal Palace, began to get nervous as well. Fearing that he might be called on to perform last rites, Father Pietro Desiderj requested instructions from the cardinal vicar of Rome, Raffaele Monaco La Valletta. The cardinal said that he was only to administer the sacraments if the king first apologized formally for having taken Church lands.

Two days later, at five minutes after noon, an official from the Quirinal arrived breathlessly at the church, saying that he had come on a matter of the greatest urgency. He handed the priest a letter written by the royal chaplain, Father Anzino, which said simply, "Give me the bag with the holy oil." But, to the royal aide's consternation, Father Desiderj refused, insisting that he could not give the chaplain the materials needed to administer the last rites without first having spoken to him.

"But the chaplain cannot leave, for the king is in danger of dying at any moment," said the aide. Their argument was soon interrupted by the frantic Father Anzino himself, who urged the parish priest to give him what he needed.

"Before I can give you what you want," the priest insisted, "I have to know whether the king has provided some kind of apology, for without one I cannot agree to your request."

Father Anzino replied that he had taken confession from the king earlier that day, following the authorization he had received from the pope by way of his sexton. In his confession, Father Anzino said, the king had told him to tell the pope that he intended to die a Catholic, that in all the laws he had promulgated he had never intended to offend the Holy Father, and that he apologized for any offense he had caused.

Still Father Desiderj would not hand over the sacraments. "First give me a written document recording what you have said, so that I can show it to my ecclesiastical superiors," he demanded.

The impatient Anzino quickly scribbled simply "I administered confession to His Majesty. I beg you to give me the Extreme Unction so that everything necessary is done."

The parish priest still held out. "I told him that such a document was not sufficient," the priest later recalled, "and I added: 'The Monsignor Vicegerent [the cardinal vicar's primary aide] lives just a few steps away. Let's go there together and let him decide.'"

They raced off, but the vicegerent, Archbishop Giulio Lenti, was not at home. The priest then forced the hapless Anzino to go to the quarters of the cardinal vicar, but he too was away. Although the chaplain was now bursting with impatience — fearing that the king might die before he returned — the parish priest would not relent, forcing him to see the cardinal vicar's secretary. The secretary, afraid to take responsibility himself for such a momentous decision, told them instead where they could find the vicegerent. The parish priest and the chaplain, now joined by the vicar's secretary, set off to find Archbishop Lenti, reaching him just before 1 P.M. in a nearby church.

Hearing of the king's imminent death and his wish to receive the holy sacraments, the archbishop asked Father Anzino whether the king had begged forgiveness for all of the evil deeds he had done to the Church.

"The king spoke to me as follows," Anzino responded. "'Tell the pope that I intend to die a Catholic, that I repent for the wrong done to him.'" Anzino added that it had been impossible to get any of this in written form, or even to have someone witness it, but he was convinced that the king had sincerely sought forgiveness. The archbishop then made his decision: under the circumstances it would have to suffice. The sacraments could be administered.[3]

Father Anzino rushed back to the parish church with Father Desiderj, where they learned that messengers from the Quirinal had been sent repeatedly to see what was taking so long. The priest dressed the chaplain in surplice and stole, and gave him the box containing the viaticum, the pouch with the holy oil, and the other materials he needed. As Anzino rushed out, Father Desiderj sent one of his altar boys with him to light his way with a lantern. The altar boy was stopped at the entrance to the palace, but the chaplain was ushered to the king's bedside, where Victor Emmanuel, breathing with great difficulty, awaited him.

A surrealistic scene unfolded. With the king was not only his son, the prince, who would shortly become king himself, but also the fiercely anticlerical government ministers — among them Mancini and Crispi — each holding a lit candle from the room's candelabras. Father Anzino administered the last rites as they looked on.[4] The king then said that he needed to rest, and as they left, an aide helped him onto a chaise longue. A few minutes later he drew his last, tortured breath. It was 2:30 P.M. Italy's first king was dead.

That evening, writing the news of the king's death to Paris, the French ambassador to the Holy See charged that it was Prime Minister Depretis and his minister of the interior, Francesco Crispi, who had prevented Bishop Marinelli from bringing the pope's salutations to the dying king. The ambassador also recalled that Victor Emmanuel, having long had a presentiment that he would be struck dead in the Quirinal, had frantically tried to get his doctors to move him to Turin or at least to his estate outside Rome. Anywhere but the palace that he had taken from the pope.[5]

For many in the Church, the king's death offered God's long-awaited response to his conquest of Rome. Turning the king's famous (if apocryphal) pronouncement on first arriving in Rome against him, *Civiltà Cattolica*, in reporting his death, envisioned him arriving at the gates of Hell and once again proclaiming, "Here we've come and here we shall remain." The Jesuit journal also noted that General La Marmora, who oversaw the occupation of the Quirinal Palace and the king's move to Rome, had himself been struck dead a day earlier. Surely it was no coincidence. And in one more sign of the Lord's displeasure, January 9, the day of Victor Emmanuel's death, was the date on which, five years earlier, Napoleon III had died.[6]

In another — equally triumphant — twist of the king's famous phrase, Davide Albertario, the legendary editor of one of Italy's most influential Catholic newspapers, Milan's *L'Osservatore Cattolico*, wrote: "'We are in Rome and in Rome we shall stay!' And in Rome he did stay, just as he himself had prophesied, but he stayed there as a cadaver." Such disrespect for the monarch was not to the liking of the clergy or the Catholic faithful, especially in a city such as Milan, where — as opposed to the former Papal States or even the south of Italy — Victor Emmanuel was regarded by many in the Church as having a firm claim to rule. A hundred priests in Milan and the surrounding area signed a petition lambasting Albertario and expressing their regrets at the king's death.

That it was Albertario and not the hundred protesting priests who was closer to the pope's way of thinking became clear when the archbishop of Turin, Monsignor Gastaldi, voiced his own regret at Victor Emmanuel's death. On January 17, *L'Osservatore Romano* made the Vatican's displeasure known: "Various newspapers have been publishing the pastoral letter of the archbishop of Turin. Being unable to associate ourselves with all the opinions expressed in it, we do not reproduce it here." Furious, the archbishop demanded that the secretary of state disassociate himself from the story. But in his response on February 1, Cardinal Simeoni informed Gastaldi that the note that he judged so offensive had been ordered by Pius himself. On the same day as the *Osservatore Romano* snub, the pope wrote a personal note to Albertario and his newspaper, lauding them for their loyal defense of his policies. This note was printed in the newspaper later in the month. Not only did the pope praise the intransigent editors for warning the faithful against the evil teachings of the Church's enemies, he also complimented them for cautioning the faithful against "others, who, using the pretext of prudence and charity, spin tales of absurd and impossible reconciliations."[7]

On January 11, *L'Osservatore Romano*, recounting the king's last rites, reported that on his deathbed he had "asked the pope's forgiveness for the wrongs for which he was responsible." Other Catholic papers followed suit, trumpeting the king's supposed repentance when faced with his Maker.

Crispi hastily prepared a counterattack. Reporting the circumstances of the king's death, he wrote in an official government statement that the Catholic press "is asserting things that are not true. His Majesty King Victor Emmanuel did not make any declaration that repudiated his glorious life as Italian king."[8] For both Crispi and Depretis, much was at stake. That the king had died a good Catholic could be used to great profit, a new demonstration of what they had long been claiming; there was no conflict between loyalty to the state and devotion to the Church. But any suggestion that on his deathbed the king had expressed regret for conquering the Papal States threatened the very existence of the Italian nation.

In the meantime Umberto, the thirty-three-year-old heir to the throne, was eager to burnish his own Catholic credentials. The day after his father's death, he sent an aide to the Vatican to thank the pope for his recent expression of interest in the king's welfare. The Vatican was dumbfounded, having long viewed Umberto as a *"mangiapreti,"* a priest eater, who was even less well disposed toward the Vatican than his father.[9]

With the king's death, the Vatican faced new pressures. Throughout the country people mourned their vigorous founding father, who had been taken from them so unexpectedly. They not only wanted a funeral fit for a king in Rome but stately funerary observances from Turin to Palermo.

The cardinals of the Congregation of Extraordinary Ecclesiastical Affairs gathered in the Vatican to advise the pope on what course he should take. Formed in 1814 after Pope Pius VII's return from his exile in France, the Congregation was the pope's primary source of advice on questions of the relations between church and state in Italy and beyond. Composed of two dozen of the most influential cardinals, its weekly agenda was set by the secretary of state and its recommendations sent to the pope for his approval. At the time of Victor Emmanuel's death, its members included not only the secretary of state but the cardinal vicar of Rome and a number of former papal nuncios.[10]

The cardinals found themselves in a difficult spot. Depretis and his government were undoubtedly eager to exploit the emotions surrounding the king's death to bolster popular allegiance to the regime. And after not only excommunicating the king but also insisting for so long that the government had no right to be in Rome, the Vatican could hardly give its blessing to a royal funeral in the Holy City. Yet having a Catholic monarch's funeral in Rome without the participation of the clergy was likewise unimaginable. They had to find a way out.

The solution, from the cardinals' perspective, depended on the claim that, on his deathbed, the king had fully repented for his crimes against the Church, begged forgiveness, and received absolution. Because they knew how vigorously the government would deny this view, the cardinals instructed the priests involved in his last rites to prepare written accounts of what had happened. The parish priest, Father Desiderj, and the vicegerent, Archbishop Lenti, lost no time in preparing detailed statements. But for the man whose testimony was most important, Father Anzino, the matter was far from simple.

The royal chaplain found himself in a terrible quandary. The same day as the cardinals of the Congregation of Extraordinary Ecclesiastical Affairs gathered, he was summoned by Crispi, a notorious anticleric, former Garibaldian, and now the powerful minister of the interior, who warned him of the gravity of the situation: the future of the Italian state and the monarchy rested in his hands. Should he claim that Victor Emmanuel expressed regret over the taking of Rome and the rest of the Papal States and asked divine forgiveness for these acts, he would be delivering a potentially lethal blow to the state and to the royal family he had long served. But Crispi was taking no chances. Unwilling to place all his faith in the priest's patriotic bent or sense of loyalty to the Savoyards, he also threatened him. Should Anzino make any embarrassing claims of royal retraction, he would find that he was a royal chaplain no more.

In stark contrast to the long statements of Father Desiderj and Archbishop Lenti, the letter that Father Anzino sent to the Vatican could hardly have been shorter. Dated Rome, January 10, 1878, it said simply: "His Majesty King Victor Emmanuel II, in the act of receiving the Holy Sacraments, expressed himself in these terms: 'I authorize you to declare that I intend to die as a good Catholic, with a feeling of filial devotion to the Holy Father. I am sorry if I caused any displeasure to His August Person, but in all these matters I never had the intention of causing any damage to Religion.'"[11]

Having drafted the note, Father Anzino first took it to Umberto. The prince expressed his approval, adding that it was a sentiment to which he could affix his own signature. "I too am a good Catholic and I want to die as one," he said. "And my position is better than my father's," he noted with some satisfaction, if unheroically, "because it was he who did everything, while I need do nothing more than preserve what he has left me." Victor Emmanuel's ambiguous apology had the virtue of serving the needs of both the Vatican and the Italian state, allowing each to offer its own interpretation.[12]

Just what Church involvement the pope would permit in the king's funeral observances remained unclear. Cardinal Simeoni sent a secret communiqué to every Italian bishop on the tenth. It forbade "any ecclesiastical service that may be ordered or requested by the Civil or Municipal authorities," but it then weakened this categorical ban by adding "especially if such a service may take on the character of a political demonstration." Two days later, citing "some uncertainty about the meaning" of the instructions of the tenth, Simeoni specified that the earlier statement "was not intended to absolutely prohibit funeral services in present circumstances, as long as there is no attempt to give them the character of a political demonstration, which is left to Your prudent judgment to determine." In any case, the secretary of state added, no funeral services should be sponsored by the Church, nor should any higher Church authorities take part.[13]

The Vatican also faced the problem of the funeral site. Much anguish could have been avoided if the government, respecting the sentiments of the royal family, had agreed to hold the ceremonies in Turin, with burial in the Savoyard mausoleum just outside the city. But Depretis, Crispi, and the other members of the government opposed such a move, for it risked provoking some uncertainty about the royal family's — and with it Italy's — claim to Rome. A stirring funeral procession through the streets of the Holy City and entombment in a place in central Rome that could become a permanent pilgrimage destination for Italian patriots was just what the government most needed. As one liberal newspaper put it, "It is the fervent wish of all Italians to place the first stone in the new national tradition, erecting it on the foundation of its ancient greatness against another tradition, which was, is, and will be forever the enemy of Italy." Citing this passage, *Civiltà Cattolica* asked: "And what exactly is the tradition that was and will always be the enemy of Italy?" It replied: "If we have not misunderstood, it is the Christian tradition."[14]

Elsewhere in Italy, the bishops found themselves in an uncomfortable position. People were clamoring for funeral observances in the only churches fit for such royal ceremonies, the cathedrals, and expected the highest Church officials to take part. It was also clear that these ceremonies would be local apotheoses of the hero of Italian unification, the king who had defied the pope and taken his very palace from him. In most cases, the bishops refused to participate and did what they could to prevent the use of their cathedral for such rites, especially in the lands that had, until recently, been part of the Papal States. In one not atypical incident, a large group of men in Bologna, irate at the news that their archbishop, Lucido Parocchi, refused to allow funeral ceremonies for the king, surrounded his residence and pelted it with rocks, shouting, "Death to Parocchi! Down with the clergy! We want to be excommunicated!"[15]

In the end, the pope agreed to bury the king on sacred ground in Rome, insisting only that none of the Holy City's basilicas be used. After considerable argument, and thanks to the mediation of Father Anzino, the Vatican permitted the use of the ancient Pantheon for the service and for the king's final resting place. The symbolism was most appropriate. The Pantheon was a consecrated church — St. Mary of the Martyrs — but long before it had become a Christian church it was a temple for worshiping Rome's secular rulers, dedicated to Augusta and Agrippa in 27 B.C.

While the government heads were pleased with the Pantheon for the king's tomb, they wanted a church with a much greater capacity for the actual funeral service. Not only did they expect many foreign dignitaries to attend, but they anticipated that patriots from all over Italy would flood into Rome. Yet on this the Vatican would not budge: none of Rome's major churches could be used.

Victor Emmanuel's body lay in state in the chapel of the Quirinal Palace; six Capuchin monks, sitting by the coffin, took turns reciting the prayers for the dead as dignitaries filed by to pay their respects. On January 17, the royal funeral procession marched through Rome's streets from the Quirinal to the Pantheon. To encourage a large display of devotion, the government offered a 75 percent discount on train tickets to Rome; 150,000 people poured into the city. Behind the coffin, a general on horseback brandished the dead monarch's sword. Just behind him, the Savoyard royal crown was reverently carried. In front of the coffin marched government officials of all sorts, members of the judiciary, and university professors. Town officials from throughout the kingdom marched, holding their municipal crests aloft, with the city councilors of Rome and Turin given pride of place. A hundred uniformed generals — some gray and bent with age — marched by solemnly, as did soldiers bearing the banners of eighty regiments. Troops lined all the streets along the route as the crowds behind them threw flowers onto the royal coffin. Immediately in front of the funeral bier strode the king's younger son, Prince Amedeo, surrounded by representatives of Europe's royal families and the diplomatic corps. Depretis and Crispi marched near the coffin. The Vatican had forbidden any clergy beyond the simple priests of the local parish to take part, so no bishop or cardinal was to be seen, nor did the pope allow any Catholic confraternities, a mainstay of such processions, to join in. Most embarrassing for the government was that the king's own daughter, Clotilde, known for her devotion to the Church, was nowhere to be seen.

The immense procession lasted four hours, with the coffin arriving at the Pantheon at 2 P.M., greeted by the priests of St. Mary of the Martyrs. (The name Pantheon was viewed with distaste by the Church as a pagan term for what had for centuries been a consecrated church.) Only foreign royalty, diplomats, members of the Italian parliament, and other high state officials were permitted inside. After the ceremony the dignitaries left, and the huge crowd outside was allowed to file in. Throughout the day and into the night, all of Rome shook with the blast of a cannon fired every minute.[16]

Some in the Catholic press, gleeful at the king's premature demise, trumpeted the point that the elderly pope had outlived him. But the pope himself was in no position to celebrate, for he was a very sick man.

Far from reconciling himself to his loss of temporal power, in his last years the pope had grown even more combative.[17] Among his strongest denunciations of the Italian state was that contained in one of his last formal allocutions, on March 12, 1877, an address that some saw as announcing a new Catholic crusade against Italy. The following year, shortly after the pope's death, *Civiltà Cattolica* cited this speech, calling it a kind of last testament. "After having proclaimed the necessity of temporal power for the independence of the apostolic ministry," the Jesuit journal recollected, "he declared that in Rome the Head of the Church must either be ruler or prisoner."

The intransigent mood of the Vatican in Pius's last months was reflected in an incident in October 1877. The famed Jesuit scholar and journalist Carlo Maria Curci, one of the founders of *Civiltà Cattolica* and once very close to the pontiff, was suspended from the Jesuit order by papal directive. In March he had written a public appeal to the pope to make peace with the Italian state and abandon the call for reestablishing the Papal States. Under Pius IX, such language was blasphemous.[18]

When Victor Emmanuel died, the elderly pope had been too sick to celebrate mass for over a month. Although a brief reprieve from his suffering allowed him to say mass on the seventy-fifth anniversary of his first communion on February 2, he quickly took a turn for the worse, and on the morning of Thursday the seventh, his doctors warned that the end was near. The pope himself, under no illusions, asked for the last rites. Dressed in white nightclothes and propped up on his bed by pillows, he alternately rested, prayed, and talked with one or another of the cardinals who came to comfort him. Just before noon, the man whom he had recently appointed as his chamberlain, Cardinal Gioacchino Pecci, asked Pius to bless all the cardinals. "Yes," the failing pontiff replied, "I bless the Sacred College, and pray that God will enlighten you to make a good choice." Grasping the small wooden cross that he always carried with him, he held it up and added, "I bless the whole Catholic world."

Shortly after noon that day, Francesco Crispi summoned Rome's police commissioner to his home to discuss the situation. He wanted to be notified the moment the pope died. At 4 P.M., the French ambassador to the Holy See, realizing that a conclave to choose a new pope was imminent, sent a telegram to Paris: "It is indispensable for the French cardinals to leave for Rome as quickly as possible." An hour and a half later, Pius IX, who had served as pope longer than any of his 255 predecessors, died. Catholics throughout the world went into mourning, although the news was greeted with relief, if not delight, in some of Europe's capitals. When Bismarck received word of Pius's death at one of his rural estates, it is reported, his spirits immediately brightened: "Let's drink to that!" he said, and told his servant to fetch a bottle of schnapps.[19]

The following day, at 3 P.M., all of Rome's church bells rang out in an hourlong funereal chorus. Even the bell tower of the Campidoglio, Rome's municipal headquarters, joined in, if only for twenty minutes. The curious poured into St. Peter's Square, which by afternoon was mobbed although remarkably quiet. Having been criticized the previous night for not closing the theaters as a sign of respect, the government shut them down. On the evening of the eighth, the pope's doctors embalmed his body, placing the heart and intestines in a special urn and injecting a preservative into the veins.

Ordinarily, the pope's body would then lie in the Sistine Chapel for public viewing, but large crowds were expected to pay their last wishes to Pius IX, and the cardinals were not willing to allow the Italian police or military into the midst of the Vatican to help maintain order. As a result, arrangements were made for the body to be on display in St. Peter's, under the protection of Italian forces. On the evening of Saturday,

February 9, the holy cadaver, dressed in white papal robes, was placed on a litter to transport it into the basilica. Beside the body lay a golden miter. The pope's hands were folded across his chest, one clutching an ebony cross, the other a cross made of ivory. Clergy bearing torches led the procession, striding slowly between two lines formed by the Swiss Guard. Behind them came the funeral litter, surrounded by the Noble Guard, who in turn were followed by the clergy of the basilica, holding burning candles, and then the members of the pontifical family. The cardinals marched two by two, carrying torches and chanting psalms, followed by a gaggle of princes and others of the Roman aristocracy. The body was placed behind a grate, with the pope's feet poking outside so that mourners could kiss them. There it remained on display from the morning of Sunday, the tenth, through Tuesday, the twelfth. An immense crowd packed St. Peter's Square and the surrounding streets, an endless line winding out of the vast basilica.[20]

For the government, it was crucial to show that the papal ceremonies could proceed smoothly. As early as September 1871, a year after Rome had been taken, the minister of the interior had sent a long list of instructions to Rome's police commissioner about what to do should the pope die. The police were to surround the Vatican, checking all those who entered. If such obvious surveillance proved to be a problem, plainclothes police were to be used as much as possible. "No demonstration, whether peaceful or not, will be tolerated either in the immediate vicinity of the Vatican or in the larger area around it . . . Newspaper and book vendors will not be permitted to shout out anything that offends religion and the papacy, or that offends public decency or in any other way is inopportune under the circumstances."

Many cardinals were opposed to allowing the Italian forces into St. Peter's, yet, aware of the immense crowd seeking entrance, they faced the choice of trying to keep out all but a relatively small number of guests or having to seek help from the government whose legitimacy they rejected. On the evening of Saturday, the ninth, a Vatican representative met secretly with Giuseppe Manfroni, the police inspector in charge of the Vatican, and told him that police were to be permitted in St. Peter's to help maintain order, but no Italian soldiers would be admitted. Manfroni, though, feared that more than a simple police guard was needed to ensure order. He would station Italian military forces outside the basilica doors, but, he said, the Vatican would have to permit him to allow the military to enter the church if needed.

Manfroni was under great pressure, as he later recalled: "My work was enormous, my position difficult. It was the first time that the body of a pontiff had been displayed to the public under the custody not of his own soldiers but of a force that the papacy insisted on considering an enemy." Veterans from opposing sides of the battles of Mentana and Porta Pia would be standing face to face, and emotions were running high.

On the morning of the tenth, with the huge crowd pushing toward the basilica's door, Manfroni told his Vatican contact that there was no way of maintaining order without sending soldiers inside. The crowd, despite the triple cordon of soldiers outside the gate and the large number of carabinieri and papal guards inside, was becoming increasingly difficult to control. Reluctantly, the monsignor agreed to let the Italian troops enter St. Peter's.[21]

In fact, order was preserved, and even the Vatican newspapers complimented the Italian forces on their dignified behavior and effective work.[22] Nor was the prime minister, Depretis, slow to trumpet this fact. At 2 A.M. on February 11, he circulated a notice to all foreign governments: "Today the solemn exposition of the deceased pope began at St. Peter's. In agreement with the ecclesiastical authorities, police agents were stationed inside the church and perfect order was maintained. The greatest tranquility reigns in the city."

Manfroni estimated that at least three hundred thousand people filed into St. Peter's to view the pope's body. Among them, or so the French ambassador reported in a telegram sent in midafternoon on the twelfth, was Queen Margherita herself, King Umberto's notoriously Catholic wife, who had gone to kiss the foot of the dead pontiff, "a curious and gripping sight." The rumor, a great embarrassment to the Italian government, prompted Crispi to send his own telegram to the Italian embassy in Paris three hours later, to be passed on immediately to the French foreign minister. The report of the queen going to kiss the foot of Pius IX was utterly fallacious, Italy's minister of the interior wrote. "The Queen did not even leave the Quirinal Palace."[23]

On Wednesday evening, following a solemn procession of cardinals and the clergy of St. Peter's and accompanied by the singing of the basilica's choir, the pope's body, clad in white papal vestments and covered by a red silk cloth, was placed in its temporary tomb inside St. Peter's. There it would remain for three years.[24]

Pius IX was dead. The object of greater adulation in the Catholic world than any pope in history, he had died a martyr in the eyes of millions of devoted Catholics, a deeply religious figure who would not trade his principles for political expediency, a man seen as God's champion on earth. In death, as in life, he was the saintly prisoner of the Vatican.[25]

But the pope's popularity was far from universal. Not only was he widely reviled in Italy for his continuing opposition to Italian unification, he had angered most of Europe's political elite as well. At his death, the *Kulturkampf*, the German government's attack on the Catholic Church, was still in full swing, as was a campaign against the Church in Switzerland. The Austrians were angered by the pope's refusal, a month earlier, to receive a member of the emperor's family who was in Rome for Victor Emmanuel's funeral. In France an anticlerical party had just come to power, and in Belgium the ruling party showed little love for the Vatican. Nor was the situation in Spain much better.

Following his predecessors' example, Pius IX had identified the Church with the monarchs of Europe and with the battle against civil liberties. But many of the monarchs with whom he had been most closely identified had been deposed and discredited, and he himself died as a self-styled prisoner of the Vatican. The question now facing the Catholic faithful, as well as the Italian government and others throughout the Christian world, was, what would his successor be like? Were things about to change or would the new pope, too, piously await the day when God would drive the revolutionaries from Rome and restore His vicar on earth to his rightful place?[26]

11

Picking a New Pope

WITHIN MONTHS OF occupying Rome in 1870, Italy's leaders had concluded that the Holy See would never make peace with the Italian state as long as Pius IX was alive. So it meant that a great deal was at stake in the choice of the new pope. Would he be more politically realistic and willing to stand up to the *zelanti*, as the intransigents were called? Or would he himself be drawn from their ranks, ushering in another decade of hostility toward the state?

In the years that followed, Italy's ambassadors met secretly with the leaders of Europe's other governments to try to devise a plan to influence the selection. In June 1871, for example, Marco Minghetti met with the Austrian foreign minister, Count Beust. Since a vacancy on St. Peter's throne could come at any time, Minghetti suggested that Europe's powers work together to ensure "that the new pope is a man of moderate and conciliatory spirit."[1] The following month, Italy's foreign minister, Visconti, urged the Italian ambassador in Paris to raise the question of a papal successor with the French prime minister. "The question of the future pope," Visconti wrote, "is of tremendous importance for both political and religious interests. Governments should waste no time in smoothing the way for the election of a pope who is well disposed to conciliation, not only with Italy, but with all of modern society."[2] At the same time, the Austrian and French foreign ministries were in direct contact with each other. Beust warned the French that, under the current circumstances in the Vatican, "the candidates of the party of conciliation had no chance, and a pope chosen from among the infallibilist cardinals would be a danger for all governments." Preventive action was crucial.[3]

The Portuguese government also wanted to be involved. In early 1872, the Portuguese were amassing historic documentation aimed at proving that they too had a right to cast a veto in papal elections. They would have a hard time getting anyone to heed them. The veto had long been the prerogative of Austria's emperor and the kings of Spain and France by dint of their claim to being the successors of Charlemagne, who as Emperor of the West had enjoyed such a right. They had exercised such a veto often over the past centuries.[4]

The Portuguese agreed with the Italian plan. As their foreign minister put it, according to a February 1872 report from the Italian ambassador in Lisbon, a prior agreement by the European powers would be extremely useful, "above all to eliminate the candidates for the pontificate well known for their membership in and devotion to the party of the irreconcilables." It would also be well to agree in advance on the election of a cardinal, he said, who, "if not the most liberal — who in current circumstances would have little chance of success — was at least one of the cardinals . . . well disposed to reconciliation." Italy, the Portuguese minister warned, was in a dangerous position. The Vatican, he said, "is doing all it can . . . to isolate Italy and to bring victory to the royalists in France and — with Henry V [then being championed by the French royalists] on the French throne together with a new pope hostile to Italy — reestablish temporal power."

The Italian leaders shared these fears. A few months later, Visconti told his ambassador to Paris that, while it was too much to hope for the election of a liberal pope, "it would be a most useful result to exclude the election of cardinals who are known for their intolerant viewpoint and their membership in the Jesuitical party." But he urged caution. The Italian government must not be seen to be the initiators of these secret European discussions.[5]

In a confidential memo dated May 10, 1872, Visconti set out the government's concerns about a future conclave, to be used in briefing Italian ambassadors abroad. At the moment, what most preoccupied him was not so much who the new pope would be but how he would be selected. Two rumors had him worried. One was the proposal, favored by a number of influential cardinals, to elect the next pontiff *presente cadavere*, that is, as soon as Pius IX had died and even before he was buried. It would mean choosing the new pope without a conclave. The other was the plan to hold the conclave outside Italy, on the grounds that the cardinals could not deliberate freely in Rome. "Any deviation from the canonical form can only diminish the authority of St. Peter's new successor," Visconti warned.[6]

Germany and Chancellor Bismarck were also involved in these secret discussions. In late May 1872, the German foreign minister had called in Italy's ambassador and read him a confidential message that Bismarck had written. It was extremely important, the chancellor wrote, for the European governments to ensure the regularity of the upcoming conclave, not least so that they would be in a position to use their veto. Its importance was now far greater than it had ever been, given the recent proclamation of papal infallibility: "How much more precious has this right become," Bismarck wrote, "after the dogmas that have recently been proclaimed! Following these dogmas, the bishops have lost all of what independence had been left to them vis-à-vis the Holy See. They have become the Pope's employees."[7]

The spring of 1873 found Visconti engaged in frenetic correspondence with his ambassadors, orchestrating confidential discussions of the next papal vacancy, now widely assumed to be near. The Austrian foreign minister charged that Cardinal Antonelli was pushing for a conclave to be held outside Italy (in this the Austrian was almost surely wrong) and urged that the European powers do everything possible to prevent it. The Italian ambassadors in France, Germany, Austria, Portugal, and Spain were all reporting that those governments wanted the next papal election to be held in Rome and wanted a moderate named as pope. But Visconti suspected that something else was going on. On May 20, he wrote a long letter to his ambassador in Vienna.

"Behind our back and unbeknownst to us," he told him, "agreements are being made dealing with the papal question that are against our interests." Above all, Visconti distrusted the French. Our goal, wrote Visconti, must be "to paralyze, at least in part, that action, unfavorable to us, that France would like to carry out."[8] He then turned to the prospect of a conclave outside Italy. Such a gathering, he wrote, would represent a triumph for the reactionary faction of the Church, for in such a gathering the election of one of their own number would be a foregone conclusion. And once elected outside the country, it was hard to imagine that the new pope's first act would be to return to

Rome, for to do so would be to admit that he was free to come and go as he pleased and so was not the prisoner of the Vatican as Pius IX had claimed. Having the new pope outside Italy, Visconti argued, would prove a great boon for fanatics, who would use it to arouse popular anger. It would mean a new Crusade, led by the pope himself. And the impact on Italy would be enormous: "All of Italy's policies would be dominated by the need for defense. Everything would be driven to the extreme." Visconti accepted as fact the reports that Antonelli was pushing for a conclave outside Italy, but he noted that Austria and the other Catholic powers — working against France — could fight the plan, profiting from the reluctance of most of the Roman cardinals to leave the Holy City, frightened as they were by the prospect of exile.[9]

Evidence that the *zelanti* in the Vatican were indeed plotting to have the next pope elected outside Rome comes from a strange visitor, received by the Austrian emperor at the beginning of September 1873. The visit also suggests that it was not Antonelli but cardinals trying to work around him who were behind the plan. For the man presenting himself as the special, secret emissary of Pius IX was not the papal nuncio to Vienna (who was directly under Antonelli's authority) but Monsignor Francesco Nardi, one of the most notorious of the *zelanti*, a fervent champion of the pope's temporal power who had grown very close to Pius IX in his last years.

Nardi informed the emperor that the pope had recently signed a secret pontifical bull ordering that his successor be elected within two hours of his death. But why, the emperor asked, would the pope send Nardi to tell him this? Because, the monsignor explained, there was still a way to avoid this unorthodox procedure. If Austria were to offer a place in its territory where the conclave could be held, it would not be necessary to abandon the traditional method of electing a new pope.

The emperor was unmoved by the monsignor's plea. He refused the request, adding that he saw no reason that a free conclave could not be held in Rome.

Nardi responded with a threat: "Well, since Austria is turning us down, we will have to turn to France."

"Do as you like," the emperor replied, but he suggested that, before leaving Vienna, the monsignor speak with Count Andrassy, who had recently succeeded Beust as Austria's foreign minister.

Like the emperor, Andrassy wondered whether Nardi had actually been sent by the pope, for he offered no direct proof, and it seemed possible that it was all part of a *zelanti* plot.

A pope elected outside Rome in dubious circumstances, said Andrassy, would face grave difficulties, for many Catholics would question his legitimacy. In any case, he told Nardi, the Imperial Government would not host such a conclave, for the election of the new pope in Austria implied "the commitment to bring him back to Rome under the conditions that he himself determined and, as a final consequence, the necessity, should it be called for, of declaring war on Italy, something that the Imperial Government absolutely refuses to do."

Nardi, his mission a failure, left straightaway for Rome.[10]

In June 1875, Visconti outlined his concerns in a letter to his ambassador to Paris. He was worried about the papal candidate whom he thought France was pushing, Cardinal Sisto Riario-Sforza, the archbishop of Naples. From a noble Neapolitan family close to the Bourbon king of Naples and made a cardinal back in 1846, at the age of thirty-five, Riario-Sforza was one of the Church's leading conservatives. Visconti described him as "narrow-minded and of limited intelligence," but he was nonetheless viewed as honest and incorruptible. "In some circles of the prelature here in Rome," observed Visconti, "he is seen as likely to fall under the Jesuits' influence. For my part, I believe that his papacy would follow the same line of conduct as that of Pius IX. But it is for other reasons that I must confess that the likelihood of the election of Cardinal Riario repels me. As a Neapolitan he was always very devoted to the Bourbons, and his social origin gives him greater prestige, and it also makes one suppose that he would be very closely tied to the Bourbon aristocracy of the South, without having to add that this complex of networks has close ties to France."[11]

In a remarkable document that Visconti sent to his ambassador to Portugal in January 1876, the Italian government offered its secret evaluation of each of Italy's thirty-three cardinals, to be shared with the Portuguese foreign minister and used in the secret negotiations then taking place in Europe's capitals. Visconti divided the cardinals into two categories. He explained that the first, List A, consisted of the names of those who, "in our view, should be excluded and whose election to the papacy seems dangerous to us both due to their fanatical and ultra-reactionary opinions and because their actions as pontiff are, for other reasons, to be feared." List B, on the other hand, "contains the names of those cardinals who, in our view, do not have against them any particular reason for the exercise of a veto." On both lists, Visconti had placed the names in the order of their probability of election, beginning with those having the greatest chances.

Among those about whom Visconti was most concerned, Cardinal Riario-Sforza again drew special attention. The head of the Bourbon aristocracy in Naples, Visconti wrote, the cardinal was the candidate of those who would like to see the South of Italy separated from the rest of the country. He was the darling of those French Catholics who most hated Italy.

By the name of each cardinal were brief — and often brutal — comments. Cardinal Costantino Patrizi had the dubious honor of being placed first on List A. "This is a poor, coarser facsimile of Pius IX. Without a heart and without a mind. He has a faction behind him, however, composed of all those who want to prolong the Vatican's current policy with even harsher and more bitter forms. To be excluded."[12]

A position on the B list did not guarantee kind treatment. Carlo Sacconi, a former papal nuncio to France, for example, while making the B list, was described as "a man of small mind, uncertain and vacillating in his convictions, if in fact he has any." But this was better treatment than that received by Cardinal Fabio Asquini, who was described simply as "having always been a moron."

In retrospect, the most notable feature of Visconti's secret list was its selection of Gioacchino Pecci as the candidate on the B list with the greatest chance of election. The archbishop of Perugia, Pecci was the man who would, in fact, in two years' time become Pope Leo XIII. "Sufficiently cultured, of rather gentle character, he was first a nuncio and then a bishop, never showing himself to be a passionate opponent of the national order, or at least he always kept a prudent reserve in order not to provoke disagreements with the Government. Having always lived outside Rome, he was not involved in the Curia's intrigues and conspiracies, and so he has no enemies in the Sacred College of Cardinals and will gather many votes for the papacy." This portrait was only slightly tarnished by its concluding comments: "While one cannot state with confidence that he has the positive qualities that would today make him an outstanding pope, the negative qualities that have marked his life make it the most suitable for the papacy, because these negative qualities are the most one can hope for in a future pope, chosen by these cardinals."[13]

While trying to orchestrate a papal election campaign with Portugal and Austria, Visconti remained deeply suspicious of the French. In early August 1876, the Ministry of the Interior's surveillance of the Vatican produced a warning that the Holy See was engaged in detailed discussions with the French government about plans to hold the next conclave in Nice.[14]

The French, knowing of the Italians' suspicions, were eager to put them on another scent. After earlier denying any knowledge of the Vatican's plans to hold the next conclave outside Rome, the French foreign minister shocked the Italian envoy in Paris by telling him that he had apparently been mistaken. "I assure you that I do not know what they want to do. I have not yet been able to discover it. I only know that various machinations are going on and that Cardinal Antonelli knows them." He directed the Italian envoy's attention to Cardinal Alessandro Franchi's recent, hastily arranged visit to Ireland, which seemed especially odd as it came at a time when Cardinal Antonelli was himself gravely ill. Franchi was one of the Vatican's major figures, a former nuncio to Spain and soon to become secretary of state with the election of a new pope. "It would not surprise me," the French foreign minister said, "if this had to do with making arrangements for holding the conclave in Malta." Franchi was scheduled to go from Ireland to London and then on to Paris. The French foreign minister reported that he was placing the cardinal under police surveillance in France, and he called on the Italians to have their ambassador in London try to find out what he was up to there.[15]

The Italian foreign minister wasted no time in contacting his ambassador in Britain, urging him to speak to Lord Darby, the British foreign minister. Darby insisted that he knew nothing of plans for a conclave in Malta. But, he added, to the ambassador's dismay, if the cardinals did decide to hold their conclave on the island, there was nothing he could do to stop them.[16]

A look at the confidential diplomatic correspondence then in progress between the French foreign minister and his ambassadors to Italy and to the Holy See makes it clear that the French government was in fact not then plotting with the Vatican to hold a conclave in France. In April 1877, the French ambassador to the Holy See met with Cardinal Simeoni to go over their understanding about the next conclave.

"It is French policy," the ambassador reminded him, "to ensure that the Sacred College of Cardinals has full freedom guaranteed in Rome, so that the traditional procedures for the election of a new pope can be followed."

"Yes, this is all well and good," replied Simeoni, "but should the cardinals sense any threat to their safety or freedom, or any hint of pressure from the Italian government, the conclave will not be held in Rome."[17]

This then was the situation when Pius IX died on February 7, 1878. The conclave that convened later that month proved to be the first of a new epoch. Although Italians still dominated, now 40 percent of the cardinals were from abroad. Just as important, developments in transportation, especially the advent of the railway, made it possible for foreign cardinals to arrive in Rome in time for the election. And something else had changed: the cardinals were now no longer selecting the ruler of an earthly state but only a religious leader, albeit one with enormous political influence.[18]

The crisis atmosphere that enveloped the Vatican after the taking of Rome affected all of the cardinals who gathered for the conclave. Many of the cardinals of the Curia — those most directly involved in running the Vatican — believed that the new pope should stick loyally to Pius IX's stance and condemn both the Italian state and all liberal ideology. But others thought it futile to continue to deny the existence of the Kingdom of Italy and believed as well that tying the Church's future to Europe's most reactionary political forces was a prescription for disaster. The lines seemed drawn for a bitter struggle.

The mentality of the intransigent faction is reflected in an article in *Civiltà Cattolica* by Raffaele Ballerini, which appeared just days before Pius IX died. It linked the taking of Rome to liberalism, portrayed as the great evil of the time. "The goal of liberalism," Ballerini wrote, "is the destruction of the Catholic Church." Liberals had "seized Rome not so much in order to defeat the Pontiff's temporal power as to defeat his spiritual power." The pope, he argued, "forced to remain closed up in the Vatican, almost in prison . . . under an enemy power . . . is no longer his own master." The occupation of Rome had "robbed Catholicism of its capital and placed the Pontiff in a violent and absurd situation." Liberalism "would like to bring Protestantism's work to Italy, defeating the monarchy of the Church. In so doing it can only be motivated by the same spirit that motivated Luther, that is, hatred for the Church of Christ."[19]

The dominance of this attitude in the Vatican was also evident in a communiqué that Cardinal Simeoni sent to all of the nuncios on the inauguration of Victor Emmanuel's successor, Umberto: "His Holiness has ordered the undersigned Cardinal Secretary of State to protest and to renew our claim to the Church's right to maintain its ancient domains intact and to protest its unjust usurpation."[20]

After years of speculation about where the conclave would be held, the time for a decision had arrived. As soon as the French ambassador to Italy heard the news of the pope's death, he went to see Depretis. The prime minister assured him that the Italian government would do everything that the Sacred College of Cardinals requested to ensure the smooth functioning of the conclave. The Austrian and Spanish ambassadors were summoned by Depretis and given the same assurances. Mancini had, the evening of the pope's death, gotten word to Cardinal Pecci, the chamberlain, who by virtue of his office was in charge of the Vatican's affairs until a new pope was elected, telling him that the government guaranteed them all the freedom and security they needed.

That same evening, the French ambassador to the Holy See went to see several of the senior cardinals in order to convey the Italian government's assurances. Among those present was Cardinal Pecci, who, on hearing the ambassador's news, "expressed neither surprise nor satisfaction." All these questions, the chamberlain said, would be dealt with the following day by the general meeting of those cardinals present in Rome.[21]

It was not only the Italian cardinals of the Curia who were suspected of scheming to hold the conclave outside Italy. Among Europe's diplomats, a good deal of suspicion fell on the head of the Catholic Church in Britain, Cardinal Henry Manning. A champion of infallibility and a fierce opponent of Catholic liberals, Manning had all the zeal of a convert, having become a Catholic only as an adult, in 1851, leaving the Anglican Church and his position as an Anglican priest. Deeply indebted to Pius, who had made him archbishop of Westminster in 1865, Manning had been disappointed that the pronouncement of papal infallibility in 1870 had not been stronger. The German historian Gregorovius, with his typical lack of charity, described the British archbishop as "the fanatic, a little grey man, looking as if encompassed by cobwebs."[22]

A month before Pius's death, the French ambassador to the Holy See told of a recent conversation he had had with Cardinal Manning, in which the British archbishop let on that he preferred holding the conclave outside Italy. Among the places the cardinals were considering, he said, were the French city of Nice, the Principality of Monaco, and one of the Catholic cantons of Switzerland. The continued existence of two powers in Rome, Manning said, was impossible.[23]

When the thirty-eight cardinals gathered the morning after Pius's death, they stood in front of the large crucifix in the Consistorial Hall and took an oath of secrecy. Cardinal Pecci then surprised many of them by taking out a packet of four documents that the pope had given him to use at this fateful moment. To be sure that his words were heard after his death, Pius had had three other copies made, each set given to a different cardinal. They consisted of the regulations governing the holding of conclaves and three documents that he himself had written to guide them, one in 1871, one in 1874, and the last just four months earlier, in October 1877. Each one was read aloud to the assembled cardinals, whose curiosity about Pius's instructions must have been great indeed.

The first of the instructions, written less than a year after the taking of Rome, contained the provisions that the Italian government and the other Catholic states of Europe most dreaded. Given the parlous situation in which the Vatican now found itself, the pope wrote, he was releasing the cardinals from the rules governing previous conclaves. The cardinals in Rome at the time of his death were to decide if the conclave should be held outside Italy, and they were authorized to elect his successor immediately, without waiting for other cardinals to make their way to Rome, if they thought it best.

Pius's second message simply affirmed his 1871 instructions. Finally came the latest document, which reflected an even greater reluctance to hold the conclave in Rome. In light of the ever-worsening situation of the Church there, the pope told them, even if they initially decided to meet in Rome, they should leave their options open. Should, in the process of organizing the conclave, any of the cardinals be subject to harassment or be prevented in any way from participating freely, the conclave should immediately be dissolved and moved, even if voting had already begun.

The pope's opposition to the conclave's being held in Rome made a big impression on the cardinals. Cardinal Camillo Di Pietro, who chaired their discussion, found himself in the minority in urging his colleagues to remain in Rome. To support his view, he produced a message he had received the previous evening from Pasquale Mancini, the Italian minister of justice. Dated Rome, February 7, 1878, 10 P.M. — just hours after Pius's death — it assured the cardinals that the Italian government would "do its utmost to ensure the Conclave the fullest security, freedom and independence." Yet the cardinals were not won over. A straw poll produced 28 votes for abandoning Rome and only 8 in favor of remaining. Cardinal Di Pietro, alarmed at the fateful decision that the agitated cardinals appeared about to make, tried to slow things down. In doing so, he stopped the cardinals from making a choice that could well have had monumental ramifications for the Church. They could not decide to hold the conclave in another country, he argued, without first determining where to go. Since it would require long discussion, he advised, they had best put the final vote off until the next day, when the merits of various alternative sites could be discussed.[24]

By then, many of the cardinals were clearly having second thoughts. When they gathered that morning, Cardinal Di Pietro began by reading the assurances he had received from the Austrian government, based on their discussions with top Italian officials, pledging that the cardinals would be entirely free to meet in Rome. The Austrians urged the cardinals not to abandon the Holy City. The French and the Spaniards were also doing what they could to discourage the cardinals from leaving Rome. A coded telegram from the French ambassador to the Vatican on February 9 reported that the Spanish cabinet had unanimously voted against allowing the conclave to be held on Spanish territory, and the French diplomatic correspondence makes it clear that the French offered no more encouragement for the idea of a conclave on French soil.[25]

Given all these assurances from the Italian government, the cardinal told his colleagues, and the notable lack of enthusiasm by the Catholic powers for hosting them, it would be prudent to hold the conclave in Rome. Should there be the slightest sign of any interference from the Italian government, he added, they would leave Italy and in doing so would have the full support of all of Europe's Catholic powers. At this point, Cardinal Monaco and some of his colleagues objected, arguing that trouble would be averted if they simply proceeded directly to the election of the new pope, *presente cadavere*. But the tide of opinion was shifting. Di Pietro asked for a new vote on the question of holding a regular conclave in Rome. This time 31 voted in favor and only 6 against.[26]

The day after Pius's death, the French ambassador to the Holy See sent a telegram to Paris, asking that the French cardinals be told to come to his embassy on their arrival so that they could agree on a strategy. Two days later, the French foreign minister, the Protestant William Waddington, sent the ambassador copies of a long message to give to each of the French cardinals on their arrival in Rome.[27]

The true interests of the Church and of France, Waddington told them, are one and the same. Pius's successor must be a man of prudence and moderation, able to calm things down. He should also be an Italian, for electing a pope from one of Europe's other Catholic powers could lead to unforeseen and unfortunate consequences at a time of great international rivalry.

Although Waddington did not mention it, the French government had decided that there was one person it would definitely veto if it looked as though he were about to be elected. The target of their concern was Cardinal Luigi Bilio, one of the architects of the Syllabus of Errors and one of the preeminent champions of infallibility at the First Vatican Council. Bilio, a Barnabite monk, was the man whom Pius had at one point indicated was his own favorite to succeed him. So notorious was Bilio — one of the intransigents' leaders — and so great were his prospects that both Austria and Spain also arranged to have his candidacy vetoed if his election appeared likely. The French foreign minister, knowing that the archbishop of Paris was a friend of Bilio's, did not trust him with the task and so asked the archbishop of Rouen to cast the veto should it prove necessary. Meanwhile, the archbishop of Toledo carried the Spanish veto and the archbishop of Vienna was given Austria's veto. Because a veto could only be exercised before a candidate won a majority of the vote, the timing of its announcement was crucial. No state wanted to squander its veto, nor create the ill will that one would inevitably cause, unless it had to, yet the danger of waiting until it was too late made it a nerve-racking affair.[28]

Within three days of Pius's death, five hundred workmen were busy preparing places for all of the cardinals to stay and readying the Sistine Chapel, where the conclave would be held. By tradition, once entered into conclave, the cardinals could not leave the premises until a new pope was elected. Because no one could predict how long the conclave might last — some in the past had gone on for months — the task of making the arrangements was complex.

The rules specified that the cardinals were to enter into conclave ten days after the pope's death, and on Sunday, February 17, the nine days of devotional services for Pius IX were concluded. On Monday morning the mass of the Holy Ghost was sung, allowing the conclave to begin. Sixty-one of the sixty-four cardinals were present. One absentee was on his deathbed. The other two — including the only American, Cardinal John McCloskey, the archbishop of New York — arrived after the election was over. All thirty-eight Italian cardinals were present, and so had a clear majority.

Sixty-four screens were placed along the two sides of the Sistine Chapel, with a numbered canopied seat and desk in front of each. Four of the canopies and seats were draped with green cloth, marking the cardinals appointed by Gregory XVI, the only ones who had previously taken part in a conclave. Each cardinal was given a ballot divided into three parts. At the top the cardinal wrote his name, in the middle his selection, and at the bottom a biblical text of his own choosing. The top and bottom were folded over and sealed so that the only visible part of the ballot was that bearing the name of his candidate. The other portions were to be used only in the case of a challenge to verify that the vote had been properly cast.[29]

As the cardinals prepared for the first ballot, speculation abounded. Would they dig in and, following Pius's wishes, elect an intransigent, committed to rejecting modern doctrines and any reconciliation with the Italian state? Or would they seek out a moderate, someone who might alter the Church's path?

Despite all of the French government's attempts to encourage the latter, two days before the conclave began the French ambassador to Italy sent a long telegram to Waddington with news of a disturbing development. The foreign cardinals, contrary to hopes, were apparently having an unfortunate influence on the Italian cardinals, who, after initial moments of recklessness, had finally been calming down. Especially alarming, he reported, were rumors that the French cardinals were most vociferously championing the intransigent cause. "I have no doubt that you feel as I do how serious it would be if the foreign cardinals, and especially the French cardinals, could be suspected of having turned the Sacred College away from the voices of moderation."[30]

Two days later, on the eve of the conclave, the ambassador to Italy sent a second telegram to Waddington. "I continue to have doubts about the disposition of the French cardinals and the influence that they are having in the Sacred College. They are trying to influence the foreign cardinals by convincing them of the danger of a pope who, by accepting conciliation with Italy, would betray the interests of Catholicism." That same day, an increasingly agitated Waddington telegraphed his ambassador to the Holy See, telling him of the news coming to him from the ambassador to Italy. Should the French cardinals help engineer the election of an intransigent pope, the French foreign minister told him, it would be a disaster. "Please hasten to clarify for me their attitude and, if the rumors that have been reported to me actually do have some foundation, appeal to their patriotism before the Conclave opens."

The ambassador to the Holy See telegraphed back immediately, presenting a very different picture from the one that his fellow ambassador was painting. "In the many conversations I have had with the French cardinals," he reported, "I have not noticed any trace of the sentiments that seem to so alarm my colleague." He went on to explain: "The foreign cardinals certainly want an Italian to be pope, but not an Italian pope. That is to say, they judge that a pope who allowed the papacy to be absorbed by and confused with Italy would be a greater danger than any other for the Church and for religious peace in Europe." The ambassador, who was well connected in high Vatican circles, also offered the first prognostication of a likely successor. "The first ballots will open with the names of Cardinal Pecci and Cardinal Bilio. If no agreement is reached on one or the other, they will look for a third."

In a telegram sent at ten o'clock that night, just hours before the conclave would open, the ambassador sent further news, attributing his colleague's alarming reports to the scheming of the Italian government. "Without revealing any details and the secrets of their deliberations, which are protected by religious oath, various Italian cardinals have assured me that the foreign members of the Sacred College, and the French cardinals in particular, have never departed from a position of the greatest moderation." Rather, he charged, "the Italian Government has been carrying out a maneuver — and hardly a new one — of denouncing the attitudes of the Austrian and Spanish cardinals to Vienna and Madrid, just as they denounce those of the French cardinals to Paris."[31]

Two factions dominated the conclave. The first, centered around some of the older Italian cardinals of the Curia, believed it critical to reinforce the policies that the saintly Pius IX had so forcefully espoused. The Church must place itself in God's hands, they believed. Some hoped for a miracle. Others thought that the worse things got in Italy, the better it would be for the Church, for it would increase the chances that the Italian state would collapse and temporal power be restored. Far from calling for a worldly man sophisticated in diplomacy, they were convinced, the times required a pope devoted to prayer and to defending sacred doctrine.

Cardinal Lorenzo Randi, who was of this view, urged his colleagues to vote for Cardinal Tommaso Martinelli, an Augustinian monk, whom he portrayed as just the saintly sort of person they needed. Yet Martinelli's candidacy did not get far, for reasons that are reflected in Bishop Soderini's portrait of the conclave: "Not that Martinelli was not a holy man, of upright intentions and pure life, but, besides a want of physical gifts, he had no experience at all of the world, lived a most retired existence, was excessively shy in speaking, fled from any conversation, and came into touch with as few persons as possible." Randi's lobbying for Martinelli was motivated in part by his dislike of Pecci, whose election he wanted to avoid at all costs. Randi and Pecci had quarreled two decades earlier, when Randi had the top government position in Perugia while Pecci was archbishop there.

The intransigents' greatest hope was Cardinal Bilio, but to their chagrin he insisted that he was not up to the job and urged his colleagues to vote for Martinelli. "These melancholy times," said Bilio, "demand that we should choose a man humble in men's eyes, so that God should directly cooperate in the work of salvation with His grace. You saw what happened at the death of Pius VI: it was the good Chiaramonti, a humble monk, known to no one, not very learned, created cardinal more because he was related to Pius VI than for any other reason, who was the one to become pope, and he governed well." Meanwhile, Cardinal Sacconi, another of this persuasion, attacked the other faction's favorite, Cardinal Pecci. Bishop Soderini, close to the man who would become Leo XIII, painted Sacconi's efforts in an unflattering light: "Not ill-favored but indeed majestic in countenance and courteous in manner, he was anything but happy in speech, even with his intimates, while he was stubborn with a stubbornness in inverse ratio to his mental level, which was certainly not above the ordinary. He went about repeating that the bishop of Perugia was too modern, too averse to the policy followed up till then, and, in addition, of sickly health."[32]

Although moderate by comparison, the other faction was also committed to the return of the Papal States, at least in some form. Yet they were convinced that Pius IX's stance had proved a dead end, that a new approach had to be tried. A pope who better understood this world was needed. If the Holy See was ever going to be able to attract diplomatic support abroad, the papacy could not continue to be seen as a vestige of the Middle Ages, opposed to all that was modern. This position was especially popular among the foreign cardinals, who were well aware that their governments strongly opposed the election of an intransigent.[33]

The moderates' choice, Gioacchino Pecci, was in fact politically astute and eager to win favor among the world's rulers. For years he had been kept far from the center of Vatican power, for Antonelli disliked him — possibly fearing him as a potential rival — and fed Pius stories that painted him as a secret liberal. It was only after Antonelli's death that the road to Rome opened up. The pope summoned Pecci to the Vatican just after the secretary of state died and then, in September 1877, named him chamberlain, giving him a new visibility.[34]

Pecci was born in 1810 in a small town near Rome, the sixth child of the only noble family living there. One of his older brothers became a Jesuit, but he decided to attend the Pontifical Academy of Ecclesiastical Nobles in Rome and enter the Vatican diplomatic service. In early 1843, Gregory XVI gave Pecci the title of archbishop and sent him to Belgium to serve as papal nuncio. But disaster struck. As nuncio he became embroiled in a dispute between the Belgian Catholic Church and the Protestant king of Belgium, who called on the pope to relieve Pecci of his duties. Worse, the episode led to Prince Metternich's view that Pecci was incompetent, in effect ending what had up to that time been a promising diplomatic career. Pecci was sent to Perugia as archbishop and, though raised to the cardinalate a few years later, remained isolated in the small Umbrian city for many years.[35]

The Perugians viewed Pecci as a rather remote and haughty figure, although the more perceptive among them saw a well-read man of sharp intelligence and prodigious memory. He was nothing if not methodical, seeking out all the information he could get his hands on and studying each question thoroughly before coming to a decision, in marked contrast to Pius. Yet, like his papal predecessor he had supreme self-confidence. Neither man would tolerate criticism.

On the morning of Tuesday, February 19, the cardinals filed into the Sistine Chapel, where they each received Holy Communion. At 10 A.M. they were at their desks and the first ballot was passed around. The three cardinals selected by their peers to verify the vote read out each form: Cardinal Pecci received the most, with 18. Cardinal Bilio, the intransigents' favorite, despite his protests that he was not suitable, was second, but far behind, with 6 votes. Fourteen other candidates received at least 1. By the second ballot, later in the day, Pecci had reached 26. His momentum could not be stopped, and the following morning the cardinal from Perugia was formally elected. Shaking uncontrollably, the new pope was led into the robing room, where he was given a glass of wine and some little cakes to help him settle down. Observing his pale complexion and frail movements, many predicted that he would not last very long. They would be proven wrong. In the robing room were three chests filled with temporary vestments for new popes until their own could be tailored. One contained robes for a tall man, one for someone of average size, and one for a small man.[36]

The cardinals drew out the vestments, replacing Pecci's purple cardinal's robes with the traditional papal vesture and skullcap. Only his shoes — scarlet with a golden cross embroidered on them — were not white. Now sitting on the papal throne, Leo XIII was approached by one of the cardinals, who removed the cardinal's ring from his hand and replaced it with the ring of the fisherman. For the first time, Leo XIII would have his feet kissed by a cardinal, mirroring the act ascribed to Jesus at the Last Supper, kissing the feet of his apostles. Each of the other cardinals then followed, repeating the rite.[37]

As pope, Pecci would show the clear signs of his aristocratic upbringing, holding himself at some distance from the faithful. An American observer, the wife of a French statesman who was able to observe both Leo and his predecessor closely, noted the differences between the two men: Pius, she wrote, "had a kind, gentle face (a twinkle, too, in his eyes), and was always so fond of children and young people. The contrast between him and his successor is most striking. Leo XIII is tall, slight, hardly anything earthly about him — the type of the intellectual, ascetic priest — all his will and energy shining out of his eyes, which are extraordinarily bright and keen for a man of his age." Leo's ascetic image was underscored by his modest diet, which contrasted with Pius's love of a hearty meal and his taste for a good cigar. It was only with great reluctance that as Pius aged, at his doctors' urging, he had given up his beloved fried foods.[38]

A firm supporter of papal infallibility at the Vatican Council, Leo instinctively felt most comfortable with top-down rule. As George Weigel, an American Catholic theologian, put it, "He had no theoretical quarrel with democracy and was quite open to its merits. However, he could not be a democrat because his life was formed by a different vision. Leo showed love for the people, but he did not trust them. For him the people must be taken care of, but they are too immature and too undisciplined to rule." Weigel added, "He definitely wanted government for the people, but it is doubtful if he wanted government by the people." Or, as a French observer noted at the time, "Leo XIII is more concerned about gaining the friendship of the powerful than the enthusiasm of the masses." Although in some ways Pecci was a man of modern times, it is telling that among his heroes was Innocent III, the thirteenth-century avatar of medieval theocracy.[39]

Finding himself in the difficult position of replacing a man who had become an object of adulation in large sectors of the Catholic world, Leo suffered from the comparisons that inevitably greeted him during his first years as pope. Henri des Houx, an intransigent French journalist, put it this way in his memoirs: "Pius IX seemed to speak to the affection, zeal, devotion, enthusiasm of the Catholic people . . . For Leo XIII, diplomacy is the master science, the supreme art, and, if the ambassadors are happy, he thinks the Church is saved." For all that Pius was spontaneous, apt to say what he thought, Leo was closed, spoke with great care, and avoided leaving any direct written evidence of his private thoughts.[40]

Since the beginning of the conclave, the Italian authorities had stationed an army squadron in St. Peter's Square. Carabinieri on horseback and a squad of cavalry patrolled the external walls of the Vatican, with orders to prevent any demonstrations. Large numbers of the curious milled around on the nineteenth, only to be disappointed to watch the black smoke rising from the chimney of the Sistine Chapel. The smoke came from the burning of the ballots, which, in the case of those that failed to produce a majority, were mixed with damp straw to blacken the wisp of smoke that was visible. But following the vote on the twentieth, as white smoke rose from the chimney, the bells of St. Peter's rang out to let all of Rome know that a new pope had been elected. Church bells throughout the city soon joined them.

Hearing the chimes, an enormous crowd rushed to St. Peter's Square, hoping to receive a blessing from the new pontiff, following a tradition whereby the new pope appeared at a balcony overlooking the square to give his first benediction to the people. No one was sure what the new pope would do. Pius IX, proclaiming himself a prisoner, had refused to make such public appearances. For Leo XIII it was a crucial decision, with little time for the kind of careful deliberation he preferred. Not to follow the tradition would mean embracing the claim that he was a prisoner. It would not only send out a powerful message to the world's Catholics and governments but would also disappoint the many thousands of Romans who had gathered. But could he so abruptly repudiate the stance that Pius had so tenaciously clung to?

Giuseppe Manfroni, the Italian police official in charge of Vatican surveillance, recounted that the new pope waited until the last minute to decide. The intransigents warned him against appearing, while the moderates urged him to observe tradition and not, in his first act as pope, proclaim himself a prisoner. According to Manfroni's sources — which remain unconfirmed — the pope decided that if the Italian government ordered the customary firing of the cannons of the nearby Sant'Angelo Castle to celebrate his election, he would reciprocate by appearing on the balcony. But the cannons remained silent, and after hours of waiting, the pope proceeded into St. Peter's basilica, where he blessed those gathered inside.[41]

Rome's diplomatic corps hurriedly sent word home of the conclave's selection, along with their first impressions. The new pontiff, wrote France's ambassador to Italy, was known for "his strength of character, love of order, and understanding of world affairs." Pecci had demonstrated his efficiency in the work he had done as chamberlain. "His orders are precise and he insists that they be carried out without delay. It is said that he loves all of the Church's pomp and its major ceremonies." Even Léon Gambetta, a towering figure of the French republican left and not fond of the Church's power, held out hopes: "This Italian, more a diplomat than a priest . . . seems to me to be a very good omen . . . If he doesn't die too early, we can hope to see a marriage of reason with the Church . . . He is a holy opportunist." Those who caught sight of him for the first time as he gave his blessing inside St. Peter's, wrote one observer, "saw a tall old man, surprisingly thin, with a waxen pallor, but having a vast and prominent forehead, thin lips, and extremely lively eyes."[42]

If those in the Vatican were offended that the Italian government was not doing more to pay homage to the new pope — the government's official bulletin refused even to mention his election — the anticlerical press was blasting Crispi for what it viewed as the excessive deference being shown the Holy See. The police had torn down public notices of planned demonstrations against the law of guarantees, and all anticlerical demonstrations were banned, as were all public gatherings deemed likely to offend Vatican sensibilities.[43]

But throughout the country the anticlerical forces were aroused. On February 24, before Leo's coronation, Rome's anticlerics succeeded in having a public meeting in a theater. Billed as a gathering of those opposed to the law of guarantees, it was justified to the police on the grounds that it was not a public but a private, invitation-only affair. Yet invitations were not hard to come by: tickets were given out freely in sympathetic bars and cafés.[44]

The meeting was called to order at noon. Among the dignitaries on the dais sat Giovanni Bovio, a champion of the extreme left in parliament. The first three speakers aimed their attacks at the law of guarantees and the government that enforced it. But the fourth speaker went further. "I spit on this putrefied cadaver that is the papacy," he thundered. Some applauded enthusiastically, but others seemed a bit uneasy. "Those who made the law of guarantees are enemies of the fatherland. We protest against the Vatican, but we protest as well against those who have made themselves their accomplices in wanting to maintain a state within a state in Italy." The orator concluded with a seditious call: "The monarchy and the papacy are in cahoots. We must kill off one to kill off the other!"

Next to speak was Bovio, who began by denouncing the Italian government for keeping parliament closed during the conclave to avoid risking any remarks being made that might offend the Vatican. "What servility!" he cried. "But the Vatican has one thing right, for it has posed the choice very clearly: either everything or nothing . . . Conciliation of Church and State is impossible, because it is impossible to reconcile faith with intelligence." Today, concluded Bovio, was a historic day, because it was the day that everyone in Europe would be put on notice that "the people of Rome, gathered at the Corea amphitheater, demanded the separation of Church and State, proclaimed the principle of freedom of conscience, and protested against the government's servility toward the enemies of the fatherland." The gathering ended with a vote in favor of ending the law of guarantees. Although some hotheads called for blowing up the Vatican, the meeting ended peacefully.[45]

Meanwhile, final arrangements were being made at the Vatican for the pope's coronation. Leo had initially given orders to prepare St. Peter's basilica for the ceremonies, and scores of workers labored hurriedly to set up the special platform and stands. An emissary was sent to speak with Manfroni about how Italian soldiers might protect those inside the basilica. It was a delicate topic for the Vatican, and the monsignor charged with the negotiations insisted that the Vatican's request be kept secret. But on March 2, just two days before the coronation, Manfroni learned — to his consternation — that the workers in St. Peter's had been ordered to dismantle everything they had just built. Someone — Manfroni speculated that it was one of the intransigents of the Curia — had leaked news to the press of the Vatican's request for Italian soldiers in St. Peter's, and the new pope, embarrassed, had immediately canceled plans to hold the ceremonies there. The rites would instead be held in the Sistine Chapel, with only the diplomatic corps, Church dignitaries, Roman noblemen, and a few other invitees attending.

If the coronation itself was not to be held in public in St. Peter's, Manfroni hoped that the pope would at least come to an internal balcony of the basilica immediately after the ceremonies in order to bless the crowd inside. Although the pope planned to do just that, and thirty thousand people crowded inside to receive his blessing, at the last minute he changed his mind. Immediately after the coronation ceremonies, Leo sent an observer to the basilica to size up the crowd and learned that the situation was too dangerous. But what the pope had not realized, Manfroni later complained, was that Italian police were scattered throughout the massive church and had the situation well in hand. "At the side of every fanatic, for or against, were police agents, ready to stop any intemperances, whether red or black."[46]

Rome's streets that night reverberated with anticlerical shouts. A crowd of thousands gathered outside the home of one of the city's foremost Catholic aristocrats, angered by the lights and decorations he had placed on the palace façade to celebrate the pope's inauguration. Perhaps a hundred, shouting "Long live Italy!" and "Down with the priests!" and "Down with the guarantees!," began to throw rocks at the palace's windows and lanterns. The police finally succeeded in dispersing them, arresting six young men.[47] Such was Leo XIII's first night as pope.

12

Keeping the Bishops in Line

ON TAKING ST. PETER'S THRONE, Leo XIII was something of an enigma, both to the public at large and within the Church itself. Fears that he might try to make a deal with the Italian state coursed through many an intransigent's veins. At the same time, Europe's diplomatic community held its breath, hoping that the new pope might depart from his predecessor's path and find a way to reconcile the Church with modern times and make peace with Italy.

Five days after the conclave ended, the French ambassador to the Holy See advised his government that Leo XIII was a man who combined "prudence and firmness."[1] The question, he said, was where this prudence would lead. Would the new pope be afraid to alienate the conservatives in the Curia, or would he see the need to be bold? The pontiff's first allocution, pronounced to a gathering of cardinals within a month of his coronation, gave liberals some hope. In contrast to his predecessor, he had devoted but a single sentence to protesting the loss of temporal power. "That Leo XIII could explicitly renounce temporal power, and immediately, and without even any sign of protest, no one could expect," wrote the Italian police inspector, Manfroni. But "milder, more bland than this, his protest couldn't be."[2]

If this was a trial balloon for the pope, it was soon punctured, for so loud was the indignation of the Church intransigents at the thought that he would change course that he quickly decided to take a step back. *L'Osservatore Romano* put out a series of articles insisting that the pope was committed to regaining temporal power. To demonstrate

Leo's long-standing devotion to this principle, the Vatican daily republished a pastoral letter that he had sent to his diocese in Perugia in 1860. The letter concluded: "To take away the pope's temporal power is to wish to make his exercise of spiritual power impossible." The French envoy to the Holy See, in reporting these developments to Paris, noted that it had been the secretary of state who had, on orders from the pope himself, instructed the Vatican newspaper to reprint his earlier remarks.[3]

Although the Jesuits of *Civiltà Cattolica* harbored deep doubts of their own about the new pope, they quickly joined in the chorus of Vatican protestations: "Hardly had the new Pontiff Leo XIII sat on Peter's throne than the liberal press began to spread confusion with its tales of a new direction," the Jesuit journal reported in late April 1878. "It kept repeating that the new pope, given his great intelligence, breeding, his knowledge of world conditions, and especially his moderate and pacific temperament, would reconcile himself to the century, would infuse new life into Catholicism and recognize the justice of the conquests of the modern State." But all these foolish speculations, the journal continued, had been shown to be groundless: "The fact is that the liberals — Jews and non-Jews — would like the pope to stop these protests, to be able to say that finally the Holy See relinquishes any right to temporal power . . . But it is one thing to act like an ass, and another the ass's driver." A few months later, still exercised about accounts in the press of the new pope's interest in reconciliation, the journal reported: "Despite the solemn denials they have received, not only from *L'Osservatore Romano* but also and principally from the pope's Encyclical, his allocutions, and by His Holiness's own actions, they persist in spreading fables to bolster their mendacious deception that, were he free to do what he liked, free from the pressure of *the intransigents,* he would easily and happily come to an agreement with the government."[4]

Leo found himself in a difficult spot, caught between his recognition that something new needed to be tried and the heavy pressure he felt within the Church not to do anything that might call into question the wisdom of his saintly predecessor's rejectionist stance. Among the forces exerting the most pressure were Italy's two major national organizations of Catholic laity, established under Pius IX — the Society of Catholic Youth and the Opera dei Congressi — both of which firmly supported the intransigent line.

But Leo was very different from Pius, as was clear to all who would but look. While Pius had barely let an occasion go by without denouncing the usurper state and heaping abuse on those, inside and outside the Church, who embraced the ideals of freedom of religion and freedom of speech and press, Leo was much more restrained. When he received groups of pilgrims he rarely strayed from his prepared text, he rarely got emotional, and he largely avoided political topics. As a result, at least in the first years, when memories of the warm and fiery Pius IX were still fresh, pilgrims found the new pontiff rather cold and uninspiring.[5]

One of the most eagerly watched signals of Leo's intentions was whether he would continue Pius's attempt to portray the pope as a prisoner of the Vatican. Might he, for example, signal a change by escaping Rome's summer heat and malarial air for the cooler, safer climes of the papal estate at Castel Gandolfo, something Pius IX had refused to do after 1870?[6]

The first real test of the new pope's commitment to the Vatican's stance came soon enough. The occasion was the decision by Umberto, Italy's new king, to set off on a grand tour of his kingdom. His father, Victor Emmanuel, had hated public ceremonies and loathed traveling from city to city to take part in them. The only city that Italy's first king had felt at all comfortable in was his old capital, Turin. But Italy's ministers were eager to build up popular enthusiasm around the new monarch, and he was amenable to the travels they planned for him.[7]

Umberto was not terribly impressive, lacking his father's brusque self-assurance and striking many as rather plain in contrast to his anything-but-ordinary-looking father. Like the Savoyards before him, Umberto had been trained for the military but not given any political responsibilities. Or, as his wife, Queen Margherita, would later put it, in the House of Savoy "one person reigns at a time."[8]

As colorless and quiet as his father was colorful and boisterous, he had a hard time becoming popular among the masses the way Victor Emmanuel was. Embarrassed by his own inadequacies, he waited until others left the room before he would sign documents put in front of him, or he found a way to go into another room to do so, ashamed of his difficulty in producing a suitably royal signature. He was an easy target for the canny Crispi, who, along with Depretis, wrote most of the speech that the king gave to parliament on his inauguration. It was they, too, who persuaded him not to follow his family's advice and become Umberto IV (the fourth in the Savoyard dynasty) but rather demonstrate his allegiance to the new kingdom by becoming Umberto I, the first to rule Italy.[9]

Up at five o'clock every morning, the king took a hearty breakfast of roast pheasant covered with meat sauce. Although uncomfortable in the world of culture — he would flee at the approach of an intellectual or artist — he knew all there was to know about horses, uniforms, and — at least so he would like to think — women. His aides tried to protect him from the latter — or at least to do what they could to avoid public scandal — but they were worn out by the king's love of horses and riding, sometimes finding themselves sore from trying to keep up with his marathon rides, which could last fourteen hours without a break.

The new king did have one powerful advantage over his father: Queen Margherita. Blue-eyed, elegant, comely, bright, and politically astute, she had little in common with her husband beyond their shared sense of Savoyard pride. Victor Emmanuel's own wife, along with his mother, had both died in 1855, leaving a ceremonial vacuum that lasted almost a quarter of a century. The appearance of the new queen was thus all the more dramatic.

If marrying Margherita was the best thing that Umberto could have done, the wedding itself was a somewhat hasty affair. It appears that his 1868 marriage to the sixteen-year-old, Umberto's first cousin — the daughter of his father's brother — was intended to bolster the sagging popularity of Victor Emmanuel in the wake of the debacle at Mentana.

While pretending a close relationship for public consumption, Umberto and Margherita could barely stand each other. Umberto had met his true love, the Duchess Litta, said to be one of the most beautiful women of the nineteenth century, when he was eighteen and she twenty-five, and she remained his lover throughout his life. He installed her in a home next to his royal quarters in Monza, outside Turin, where she bore him a baby who died in childhood. When in Monza — which was a good deal of the time — he went to her every evening. Nor was Litta his only female companion, for in Rome he had relations with a series of women, arranging for them to be brought to an apartment set up for the purpose in a wing of the Quirinal, where, according to his close aide, he insisted on making the bed himself the next morning.[10]

Margherita wanted the royal couple to become the center of social and intellectual life in Rome, something Victor Emmanuel had disdained. They held regular banquets and formal balls at the Quirinal, sponsored charitable organizations, and held salons for the artistic elite. Margherita appeared as a vision of royal beauty: covered with jewelry, wearing a spectacular white dress with gold trim and a long train and a fur stole draped over her slender shoulders. While many observers were enchanted, others were less impressed, thinking her extravagance unseemly. Among those in the latter camp, the Frenchman Ernest Tissot complained that she dressed with "poor taste." At her frequent balls, she wore fifteen strands of pearls around her neck, huge pear-shaped earrings, and a corset covered with brooches and tangles of diamands. The queen, he remarked, "is adorned to look like a votive statue." Others, seeking to puncture the highly touted image of royal beauty, carped that the queen had short legs (which she tried to conceal by strategic dressing) and a hooked nose and that her supposedly blond hair was in fact simply mousy. Whatever her appearance, it was clear that the queen had an iron will joined to aristocratic, autocratic instincts, and she knew how to get her way.[11]

In addition to cultivating an image of the devoted wife and gracious queen, Margherita reveled in her reputation as a devout Catholic. A year after Umberto became king, the French ambassador to the Holy See reported that, at the queen's urging, the pope had lifted the ban on holding mass in the Quirinal. "The Queen," wrote the ambassador, "is very pleased by the decision and she plans to hold mass every morning." At Margherita's appearances at Church functions, cries of "Long live the Catholic Queen!" greeted her. By contrast, although Umberto went to mass often enough — believing it appropriate for a king to do so — he had a visceral distaste for the Vatican, the Church, and the priests. A close aide described him as a *pretofobo,* a priestophobe, reporting that Umberto once told him that all priests should be castrated.[12]

From the Vatican's perspective, the new king had no right to rule anywhere other than northern Italy, along with the island of Sardinia, and even this claim was undercut by the Savoyard monarchy's treachery in robbing the pope of his domain. While Umberto sought the legitimacy that would come from rituals of the sort that the Church had been furnishing monarchs for many centuries, the Vatican was eager to deprive him of any such support. Yet, maddeningly for Leo, this proved impossible, so fiercely did so many of Italy's bishops resist his orders.

In the short time between Umberto's accession to the Savoyard throne and Leo's own coronation, the Vatican had already begun to feel pressure from the Italian bishops. In one such case, the bishop of Parma wrote to the secretary of state for instructions: "I am under great pressure to order the singing of a *Te Deum* [a prayer of thanksgiving] in my cathedral . . . to mark Umberto's elevation to the throne." He added that he had also heard rumors that the new king would soon be paying a visit to Parma and noted that he would be expected to appear with other dignitaries to pay his respects.

"I have referred your queries to the Pope," responded the secretary of state, writing on the very day that Pius IX died. The bishop was not to take part in any Te Deum rites, and he was ordered to refrain "from any act of homage that might be interpreted as a sign of adherence to the current order of things." The reasoning was clear: "The king's voyage will clearly be aimed at better entrenching the work of the revolution, which today no longer aims merely at undermining the legitimacy of the deposed Princes, but at undermining the rights of the Church and of the holy Pontiff himself." It was therefore imperative, wrote the secretary of state, "for the bishops to abstain from any act that could contribute to the attainment of such a perverse goal."[13]

By the time the bishop received this letter, the Church and the whole Catholic world were in mourning, and for the next few months the pope's death and funeral, the conclave to elect his successor, and the period of the new pope's settling in would overwhelm all else. But by summertime the issue of what to do about the new Italian monarch came once again to preoccupy the Vatican, as news arrived of Umberto's plan to visit each of the cities in his domain.

The summer presented another difficulty for the Holy See when the surprising news came of yet another death. On July 31, Leo's first secretary of state, Cardinal Alessandro Franchi, a man known for his moderate views, died. The fifty-nine-year-old cardinal had passed so rapidly from florid health to his death throes that — in Rome's overheated atmosphere — rumors that he had been poisoned by the intransigents spread quickly. After some hesitation, the pope selected Cardinal Lorenzo Nina as his new secretary of state. A less imposing figure, he was known both for his deep theological learning and his prudence, though some would say timidity.

In August, in a letter that he made public, Leo wrote to his new secretary of state with instructions on the conduct of his office. The pope bemoaned "the extremely difficult condition in which the Head of the Church finds Himself in Italy and Rome in the wake of the seizure of his temporal dominion, which Providence had given him for so many centuries in order to safeguard the freedom of his spiritual power." He went on to complain about a series of government measures, from the suppression of the monasteries to the law subjecting Catholic seminarians to military conscription, bewailing as well the government's decision to allow other religions to erect their own temples and churches in the Holy City.

The liberal press, until that time nursing some hope that the pope would take a different approach from that of his predecessor, began to lash out at him, seizing in particular on his calls for help from foreign governments to accuse him of wanting to foment a war against Italy. *La Libertà* wrote that the pope's letter to his secretary of state showed that the Vatican's true goal was "peace with everyone else at any cost; war with Italy at all costs and at all time." It charged: "The Vatican's game is clear: it aims to isolate Italy. Having made peace with all the Powers, the pope hopes to turn all of them against us." *La Riforma* put the matter more personally: "This pope is dangerous, we've already said it, because he is a calculator, perhaps also a skeptic. Pius IX was a man of faith; Leo XIII is a man of tricks."[14]

Meanwhile, the problems caused by the king's travels would not go away. On August 10, Leo XIII sent instructions through his new secretary of state to all of Italy's bishops, forbidding them from participating in any rites for the usurper king. This act prompted an immediate, heated reply from the archbishop of Cagliari, Sardinia's capital. Using an argument that dozens of other bishops would make in the coming months, he insisted that his situation was unique, and that applying the pope's directive would be disastrous. "On the island of Sardinia in general, and in the city of Cagliari," the archbishop wrote, "even today there is the greatest popular veneration for the King and for the entire royal House of Savoy. If the King comes here, as is likely, and I do not pay him any act of homage, not even a private visit, it would be viewed very poorly, and greatly irritate the large majority of the population." What would he tell people, he asked, when they pointed out that in the king's recent visits to Lombardy and Venetia he had been greeted publicly by bishops, patriarchs, and cardinals? To fail to greet the royal couple would be impossible for him, not only because the palace in which the new monarch would be staying was contiguous to his own residence, but because he had known the queen for a long time, having in fact presided over her confirmation in Turin years earlier. The only way he could obey the papal directive, he concluded, would be to leave the island altogether before the king's visit, something he was clearly not eager to do.[15]

With similar pleas arriving in great quantity from throughout Italy, Leo had Cardinal Nina convene the Congregation of Extraordinary Ecclesiastical Affairs on Thursday morning, August 22. The secretary of state set the meeting's tone by preparing a report for discussion; it began by noting the "painful impression" made by the bishops in northern Italy who had participated in welcomes to the king on his recent travels. The harm was all the greater in the diplomatic world, for Europe's royalty had shown restraint in refusing to visit a king "who has not only usurped the Temporal Dominion of the popes, but who still finds himself in open war with the Holy Pontiff." How, asked the cardinal, could the pope expect foreign royalty to shun the king when his own bishops and cardinals were going out to welcome him? Nor was it any use arguing that such deference was acceptable as long as it took place only in the northern lands to which the king had legitimate claim, for the king himself was in a state of war with the Church, his residence the pope's own palace in Rome.[16]

The cardinals of the Congregation were deeply divided. First to speak at the meeting was Cardinal Luigi Bilio. Although he might have been expected to take a hard line, he came from Piedmont, the home of the Savoyard monarchy, and cringed at the prospect of bishops snubbing the king.

"Bishops should try to refrain from paying visits to the King," he said. "But, if this proves impossible without provoking even greater evils for the Church, they should go ahead, albeit in the least solemn way possible." It was one thing to have such a strict rule in place immediately after the usurpation of the papal lands, he argued, but it had now been so long that continued insistence on such a policy would be counterproductive. The pope ran a greater risk, "the danger of not being obeyed [by the bishops], which would truly produce a terrible scandal."

A number of the cardinals insisted that a distinction be made between the bishops in the lands the king ruled legitimately and those in the lands that had been stolen from the Church. In the latter group, Cardinal Ledóchowski argued, no bishop should ever greet the king, while in the former, if bishops were clearly forced by circumstances to do so, people would understand. Others disagreed. "You're too worried about public opinion," complained Cardinal Ferrari. Much more important, he insisted, was respecting the sensibilities of good Catholics, who would understandably be offended at the sight of a bishop paying homage to the king anywhere in Italy.[17]

Informed of the cardinals' conflicting views, the new pope released a set of instructions for the bishops in lands that had been usurped from the Papal States. "It would certainly be best if the bishops abstained from taking part in any act of homage to the sovereign invader," the text began. It might be made easier if the bishop absented himself when the king visited his city. However, should the bishop judge his failure to appear to be likely to provoke popular demonstrations against him, it would be acceptable for him to pay the king that degree of courtesy deemed indispensable while taking care that nothing be done that could offend good Catholics. In no case, the pope added, were bishops to permit the Te Deum to be sung or other Church rites performed in the king's honor.[18]

A few days later Archbishop Agostini, the patriarch of Venice, wrote a long, defensive letter to the secretary of state. The king had recently visited Venice, and the patriarch had agreed to pay him a personal visit, much to the horror of the Catholic press.

When he had been invited to be received by the king, the patriarch recounted, he reflected that the archbishops of Turin and Milan had both recently paid public homage to the king in their cities. And he had an even greater reason not to want to snub the king, for he was still awaiting the government's authorization to give him legal claim to his post. The fact that an invitation addressed to "the archbishop of Venice" — albeit without his own name on it — had been delivered to him on behalf of the king, he argued, was an important step toward the government's official recognition. And it was only right that he pay homage to the king, for Venice — unlike Rome or Bologna — was legally under the king's control. "As for me," he continued, "I am of the opinion that a bishop who does not pay public homage to a legitimate king would infringe upon a principle propounded in the Holy Scriptures, where it speaks of respect for authority, and it would offer a bad example to the faithful." As a result, on the king's arrival in Venice, the archbishop had ordered all of the bells of the city's churches to toll, and, seated in his own gondola, he joined the flotilla of dignitaries that glided out to meet the monarch.[19]

In an effort to stop the damage done by such episodes, Leo and his secretary of state began to warn bishops before the announced royal visits. On August 30, in one such case, Cardinal Nina wrote to the bishop of Brescia, in Lombardy, telling him that the pope, having learned from the newspapers of the king's planned visit, wanted to be sure that the bishop had the latest instructions. The secretary of state added a warning about one of the bishop's colleagues nearby. "From the press Your Reverence will have learned some details regarding the conduct of the Eminent Archbishop of Verona during King Umberto's visit to that city," Nina wrote, adding: "I cannot conceal the fact that this produced a rather painful impression on the Holy Father." He then asked the bishop of Brescia to investigate the archbishop of Verona's recent behavior and report back on what he learned.[20]

That same day the secretary of state sent a blistering note directly to Verona. People in Rome were distressed at the news of his recent encounter with King Umberto, Cardinal Nina told the archbishop. "Your Eminence will well understand that such accounts in the press have been greeted here with great reserve, all the more so as they involve a cardinal, bound by strong ties to the Holy See and to the Person of His Holiness." As he did not have sufficient information to rebut these charges, the secretary of state wrote, "I pray Your Eminence to furnish me with all the details regarding the supposed encounter so that I will be in a position to dissipate any of the less favorable impression that the above-mentioned news has produced in the Holy Father's soul and among the Diplomatic Corps."[21]

Cardinal Nina did not have to wait long for the archbishop's angry reply. "After the bombs, after the satires, after the articles in the yellow press, after the demonstrations, after the threats — even of death — that I have suffered for my strong public attachment and deep devotion to the Holy See and its venerated Head," he wrote, "I would never have believed that I would have received the words contained in your message of yesterday, which arrived this morning."

He explained that the local prefect had sent a letter inviting him to be at the train station on the king's arrival. Umberto simply planned to stop for a few minutes before continuing on his journey. "I went there, dressed in black, with only a large red cloak, as I didn't know what else I could wear." He had decided to go, he said, for three reasons. First of all, in Verona Umberto was a legitimate king. Second, the archbishop argued, a dozen years earlier Umberto, then a prince, had been a guest at his residence, and so "it seemed discourteous to me not to pay him a brief visit." But third, it had occurred to him that given his familiarity with Umberto, he might take advantage of the opportunity to urge the king to find a way to reach a modus vivendi with the Holy See. And he had begun to do that very thing when he was interrupted by a general who tore the king away from him.

But now, for having acted in a way that he believed was in the best interest of the Holy See and the Church, he was being vilified. It was too much. He begged the secretary of state to inform the pope that he wanted to be relieved both of his cardinal's hat and his appointment as bishop. He wished simply to retire to his home "to prepare myself for that death which I sense is not far away. There, as a simple priest, I will help the bishop assigned to be my successor as much as I can." He pleaded: "If only I could return to being a simple priest! I am entirely nauseated by the world." [22]

The Verona cardinal may have also been aware that, at the Vatican's request, his colleagues were spying on him. On August 28, the secretary of state received a confidential report from Verona. A priest whom he had asked to investigate the cardinal had been instructed to send his reply on the same sheets of paper the request had come on, to ensure its secrecy. The king had stopped at the Verona train station at 2:10 P.M. on August 7, the investigator recounted, spending about fifteen minutes there before the train pulled out. "His Eminence, wearing the cardinal's vestments, was at the station with the other Dignitaries." On the king's arrival, the very first person to speak to him was the cardinal, "whom King Umberto greeted with great affability and kindness." After paying his respects to the queen, the cardinal kissed the little prince and gave him a red case containing a little silver statue of Saint Joseph." The informant added that the newspapers had complained that it was not right that the cardinal was the first to greet the king; this honor was due the mayor. [23]

Meanwhile, the bishop of Brescia found himself in an exceedingly embarrassing position when he received the secretary of state's letter telling of the pope's anger at the archbishop of Verona and requesting his own confidential investigation. The Brescian bishop had a transgression of his own to confess, as he did in a letter to Cardinal Nina on September 2. He, too, had received an official invitation to be at the train station to receive the king. "I have nothing to reprove myself for," the bishop argued, "neither from the few words that I addressed to His Majesty nor from the circumstances of that very brief encounter." Yet, in light of the secretary of state's letter, he wrote, "I confess my mistake and beg forgiveness from His Holiness and Your Excellency and from my fellow clerics who were led by my example to commit the same mistake." In the future, he promised, he would never let this happen again. "As a consequence of what I have told you here regarding my own behavior," he concluded, "I must believe myself dispensed from the delicate task that Your Excellency commissioned me to undertake." He could hardly launch a secret investigation of the behavior of the archbishop of Verona when he himself was guilty of the same misdeed.[24]

Yet not all of Italy's bishops were so eager to pay homage to the king, and some — much to Leo's relief — proudly informed him of their loyalty. Such was the case of the bishop of Piacenza. On August 31, the king had paid a visit to that northern city, where he stopped at the train station for official ceremonies. Displeased to learn that the city's bishop was not there to greet him, Umberto lamented his absence to the mayor and the prefect. Rather melodramatically, at this point in telling the story of his principled stance, the bishop added, "Up to now I have not been molested, but whatever comes, I am at peace and ready even for death in order to keep my sacred ministry untarnished, and to scrupulously follow the orders, advice, and instructions of our beloved Holy Father."

But the bishop did not stop there. He went on to complain about his colleagues' behavior. Inexplicably, the clear, sage instructions that the pope had sent them all "had not prevented other bishops, archbishops, and cardinals, not only from paying homage to the sovereign, but from doing all they could to show their attachment to the man who continues to inflict so much pain on the Holy Church. This is creating confusion among the people, making the position of the bishops who want to faithfully serve the Holy See much more difficult." He concluded his letter to Nina: "Oh! Eminent Prince, if we could only achieve uniformity in our behavior, how much we would gain in decorum, how much bitterness would be avoided, and how much more powerful would the Sovereign Pontiff's words of protest be, supported in this way throughout the land by the conduct of the episcopate."[25]

At the same time, the pope was under great pressure to soften his stance. On September 9, the archbishop of Catania, in eastern Sicily, wrote to the secretary of state a long letter pleading to be allowed to take part in the ceremonies surrounding the king's impending arrival. Here in the South and especially in Sicily, the archbishop explained, "the visits of Sovereigns assume a very special meaning. Here the mass of people, who are religious and know absolutely nothing of politics, believe that a king, whoever he is, should show respect toward the Church, and enter it with the necessary pomp." The archbishop went on to recall that in January, after Victor Emmanuel's death, he had received the Vatican's instructions not to participate in any funeral observances. But he and his colleagues had concluded that following such orders would be disastrous, and they had been proven right. Where bishops took part in the ceremonies that honored the dead king, respect for the Church had been maintained, but bishops who boycotted the rites had provoked popular anger and hostility.

None of the secretary of state's suggestions for how to avoid unpleasantness in refusing to greet the king would help, the archbishop argued. He could hardly claim to have pressing business elsewhere and so be absent from Catania when the king arrived, for everyone knew that September was the time when the peasants were busy in their vineyards and that bishops never made rural parish visits then. And writing a letter explaining his refusal to greet the king, attributing it to the poor relations existing between the state and the Holy See, as the secretary of state's instructions had suggested, was impossible, because everyone knew that the archbishops of Turin, Milan, and Verona, as well as the patriarch of Venice, had all paid their respects to the king on his northern tour.

To snub the king and the civil authorities risked ruining much of the work of his archdiocese. He had good relationships with the municipal authorities, who allowed him to continue to run Church seminaries, schools, and charities. All would be placed in jeopardy. And who, he asked, would benefit the most from such a refusal? It would not be the good Catholics of Catania but the radical anticlerics, republicans who opposed the monarchy. "They would applaud my absolute abstention while on the other hand, many well-intentioned people believe that the king, whoever he is, represents the last vestige of civil authority, and they would like it respected, as the only safeguard against a social cataclysm."[26]

The archbishop's arguments failed to impress Leo, who had Cardinal Nina prepare a lengthy rebuttal. The archbishop's letter, wrote Cardinal Nina, was filled with references to special local conditions, but the pope had a responsibility to look after the larger interest of the Church. The Church had to present a united front if it was to show the world how much suffering it was being forced to endure at the hands of the Italian state; only from such a demonstration could they hope to get help from foreign governments. "And here I must add," wrote the secretary of state, "that it was precisely by having diverged from such conduct on the occasion of the funeral ceremonies for King Victor Emmanuel — which did not afford the least relief from the deplorable conditions in which our Religion finds itself in Italy — that our adversaries were given ammunition to support their claims. The same thing happened again when some bishops of northern Italy recently paid private visits to King Umberto." The Holy Father, Cardinal Nina wrote, could not tolerate any deviation from this policy on his part, for his would be a powerful example to the other bishops in Sicily.[27]

The pope had his secretary of state send similar replies to the archbishops of Cagliari and Sassari in Sardinia, as well as to the archbishop of Bari on the southern mainland. No local circumstances could justify having a member of the ecclesiastical hierarchy engage in normal relations with the king.

Meanwhile the king continued on his royal progress, which took him from Rome through the northwest — Genoa, Turin, Milan — east to Venice, then down through Tuscany and central Italy before entering the South in Puglia. In the smaller cities his train stopped only long enough for the authorities to pay their respects and for Umberto to salute the throngs eager to catch a glimpse of their new monarch. In the larger cities he was the guest of honor at a frenetic round of banquets, special displays, reviews of the troops, and receptions where town councilors and assorted dignitaries jostled for the honor of addressing him.

The embarrassment felt by the archbishops and bishops who failed to pay homage to the king when he passed through their cities is clear from messages that the king received from them, explaining their absence. When Umberto was in Florence, on November 6, he received a letter from the archbishop, explaining that he was constrained not to make any display of greeting in public due to the conflict between church and state but assuring the king that, were he free to follow his own feelings, he would not have failed to participate in the celebrations honoring him. The day before, the bishop of Parma had sent the king a similar note, explaining that he was distraught that he could not personally pay his respects to the king and promising him that, just as soon as the longed-for reconciliation of church and state occurred, the king would find that he had "in the bishops one of the strongest sources of support of his Power."[28]

Urged on by the ministers of the left, who were eager to link the king's legitimacy to the devotion of his subjects, Umberto spent a full three weeks traveling in November. But the highlight of this national consecration of his new reign, and of the kingdom itself, was planned for November 17 in Naples, the old capital of the South, when the king was scheduled to make a triumphal entrance through the city with Benedetto Cairoli, the prime minister, at his side.

That evening, the shocking news of what happened that day spread through the country. A telegram from the minister of the interior told the story:

A little after the royal procession had left the Naples train station, a young man of sinister appearance threw himself on the carriage of His Royal Majesty, trying to stab His Majesty in the chest with a sharp knife whose handle he kept covered in a small red flag. He succeeded in grazing the skin of the King's upper left arm and lightly wounding the right thigh of the Prime Minister, while His Majesty with his usual quick thinking and iron nerves struck him on the head with his saber and the Honorable Cairoli, with similar energy and alacrity, grabbed him and held him by the hair. The assassin was meanwhile wounded as well by the Captain of the guard who handed him over to the Police. The name of the assassin is Giovanni Passanante, a cook, aged 29 and a native of Salvia, province of Potenza.[29]

The government acted swiftly to use the assassination attempt to generate popular sympathy for the king. Again the Vatican found itself in an awkward position. Having long warned that the Savoyard kings were putting themselves at the mercy of the revolutionaries who had robbed the pope of his temporal throne, papal defenders took an I-told-you-so attitude. *Civiltà Cattolica,* in its account, reported: "Now they understand that you shouldn't play with fire." The Jesuit journal gave its version of what had happened: "A villain, a bit dimwitted certainly, but filled with the principles of the socialist diatribes against the King and the Emperors, decided to gain everlasting fame for himself by killing His Majesty, King Umberto, in broad daylight." Passanante had used a kitchen knife — not being able to afford anything special for his task — covered with a red cloth on which he had written: "Long Live the International Republic!" *Civiltà Cattolica* informed its readers that since the revolutions of 1848, there had been twenty-eight major assassination attempts against emperors, kings, and other heads of state. "Now among all of these assassins and regicides," the journal pointed out, "one would search in vain for a *clerical.* They are all the work of *liberals.*"[30]

The pope faced a ticklish problem. The narrowly avoided royal assassination produced an overpowering desire among the king's subjects to thank God for having saved him, and throughout the country, people were demanding that churches hold special services of thanksgiving. On the day after the bungled attempt, the secretary of state issued instructions to the cardinal vicar of Rome: "The Holy Father, after having taken into consideration all the reasons . . . regarding the singing of the Te Deum, has ordered me to inform you that Your Eminence may tolerate the singing of the Te Deum in the Church of St. Silvester at the simple request of private persons." He went on to explain that the Te Deum could not be chanted in any of Rome's other churches, given the risk that such ceremonies would be turned into political demonstrations on behalf of the usurper state.[31]

No prelate was placed in a more difficult position by these orders than the archbishop of Naples. On November 18, the archbishop sent the secretary of state an urgent letter describing his "exceptional and precarious position." Naples was in turmoil. The streets were filled with one demonstration after another, denouncing the attempt made on the king in their midst. "Now the craving has come for the Te Deum to be sung. Ever since yesterday, I have been bombarded by requests to permit this rite." The archbishop had received the pope's orders but, he said, obeying them would invite disaster. "To avoid the danger of scandalous pressure, to avoid noisy demonstrations in the churches, and to protect me and my Clergy from any violence, this morning, after a meeting that I had with all of Naples's parish priests . . . it was decided that tomorrow we will sing a Te Deum to thank God for having saved Naples from a bloodbath, which would have flooded all the city's streets if the assassination had been successful." The archbishop quickly added that to ensure that the masses were not misinterpreted, he had arranged for various newspapers to explain why he was authorizing them.

Two days later, having not heard the pope's reaction to his letters, he wrote to the secretary of state again with further exculpatory details. The archbishop hastened to assure the pope that he had refused to participate in any of the Te Deum services himself, forbidden the chanting of the Te Deum in the city's cathedral, and prohibited the saying of the traditional prayer for the king. "I place my hands together and beg your Excellency," he pleaded, "to write me as soon as possible to let me know if I have earned Your Excellency's approval, just as, should the opposite be the case, I am ready to humbly receive any criticism, should you decide that it is merited." On the twenty-second the secretary of state responded, telling the archbishop how much the pope appreciated his refusal to take part in the Te Deum himself but studiously avoiding any similar support for the decision to allow such ceremonies to be held in the city.[32]

The would-be assassin remained in jail awaiting trial. Not connected to any revolutionary or republican organization, Passanante shared an old anarchic streak that had long marked southern Italy's poor. Amid all the poverty and misery, the king's opulence was, in his eyes, an affront that had to be avenged, a feeling likely nourished by the propaganda against the monarchy then being spread in anarchist and socialist circles in Naples. At the conclusion of his trial in March 1879, unmoved by the defense attorney's pleas for mercy, the court sentenced Giovanni Passanante to death. His appeal rebuffed, the date for his execution was set. But at the last minute the king himself, in an act of royal benevolence, commuted the sentence to a lifetime of hard labor. Yet Umberto was clearly shaken, living the rest of his life in fear that another assassin lurked in the crowds that always surrounded his carriage, commenting — prophetically, it turned out — that one day a would-be assassin would trade in Passanante's knife for a revolver, to deadly effect.[33]

The pope, meanwhile, continued to be torn. While under heavy pressure from the intransigents in the Church and trying — not altogether successfully — to keep Italy's bishops in line, he realized that something new had to be tried.

Among the pillars of Pius's rejectionist policy was the *non expedit*, the papal ban on the participation of Catholics in Italian national elections. The status of this prohibition on running for parliament and on voting had been a bit murky in the immediate aftermath of the taking of Rome, but in 1874 Pius IX emphatically stated that no good Catholic could enter the Italian parliament, not least because doing so required taking an oath of loyalty to the usurper state.[34] The negative side of a Catholic boycott of national elections was obvious, and early in his papacy, Leo wondered whether it would not be wise to allow loyal Catholics to take part in national politics. Might it not be helpful to form a Catholic party, as had recently occurred in Germany, which could then be used as leverage in demanding concessions from the leaders of the Italian state?

It was a delicate matter. In May 1878, when newspapers reported that the pope had sought the opinions of several bishops on this subject, *L'Osservatore Romano* immediately published a denial. But in October the pope had his secretary of state send secret instructions to the archbishop of Turin to pass on to the editor of that city's Catholic newspaper, *L'Unità Cattolica*. The editor, Father Margotti, was told that he should begin to habituate Catholic opinion to the possibility that the *non expedit* would be lifted, that under certain circumstances the pope might want to encourage Catholics to vote and to run for office. Margotti was chosen because he had come up with the famous phrase linked to the *non expedit* policy: *"né eletti né elettori,"* Catholics should be neither elected nor electors.

Margotti lost little time acting on these instructions, on October 29 publishing an article of his own on the subject, altering the paper's previous embrace of the *non expedit* and raising the possibility that the Vatican might lift the ban. He was dumbfounded the next week when, instead of getting the papal praise he expected, he got a severe reprimand from Cardinal Nina via the archbishop of Turin. "From reading the article," the secretary of state wrote, "I noticed, not without surprise, that he had not exactly followed the instructions he received, which were to the effect that there was to be a gradual evolution of the theory that he had proclaimed of 'neither elected, nor electors,' so that,

bit by bit, the Catholics would be prepared to embrace the new program." This goal, Nina went on to suggest, might have been accomplished by such means as publishing "a letter from some Catholic who
questioned the matter . . to which, responding, he would have been
able to prepare the way for a change in ideas." But "instead, the valiant
writer proclaimed, all of a sudden, the contrary political theory in a
way that was too explicit and too decisive." Rather than risk the intransigents' ire, the pope ordered a hasty retreat. Margotti was instructed to
publish no more on the subject until further notice.[35]

Leo XIII was clearly wary about taking the plunge, but he did not
give up. Within weeks he called on a commission of cardinals to study
the matter and offer advice. Presided over by Cardinal Nina and including the pope's own brother, Giuseppe — whom he would make a
cardinal the following year — the commission met in November and, it
appears, advised Leo to reverse the Vatican's policy and allow Catholics
to participate in parliamentary elections. Excitement about a possible
papal change of direction grew when, on December 28, Leo released an
encyclical stressing the importance of harmony between the religious
and the political spheres if social disorder was to be avoided, a message
that was interpreted by many enthusiasts as calling for an agreement
between Catholics and moderates in the government.

By the beginning of 1879, encouraged by these signs of a new era, a
group of Catholic nobles and others of Italy's Catholic conservative
elite were meeting secretly to plan a new Catholic political party. Yet
their hopes were short-lived. For reasons still not entirely clear, on February 22, 1879, in an address to a group of journalists from the Catholic
press, Leo surprised many by energetically demanding the restoration
of temporal rule and lashing out at those who presumed to take any action that contradicted his expressed wishes. The Catholics who had
been feverishly working to launch a conservative Catholic party, in the
expectation of receiving the pope's blessings, were flabbergasted.

Clearly the pope was having second thoughts about where a political
party might lead. The promoters wanted a national party that, while
devoted to the Holy See, would not be directly under papal control.
What he apparently had in mind was something like Germany's Center
party, which covered a broad political spectrum, united not by economic interests or political philosophy but by its devotion to the
Church and its interests. Yet many promoters of the plan envisioned a

Catholic conservative party that would fight alongside other conservatives in parliament against the left. The pope had another fear as well, one that he could never voice publicly. To field a Catholic party blessed by the Vatican, the pope realized, meant putting to the test the Holy See's oft-repeated claim that the majority of Italians were for the pope and against the new state. He feared that such a party would in fact gain only a small minority of the vote.[36]

One of the casualties of the pope's change of heart was Cardinal Nina, known to be a proponent of the conservative party strategy. In October 1880, Leo dismissed Nina and replaced him with a figure more in tune with the rejectionist line, Cardinal Ludovico Jacobini, who became his third secretary of state in less than three years. Champions of Catholic involvement in Italian politics interpreted the pope's move as a final repudiation of their efforts.[37]

The intransigents' triumph was evident in *Civiltà Cattolica*. In January 1881, Father Gaetano Zocchi put it this way: "There is the Rome of the Popes and the Rome of the Freemasons. There is the Rome that prays and the one that swears, Rome of the martyrs and Rome of the tyrants; blessed Rome and cursed Rome. There is the Rome made of granite and the Rome made of papier-mâché, eternal Rome and the Rome that, born yesterday, is unsure it will see tomorrow. There is the Rome of Christ and the Rome of the Anti-Christ." Was there any chance of reconciliation between these two Romes? he asked. Only people lost in a fantasy world could think so. "And no conciliation between them being possible, which of the two will emerge as the winner of the battle?" the Jesuit journal asked. "Which will live on even more glorious and more beautiful and which will be smashed to pieces?" The question, of course, was rhetorical, the winner divinely ordained. And there could be no doubt of Leo XIII's resolve, Zocchi continued. "He is as firm as can be in continuing the glorious struggle sustained by his saintly Predecessor against those who call themselves *Italy*, but who are instead revolution, Freemasons, satanism."[38]

13

The Pope's Body

A FEW DAYS BEFORE he was elected pope, Gioacchino Pecci, in his role as chamberlain, called in the dead pontiff's relatives for a reading of his last testament, eleven sheets of paper written in Pius's hand, bound by a silk ribbon. To the surprise of some who heard it, Pius asked that he be entombed, not in one of Rome's great churches, but in the modest basilica of San Lorenzo, outside the city walls. He specified the exact location in the church that he had chosen and instructed that no more than four hundred scudi be spent to build the shrine. The inscription was likewise to be modest: "Here lie the bones and mortal remains of Pius IX," along with the dates of his papacy and the date of his death. The only symbol to be placed over the inscription was a death's head. In the meantime, as was the custom, the pope's body was placed in St. Peter's.[1]

Just what it was that led Leo XIII to decide to hold the funeral procession three years after Pius's death remains unclear. It was customary to wait until the death of a pope's successor for such a reburial ceremony, but the three cardinals Pius had named as his executors were, for some reason, impatient. Yet in their haste to have his body taken to San Lorenzo, they recognized the risks they were running. Such a move would require a procession through the entire city. Given what Pius IX, the last pope-king, represented to the people of Rome, the prospect of provoking violent anticlerical demonstrations surely occurred to them. Nor was it clear initially that the Italian authorities would allow such a rite, although the law of guarantees assured the pope the same honors as those given the king. Since 1876 the government had forbidden all outdoor religious processions in Rome, arguing that they threatened the public order. And, given the hostile climate, the Church leaders themselves had not been eager to face the taunts and worse of the anticlericals by marching through the city streets. It was for this reason that ever since 1870, even the annual Corpus Domini procession, normally one of the most impressive public rites in the Holy City, had been abandoned.[2]

Pius IX's executors could hardly have been better placed in the Church: Raffaele Monaco la Valletta, cardinal vicar of Rome, Giovanni Simeoni, Pius's secretary of state, and Teodolfo Mertel, who, along with Antonelli, was one of the last men to serve as a cardinal without ever having been ordained a priest. In the recriminations and finger-pointing that followed the funeral events, some charged the three cardinals with having pushed a reluctant pope into approving the procession. Whatever the case, in discussing the plans with the pope and his secretary of state, the executors concluded that it would be too risky to hold the procession in daylight. It also appears that the pope thought it best to keep the rite as secret as possible to minimize the risks of confrontation or violence on the city's streets.

As cardinals, the executors could not enter into direct negotiations with the Italian authorities, so they deputized a layman, Virginio Vespignani, a Roman architect from a noble family, as their intermediary. On June 23, 1881, he wrote to Rome's prefect on their behalf asking for authorization to transport Pius IX's body from St. Peter's to San Lorenzo on a night between July 1 and July 16. On June 28, the prefect responded that as soon as they informed him of the specific night, he would make the arrangements. On July 5, the architect again wrote to the prefect, setting the date for midnight on Tuesday, July 12, and describing the route to be taken. According to the architect, the procession would be modest: "The cortège will consist of a wagon with the coffin covered with a funeral pall, drawn by four horses, and two or three carriages following. There will not be any external sign. All will proceed in a totally private fashion." With the date and route fixed and the pledge that it would be only a small, private ceremony, the prefect gave his approval. He would see that the necessary security was provided.[3]

Just what assurances the Vatican gave the Italian authorities remain one of the points in the dispute that followed. Two days after the violent events on the night of the procession, an emergency inquiry was conducted at the behest of Depretis, the prime minister, who also served as minister of the interior. As part of the inquest, Signor Bacco — who as *questore* served as the head of the police services for the prefect of Rome — described how he was first informed of the plans. "On the 9th, at just about the same time, I was called in both to see the general director of public security for the minister of the interior and to the prefect's office. I went first to the ministry, where Commissioner Bolis [head of the police in Rome] told me that the transport of Pope Pius IX's body was going to take place in an absolutely private manner, and he gave me responsibility for taking some purely precautionary measures, as there was nothing unusual to be worried about."

Bacco recalled voicing some concern: "I replied to Commissioner Bolis that it was a mistake to think that the transport would take place quietly, without a crowd of followers, since there was already great ferment among Catholics, for the news of the transport had reawakened all the devotion and sympathy that these people felt for the Pontiff." And in this recollection, recorded in the wake of the disaster and with the knowledge that heads would have to roll, Bacco made sure to cast the blame elsewhere: "Commissioner Bolis in the end did not believe that at midnight many people would gather to follow a long route such as that from St. Peter's to San Lorenzo."

By the following day, signs of trouble appeared. The prime minister was getting reports that, despite the Vatican's assurances, the "private" procession was going to become a mass demonstration of loyalty to the last of the pope-kings. Rattled, the secretary-general of the minister of the interior called in Bacco. "I wouldn't like to see the procession assume — due to the clericals' involvement — the nature of a political demonstration," he said. "True, there are not a great many of them, but in any case it would make a bad impression to hear it said that Rome is still today devoted to the pope." Bacco was told to ensure that all went quietly.

But Bacco was uneasy. Were he to try to prevent people from taking part in the procession, the Church would certainly complain that the government was keeping the faithful from a funeral rite. "I also said," the *questore* recalled, "that there should be no illusions about the number of Romans who remained loyal to the Pope, for there are a great many of them."

He was then escorted to the prime minister's office. Described by Bacco as both listless and brusque, Depretis asked him whether he thought the funeral cortege could proceed in such a way that it would avoid attracting attention, "since it would not be good if there were much hubbub and it was given much importance."

The following day, Monday, the eleventh, Bacco received a series of disturbing reports from his informants. A meeting had been held at one of Rome's radical clubs, with two parliamentary deputies present. The radicals were convinced that if the funeral cortege proceeded without protest, it would give the impression that the government was in league with the Vatican. Worse still, the world would conclude that the Romans were devoted to the pope. Bacco was also told that news of the supposedly private cortege had spread among Rome's loyal Catholics, who were planning to turn out in great number.

That day Bacco received two unexpected visitors, Cesare Crispolti and Alessandro Datti, two of Rome's most prominent lay Catholics. The fullest account we have of their visit comes from a report they made to the Vatican secretary of state a few days later, at the height of the procession polemics. On Sunday evening, they recalled, while talking with friends, they had decided that it would be best to notify the authorities that what they had initially thought was going to be a small, private funeral cortege was clearly turning into something very different. After receiving approval from (unspecified) Vatican authorities for their plan, Crispolti and Datti were deputized to speak to the police authorities. At 6 P.M. the next day they were ushered into Bacco's office.

They had come, they said, in a private capacity — although it is hard to believe they would have engaged in such a mission without the Vatican's encouragement — to be sure that the authorities allowed all those Romans who so desired to join the funeral procession. Bacco expressed his consternation that the supposed secret had become so publicly known, pointing out that even the morning's newspaper had carried a story about it. Would the participants be carrying torches and singing songs? he asked. Yes, the men replied, they would be carrying torches, singing songs, and reciting the rosary. "He then observed," Crispolti and Datti recalled, "that police regulations in fact prohibited such a funeral procession because they specified that after 11, the city should remain quiet. Nonetheless, persuaded that all would unfold in a satisfactory manner, he left us complete freedom to do what we had told him was planned."

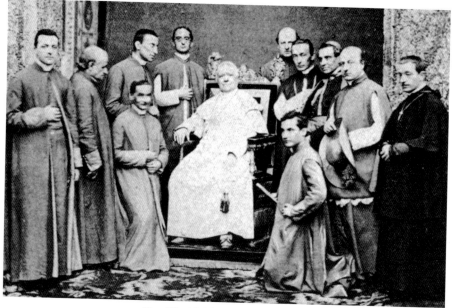

Pius IX with his court in the 1850s.

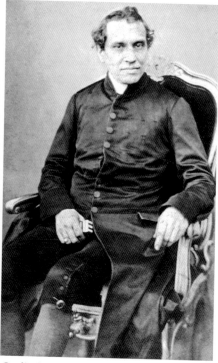

Cardinal Antonelli, secretary of state, in the 1850s.

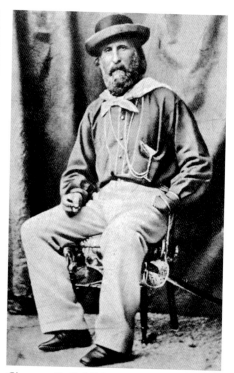

Giuseppe Garibaldi, in a red shirt, at the time of his expedition to Sicily, 1860.

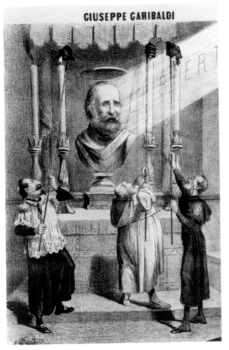

GIUSEPPE GARIBALDI

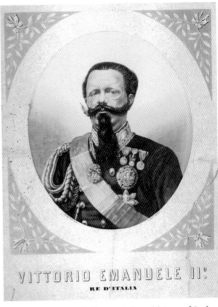

VITTORIO EMANUELE II:
RE D'ITALIA

Victor Emmanuel II, proclaimed king of Italy.

This satirical image from 1863 shows Pope Pius IX and Napoleon III unsuccessfully trying to prevent the heavenly light—labeled "Freedom"—from shining on Garibaldi, the object of popular adulation.

The satirical magazine *Il Lampione* regularly skewered the pope. In this caricature from 1861, King Victor Emmanuel II rescues Rome (portrayed as a half-naked woman) from the grasp of Pius IX, whose tiara is falling off. The legend reads, "The rape of the Sabines, by Giambologna, as revisited and corrected by *Il Lampione*." The image is based on a famous statue by Giambologna in Florence. The *Lampione* caricatures shown here were originally in color.

IL RATTO DELLE SABINE (di Gino Bologna riveduto e corretto dal LAMPIONE.)

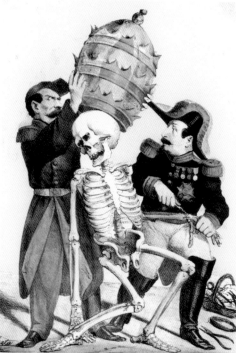

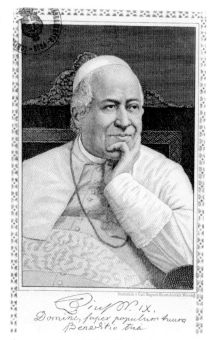

An engraving of Pius IX with his signature.

Il Lampione (1861) shows French troops, under Napoleon III, trying to put the papal tiara on the skeleton of temporal power.

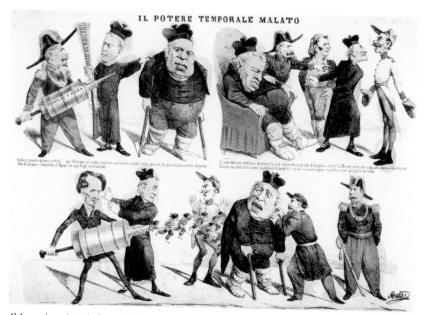

IL POTERE TEMPORALE MALATO

Il Lampione (1861) shows "The Sickly Temporal Power." Napoleon III comes to Pope Pius IX's aid, but his troops' attempts to prop up the ailing pontiff are bound to fail.

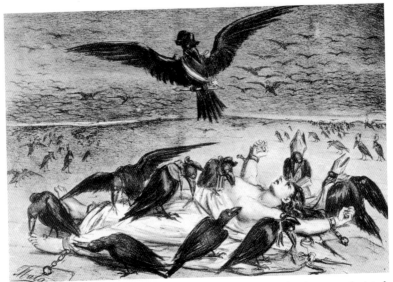

Il Lampione's view of the Vatican Council in 1870. The Catholic clergy are depicted as voracious ravens picking at the half-naked body of Italy. The legend reads: "Italy and the Ecumenical Council: Here we see Italy's true position without its Rome. Will it end up being devoured by the ravens?"

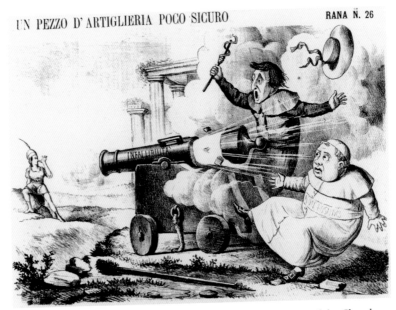

UN PEZZO D'ARTIGLIERIA POCO SICURO — RANA N. 26

La Rana, Bologna's satirical weekly, regularly carried caricatures of the Church-state battle. Here, in an image from July 1, 1870, the Vatican Council's proclamation of papal infallibility is skewered. The pope, with a Jesuit at his side, fires the cannon of "Infallibility" at the female figure of Progress, who is thumbing her nose at them. The legend says, "The shot will leave infallibly, but instead of hitting Progress, bam! . . . the piece of artillery cracks and . . . flies into pieces."

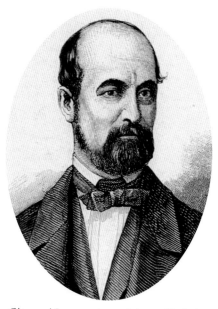

Giovanni Lanza, prime minister of Italy in 1870, urged the reluctant king to send Italian soldiers to take Rome from the pope.

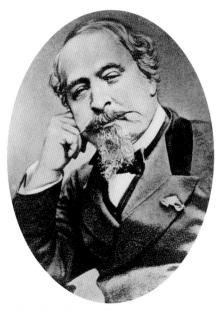

Napoleon III in his last days as emperor of France, around 1870.

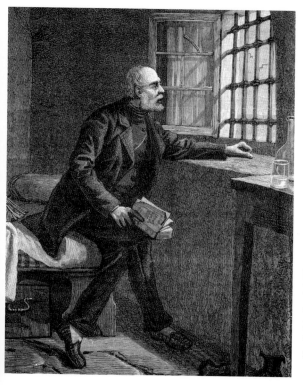

Giovanni Mazzini, a great theorist of Italian nationalism, was imprisoned at Gaeta on orders of the Italian government while its troops marched on Rome.

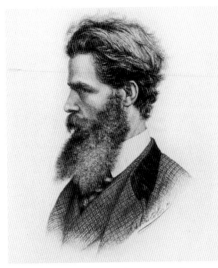

Ferdinand Gregorovius, the German Protestant scholar, lived for many years in Rome while he worked on his multivolume history of the city. With acerbic wit and jaundiced eye, his diaries recount the events surrounding the Vatican Council and the taking of Rome.

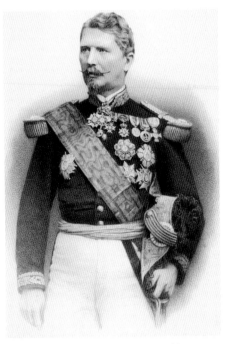

Hermann Kanzler, the Swiss general in charge of the papal troops protecting Rome.

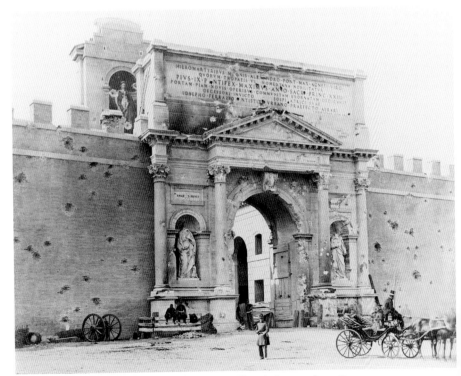

Porta Pia, showing the holes made by Italian artillery in its assault on Rome.

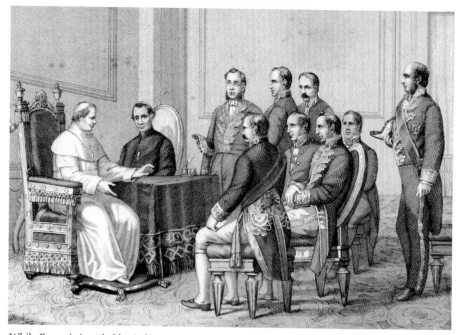

While Rome is invaded by Italian troops on the morning of September 20, 1870, foreign ambassadors console Pius IX. Cardinal Antonelli is at his side.

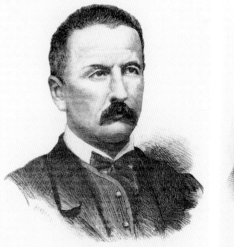

Nino Bixio, who had commanded one of Garibaldi's two ships in the 1860 assault on Sicily, was made a general in the Italian army despite his reputation as a hothead and a fierce anticleric. In leading one portion of the army's assault on Rome ten years later, he had no compunction about aiming cannonballs perilously close to St. Peter's.

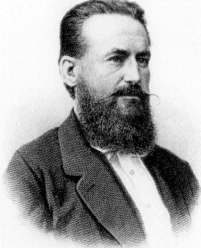

Harry von Arnim, Prussia's ambassador to the Holy See, pictured in 1870, was suspected by the Italians of plotting the pope's return to power.

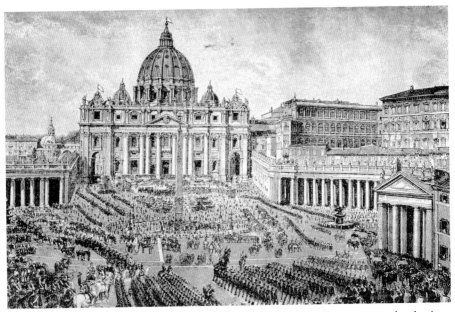

The pope blesses his defeated troops in St. Peter's Square on September 21, 1870, as they begin their march out of Rome, bound for their countries of origin.

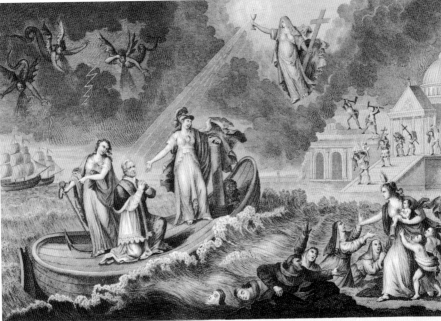

PIO PAPA IX 1871

In this religious image of 1871, a praying Pius IX, in stormy seas, receives heavenly blessings as demonic figures swarm in the dark sky, and monks and nuns try to save themselves from drowning.

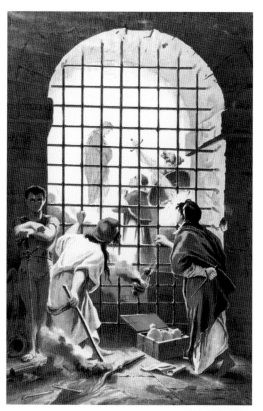

Pius IX portrayed as a prisoner, praying to the Madonna.

"Changes in Residence." In May 1871, as plans went ahead to shift the capital from Florence to Rome, *La Rana* shows Prime Minister Lanza moving in; the pope must take all his belongings out. These include a book marked "Index," bellows marked "Reaction," and a broken pot marked "Excommunication."

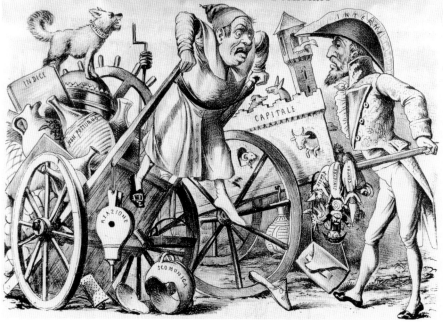

(Maggio) CAMBIAMENTI DI DOMICILIO

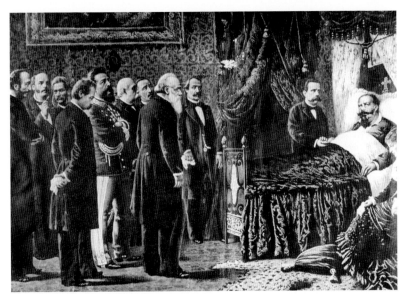

Umberto, the king's heir, holds his father's hand on his deathbed, in January 1878, as members of the cabinet, including Prime Minister Depretis (with white beard) and Minister of Internal Affairs Francesco Crispi (bald with white mustache, behind Depretis), look on. The excommunicated king's bed has a cross on the headboard.

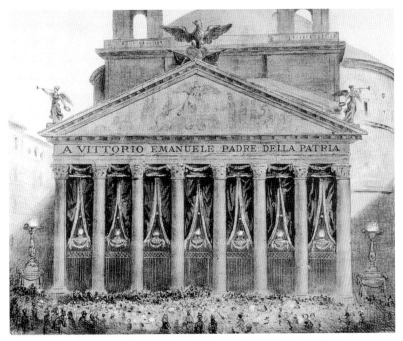

The Pantheon, site of Victor Emmanuel II's funeral. The Latin inscription atop the pillars has been covered with the new words "To Victor Emmanuel, Father of the Country."

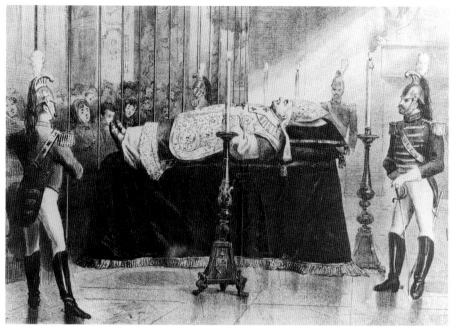

Pius IX's body on display in St. Peter's. His feet were placed so that the faithful could kiss them while filing by.

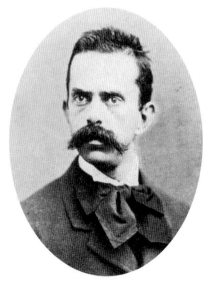

King Umberto I as a young man.

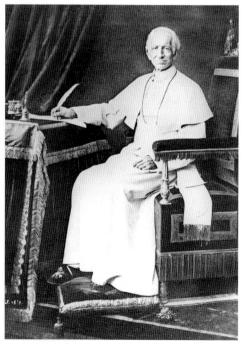

Leo XIII at his writing desk shortly after becoming pope in 1878.

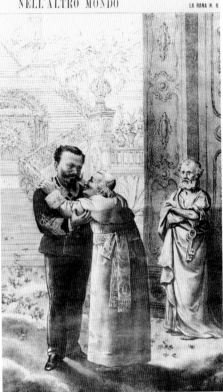

NELL'ALTRO MONDO — LA RANA N. 8.

The two old antagonists embrace at St. Peter's gate. Pius IX exclaims, "Victor! Victor! Up here I will deny you no longer, but I ask you to give me an affectionate hug." From *La Rana*, February 1878.

"In This World." In contrast with the reconciliation that could be achieved in heaven, *La Rana*, on March 1, 1878, depicts the new king, Umberto I, and the new pope, Leo XIII, being prevented from reaching the reconciliation they both desired by the evil figure of the Jesuit. The stormy skies and scorched earth signify the Vatican's commitment to reinstate the pope's "temporal power."

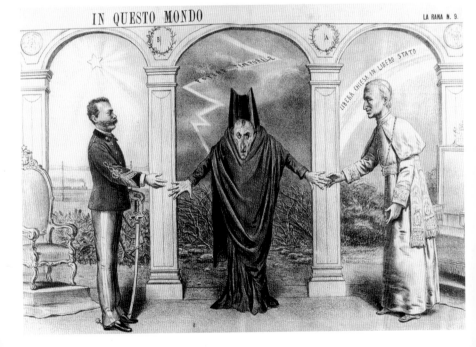

IN QUESTO MONDO — LA RANA N. 9.

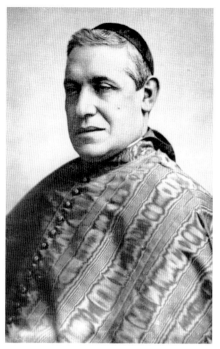

Cardinal Mariano Rampolla del Tindaro, secretary of state to Leo XIII from 1887 until the pope's death in 1903, aimed to regain Rome for the pope.

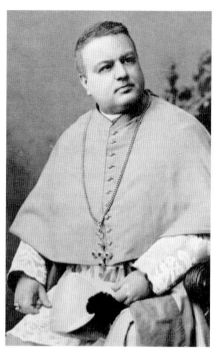

Luigi Galimberti championed a Vatican alliance with Austria and Germany and peace with Italy. Galimberti, whose own hopes for becoming secretary of state in 1887 were dashed, long remained Cardinal Rampolla's rival for the ear of Leo XIII. This photograph was taken in the 1890s, when he had become a cardinal.

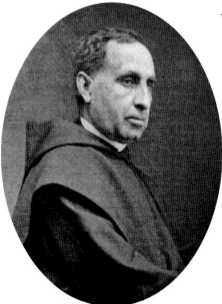

Luigi Tosti, a monk who had long known Leo XIII, only thought he was helping the pope by publishing a call for reconciliation with Italy in 1887, but he was denounced by the Vatican.

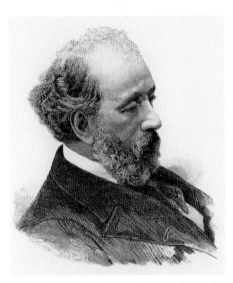

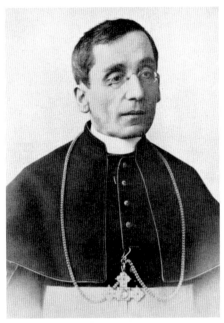

Alberto Mario, an anticlerical journalist and organizer, who at a rally in 1881 praised the anticlerical demonstrators who had come so close to throwing Pius IX's "carcass" into the Tiber.

Giacomo Della Chiesa as a young priest, around the time in 1887 when he was sent on a secret mission by Leo XIII. In 1914, Della Chiesa would become Pope Benedict XV.

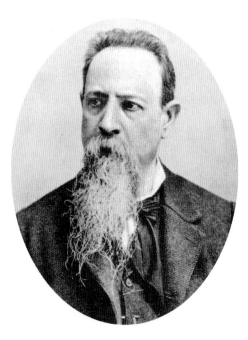

Giovanni Bovio, member of the left in parliament and famed anticlerical orator whose inscription adorns the statue of Giordano Bruno in Rome.

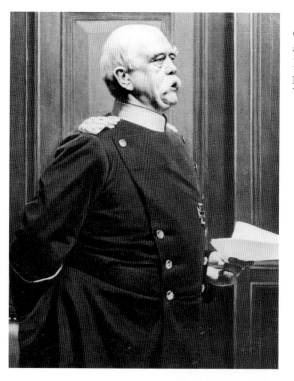

Chancellor Bismarck addressing the German Reichstag, in an 1886 painting by Anton von Werner.

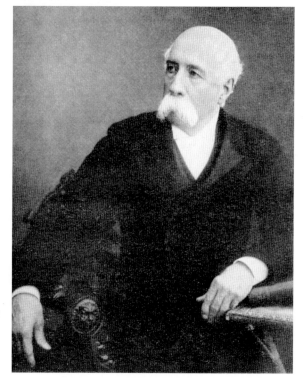

Francesco Crispi as prime minister. It was often said that Crispi looked like Bismarck. One observer wrote that although there was a resemblance, "Crispi gives all the appearance of wanting to charm his visitors, . . . Bismarck would like to terrorize them."

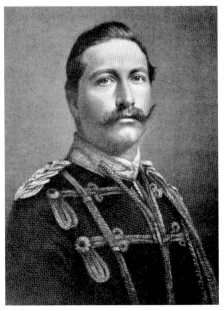

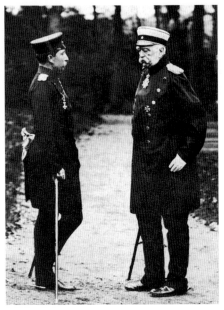

Wilhelm II. Within months of becoming emperor of Germany in 1888, Wilhelm was the first European sovereign to defy the pope and visit the Italian king in Rome.

Chancellor Bismarck and Wilhelm II in Friedrichsruh, Germany, on October 30, 1888, shortly after their return from Rome.

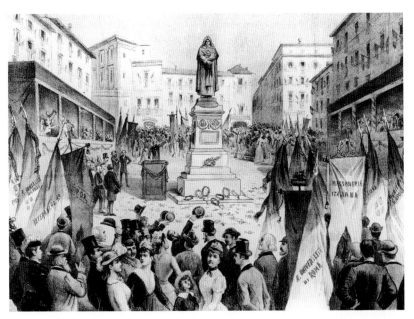

The 1889 dedication of the statue of Giordano Bruno in the Campo dei Fiori, where Bruno had been burned at the stake almost three centuries earlier, enraging the pope. Many believed it was the last straw, that the pope would soon leave Italy, to return only after Rome was taken from the Italians and returned to his control.

Did they expect there to be a large crowd? Bacco asked them. Yes, Crispolti and Datti replied, they thought it would be very large. But they hastened to add that the Vatican authorities had done nothing to encourage a mass gathering and had done all they could to discourage people from joining in. "Indeed, the cardinal vicar sent some Catholic organizations express instructions not to take part." Bacco told them that he had already made plans to have a large number of police lining the entire route and that many plainclothes police would be mixed in with the procession itself.[4]

In his own testimony to the government's investigative committee, Bacco gave a slightly different account of this meeting. The two lay Catholic leaders came to see him on the eleventh, he recalled, but their mission had been to request that those following the funeral cortege be allowed to carry lit candles. He told them that they could, and then, he said, he sent news to the prefect "that the clericals were highly excited and planning to take part in the procession in great numbers, and that the well-known agitators were making plans to disrupt the funeral procession." However, in the police archives, Bacco's only telegram sent to the prefect on the eleventh reads rather differently: "I know positively that a great many people will be going to accompany the body of Pius IX from St. Peter's to San Lorenzo, following behind the coffin with torches and reciting prayers. There is so far no plan for political demonstrations or plans to promote disorders." It went on to say that he would submit a plan for the prefect's approval the following day for "a very strong contingent of police officers and agents at St. Peter's, behind the cortege, and along the streets through which it will pass on its way to San Lorenzo, so that we are in a position to provide for any emergency."[5]

Despite receiving this warning, on the morning of the twelfth the prefect did not seem to fully register the magnitude of what was about to take place, for he wrote that "all ought to proceed in a totally private manner." Yet, while not entirely aware of just how explosive the situation was, the prefect stressed to Bacco the need to ensure that nothing disturb the procession. "I especially urge you to see that at both the Vatican basilica and at San Lorenzo there is a highly alert and sizable contingent of oversight and that this also extends along all of the roads through which the cortege will pass and is in a position to be able, in any eventuality and at any point of the route, to take prudent action to prevent or immediately stop even the smallest disorder." Should Bacco believe that the police under his command were insufficient to guarantee that there would be no public disturbance of any kind, the prefect wrote, he should let him know so that arrangements could be made to call up the troops.

Clearly nervous, Bacco made one last trip to the Ministry of the Interior, where, according to his own later account, he received some good news. The secretary-general and the Rome police chief told him that they had received new information assuring them that, despite the earlier threats by anticlerical groups, there would be no disorders. But, still uneasy, at 2:10 P.M. Bacco sent a new telegram to the prefect, taking up his offer and asking that nine military squadrons of a hundred men each be placed at strategic points along the planned route. As soon as he received the request, the prefect sent urgent orders to the commander of the Military Division of Rome to furnish the troops. He then contacted Rome's mayor and asked him to have all available municipal police on hand to help. He also made arrangements with the Vatican's lay emissary, Vespignani, so that only those on a list that he provided would be allowed to enter the church of San Lorenzo with the pope's casket.[6]

Until the morning of the twelfth, the route of the procession had been kept secret, but that morning news of it spread through the city, in the words of *Civiltà Cattolica*, "with the speed of light." As the journal put it, "Everyone's hearts were beating loudly, they could barely wait, so universal was the desire to accompany the venerated body to San Lorenzo." And although Leo had wanted to avoid a large demonstration, by the morning of the twelfth Catholic groups were distributing printed invitations calling on all good Catholics in Rome to show their respect for the dead pontiff by joining the cortege.

All day long itinerant vendors crowded St. Peter's Square, doing a brisk business in candles and torches. By shortly after eleven, in the estimation of the Jesuit journal, at least one hundred thousand people had crowded into the area between the steps of St. Peter's and the bridge in front of Sant'Angelo Castle. While this number seems suspiciously large, there is no question that the small ceremony had turned into something much different. Whatever the total number, not all were there out of devotion to Pius. Some were simply curious and wanted to see the strange and unusual event, or perhaps they knew of the battle to come and did not want to miss it. Others had a more mischievous intent.[7]

At nine o'clock, inside St. Peter's, in the mausoleum beneath the main floor, the wall covering Pius IX's temporary resting place was demolished. Attendants struggled to extract the heavy bier, made of lead, and the prelates checked to see that the seals were intact.

With the funeral bier scheduled to appear from the left door of St. Peter's, about three thousand members of Rome's Catholic lay associations, bearing torches and candles, formed two lines stretching from the door down the steps. As midnight struck, the prelates with the pope's bier stepped out of the basilica and walked down the steps between the lines of the faithful. They placed the bier in the waiting wagon, covering it with a red cloth bearing the pontifical insignia. Flares shot into the sky, signaling the procession to begin. Two pairs of black horses pulled the huge wagon, the front horses each carrying a black-suited rider wearing a pointed hat.

Giuseppe Manfroni described his feelings of helplessness: "St. Peter's Square was packed, and the police (a hundred men in all) — submerged in a vast sea of people — were impotent." The carriage carrying the pope's body, with four official Vatican carriages behind it, was followed by two hundred carriages of the Catholic faithful and three thousand candle-bearing marchers chanting prayers in Latin and Italian and reciting the rosary. But the procession had no sooner left St. Peter's Square than anticlerics began to drown out the mourners' prayers with shouts and songs. At Sant'Angelo bridge, fears mounted that the assailants might succeed in tossing the papal bier into the Tiber, with two to three hundred anticlerics bellowing, "Into the river! Into the river!"[8] The police desperately tried to separate the anticlerics from the processioners, but, as Bacco reported in a telegram sent to the prefect, "it was not possible because they were all mixed in among the carriages and the crowd."

A police captain described the scene as the procession reached the other side of the river: "The demonstrators became much more aggressive, one heard loud whistles, hostile shouts against the priests, and all of a sudden almost everybody was swept up into the demonstration, people taking one side or the other, not only in the street but from the adjoining houses as well." The police did their best to keep the protesters away from the procession once it reached the other bank, but by Piazza Pasquino what had already become unruly and embarrassing turned into something much more dangerous. In Questore Bacco's words, "The shouts on the one side and on the other were growing louder and ever more threatening. The horses of one carriage reared up in fear, and in that narrow piazza, packed with people, there was great confusion." Meanwhile, all along the way, many homes — just how many was part of the polemics that would follow — had placed special lights and decorations outside their windows to mark the occasion, and from some of them people tossed flowers onto the funeral bier. But the lanterns perched on the windowsills were tempting targets for the protesters, whose well-aimed rocks showered shards of glass onto the street. Outside the palaces of those noblemen who lived on the route, servants bearing torches and dressed in their most formal livery had been instructed to form a line to pay their respects. They too faced jeers and worse.

The police tried to summon the military squads that had been placed in reserve along the route, but so great was the crush of the crowd that they could not get through. Near Piazza del Gesù, faced by an angry crowd, a panicked municipal guardsman unsheathed his sword, provoking shouts of outrage. His horrified captain rushed in and pulled him away.

The procession soon reached Piazza Termini, where the protesters began hacking away at a pontifical crest that a devout storekeeper had placed over his shop. When police intervened, the violence grew worse. Rocks rained on the carriages of the funeral procession, and angry demonstrators shouted, "Death to the priests!" Two military squads finally succeeded in entering the piazza and separating the protesters from the funeral cortege. But with the protesters rushing through side streets to try to reassemble farther down the route, the police urged the funeral wagons to hasten their pace, leaving many of the faithful, now disorganized and the target of hostile whistles and shouts, straggling well behind in the last stretch leading to San Lorenzo. By 3 A.M., the wagon with Pius IX's remains, accompanied by the carriages of the Vatican dignitaries, entered the piazza outside San Lorenzo, where another group of demonstrators waited. The police, in considerable force, were ready and succeeded in keeping them away from the cortege and the church door.

There were many arrests, not all of them among the anticlerics. In fact, the first person listed in the original report of the commander of the carabinieri was Giuseppe Riedi, age fifty-seven, a pensioner of the pontifical state living near the Vatican. Described as part of the

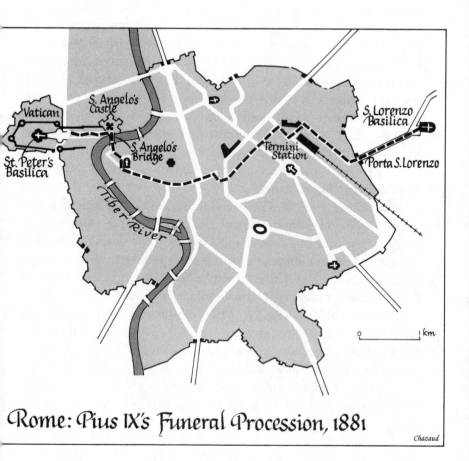

Rome: Pius IX's Funeral Procession, 1881

Vatican
S. Angelo's Castle
S. Lorenzo Basilica
St. Peter's Basilica
S. Angelo's Bridge
Termini Station
Porta S. Lorenzo
Tiber River
km
Chazaud

"clerical party," he was charged with refusing to obey police orders. But most of those arrested were anticlericals, and almost all were young men. They included an eighteen-year-old butcher, a twenty-year-old baker, an eighteen-year-old goldsmith, a nineteen-year-old hairdresser, a twenty-two-year-old clerk, and a twenty-nine-year-old municipal employee. Several people had also been injured, although none too seriously. A twenty-two-year-old cook for the priest who ran the Church's institute for Jewish converts had been hit by a blunt instrument near San Lorenzo; a twenty-four-year-old university student had been hit by a club. More embarrassing for the government, the pope's nephew, Count Pecci, had been hit by a rock in his wagon and, bloodied, been forced to flee.[9]

A major public relations disaster loomed, as Depretis realized before the dawn. There is some evidence that this is exactly what those in charge of the funeral procession had in mind. In a series of reports to the British foreign minister, the British envoy in Rome reported on two conversations he had had, one with a canon of St. Peter's, who had been involved in the preparations, and another with one of the Curia's most influential cardinals. Leo XIII, according to both sources, had never been comfortable with the plans for the cortege and "highly disapproved of the proposed proceeding. His Holiness foresaw the consequences which probably would, and actually did, result from it. His Holiness never sanctioned it — but was silent." It was the Catholic clubs of Rome that had organized the marchers bearing torches. "The effect of the clubs was to create a political demonstration, which they knew beforehand would be a provocation of the national feeling, and would probably give rise to scenes which would enable them to proclaim that there was no security for religion, or for the Church, in Rome." It had all been the work of the intransigents, the *zelanti*, and, the envoy added, "they had only too well succeeded in their purpose."[10]

On the government's side, those most directly involved each tried to blame someone else. At 5 A.M., Bacco sent the prefect a long telegram describing the mayhem but trying to play it down, stressing that the only known injuries were to "a priest and another person, both hit by rocks, and a young woman who received a blow with a lit torch," adding that their injuries were all minor. Receiving the telegram a half-hour later and by now realizing the gravity of what had just taken place, the prefect hastened to send the telegram on to Depretis, along with a note: "From this brief report it appears that some very serious things happened that would not have happened if greater precautions had been taken. Either my orders were not precise enough, or they were not fully followed. Given what has happened, I would like Your Eminence to order a rigorous inquest."[11]

Depretis was feeling great pressure. That same day two senators interrogated him on the Senate floor. The first to speak was Senator Carlo Alfieri.

"I believe that I express my colleagues' unanimous feelings," he said, "in deploring in the strongest terms the fact that, in the Kingdom's capital, a funeral cortege was unable to proceed in perfect tranquility and perfect decorum. Considering moreover that this funeral convoy was for a person who was not only of the highest status, but of such high virtue, worthy of respect and veneration even by those having very different opinions and convictions from those of the illustrious Pontiff, the deplorable events of last night assume even greater gravity." Senator Cambray-Digny then followed, seconding Alfieri's comments and asking Depretis "how was it that, knowing how important it was that this cortege proceed solemnly, the necessary precautions were not taken to effectively prevent the disorders that were all too easy to foresee?"

The prime minister rose to reply. "I too," he said, "hasten to say that I deplore the painful events that took place last night no less than the senators who have spoken." But Depretis tried to minimize the commotion and to cast the blame elsewhere: "During the funeral cortege a few irresponsible people disturbed the holy ceremony. But nothing serious occurred. The authorities intervened and enforced respect for the law. Despite this, some disorders did take place which, especially in the capital of the Kingdom, under the very eyes of the Government, ought not to have occurred." Depretis went on to explain how this had happened.

The government had been informed of Pius's funeral wishes, Depretis recalled. "Yet only yesterday the Government learned that invitations were being sent to the faithful to encourage them to take part in the holy service. The Government made the necessary arrangements, but in a stretch of road such as that running from St. Peter's all through the city to the church of San Lorenzo outside the opposite wall, it was impossible to prevent disorders at all points along the way."

Just who was responsible, Depretis went on to say, remained unclear. He had ordered an inquiry to find out and to determine whether any of the public security forces had failed to carry out their explicit instructions to maintain order. Should the latter prove to be the case, he pledged, appropriate punishment would be meted out.[12]

When, two days later, the principal inspector for the minister of the interior arrived at Bacco's office, Bacco must have already had some idea of his purpose. Yet he proved to be a difficult witness, for he kept resisting the inspector's requests that he acknowledge that it had been the Catholics who were responsible for the mayhem.

"On my honor," Bacco replied, "I cannot say that the clericals provoked it, for they kept the agreements they made." Nor would he agree that the procession was political: "I could not see this as a demonstration against the institutions and against the State, because it was only a funeral transport followed by the faithful."

"It hardly seems possible to me," said the inspector, "that a *questore*, knowing of the numerous and close-knit clerical associations existing in Rome, did not know that they were preparing a political demonstration and that it would become a provocation."

"I believe that you begin from a false premise," replied Bacco. "I did not fail to warn the minster and the prefect of the many people on the *clericali*'s side who would take part in the procession." But, he added, he had been told not to interfere. "The secretary general of the minister of the interior told me that I was exaggerating the number of *clericali*, and when at the last moment he saw that we had all erred in predicting how many there would be, I asked in vain for instructions." Yet, even with all of the *clericali* there, he added, "it would not have affected public order had there not been provocation."

"But," replied the inspector, "the provocations came from the *clericali* who shouted, 'Long live the Pope-King!'"

"As far as the shout 'Long live the Pope-King' goes," said Bacco, "it was limited and came only in response to great provocation. For the most part people were shouting 'Long live Pius IX! Long live the Pope!'"

"So you persist in making all these statements?" the inspector asked.

"Completely."

Depretis had found his scapegoat. On July 29 he reported to parliament that the investigation into the affair had been completed and appropriate action had been taken against those who had failed to carry out the government's instructions. Bacco was relieved of his duties that day.[13]

Although those around the pope felt genuine outrage at the anti-clerical sacrilege of that night, they were also excited by the political ammunition it offered. Cardinal Jacobini, the secretary of state, certainly lost no time using the episode to bolster the Vatican's cause. Within hours of the procession, he was sending coded telegrams to his nuncios, urging them to help organize a worldwide protest, although he cautioned them to be discreet. The protests had to be viewed as spontaneous.[14]

On July 15, Jacobini sent a long account of the events both to his nuncios in Europe and to his emissaries in the Americas. He then highlighted the main lesson to be drawn from the affair:

> From all this you can easily deduce just how much protection Catholics are offered in Rome in carrying out their duties, how much respect and freedom is provided the pope, who among other things is by law accorded the rights and honors of a Sovereign. If they let those paying their last homage of filial respect to a dead pope, a man loved and revered by all Romans, to be injured and attacked, what disorders would darken the streets of Rome if they were traversed today by the living pope? What disorders would break out if the Holy Father wanted to visit His basilicas and carry out the sacred rites in the midst of His devoted population with all of the majesty of His court? The pope's imprisonment has received full confirmation by these sad, but inevitable, events.

He concluded by instructing his nuncios to read his letter to the minister of foreign affairs in the country they served and then leave him a copy.[15]

The same day, Pasquale Mancini, then minister of foreign affairs, sent out his own lengthy message, addressed to all the Italian ambassadors in Europe. "This telegram," he explained, "is for your information and to put you in a position to correct the erroneous versions of what happened on the occasion of the transfer of the remains of Pius IX from the Vatican to San Lorenzo." The facts he went on to recount were rather different from those in Jacobini's circular. Rome's prefect had received a request for a small, private transfer of the body of Pius IX to his final resting place, to be held without anyone following it. Authorization was given with these assurances. "But at the last minute a political demonstration was organized through calls by the heads of the clerical party, of which I possess various copies, and a large and noisy procession of over two thousand people" followed. "Some groups of youths reacted against the provocateurs at various points along the route. Some jostling, which led to no injury, followed, as the police intervened immediately to protect the funeral procession, assuring its march to San Lorenzo, where the inhumation and religious ceremonies were conducted in tranquility." Mancini went on to report that the young men who had been arrested for disturbing the procession had been quickly brought to justice and that six of them had already been sentenced to two to three months in prison.[16]

While the Catholic press throughout Europe denounced the Italian government and cited the chaotic procession to support its argument that Rome must be retaken, the secular press was divided. Some papers criticized the Italian government for allowing the disorders to occur, but many lashed out at the Vatican instead. Vienna's nuncio reported on a number of these stories on July 21. The German newspaper *Fremdenblatt*, like many others, asked how the Vatican could criticize the Italian government for failing to obey the law of guarantees when Pius had himself so loudly rejected it. The Austrian *Wiener Allgemeine Zeitung* charged that the Church was using the event cynically, to support its "fable" that the pope remained a prisoner. If the Italian government was to be accused of anything, the paper argued, it was for being too lenient toward those who would hold demonstrations in favor of the pope's temporal power. "The hypocritical complaints of violence committed against the pope will everywhere be received with a courteous shrug of the shoulders." The pope, the newspaper argued, "has the fullest freedom, no one threatens him, no one places obstacles in his way." And it concluded: "The 19th century will not see any crusade for reestablishing the popes' temporal dominion."[17]

If Leo was hoping to use the frenzy to gain support for his efforts against the government, the initial signs were not promising. After a visit by the papal nuncio, who presented the Vatican's protests, the French foreign minister sent a letter to his ambassador to the Holy See. The disorders of the night of the twelfth, he said, were most regrettable. However, he noted, the Italian government was doubtless just as angered by the actions of the anticlerical rowdies as the French govern-

ment was, and unfortunately in a large city such things could sometimes not be prevented.[18]

But not all was going well for Depretis and his colleagues. The image
of a holy funeral cortege, and that of a pope no less, being pelted with
rocks and disrupted by obscenities was a great embarrassment. The
Italian ambassador to Berlin shared in this discomfort and was angered
by his government's excuses. Writing to Mancini, he was blunt: "As
Your Excellency has encouraged me to speak frankly, allow me to add
that your telegram [giving the official government account] produced
a poor impression on me." That some people would try to mount such
a noisy protest could not have been unknown to the government, and
the scandal that would follow could have been entirely foreseen. "Police who serve only to put down disorders rather than try to prevent
them from occurring in the first place," wrote the ambassador, "are ne-
glecting an essential part of their job. I cannot help but lament," he
added, "that we have given fodder to our enemies who are searching
for just such pretexts to harm us. At the same time, we have paralyzed
our friends — and certainly they are far from numerous — who also
have to cope with the sentiments of their own Catholics who, in these
circumstances, will not fail to exploit the matter to our detriment."[19]

Sensing that it was gaining ground, the Vatican tried to step up the
pressure. In a new circular, sent in code to the nuncios on July 30, the
secretary of state raised the old threat of leaving the Holy City. The few
malefactors who had been arrested for the violence, he reported, had
received minimal sentences and had been released without bail, pend-
ing an appeal. The investigation that Depretis had promised the Senate
had been conducted by one of his own men, who failed to interview
any of the Catholics who had been attacked. The government's unofficial newspapers had joined the radical press in Rome in their polemics against Catholics, and various anticlerical clubs had recently been
formed "with the goal of uniting all the enemies of the Church and the
papacy." The secretary concluded on an ominous note. The nuncios
were to inform Europe's foreign ministers that "because the position of
the Holy Father in Rome has become so difficult, there are discussions
in the councils of the Holy See seriously deliberating whether departure from the capital has become necessary."[20]

Rome remained tense. The funeral fiasco had fanned the intransigent flames in the Vatican, and now no rhetorical flourishes were being

spared. In a long, combative article on August 4, *L'Osservatore Romano* called for the government to give the Holy City back to the pope. "No, Italy has no need of Rome as its capital. Italy can stay in Florence or go to Naples, it could be in Milan or Ravenna." The pope was a prisoner in today's Rome, the paper charged; "his imprisonment has been shown to be truer and more complete than ever. And so the dream of conciliation between the Papacy and the New Italy is impossible." The paper's language could hardly have been more melodramatic: "The pope is a prisoner, the Italian government his jailer." The article ended with a thinly veiled warning: "The Kingdom of Italy presents itself as if it were made of granite, but its base is made of clay, and the night of July 13 proved that at any moment the rock might slide off the mountain and will deal it the fatal blow."[21]

In this overheated atmosphere, the police tripled the guard around the Vatican, having heard rumors of plans by anticlerical groups to destroy what they called "the vipers' nest." At the same time, known anticlerical agitators were ordered to be tailed.[22]

The police also learned that a huge anticlerical meeting was planned for Sunday, August 7, at the vast Politeama Theater, a meeting that would gain international attention. The government had banned all outdoor political demonstrations and rallies, but to ban an indoor meeting risked both undermining its claim to be supporting basic political freedoms and angering the more anticlerical of its supporters. The organizers provocatively addressed invitations to "all patriots, all former political prisoners from the reign of Pius IX, and all the relatives of the victims of the former pontifical government." In the evenings before the event, anticlerical youths covered the walls of the Holy City with epithets directed at Leo XIII and Pius IX, and several images of the Madonna and assorted saints on the streets were smashed or defaced.

The ingredients for another public relations disaster for the government had been assembled. The Italian ambassador to Vienna, who had been busy trying to repair the damage done by the funeral disorders, wrote to Mancini on August 4 to warn him about further demonstrations. "There is no point," he argued, "hiding the fact that the Vatican, taking advantage of the events of the night of July 13, which they so ably provoked, is trying to trigger Catholic agitation against Italy." While the Austrian government had so far resisted this campaign, he reported, "it is no less true that given current circumstances inside the Empire, clerical agitation could create serious embarrassment for the Government."[23]

Three thousand people crowded into the Politeama Theater, in Rome's Trastevere neighborhood, on the morning of the seventh for an event such as the Holy City had never seen. At ten-twenty the leaders climbed onto the stage. The chair was Giuseppe Petroni, a lawyer from Bologna who had spent seventeen years as a prisoner of the Papal States; he had originally been sentenced to death for his role in organizing an abortive uprising in 1853 and only released from prison when Rome was taken in 1870.[24] A variety of other anticlerical heroes accompanied him, including the old Garibaldian firebrand Alberto Mario, along with two of Garibaldi's sons — Menotti and Ricciotti — and three members of parliament. Enthusiastic applause greeted them.

Petroni opened the meeting and helped set its tone. After recounting the hardships that he and his comrades had endured in prison, he turned to the law of guarantees. "While we thought we would have guarantees of freedom, of civil progress," Petroni told them, "we found instead the guarantees of despotism, obscurantism, and corruption." The law of guarantees, he insisted, must be abolished.

Petroni proceeded to read two telegrams. The first, from Garibaldi himself, was short but powerful: "I support the abolition of the Guarantees and the Guaranteed" — the latter referring to the pope himself. In fact, just the year before, angry at the government he believed had betrayed the ideals on which the nation was based, Garibaldi had resigned his seat in parliament. He explained his action in a letter to his constituents: "I cannot continue to serve any longer in the legislature of a country where freedom is trampled and the law serves, in practice, only to guarantee the freedom of the Jesuits and of the enemies of Italian unity."[25] The second telegram that Petroni read, from France, offered Victor Hugo's support: "French democracy is forever united with Italian democracy in combating the Vatican."

But the meeting's highlight was the speech by Alberto Mario, the editor of Rome's most fiercely anticlerical newspaper and Garibaldi's close friend and comrade. Mario was not to be equaled in his vilification of the papacy. The day after the funeral procession, in his paper, he praised the attack on Pius IX's "carcass" and added that "we would have applauded even more if the remains of that great fool had been thrown from the Sant'Angelo bridge into the Tiber."[26] At the Politeama, Mario quickly warmed to his theme. "The Vatican," he said, "is a refuge and sanctuary for evildoers beyond the reach of the police." The government had allowed "Signor Pecci — at this disrespectful reference to the pope the delighted crowd laughed heartily — the freedom to publish letters and allocutions in such a way that Signor Pecci and his clergy are at the head of a separate state of 100,000 well-organized men. It is for this reason that suppressing the law of guarantees is a humanitarian act: for fourteen centuries the papacy has been eating away at Italy and Europe." What had the popes done to the pioneers of science and freedom? Mario asked. They had Giordano Bruno burned in Campo dei Fiori and forced Galileo to deny that the earth moved around the sun, "a truth that the Church has still not officially recognized." As for Pius IX, it was he "who called on four foreign powers to reduce Italy to slavery in order to prop up his tottering temporal rule, and who issued the Syllabus to combat modern civilization."

"Every people has its role in history," Mario proclaimed. "Italy's is to suppress the papacy and with the abolition of the guarantees we will reach this goal."

Mario then turned to the pope's threats to leave Italy: "Have you read the allocution Signor Pecci gave yesterday? It appears that he is considering fleeing." To this the audience responded with laughter, sharp whistles, and shouts of "Would that it were so! Into the river!" Mario continued: "'To the enemy who flees, a golden bridge,' goes the saying, and if he would only let us know the day he is leaving Rome, all of Rome would be there to wish him a pleasant journey." A sea of "Yes! Yes!" drowned out his next words.

Mario reminded the crowd of the polemics over Pius IX's funeral procession. "The pope has told a lie," he said. A voice called out, sarcastically, "But the pope is infallible!" "He is an infallible liar," replied Mario, to the crowd's delight. "Signor Pecci has said that a few of the faithful, praying, accompanied Pius IX's body. And herein is the lie. It was the clerical party, who took advantage of the opportunity of transporting Pius IX's body to mount a demonstration hostile to Italy. But in illuminating the carcass of Pius IX, they shed light on the whole history of this despicable pontiff."[27]

Adriano Lemmi, long a friend and financial supporter of Mazzini's and soon to become national head of the Italian Freemasons, followed

Mario to the podium. Lemmi began to read the resolution that was to be voted on. It began with a preamble: "Considering that the papacy and Italian unity are mutually contradictory historically and politically — the popes called in foreign forces 35 times —" Here Lemmi was interrupted by a loud, angry shout: "Assassins!" And considering, he continued, that the papacy undermined national sovereignty, "the people of Rome want that law [of guarantees] abolished and the Apostolic palaces occupied."

But in calling for the taking of the Vatican, Lemmi had gone too far. A police official who, with a cadre of officers, had been monitoring the meeting, rose and tried to silence him. Pandemonium followed. "Long live the Inquisition," one outraged anticleric shouted; others whistled. Petroni got up and tried to restore order, but his voice could not be heard over the din. Ricciotti Garibaldi stood on two chairs and tried to get people's attention but failed. Finally, one of the meeting's less illustrious leaders, who, however, surpassed his comrades in vocal volume, cried out. He recited the rest of the proposed motion and concluded by putting the question simply: "Do you want the abolition of the guarantees and the occupation of the Apostolic palaces?" A storm of applause and whistles of approval were only partially drowned out by the efforts of the police to clear the room. A squad of police reinforcements arrived, and by noon the Politeama was empty

The next day, the newspapers that published the rally's speeches were confiscated by the police. Among the offices raided were those of the Vatican's *Osservatore Romano*, for its edition had contained excerpts — with suitable outraged commentary — from the speeches. And so, much to his consternation, the director of the Vatican daily found himself condemned by court order for having violated article 2 of the law of guarantees: he stood charged of offending the pope.[28]

14

Rumors of a French Conspiracy

IN THE WAKE OF THE EVENTS of July 12–13, the Vatican ratcheted up its stark imagery of a besieged Church battling the forces of evil. Typical was *Civiltà Cattolica's* language: "There are two Romes: one pagan or, more precisely, apostate, the other Christian; the one that oppresses, the other that is oppressed, the one composed almost wholly of foreigners, the other composed of the descendants of the true Romans." While pagan Rome "has its parliamentarians, its laws, and its materialist, atheist schools, Christian Rome has as its head Peter's successor, who since 1870 has been a prisoner in the Vatican . . . For more than a decade these two Romes have stared each other in the face. The one curses the Pontiff, the other goes reverently to kiss his feet; the one insults, the other weeps and prays."[1]

Just where the battle between the anticlerics and the Church would lead was not clear. On August 17, 1881, the British envoy, reporting from Rome, wrote ominously to the foreign minister in London: "I regret to inform your Lordship that, whether with or without the connivance of the authorities, the quarrel between Papists and anti-Papists is daily assuming more important dimensions, and, if allowed to continue, may lead to consequences far more serious than the Italian government appears to have the necessary sense to foresee." Rumors of the pope's impending departure had again begun to spread, although in the envoy's view, Leo had little desire to leave, and the Italian government had every interest in his staying. Only should things get worse, he reported, would the pope flee, his likely destination being Austria.[2]

In preparing the circular to the nuncios on the papal funeral procession in late July, the pope had consulted with the cardinals of the Congregation of Extraordinary Ecclesiastical Affairs, and they again raised the question of departing from Rome. Cardinal Camillo Di Pietro, arguing that it was futile to send out yet more protests against the sorry situation to which the Holy See had been reduced, suggested that the pope immediately seek asylum in another country. The cardinals were divided about the wisdom of such a move, but they urged that the possibility of flight be further explored and debated whether it would be helpful for the pope to use the threat of departure in his upcoming allocution.[3] In the end, the circular included just such a threat.

Following the instructions in the circular, the papal nuncio in Vienna met with Austria's assistant foreign minister. Impatient with the minister's generic expressions of sympathy, the nuncio invoked the specter of papal flight. As he recounted in his report to Jacobini: "I could not help but add that the future looked rather bleak, and if things continued to go the way it looked like they were heading following the important events of July 13, it was not unlikely that considerations of his own dignity and security would prompt the Holy Father to leave Rome."

The Austrian official was not impressed. "Ah! No!" he replied. "We hope that such an eventuality will not come to pass and that such deplorable events as occurred on July 13 will never be repeated."[4]

The pope's supposed plans to leave Italy quickly became the subject of animated discussion in the press, a weapon used by all sides. On August 10, just three days after the Politeama protest meeting, the Roman daily newspaper *Il Diritto*, widely viewed as the unofficial mouthpiece of Depretis himself, reported that Leo had in fact made the fateful decision to leave Rome. The pope, the long article continued, had made up his mind shortly after the funeral procession disorders and had communicated it to a number of foreign powers. Leo had also decided where he would go — to Malta. The cardinals, who were consulted on the matter, were in full accord. "Political circumstances may speed up or delay his departure," *Il Diritto* related, "but it seems that it is unlikely that they will prevent it."

The Vatican press was not denying these rumors. On August 10, the French Catholic news agency, Havas, angered the Vatican by reporting that the pope had decided to stay in Rome. In recent days, the agency claimed, "the pope has declared to many members in his retinue that he is resolved not to abandon Rome unless made to do so by force. Instructions have been sent to the nuncios telling them to reply in this fashion if they are asked." *L'Osservatore Romano* dismissed the story curtly: "We are in a position to state that the whole content of this article is pure invention." But in the wake of the funeral disaster, the Vatican paper itself was brandishing the threat of papal departure, observing: "History teaches us that every time that the pope, forced by the tyranny of either the plebes or governments, left Rome defeated and humiliated, he returned there triumphant and covered with glory."[5]

Although the Italians were then accusing the French of plotting the pope's departure as part of their efforts to weaken the Italian state, French diplomatic correspondence makes it clear that such charges were groundless. In response to the new wave of stories about the pope's leaving Rome, the French foreign minister sent instructions on August 14 to his envoy to the Holy See. "The pope's abandonment of the traditional seat of the papacy would have the most unfortunate consequences," he wrote. "His departure from Rome would become the signal for a popular uprising against Catholic institutions in Italy which the royal government would most likely be unable to quell. This revolutionary movement would be very dangerous for Italy itself without thereby benefitting the papal cause. It is impossible in any case to predict how long the agitation that would follow might last, what course it would take, and how long the period of exile would be to which the papacy would have condemned itself." The foreign minister also worried about the impact that the pope's departure would have elsewhere in Europe, for Catholic sentiment would everywhere be inflamed. He concluded by telling his envoy to convey these thoughts — unofficially — both to the pope and to the cardinals he knew.[6]

In fact, unknown to most Italians, their government was then in the early stages of forming a Triple Alliance, aligning with Germany and Austria, aimed in good part against France. This action was in some ways unexpected, for it was France that had helped the Savoyard monarchy unite Italy by fighting against Austria, the main foreign foe of unification. That it was a government of the left that engineered the alliance against the French also had much to say about the abandonment by men like Depretis, Crispi, and Mancini of their old republican principles, for they were now taking the side of a German king and an Austrian emperor against republican France.

But various developments in 1881 helped push the Italian government into the Triple Alliance, which would be sealed in a treaty the following year, its secret provisions becoming public only many decades later. The anticlerical disorders of the summer, identified with the republicans, whose fondness for the Savoyard monarchy was only slightly greater than their regard for the papacy, frightened Umberto and his court. The central powers seemed to offer protection against the threat to the monarchy. Forming an alliance with Austria and Germany also meant removing the danger that either one of these major powers might take the Vatican's side against Italy. Another big factor was the aggressive foreign policy then being pursued by France. Depretis himself had become prime minister in 1881 only because the previous government had fallen in the spring after the French occupation of Tunisia, which Italians viewed as properly a part of their own sphere of influence. In this atmosphere, it was easy to stir up patriotic sentiment against the French.[7]

On August 15, the French ambassador to Italy sent his foreign minister copies of two recent Italian newspaper stories accusing France of plotting with the pope against Italy. He was especially alarmed by the piece in *La Riforma*, a paper viewed as under Crispi's control. France was planning a war against Italy, the paper reported, and was preparing "to lead the pope back into Italy in the midst of the French army!" Of course, it would first be necessary for the French to get the pope out of Italy, and, according to *La Riforma*, this was exactly what the French ambassador to the Holy See was secretly working to do. It was he, the paper charged, who had been behind the arrangements for Pius IX's funeral procession, knowing that the resulting chaos would offer Leo XIII a pretext to declare that he could no longer live in Rome. "Crispi's newspaper," the ambassador reported, "ended its article by asking that the Italian army be readied."[8]

At the Vatican, the summer's events had left everyone on edge. Eager to demonstrate that most Italians were on the pope's side, various Catholic associations organized pilgrimages to the Vatican, an effort that continued throughout the next decade. The tension was palpable. A secret police report told that, following the disorders, "the wall near the Vatican gardens was being guarded for fear that it would be

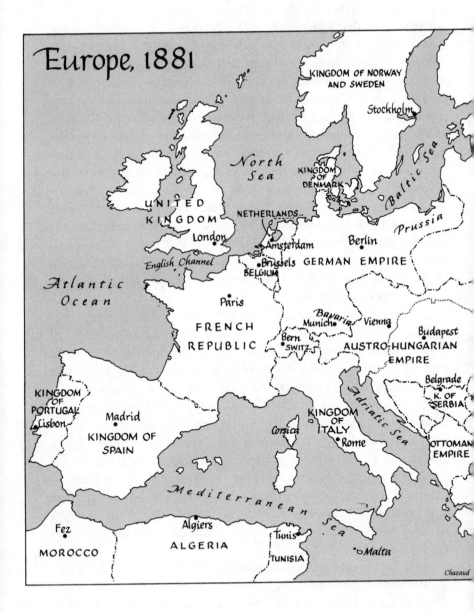

climbed and a sudden assault made without the Government's knowledge." It concluded: "In the Vatican they fear that the republican and
socialist party have already infiltrated the army and the civil authority
itself . . . they do not believe that even the Savoyard dynasty is safe."[9]

It was a dangerous moment for the papacy, for the new Italian state,
and for much of Europe. Italy was in an uproar about the French invasion of "its" Tunisian territories, and murmurs of war with France
were growing ever louder. Although to this point the French had been
working behind the scenes to calm the Vatican waters, they now began to see some advantage in roiling them. On Monday, October 17,
the French chargé d'affaires in Rome, the marquis de Reverseaux, reported just how tense the city was. The previous day, the pope had received a large number of Italian pilgrims in St. Peter's. The Italian
authorities were worried that anticlerics might infiltrate the ceremonies, and for good reason. "Just one shout hostile to the Holy Father," the envoy wrote, "could have led to a clash in the church itself
whose consequences would likely have been the pope's departure from
Rome."

What he then went on to suggest to his foreign minister shows that
something had changed radically in the relations between France and
Italy in two months. The envoy predicted that Italy's Catholics would
try to form an unholy alliance with the republicans aimed at destroying the Italian monarchy. The Holy See, he wrote, believed that such a
development would be in its interest, for the demise of the kingdom of
Italy would give rise to a weak federal republic, allowing the Vatican
"once again to take possession of the Papal States or, at least, remain
the master in Rome."

What should the French do about this prospect of Italy's descent
into civil war? "We need not take the side of one or the other of the two
adversaries," wrote Reverseaux, "but we can hope that in this duel to
the death, the papacy is the victor. Each day we see the disadvantages
of having unified Italy, and to the extent that this unity becomes better
established and stronger, we will have more to fear from its hostility.
We therefore can only rejoice at all the causes that lead to a weakening or disorganization in Italy's current structure. And, among these
causes, the most important is the struggle between the State and the
Vatican."[10]

Remarkably, Vatican officials had indeed been secretly discussing the possibility of encouraging a republican revolt in Italy as a way to regain control of Rome. In a meeting in March 1881, the cardinals of the Congregation of Extraordinary Ecclesiastical Affairs had met to advise the pope on the best strategy for regaining temporal power. Among the scenarios envisioned was just this possibility: a republican victory leading to an Italian confederation. For the plan to succeed, more than one cardinal warned, the Vatican's role had to be kept completely secret. And for it to work, as another cardinal pointed out, it was "indispensable for the pope to leave Rome first."[11]

There was some irony in the French government's incipient plan to side with the Vatican, for at that very time the anticlerical majority in the National Assembly was busy scaling back the privileges enjoyed by the French clergy in an effort to promote a more secular state at home. In a royal audience in late November, King Umberto grilled the French ambassador to Italy on reports of an approaching rupture between the Church and the government of the notoriously anticlerical French prime minister, Léon Gambetta. "As for us," said the king, "we live on as good terms as possible with the pope, who is of superior mind and animated by great patriotism, and who understands that by allying himself with the kingdom's enemies, he is not only compromising the existence of Italian unity, but of the papacy itself." Umberto, it appears, had a weakness for wishful thinking, or perhaps it was a weakness for wishful speaking.[12]

Talk of the pope's imminent flight was again sweeping the country. "These rumors . . . ," the French chargé d'affaires informed Gambetta in late December, "repeated with increasing insistence in the past days, do not fail to leave an impression on the government and the king, as do the words attributed to the pope 'I hold the future of the house of Savoy in my hands,' which seems to many Italians to portray the situation exactly. The pontiff's departure could, in effect, trigger an upheaval, whose result would be fatal for the monarchy while working to the advantage of a republic. Now, the Vatican is not far from wishing for this solution."

While the German and Austrian governments were secretly warning Italy of France's attempts to induce the pope to leave Rome and so destabilize the Italian state, the French envoy was pointing the finger at Bismarck. He had learned, Reverseaux wrote, "that the Chancellor's secret agents were actively working for the pope's departure . . . it seems that most of the members of the Sacred College are disposed to heed these suggestions, thinking that in this way they can force the Powers to impose a settlement."[13]

Although this allegation was groundless, the possibility that the pope was scheming to go into exile as a way of fomenting chaos in Italy was being seriously discussed in high German government circles. Germany's major Catholic newspaper published a booklet at the time that proposed just such a scenario. The plan it set out called for restoring the pope's rule over the Holy City and its hinterland by having the pope first abandon Rome. This move, it was thought, would lead to an uprising by Italian radicals who, in their anticlerical and republican fervor, would destroy the monarchy. The resulting anticlerical republic would be so radical — and outrage at what had happened to the Church and the pope would be so great — that it would inevitably provoke a European war that would end in the pope's restoration. The Italian chargé d'affaires in Berlin, in reporting all the attention that the booklet was getting in Germany, complained that the German government had so far done nothing to indicate its own repugnance for such a prospect. The Italians were all the more concerned because in recent months, Bismarck had been seeking to make peace with the Vatican and to bring the *Kulturkampf* to an end. Many worried that he could not be trusted.[14]

The pope himself ended 1881 with a belligerent address to the Sacred College of Cardinals. In reporting the speech, France's ambassador to the Holy See wrote that Leo had never before spoken out so strongly against the Italian government nor ever made his commitment to the restoration of temporal power so clear. The ambassador noted as well that a recent series of articles in *L'Osservatore Romano* had been devoted to the impossibility of the Italian king and the Roman pontiff sharing the same capital. "Does he hope," asked the ambassador, "that his protests will lead the Italian government to retreat in the face of the papacy and, as the religious press demands, leave him at least Rome and an outlet to the sea through Civitavecchia?"[15]

Civiltà Cattolica, in its report, expanded on why the pope could not remain in a city that was controlled by the Italian government. Those who had taken Rome, it argued, had done so "in order to destroy the Catholic Church." It then listed all the ways the Italian government had sought to bring about this end: it had suppressed the religious orders and seized their property; it had secularized the charitable institutions of the Church and removed the teaching of religion from the schools; it had reduced the pope to a prisoner, unable to venture out of the Vatican. But the story ended on a positive note. Good Catholics should not despair, for the Church's ultimate triumph was not far off. Next to the majesty of the pontiff, the king was a mere pygmy.[16]

15

Preparing for Exile

*T*HROUGHOUT THE 1880s, Leo repeatedly turned to the cardinals of the Curia to advise him on whether the time had come for him to flee Rome. His near obsession with whether he should go and his worries about which country would take him in are not easy to explain because he was far from eager to leave the Holy City. Despite a great deal of diplomatic bluster and the defiant claims in the Catholic press, Leo had few illusions about being able to repeat his predecessor's success in rallying foreign powers to return him triumphantly to his capital. Indeed, when he sent a list of questions to the cardinals of the Congregation for Extraordinary Ecclesiastical Affairs in early 1882, seeking their advice on flight, he prefaced them with the statement that "it can be held to be certain, without need of demonstration, that no power today would use its material force against Italy in order to restore Rome to the Pontiff in exile . . . Therefore it would today be a great illusion to hope that such a restoration could be brought about through governments' armed force."[1]

The pope's preoccupation with the possibility of leaving Rome had the effect of keeping the governments of Europe in a state of permanent agitation. Not wanting to believe that the pope would actually abandon the Holy City, yet alarmed at the destabilizing effects that such a departure would have on all of Europe, they peppered the Italian government with pleas not to do anything that might make the pope decide to go. This response was no doubt intended by the diplomatically savvy Leo XIII, acting as a brake on the more anticlerical actions being contemplated by the Italian government.[2]

In August 1884, Leo XIII issued a *motu proprio,* a secret proclamation in his own hand, "with dispositions and provisions for the Holy Congregations and Ecclesiastical Tribunals, for the case in which the Holy Pontiff's access to the faithful is interrupted, or that he is taken as a hostage." He explained that given the ever-increasing dangers faced by the Holy See, he believed it necessary to make plans that would allow the Church to continue to function if such misfortunes occurred. He proclaimed that in his absence a three-member commission of cardinals would guide the Church, listing in order of priority the cardinals who were to be appointed to it.[3]

Individual letters were then prepared by the secretary of state to each of the cardinals on the list, as well as to the papal nuncio in Vienna, explaining the two envelopes, sealed with wax, that they received. One contained instructions for the next conclave; the other contained the *motu proprio.* The first envelope was to be opened only at the time of Leo's death, the second, only on receiving further instructions; should the pope die first, it was to be returned unopened to his successor. The pope also had lengthy instructions prepared for the marquis who would be responsible for the care and protection of the Vatican in his absence.[4]

Two years later, in November 1886, Leo charged yet another secret commission of cardinals with the task of advising him on fleeing Rome. To guide them, he had a report prepared on "the current condition to which the Holy See and the Pontiff have been reduced in Rome." It is clear from subsequent discussion by the cardinals that this report presented the views of the pope himself, so it offers us a priceless peek into Leo's outlook eight years into his papacy.

"The revolution," as the report labeled the unification movement, "having occupied the Papal States, took over this Capital of the Catholic world" and left the pope "in the power of his enemies." Strikingly, the secret document acknowledges that the people of Rome were no longer on the pope's side in his battle with the Italian state. Thanks to the malevolent influence of the sects, it explained, religious indifference was widespread, and the love for the Church and the papacy had greatly declined, especially among the middle classes. Fewer and fewer people believed that it was good for the pope to have temporal power. "The constant work of these same sects, together with the liberal party, has succeeded not only in spreading doubts in Italian souls about its necessity, but has led them to contest it openly with exaggerated ideas of national independence. Even most Romans no longer share their ancient devotion to the Pontiff, their sole legitimate Sovereign."

But there were still grounds for hope. If things looked bleak in Italy, the situation abroad — notwithstanding the cowardice of Europe's governments — was very different. Outside Italy, the pope's cause was more popular than ever. And with Catholics feeling so strongly about the pontiff, their rulers could not long resist the pressure to come to his aid. All this afforded good reason "to hope that, whatever happens, the Pope's cause will not be abandoned, and that one day he will recover the place in Rome that is properly his." Paradoxically, even in Italy, where godless forces were making the Church's life so difficult, a glimmer of hope appeared, for the situation might have to get worse before it could get better. "Since the revolution continues, it corrupts the popular masses more every day and so ineluctably pushes them to socialism and anarchy." But once the direction they were heading in became clearer, the report argued, Italians would finally "shake off their lethargy and inertia. They will refuse to tolerate religious persecution or the Freemason's yoke any longer." They would at last realize that the pope was their only hope, that only the pontiff could bring stability to Rome, to Italy, and to Europe.[5]

The commission met on November 1, 1886, to consider this report. The pope and the whole Church, the first cardinal to speak lamented, find themselves in a pitiful condition. "The painful situation of the Holy See, more or less openly besieged for sixteen years in Rome, and almost for twenty-six in all Italy, is only getting worse."

We should have no illusions, he warned. Italy had become a unified state only through the occult efforts of the various sects and the Masons, committed to the extermination of the Church "either through open violence or through the hypocritical ploys of which the sectarians are the finest masters." A new ruling class of unbelievers, "moved by a blind hatred of the Church," had arisen in Italy. The cardinal then gingerly criticized Pius IX and his mystical faith in divine intervention: "Who knows what would have happened if, after . . . denouncing to the whole world the nature of the Revolution whose victim he was, the octogenarian Pontiff, so popular everywhere, had taken the path of the pilgrim, leaving his city behind him?" But today it was too late. "If I raise this hypothesis now," he said, "it is to illustrate how, when we had the chance to destroy the evil work of the government, we perhaps failed to figure out how to do it."

Might Leo, the cardinal asked, be able to turn to Europe's other powers for help? The continent's two major conservative forces, he observed, were Germany and Austria, but the first was Protestant, and the second, while Europe's foremost Catholic power, had a government that was not well disposed to the Church.[6]

What most worried the pope in these months was that a major war would break out in Europe, one in which Italy would be a combatant. A year earlier, the monarchists had won a major victory in the French parliamentary elections and installed a wildly popular new minister of war, General Georges Boulanger, who was known for his desire to avenge France's humiliating defeat by Germany. At the same time, Austria was embroiled in a tense struggle with tsarist Russia over control of the Balkans, and war seemed increasingly likely.

At a mid-January 1887 meeting of the pope's secret commission, a cardinal warned that, given all the tensions plaguing Europe, a general conflagration could erupt at any time. If that were to happen, he said, the pope should immediately announce his departure from Rome, explaining that it was necessary both to ensure his ability to perform his religious mission freely and to put himself in a position to play the role of peacemaker. As for where he should go, it was important that he find a party not at war. The cardinal suggested two possibilities: Monaco and the Italian-speaking canton of Ticino in Switzerland.

But the cardinals were divided. Any flight from Rome under such circumstances, said one, risked outraging the Italians, who would accuse the pope of going abroad so that he could better conspire with foreign nations against them. Another questioned the choice of destination: Monaco was fine, but not Ticino, for Switzerland was swarming with the very sects that were the Church's worst enemies

At this point Leo asked Father Giuseppe Graniello, a Barnabite monk whose advice he greatly valued, to prepare a report on these issues to help guide their discussions. The report, a remarkably rich document, was presented to the cardinals in mid-February.

The effect that a European war would have on Italy, wrote Graniello, was not easy to predict. Italy might end up on the winning side, but there was a good chance that it would be defeated, in which case foreign armies would certainly occupy the Italian North. Of particular concern to the monk was the distinct possibility that, in the face of this occupation, popular revolts would sweep the rest of the peninsula, leading to the fall of the monarchy and leaving Rome at the mercy of the republicans and other anticlerics.

Rather than hasten the return of temporal rule, Graniello warned, the pope's leaving Rome might well make it more difficult. Should Italy win the war, there was of course no chance that temporal power would be restored to the pope. But if the pontiff had in the meantime fled Rome, Graniello warned, "the government would place the most humiliating and harshest conditions on his return." As a result, he would have to remain abroad "as long as the sacrilegious usurpation lasts."

If, on the other hand, the Italians lost the war but still held on to Rome, Graniello advised, the crucial question was whether an armistice would mandate an international congress to determine Rome's final status. If such a congress were held, the pope's temporal power might be restored, at least in some form. Yet even in this situation, Graniello warned, much could go wrong. Many European governments, he noted, were in the grip of the sects. They were hardly interested in restoring the papacy's powers and cared nothing for public opinion. And there was another problem. Even if they sympathized with the pope's plight, the European powers were likely to be influenced more by their own political calculations. From their perspective, a territorially reduced Kingdom of Italy whose legitimacy continued to be contested by the Church was an attractive prospect, for such a state would be perennially weak.

Yet, the monk acknowledged, there were some grounds for hope. An international postwar conference might well decide to return Rome to the pope. For one thing, Europe's governments were tired of being pestered by their Catholic populations about the pontiff's imprisonment. Second, all were worried about the revolutionary movements that were sweeping Europe. They saw the pope and the Church as bastions of the conservative social order and the main source of legitimacy for authoritarian regimes, especially in the Catholic portions of the continent. A pope restored to the fullness of his power could work to their advantage. It was also in these governments' interests, Graniello argued, for Italy to be stable. As it was, Italy was a cauldron of unrest, and the embattled state of the papacy simply encouraged further instability.

Clearly, the best outcome of a war for the Holy See would be, not only Italy's defeat, but also the seizure of Rome by foreign forces in the course of the fighting. In such a case, he concluded, the restoration of the Papal States, at least in the area around Rome, was "very probable."[7]

When the cardinals began discussing this report, the politically savvy, aristocratic Wlodzimierz Czacki, whose aunt had married one of Rome's foremost noblemen and who had recently served as papal nuncio to Paris — a Pole surrounded by Italians — was the chief opponent of any departure from Rome. Picking up on Graniello's own hesitations, he asked where Leo would go. No one was eager to take him in, he said. All were urging him to stay in Rome, and all feared that having him in another country would undermine Europe's balance of power. "Any power that took him in for long would ruin its relations with other powers and with Italy. It would have to do a great deal at home to rein in the enthusiasms of the one side while repressing the sectarian hatreds of the other. No power would want to give the pope extraterritorial rights, nor allow a foreign diplomatic corps accredited to him, a precious legacy of temporal power." It appears that what most worried Czacki, one of the foremost champions of French Catholic interests in the Vatican, was the chance that the pope might end up in Germany. Such an exile, as some had suggested, Czacki warned, "would place us in the worst light in the eyes of all the Catholic powers, who would accuse us of having put ourselves at the service of a Protestant Power." And, he added, if the pope were to flee, the Italians would likely seize all of the Vatican's treasures, claiming them as part of the national patrimony.

Cardinal Monaco, the commission's imposing president, said that the critical question was whether, if the pope were to leave Rome, he would be able to return fairly soon, and to return with honor. Even if Czacki's fears about the Vatican palaces were exaggerated, Cardinal Monaco warned, "it is nonetheless certain that the Powers would not lift a finger if the Holy See were robbed of its property, and nothing suggests any improvement in their behavior in the future. Now, given the current state of things, there would be no certainty of any sufficiently rapid return, much less a return with honor." And so, he concluded, "the Pope should stay, except in the case of extreme violence."

But not all of Cardinal Monaco's colleagues agreed with him. To await the outbreak of war before taking action would be reckless, said one cardinal, for it would expose the pope and the members of the

Curia to great danger. Once war began, departure might well become impossible, and so, he urged, the pope should leave immediately. History held many examples of such departures from Rome, the cardinal pointed out, and they had all ended well, with the pope back in Rome and the Papal States restored.

Although most cardinals shared the more cautious views of Czacki and Monaco, they dutifully turned to the pope's question of where he might go. The principality of Monaco was dismissed as being defenseless and lacking suitable quarters. One cardinal proposed Malta, but it was deemed too isolated by the others. Gradually the cardinals converged on the choice of Spain. True, it had a liberal government that was not sufficiently respectful of the Church, and some of its political parties were hostile. But in Spain, they were sure, the people would venerate the pope and feel honored to have him in their midst. If a proper agreement on conditions could be reached with the Spanish government, they concluded, the pope and his Curia could feel safe there.[8]

16

Hopes Dashed

ALTHOUGH LEO XIII SAW HIMSELF as strong-willed, he was painfully torn. Something, he thought, had to be done to save the Church. Simply hewing to Pius IX's uncompromising stance, he realized, risked isolating the Church further. Surrounded by intransigents urging him to reject all compromise with the Italian state, the pope was tempted to try to find a way of making peace.

He was encouraged, not only by a number of churchmen whose advice he valued, but also by some signs of an opening on the part of the Italian government itself. The visceral anticlericalism of its leaders — men like Depretis and Crispi — had not changed, but they were increasingly coming to appreciate how much could be gained by reaching an agreement with the Church. The Vatican's opposition meant that Italian diplomats were constantly on the defensive. And the rift with the Church was exacting new costs in the 1880s, for Italy's rulers were beginning to dream of a colonial empire, something they thought no self-respecting European power could do without. With Catholic missions scattered throughout many of the lands the Europeans sought to colonize, the Italians realized that Church support could be tremendously helpful.

On the Vatican's side, too, were those who believed it was time — more than a quarter of a century after the founding of the Kingdom of Italy — for the Church to find a way to recognize the state. Most notable of these champions of reconciliation was Monsignor Luigi Galimberti, by 1886 the secretary of the Congregation for Extraordinary Ecclesiastical Affairs and the man who in 1887 would go to Berlin and successfully negotiate an end to the anti-Church *Kulturkampf*. Born in Rome to a modest family in 1836, as a young priest he became professor of Church history at the college attached to Propaganda Fide, the congregation in the Vatican that oversees the Church outside Europe — thus explaining the derisory characterization given him by the noble Cardinal Czacki, who called him "that little teacher of Negroes." Galimberti came to the attention of the pope soon after his elevation to the papacy and quickly rose to influence.[1]

Galimberti distrusted the republican French government, believing that the two central empires of Germany and Austria offered the Church greater protection in the long run. He also distrusted the French Catholics, whose strident opposition to the Vatican's reconciliation with Italy he thought posed a great danger. These feelings were fully reciprocated by France's conservative Catholics. One of the more acerbic of them characterized Galimberti in the darkest of terms: "There is also in the Vatican a spy of the [German] chancellor, masquerading as priest, who has as his mission that of playing on the pontiff's pride. This ecclesiastic is named Galimberti . . . It is he who works to make of the present [papal] reign one of the most inauspicious ever." Several years later, one of France's correspondents in the Vatican described Galimberti — by then a cardinal — more charitably:

> Cardinal Galimberti has a fox's brain in an artist's head. He offers a contrast with Cardinal Rampolla, his rival. A historian, he has read Machiavelli and Gioberti [a liberal Italian priest and political philosopher of the 1830s and 1840s] above all. A diplomat, he has frequented the courts of Vienna and Berlin. A philosopher and a man of the Church, he has the soul of an old-fashioned liberal and idolizes the Italian and Roman traditions. A lucid mind . . . lover of all that is beautiful and elegant; a tactician of the highest order, Cardinal Galimberti is not the skeptical opportunist that his enemies would like to paint him as. He has a clear, precise, particular view . . . He is an 1830s liberal in the body of a sixteenth-century prelate.[2]

Galimberti was not alone in pushing the pope toward reconciliation. Geremia Bonomelli, the highly respected bishop of Cremona, sent Leo a note of Christmas greetings in 1886. "In the brief span of little more than eight years," he told the pope, "you have accomplished many great things . . . above all finding a way to end so many serious conflicts that had arisen between other States and the Holy See." Following this effusive preface, he got to his point: "Holy Father, in this most propitious year of Your Jubilee, you can crown your achievements with the most arduous yet most necessary of all work, the pacification of our Country, offering relief to all people of good faith." Time was short, said the bishop: "Let us not delude ourselves, today's educated youth, who one day will be the leaders of Society, are slowly growing ever more distant from the Church, setting the stage inevitably for the apostasy of the entire nation. What then will become of the Holy See, in the midst of a society made up not only of unbelievers but of those who are fiercely hostile?"

The pope replied in a letter that, together with the bishop's note, was widely circulated in the Italian press: "That you pray for help from the Father so that peace can also be procured for our own lands from the war [against the Church] that has afflicted us, corresponds perfectly to Our own wishes, for seeing the harsh condition of things, we can only put our faith in God's help." This typically ambiguous papal reply was viewed by some as suggesting that Leo might in fact be contemplating a new approach to the Italian state.

Hopes of conciliation sprang from another source in late January 1887 as a result of events in Ethiopia, connected to Italy's early (and characteristically disastrous) colonial exploits. Five hundred Italian soldiers, on their way to relieve their comrades in Eritrea, were massacred. At scores of funerals and commemorations for the victims back home, the mixture of Catholic clergy, Catholic rites with patriotic themes, and government officials led to a growing belief that a way would be found to end the church-state divide. Among the most widely reprinted patriotic remarks were those given at one such ceremony by Bishop Bonomelli in Cremona.[3]

The intransigent forces in the Vatican were growing increasingly alarmed, blaming Galimberti for the pope's vacillation. Meeting on March 4, the cardinals complained that Leo seemed to be entrusting the Church's affairs to Galimberti and in so doing was insulting the Sacred College of Cardinals. They were all the more concerned because Cardinal Jacobini, the secretary of state, had died a few days earlier, and there was widespread speculation that Galimberti would take his place.

On the Italian side, those favoring conciliation were convinced that it was now time for a new government initiative. On April 10, Giuseppe Toscanelli, a member of parliament known for favoring the Church, wrote to the prime minister, Depretis. His letter soon appeared in the press.

Arguing that the current law of guarantees was inadequate, Toscanelli proposed a solution: "I believe that, if one recognizes that the supreme Head of the Catholic Church is both the sovereign by right and the de facto sovereign of the Vatican, and if he were given land stretching out toward the countryside, sufficiently large to construct the buildings that form part of the universal Church, as for example those for Propaganda Fide and the headquarters of the religious orders, then one would have a profane Rome and a sacred Rome. Foreign rulers, coming to Rome, would visit both of the sovereigns." Toscanelli went on to assure Depretis that he was not proposing a return to the old temporal power of the pope but something much more modest: "In this way, which would change the current situation of our government very little and would greatly improve that of the universal Catholic Church, there would be, in addition to the Republic of San Marino, a Catholic republic with its elected sovereign, and peace would return between State and Church." Later, Toscanelli recalled telling Depretis that "the whole question came down to a strip of land that gave the Vatican access to the sea, it being understood that the strip remained Italian territory, although Vatican immunities would be extended to it."[4]

Other signs of a possible breakthrough also appeared in April. When the government discovered that the new equestrian statue of Victor Emmanuel II, scheduled to be unveiled in Venice, had a decidedly anticlerical cast — the papal tiara and Saint Peter's keys were shown being trampled beneath one of the horse's hoofs — the dedication ceremonies were postponed and the papal symbols ordered removed.[5] That same month, the king and his ministers participated in the unveiling of the restored façade of the cathedral of Florence, Santa Maria del Fiore, standing alongside the archbishop of Florence and many of Tuscany's bishops. The day before the ceremonies, the archbishop went to greet King Umberto, who, in gratitude, gave him five thousand lire for one of the archbishop's charities. During the singing of the Te Deum, King Umberto and the archbishop publicly shook hands, and the queen and the prince kissed the archbishop's ring. Word of the encounter quickly spread, with the handshake between king and archbishop transformed by popular imagination into a hearty embrace. A colorful image of the king and the pope, arm in arm, chatting affably, soon became one of the most popular prints sold on street corners throughout Italy.[6]

Other evidence of reconciliation comes from Germany. The grand duke of Baden, writing to Galimberti several years later, asked if he recalled a conversation they had had in Berlin in March 1887: "Among the questions that we discussed there was one that, at the time, assumed great importance. It was the question of a neutral territory joining the Leonine City with the sea! Do you think that the time was right then for the realization of that project?"[7]

The major Catholic newspapers were, meanwhile, showing their uneasiness at any such talk. On May 19, the Vatican's *Osservatore Romano* disputed the rumors, adding that all the proposals being discussed had come from the "liberal" party, their true purpose being "to destroy the Catholic Church in Italy in general and in Rome in particular."[8]

Events soon came to a head. On May 23, 1887, the pope addressed the cardinals gathered for the naming of new members of the Sacred College. After expressing his pleasure at the recently concluded agreement with the German government, he turned his attention to Italy: "As We have indicated on various other occasions, We have long fervently desired security and tranquility for all Italian souls, and wanted the ruinous discord with the Roman Pontiff finally ended, but always remembering that this can only be done in keeping with justice and dignity for the Apostolic See . . . the only path to harmony is by ensuring that the Roman Pontiff is not subject to anyone else's power and enjoys full and true freedom." Such an arrangement, Leo XIII argued, "would not only not damage Italy's interests in any way, but, on the contrary, would increase its safety and well-being." That the pope would speak of possible reconciliation without explicitly demanding the return of temporal power came as a surprise. As one of those present later recalled, the pope's words "shocked all of the cardinals there." *L'Osservatore Romano* quickly tried to reassure the intransigents of the Church: the pope had been clear, conciliation could only come about if the state dealt justly with the Church. "Justice demands one thing and is inflexible . . . it requires the reestablishment of the temporal power, especially over the city of Rome."[9]

Seven days after the pope's ambiguous remarks caused such an up-roar, another event took place, which was widely viewed as part of his unfolding plan to strike a deal with the government. A Benedictine ab-bot, Luigi Tosti, known to be close to the pope, published a booklet, "Conciliation," which urged Leo to mark his fiftieth anniversary as a priest in 1888 by ending the hostility between the Holy See and the Ital-ian state. Tosti, born in Naples in 1811 to a noble family, had first met Gioacchino Pecci in 1839, decades before he became pope. They quickly became friends. At that time, before the revolutions of 1848, Tosti had enthusiastically supported the idea that Italian unification could best come about by creating a confederation of small states under the presi-dency of the pope himself. After the proclamation of the Kingdom of Italy in 1861, Tosti was eager to find a way to bring about conciliation between the papacy and the monarchy.

Pius IX had also been fond of the aristocratic abbot, referring to him affectionately as "that good nut Tosti." But given the gulf between Pius's politics and Tosti's, the abbot's earlier hopes of becoming a car-dinal were crushed, and he would remain a simple priest. His political inclinations and his connections with men high in the government were, nonetheless, exploited by both Pius IX and later Leo XIII. A use-ful intermediary, he is credited with saving numerous Church insti-tutions in Rome from government expropriation. At one point, the Italian government even named him as the superintendent of sacred monuments in the Holy City. At the time "Conciliation" was pub-lished, Tosti worked in the Vatican as vice-archivist of the Holy See.[10]

When the booklet came out on May 31, it was widely believed that the pope had already read a copy and given his tacit approval, using Tosti to launch a trial balloon. Just four days earlier, the pope had sent Tosti to see Francesco Crispi, the minister of the interior, on a mission similar to many he had performed in the past: he was to convince the government to reverse a decision to take control of one of Rome's Church properties. The unofficial nature of the encounter is reflected by their meeting in Crispi's home. But Tosti did not limit himself to this request, as later recalled by Crispi himself:

"The abbot had advised Leo XIII to enter St. Peter's and once again perform his ecclesiastical duties in public. His Holiness was not [said Tosti] opposed. He however first wanted to be sure that the Govern-ment would guarantee the peaceful exercise of his duties. The pope would take advantage of his upcoming jubilee to present himself to the public. That occasion seemed most propitious to the abbot for the pope and the king to meet. Just as had happened at the cathedral of Florence, where the king was received by the archbishop, the king would be received by the pope. If this proposal were accepted in principle, one could later work out the exact conditions and terms."

"I replied," wrote Crispi, "that I would guarantee public safety. The pope would have nothing to fear in the exercise of his ecclesiastical duties . . . But I cannot say the same regarding the appearance of the king and queen in St. Peter's. It is a subject that must be discussed with the prime minister and perhaps by the whole cabinet. I would also have to talk to the king. After I have done so, we can speak of it again."[11]

Two days later, Crispi did speak to the king, and Umberto expressed his interest in the abbot's proposal. Crispi then sent Tosti a note encouraging him to go ahead, writing that he looked forward to "a favorable solution." On June 4 the men met again for two hours. There was reason to believe that a historic agreement between the Holy See and the Italian state might finally be at hand.[12]

But any hopes for a breakthrough were soon disappointed. L'Osservatore Romano published a violent attack on Tosti's booklet, which had produced a chorus of outrage from the powerful intransigents in the Curia and beyond. Pressure mounted on the abbot to retract the work and on the pope to make clear that it did not reflect his own sentiments, that he remained committed to the need for temporal power. The Vatican newspaper announced that Tosti would soon publish a retraction, but the note that Tosti furnished was deemed wholly inadequate. Alongside his note, the newspaper published a column denouncing his booklet, which it said had "disgusted the souls of sincere Catholics." It concluded: "For these reasons all individuals of good sense know just how ludicrous is the claim by certain newspapers that this booklet was, if not inspired by, at least known to the Vatican before its publication. And we are authorized to state that such a claim is completely false."[13]

Did the pope read the text before it was published? There is some reason to think that he did not, although Tosti almost certainly told the pope that he was preparing it and was given some kind of tacit approval. In a letter to Crispi on May 28, Tosti reported: "My little booklet on behalf of conciliation, while not read, is in harmony with the

Vatican's desires." A well-informed source of the time offers an insight about what most likely happened. In this account, when the pope heard that Tosti was about to publish his booklet, he asked to see it. Tosti demurred, responding that it would be better if the pope could say he never read the text in advance, and so avoid responsibility for what it contained.[14]

The Vatican's pressure against conciliation had been intense even before Tosti's booklet came out. In late May, after the pope's seeming — albeit timid — opening to conciliation in his address to the cardinals, *L'Osservatore Romano* had already tried to calm the waters. The pope, the paper insisted, had in no way meant to suggest that the return of temporal power was unnecessary. At the same time, Rome's other major Catholic daily, *La Voce della Verità*, explained that the pope's generic invocation in his remarks of the need for justice "implied the restoration of temporal power, especially over Rome." In response, the Roman newspaper most closely identified with the royal court, *Fanfulla,* charged that the two Catholic newspapers' remarks "do not correspond either to Leo XIII's words nor to his sentiments . . . The Holy Father has been pained by the wholly arbitrary behavior of those behind these papers." Leo again found himself in a difficult position. Things were getting out of control.[15]

The pope had a decision to make, one that would have great consequences. Both the intransigents and those favoring reconciliation were nervous about whom the pope would choose to be the new secretary of state. Cardinal Jacobini had died at the end of February, and Galimberti had been functioning in that role ever since Jacobini had first taken ill, the previous summer. Galimberti's appointment would be a sure sign that the pope wanted to bring about reconciliation with the Italian state.

On April 18 the pope called Galimberti in to discuss the future. Recently returned from his triumphs in Berlin, Galimberti hoped that the pope would tell him of his appointment as secretary of state and the cardinal's hat that would go with it. His hopes had been given a boost earlier in the month when word leaked out that the pope had asked his Perugian advisers — the group of aides who had followed him to the Vatican from Perugia — to investigate the precedents for appointing a prelate to the secretary of state post who was not yet a cardinal. They reported back that Pius VII had set just such a precedent when he appointed the man regarded by many as the greatest secretary of state of modern times, Ercole Consalvi. Consalvi was made a cardinal only after his appointment.[16]

But Galimberti was in for a great disappointment. With a tone of regret, the pope told him simply: "They advise me to appoint Rampolla."

Galimberti was devastated. Mariano Rampolla, the up-and-coming intransigent, was one of the last people he wanted in that position.

"Well then, Holiness," Galimberti replied, "I'll go to serve as a canon in St. Peter's."

Leo tried to reassure him that his diplomatic services were still valued: "No, my dear don Luigi, we have a post worthy of you," said the pope. "We are sending you to Vienna." And, before the crestfallen bishop left Leo's quarters, the pope offered him some consolation, at least according to Galimberti's later report to his friend, the Bavarian ambassador: "Should Cardinal Rampolla not work out," said the pope, "I can always recall you to Rome at a moment's notice." Galimberti was far from mollified. "For over six months," he confided to a friend, "I have, more or less alone, conducted all the [Vatican's] international political affairs, and now all of a sudden I am supposed to be . . . subordinated to a secretary of state who knows absolutely nothing of all of these matters."[17]

Kurd von Schlözer, Berlin's ambassador to the Holy See, to whom Galimberti directed these remarks, could not have been too surprised. Several months earlier, in October 1886, in reporting Jacobini's physical inability to do his duties as secretary of state, he had written to Bismarck of the infighting at the Vatican: "In recent times the group of intransigents and other Vatican factions have repeatedly tried to distance Monsignor Galimberti from the vicinity of the pope . . . The Jesuits are doing everything they can to impose as the pro-secretary of state their favorite, Rampolla, currently nuncio in Madrid."[18]

And so Galimberti, proponent of conciliation, was sent off as nuncio to Austria, where he would come under the heavy thumb of the new secretary of state. Rampolla's appointment was announced on June 2, in the midst of the uproar over Father Tosti's *Conciliazione*.[19]

Described by the German ambassador as a "vibrant soul with a cool head," Rampolla had recently returned from five years as papal nuncio to Spain. Forty-four years old, he had been made a cardinal only two months earlier. The speedy promotion engendered considerable jealousy among his colleagues, offset only partially by the satisfaction many of them drew from seeing a committed intransigent become secretary of state. Born into an aristocratic Sicilian family, Rampolla had spent most of his youth in Rome and from early on had been on the fast track of the Vatican diplomatic service. Polyglot, pious, known for his extraordinary capacity for work, he would serve as secretary of state for fifteen years, until Leo's death in 1903.[20]

The full implications of Rampolla's appointment were not immediately clear. Ever since his elevation to the papacy, Leo had surrounded himself with a tightly knit group of trusted advisers whom he brought with him from Perugia; they were known in Vatican circles as the Perugians and viewed as the pope's secret cabinet. These men had great influence, for the pope made no diplomatic decision without consulting them. All three of his previous secretaries of state had been rather weak figures, a product of the pope's heavy reliance on this secret cabinet and his desire not to repeat what he saw as his predecessor's mistake in allowing his secretary of state to become so powerful. Leo wanted to keep close, direct control of all of the Vatican's diplomatic activity.[21]

How much difference would the choice of Rampolla make? And how much influence might Galimberti — known to be very close to the Perugians — continue to have, even from abroad? There were those who underestimated Rampolla, believing that Leo had appointed him thinking him to be young, weak, and unassertive. The French ambassador to Spain, who had observed the new secretary of state as nuncio in Madrid, described him as a tireless worker but lacking in any initiative of his own. "He carries out the instructions he has been given with the stubbornness and craftiness of a peasant," he wrote to Paris just weeks after Rampolla's appointment, but, he claimed, the pope had not deemed him sufficiently strong to serve as his nuncio in Paris. Nor was the new secretary of state especially well liked in the diplomatic community. As the Bavarian ambassador to the Holy See put it, describing the impression gained from Rampolla's first meetings with the foreign diplomatic corps at the Vatican: "Cardinal Rampolla is judicious, circumspect, and very unpleasant."[22]

But if Rampolla began his fifteen-year reign in a rather weak position, with the pope's Perugian secret cabinet continuing to have a great influence over the pope, the balance would soon change. With Leo becoming ever more slowed by age over the next years and with Rampolla increasingly gaining confidence, the pope found himself the subject of the same kinds of gossip that had plagued his predecessor. Bishop Bonomelli, no friend of the intransigent Rampolla, would lament in a letter to a friend: "It has always been a mystery to me whether Rampolla guided Leo or if Leo towed Rampolla along." But this comment came years later. For the moment, the battle was still joined, the victor not yet clear.[23]

If the situation in the Vatican was chaotic in these weeks, the Italian government was hardly more harmonious. Informed of Tosti's mission, King Umberto and the royal court hoped that reconciliation with the Church might finally be at hand. But the king did not trust Crispi, not only because of his notorious anticlericalism but also because of his penchant for acting in his own self-interest. And so the king sent one of his aides to feel out the Vatican directly, without informing his minister.[24] Given Crispi's dense network of informers, it was not long before he learned of this move. When, on June 9, Crispi next met with Tosti, by now the object of fierce attack in the Vatican and Catholic press, he castigated him for dealing with the royal family behind his back. The beleaguered abbot tried to defend himself, insisting that he had only done what the king had asked of him.

The following day Giovanni Bovio, parliament's most prominent anticlerical deputy, rose to question the government about the stories of secret dealings with the Vatican. It is possible that Bovio was prompted by Crispi himself, who by this time was worried that matters were getting out of his control and wanted to prevent the king from striking a separate deal. What, asked Bovio, did they hope to accomplish by negotiating a formal agreement with the Vatican? Wasn't the current legislation sufficient to guarantee freedom of religion and the freedom of the Church? Such a deal, he fumed, would produce the worst of both worlds, "a pact of mutual mediocrity between State and Church, a pope who is half a prince, a State that is half Catholic, in a common morass of half institutions, half men and half religion."

Crispi rose to reply. The law of guarantees, he said, already offered the Church full protection. "We do not ask for any conciliations, nor are they needed," he insisted, "because the State is not at war with anyone." Cries of "*benissimo!*" rang out from the left. "Nor do we know or want to know what those in the Vatican think. Leo XIII is not an ordinary man. The times are changing, they are softening, extinguishing the fiercest animosities, and this might lead to greater understanding between Church and State. But for our part, none of the national law sanctioned by the plebiscites will be touched. Italy belongs to itself, and to itself alone. It has but one head: the king." With this final flourish, the banks of the deputies erupted in loud voices of assent.[25]

The Vatican charged that Crispi's combative speech had finally made his allegiances clear. He was, they said, a tool of the Freemasons, part of the conspiracy of the sects against Christianity. Although overdrawn, the charge had some credibility, for by the late 1880s the Freemasons were becoming increasingly influential in Italian politics, and Crispi himself had not only long been a mason but was an old friend of the dynamic new Italian grand master, Adriano Lemmi.

For years Lemmi, a wealthy banker from a Jewish family in Livorno, had funded a variety of republican and anticlerical organizations. But even before he became grand master in 1885, the masons' opposition to the Catholic Church was deeply entrenched.[26] In early 1882, for example, the grand master of the time, Giuseppe Petroni — the same former longtime political prisoner of the Papal States who had chaired the Politeama anticlerical meeting a few months earlier — sent out a long letter to all the Grand Orient lodges in Italy. "The intolerance, the haughtiness, the unbridled ambitions of the Church of Rome, its avarice for honors and riches, its immoral dealings with the most despicable tyrannies, its most irrational superstitions, hatred for work, for science, and for truth have delivered the final blow." By contrast, the Freemasons, in Petroni's depiction, championed "the immortal principles of justice, of civilization, of progress, tolerance, freedom, equality, and human brotherhood." In many ways, although Petroni would not appreciate the comparison, the Freemasons' language echoed the Church's: each believed it was locked in a historic battle between good and evil, and each branded the other a demonic sect.[27]

When, shortly after Lemmi became grand master, Crispi became prime minister, Lemmi began firing off letter after letter to his old friend, urging him to resist efforts at compromise. A flavor of these missives comes from Lemmi's warning to Crispi in November 1887 about a prefect in the northern city of Pavia who, he complained, was too soft on the Church. He told Crispi that, despite the ban on the Jesuit order, Jesuits had set up schools and colleges in Pavia. Its city council and mayor had objected, and popular protests had filled the streets, but the prefect, who was responsible for such matters, had done nothing. Lemmi urged Crispi to act immediately. "Send the prefect of Pavia to Hell," he wrote, "and the others will realize that they can no longer get into bed with the priests." The government's task was clear: "The only enemy of our Institutions is the papacy. It is necessary to combat it and its allies without respite."[28]

If the Freemasons were outraged by the prospect of reconciliation, the French were displeased as well, if for very different reasons. Both the French Church hierarchy and, especially, Catholic organizations and publications were strong proponents of the intransigent line. When they learned earlier in 1887 that the pope might be opening the door to reconciliation, they were confused and upset. Nor was the French government — in the hands of men not known for their love of the Church — any more eager to see a reconciliation, especially now that Italy was part of the Triple Alliance. Italy's continuing battle with the Holy See meant the continuing weakness of the Italian state, something they welcomed. And France's ability to expand its own colonial empire — a national priority at the time — would be compromised if the Vatican's resources abroad, through its missionary network, were deployed on behalf of the Italians.[29]

A book published the following year by Jules Cornély offers a clear — if chilling — view of the thinking then current among France's Catholics. He was convinced that reconciliation of the pope with Italy's king would be catastrophic. On the day that the pope first emerged from the Vatican and traveled through Rome's streets, he admitted, there would no doubt be "delirious enthusiasm such as to shake the Coliseum from its ancient supports." But the Catholics' elation would soon turn to despair, he predicted, for despite the pope's best efforts, and even those of the Italian royal family itself, the pontiff would inevitably become a mere vassal of the Italian king. "St. Peter's successor," Cornély argued, "would be no more than the first among the Italian bishops." Europe's rulers would then understandably become suspicious of the devout Roman Catholics in their midst, viewing them as at the bidding of the Italian king. Fearful of such disloyalty, Europe's governments would establish separate, national churches in their countries. It would certainly be the case in France, where any reconciliation of the pope with the Italian state would produce a schism, a national French Catholic Church forming in opposition to a philo-Italian Roman Catholic Church. From the French Catholic point of view, then, reconciliation was the last thing to be desired. A captive pope was still a pope, proud and independent, concluded Cornély, but a "pope free and venturing outside the Vatican is a pope who is an Italian subject, that is a submissive pope, and a submissive pope is no longer a pope."[30]

Leo was now in full retreat. The time had come to make his rejection of conciliation clear, and he decided to do so in a letter formally addressed to his new secretary of state. That Leo's intended audience was in fact the larger Catholic world is clear, for the letter quickly found its way into the pages of newspapers across the continent. When it first appeared, on July 26, a number of observers expressed skepticism about its date, June 15, speculating that the pope had predated the letter to create the impression that he had abandoned his efforts at reconciliation earlier than he had in fact done so.[31]

The letter could not have been any clearer: no pope could give up the claim to temporal power. "Defending and maintaining civil sovereignty," Leo XIII wrote, was his "sacred duty" as pontiff.

> With divine help, we certainly will not fail in our duty and, until there is a return to a true and effective sovereignty, which Our independence and the dignity of the Apostolic See requires, we do not see any other room for agreements and for peace . . . Up until now the only means that Providence has provided for ensuring . . . the freedom of the popes has been their temporal sovereign power, and when this means was lacking, the Pontiffs were always either persecuted, or imprisoned, or exiled or certainly in a condition of dependence and in continuous danger of seeing themselves cast on one or the other of these paths. The whole history of the Church attests to this.

Were Italy to give the pope the position that was rightfully his, wrote Leo, it would benefit enormously, for having been blessed by Providence with being "the nation closest to the papacy, so it is destined to receive the greatest reward if it does not combat or oppose it." Those who argue that restoring the pope's sovereignty would undermine Italian independence, he said, could not be more mistaken. "It is incontrovertible that the cities and the regions formerly subject to the pontiff's civil authority were for this very reason the same ones most often saved from falling under foreign domination, and they have always retained their purely Italian character and customs. Nor would it be any different today."[32]

The publication of this letter came only after the pope and his new secretary of state had laid the groundwork for a new Church offensive throughout Europe. In one of a number of such dispatches to his nuncios, Cardinal Rampolla wrote on July 17 to Galimberti in Vienna with word of the upcoming papal pronouncement and instructions for organizing support. "The Holy Father," the letter began, "is planning in the near future to publicize an act of the greatest importance . . . which will in effect contain the program that the Holy See plans to follow in its beneficial action toward the various peoples and governments, and that will at the same time give the last authoritative word on the Roman question, aimed at removing any equivocations and illusions." Rampolla then spelled out the pope's message: "He will insist in the clearest and most explicit way on reclaiming territorial sovereignty as the indispensable means needed for the free exercise and independence of the apostolic ministry, and in particular Rome, destined by Providence to be the permanent seat of the Vicar of Jesus Christ."

The reason for alerting the nuncios to the upcoming papal announcement was to give them time to organize local support for the pope. "It is easy to predict that an act of such importance will provoke the ire and the complaints of the liberal and sectarian press, anger and complaints that will find an echo, albeit weaker, in the Austro-Hungarian Empire . . . It is therefore necessary to begin immediately making plans for a proper defense so that the first impressions are favorable to the Holy See's cause." Rampolla went on to specify what exactly he had in mind: "Use all of your zeal in preparing a splendid campaign, both through articles, which you might very well write yourself, to publish in the newspapers, and through the publication of booklets written by someone who is highly respected . . . In a word, use all means possible."[33]

But of equal concern to Leo was the state of the Church in Italy, where he feared that, outside the Vatican, his new intransigent stance was likely to meet resistance. Although he most enjoyed the world of international diplomacy, he knew that he had to tend as well to the thorny politics of the Italian Church hierarchy. Something had to be done to ensure that Italy's bishops — not known for their discipline or for their interest in working together — hewed closely to his new line.

17

The Bishops' Lament

ON JULY 20, 1887, Leo XIII instructed his secretary of state to arrange for a secret mission. The man they chose for the delicate task, the thirty-two-year-old Monsignor Giacomo Della Chiesa, was not coincidentally a close friend and protégé of Rampolla. Having recently served as Rampolla's secretary in Spain, Della Chiesa had returned to Rome with him just two months earlier. As it turned out, Della Chiesa was a man with a bright future: a quarter-century later, he would become pope himself. Recognizing his talent, Leo and Rampolla entrusted the young priest with a series of private meetings with the archbishops of Florence, Bologna, Venice, Genoa, and Turin. The central message he was to convey, Rampolla told him, was simple: "The Holy Father declares authoritatively that Italy's reconciliation with the papacy is impossible except on the sole basis of the restitution of territorial sovereignty and the restitution of Rome to the Holy Pontiff." The archbishops were to see to it that the bishops under their jurisdiction kept their flocks from being seduced by the reconciliation movement.

The papal envoy arrived at his first destination on Friday morning, July 22, and presented the archbishop of Florence, Monsignor Lecconi, with a letter from Rampolla. "When I mentioned the need for the Episcopacy to show itself more united with the pope than ever," Della Chiesa later reported, "he observed that this was indeed even more necessary now that the liberal newspapers seem to want to divide the bishops into two parties, praising those whom they suppose are more devoted and loyal to the Savoyard dynasty, and holding in contempt those who avoided having contacts with the Italian Sovereigns."

Della Chiesa replied, "The pope declares authoritatively that the reconciliation of the papacy with Italy is not possible except on the sole basis of the restitution of the temporal dominion and of Rome to the Holy Pontiff."

"I'm pleased to hear it," said Monsignor Lecconi, saying that these views accorded fully with his own. He added that he had been disturbed by the way the press had twisted the pope's May 23 comments to the Sacred College to suggest that he was willing to renounce his claim to temporal power.

The papal envoy then tried to turn the archbishop's attention to a plan of action, asking what help the pope could expect to come from Florence. Might, for example, local lay organizations be mobilized? Monsignor Lecconi's militancy quickly cooled.

"I'm afraid that we are not in good shape there," he said. "There is a Catholic club, but it is made up of young people — good certainly, indeed of an intransigent bent — but still youngsters who don't actually accomplish anything. They make big speeches, they vote many motions, but they don't do anything in practice."

The archbishop assured the papal emissary that he would talk privately with local aristocrats to see what kind of support he could muster. But, he added, there were problems with this group as well. "Unfortunately here in Florence there are many who say: 'The situation is harmful for both sides. Oh! Why doesn't the pope realize it?' It is a bit difficult to reason with such people and persuade them that there is only one just solution."

Della Chiesa pressed on. The pope, he said, wanted the archbishop to arrange to have "a person of prestige and literary ability" write a booklet to support his position. But again the archbishop demurred.

"Whom am I supposed to ask? In fact, I have few Catholic writers or journalists here. As for the clergy, I would divide them into the old and the new. The old still feel the effects of a hundred years of the Leopoldine legislation [of the Grand Duchy of Tuscany, in effect until 1859], and they are inclined to think that the clergy depend ecclesiastically on the civil authority as well as on the religious. They read the liberal press and are no lovers of ecclesiastical discipline. Indeed, rather than being a help to me, they are a heavy burden. I don't say the same about the younger clergy, but they too exhibit the laziness that is so much a part of the Tuscan character."

Frustrated, Della Chiesa asked the archbishop if he couldn't at least find a loyal lay Catholic to write such a booklet. After all, it might even be better if it were written by a prominent noncleric.

Well, replied Monsignor Lecconi, there is one prestigious Catholic who wrote with great literary flair. But he would certainly not write such a piece, for he too was "enamored with Italy" and thought that the pope should be making peace with the Italian state.

Finished in Florence, Della Chiesa took the train to Bologna, where he arrived that same evening. Learning that the archbishop, Cardinal Battaglini, was visiting a small parish three hours away, Della Chiesa set off the next day to find him. When they met, Battaglini told the papal envoy how pleased he was that the pope's commitment to temporal power was finally being made clear. There had recently been a great deal of confusion, he said. Some had argued that the pope would be satisfied by regaining control of Rome alone, while others had even claimed that he would be willing to settle for just part of Rome. Della Chiesa assured the archbishop that such rumors were merely misinformation being spread by the Church's enemies to sow confusion in the Catholic ranks.

Yet when the envoy raised the issue of taking action, he found the Bologna archbishop's reaction remarkably similar to that of his colleague in Florence. Hard-line militancy instantly dissolved in a stream of excuses and equivocations. Asked to organize a campaign to stamp out opposition to the papal line among the Catholic faithful, the cardinal replied, "Frankly, I would prefer to keep to the general, partially because it might make a bad impression on some people for me to say baldly: 'There is no other path than that of the restitution of temporal dominion.'"

From Bologna the envoy made his way to Venice, where he met with the city's patriarch on July 24. Two days later he was in Genoa, meeting with the archbishop, Monsignor Magnasco. There he received a bit more encouragement.

"No sooner had he understood the subject of the meeting," recalled Della Chiesa, "than Monsignor Magnasco said that he was fed up with the topic of conciliation because he did not believe that any conciliation was possible other than on the basis of Italy's complete submission to the Holy See." The archbishop went on to complain about the Vatican's timidity in making its position clear. Della Chiesa hastened to say that this was the exact purpose of his visit.

It was difficult for Della Chiesa to speak without being interrupted by the agitated archbishop, as he recalled: "Monsignor Magnasco reiterated with great vehemence that everything would be possible if only one spoke clearly, that neither he nor the people of Genoa liked statements that, albeit against the wishes of their author, could, due to the way in which they were written, be interpreted in two different ways."

"If the pope were to clearly say 'Do not hope for Italy to reconcile itself with the papacy unless it restores its temporal power,'" the archbishop told him, "I promise you that the Catholic clubs in Genoa would show their strong support for the Pope!"

The envoy's last stop was in the old capital of the Savoyard monarchy, where, on the morning of July 28, he met the archbishop of Turin, Monsignor Alimonia. Della Chiesa undoubtedly knew that the pope's message would not be popular with Turin's elites, who were traditionally closely tied to the king.

When told of the pope's wishes, Monsignor Alimonia grew uncomfortable, mumbling something about there being some confusion about exactly how large a portion of the old Papal States had to be restored to the pope.

When asked how much popular support could be drummed up for the pope's campaign, the archbishop again became uneasy. He said, Della Chiesa reported, "that he could not hide the fact that in Turin the majority of the good people consisted of moderates who were extremely devoted to the monarchy and the house of Savoy." For this reason, the envoy wrote, "the cardinal fears that there is little hope for a demonstration of religious-political loyalty to the pope in Turin."[1]

Della Chiesa's mission was now over, having produced modest results at best, but before the pope could move to the next phase of his plan, he was confronted with an important change in the Italian government. Agostino Depretis, the central architect of the left's victory in 1876 and eight-time prime minister since then, died on July 29. On August 7, the king named the strong-willed Francesco Crispi, a man viewed with great suspicion by the Vatican, as the new prime minister.

Crispi was unusual in coming from a Sicilian family of Greek-Albanian origin, his paternal grandfather a Greek Orthodox priest and he himself baptized in the Greek Orthodox church. Crispi's personal credentials were not improved by the scandal that erupted in early 1878 when, while serving as minister of internal affairs, he got married. "Bigamy!" screamed the newspapers, for they pointed out that twenty years earlier he had married a woman in Malta, that he had lived with her as man and wife for many years, and that she was still alive (legal divorce would not be possible in Italy for another century). The case went to court, and although Crispi was acquitted, the reasons did nothing to help his reputation. The court ruled that at the time of his recent wedding he was free to marry, for the marriage he had celebrated in Malta had itself not been valid because he had then been married to yet another woman. Because his first wife had, in the meantime, died, there was now no legal impediment to his recent marriage, for he was legally a widower. The outrage the case provoked forced Crispi to resign, a disgrace he would never forget.[2]

Sixty-eight years old at the time of his selection as prime minister, with white hair and a bushy mustache, Crispi looked a bit like Bismarck, a similarity much noted in the press. As a French journalist, three years later, described him: "his mouth is large, his face is long, his jowls fleshy and closely shaven, his nose strong, dominating his face above his short white, bristly mustache. His forehead is balding, as is his head, revealing his tendency to blush as soon as he gets irritated. His gaze is piercing, intelligent, changeable, different, the eyes of a very strong man, very crafty, very cunning. But something is missing! Monsieur Crispi has no eyebrows . . . He resembles Monsieur Bismarck without the eyebrows . . . Very shrewd, very intelligent, very Italian, very much a lawyer, he has no need for the eyebrows that give the other [Bismarck] the air of a man who is very strong, very brutal, very German, and very military! Monsieur Crispi gives all the appearance of wanting to charm his visitors; Monsieur Bismarck would like to terrorize them."[3]

In fact, Crispi was extremely sensitive about his appearance, spending two hours on his toilet each morning, and dressed with great care. Although he could be courteous and cordial in private, he had a reputation for impatience, bellicosity as an orator, and ruthlessness in seeing that he got his way, using outbursts of anger and indignation — pounding his fist on the table — to intimidate people. An old republican and revolutionary, Garibaldi's man in Sicily during the fateful year of 1860, Crispi had come to support the monarchy as the best way to unify Italy. But he would never have much regard for the royal family. He was not bashful about haranguing the king, and he bowed to the king and queen as little as possible. Nor was he known for his good manners. When King Umberto and Queen Margherita were receiving Queen Victoria at their villa in Florence in 1888, Crispi came barging into the room, unannounced and unbidden, and to the discomfort of both the British and Italian queens, did not take the hint to leave. Victoria later wrote that, after Crispi had finally gone, Umberto and Margherita "were most kind & amiable, making many excuses for Crispi's behaviour . . . the King saying that he was a very clever man, but had no manners."[4]

Crispi's ascent to power only increased the sense of urgency in the Vatican. Everything possible had to be done to drum up Italian Catholic support for the pope's hard line. On August 9, two days after Crispi began his first four years as prime minister, Rampolla wrote to the archbishop of Palermo, telling him to ensure that all of Sicily's clergy and laity conformed to the stance against conciliation. The archbishop was instructed to have ten to twelve thousand copies of the pope's letter to Rampolla printed and distributed throughout the island by parish priests. Funds would be provided for this purpose. "The press, the Catholic associations, and, in certain places, the town governments," Rampolla wrote, "ought to take part as well."

On the twenty-first, the archbishop reported on his progress. Four thousand copies of the papal letter against reconciliation had already been distributed to the priests on the island, and more were being printed. In addition, the Catholic press throughout Sicily had reprinted the letter. But, the archbishop acknowledged, the interest in the pope's cause that they had hoped to generate had so far been lacking, a fact he blamed on the cholera epidemic then sweeping the island, and absorbing everyone's attention. The archbishop also told Rampolla that he would not willingly follow his request that he have all of his bishops write pastoral letters to their flock calling for the return of the pope's temporal power. Should they issue such letters, he argued, they might well be arrested and charged with "wanting to excite hatred of the state institutions." Instead, he suggested, he could ask the bishops to sign a public letter of generic support addressed to the pope. Yet even this milder measure would be opposed by quite a few of the island's bishops. They were especially worried that municipal governments would pounce on any sign of their lack of patriotism in order "to fan the flames so that they could sequester the bishops' revenues in order to fatten their own administrations' coffers."[5]

Facing such foot-dragging, in late September, the pope organized another secret mission. Although his envoy is not specifically named in the archives, it was almost certainly still Giacomo Della Chiesa, for the emissary is referred to as having recently returned from a papal diplomatic position in Spain. Della Chiesa was charged with visiting a dozen archbishops and bishops from Bologna in the North down to Naples and Bari in the South, between late September and early November. At each stop, he began by handing the local prelate a letter expressing the pope's views. It painted a grim picture: "The religious situation in Italy becomes worse every day. Due to a sad series of circumstances, the revolution has obtained its goal, and the sects who are its principal instrument, after having devastated the Church and destroyed the civil rule of the Roman Pontiff, have taken over all public life." The ultimate aim of these ferocious attacks on the Holy See's temporal power was no longer a mystery: it was "the destruction of [the Church's] spiritual power . . . the suppression of Christianity."

The prelates were told that the Church could prevail only if they faithfully followed the pope's wishes and ensured that their flocks did so as well. Many Catholics had resigned themselves to the current situation, which could be attributed only "to the lack of understanding that many have of the question of the temporal dominion of the Holy See. It is almost as if this were a matter that was extraneous to the defense of religion and perhaps even damaging to the prosperity of the Italian nation . . . Everyone, each in his own sphere," the bishops were told, "must, under the Holy See's guidance, take action that, while prudent and within the bounds of legality, is energetic, assiduous, and efficient." They were to ensure that the priests under them followed these instructions, they were to activate Catholic lay organizations and parish committees, and they were to have the local Catholic press spread the word.[6]

The first of this new round of visits took place on September 27, when the papal envoy again met with Cardinal Battaglini, in Bologna. The pope, the envoy told him, was unhappy at how little the Italian bishops and cardinals had done in response to his directives of July. Leo wanted Battaglini to oversee the sending of a formal letter of support to the pope, to be jointly signed by the bishops of Romagna, the Marches, and Umbria — all regions that until 1859 were part of the Papal States. The letter, the envoy said, was to express "the wish that the pope's situation be improved, and that the ruinous conflict between Italy and the papacy be ended, which cannot happen without the restoration of the pope's true territorial sovereignty." The pope also wanted all the bishops to help ensure the success of a popular petition directed at the Italian parliament that was being organized by the main Italian Catholic lay organization, the Opera dei Congressi Cattolici, which was based in Bologna. It too called for restoring the pope's rights.

Wherever he stopped, Della Chiesa heard the bishops and archbishops complain about the spread of religious indifference in their dioceses and the difficulty of getting good Catholics to stand up publicly for the restoration of the pope's domain.

At Perugia, he went to see the man who had taken Gioacchino Pecci's place when he was elevated to the papacy. Given that the pope had spent so many years in Perugia, the picture painted by the new archbishop was not only unsettling, it was embarrassing.

"The Holy Father," Perugia's archbishop told Della Chiesa, "well knows the Umbrians' character, which is difficult in any case, and he would easily be persuaded that in Perugia one can do very little with regard to the Opera dei Congressi petition."

Della Chiesa disagreed, saying that the pope would certainly have special reason to expect some sign of affection from the people of Perugia. But the archbishop remained unmoved.

"The Perugians may have affection for the Person of the current Pontiff," he responded, "but they are not very devoted to the institution that he represents."

After returning to Rome for a rest, the papal envoy headed south, arriving at the small town of Aversa, just north of Naples, on October 21. There he heard some disturbing news: Catholic attempts to distribute their petition in Naples had prompted police intervention, threats, and fear. Responding to a newspaper report that the priests were distributing a call for the return of the pope-king, the police chief of Naples had paid a call on a nearby church. There he made the parish priest show him the petition so that he could check it for seditious content. Monsignor Caputo, the bishop of Aversa, told the envoy that once word of the police visit had gotten out, people had grown suspicious. What made things even worse, he said, was that in sending copies of the petition to the parish priests, the archbishop of Naples had not attached any letter of explanation. As a result, said Monsignor Caputo, "many priests doubted whether the petition had the pope's approval; indeed, they came to doubt that it even had the approval of the cardinal archbishop himself." A second story, carried by the liberal Neapolitan newspaper, *Roma*, had further scared off potential signers of the petition: "We have been assured," the paper reported, "that the government will denounce to the judicial authorities the authors and the signers of the petition calling for the reestablishment of temporal sovereignty in Rome. That petition is said to be viewed as an incitement to violate the basic laws of the state, and an offense directed against the person of the king of Italy."

In any case, the bishop said, not much was to be hoped for from the dioceses of the South. There, he explained, "the terrain is not naturally well disposed to produce outbursts of zeal or manifestations of interest in the pope, because few there recognize the connection between temporal dominion and the Church's prosperity."

Well then, said the envoy, it is clearly the clergy's job to teach the people why the pope's temporal power is so necessary.

The bishop shook his head. The state of seminary training in the South was a disgrace, he said, and until it was radically improved, they could expect little of the priests. "If I were to call a Seminarian here and offer him free room and board," said Monsignor Caputo, "on the sole condition that he sign the petition of which we have been speaking, he would refuse."

When the envoy met with the archbishop of Naples later that same day, he decided it best not to mention this earlier conversation. Cardinal Guglielmo Sanfelice painted a picture as bright as his Aversa colleague's had been bleak. When the archbishop assured Della Chiesa that the petition "would have a brilliant result in Naples," his visitor, rather than mention what he had heard from Caputo, asked about the recent newspaper stories. Cardinal Sanfelice, shocked that the envoy knew about them, grew wary.

"Is this the real reason that the pope sent you to Naples?" he asked.

"By no means," Della Chiesa replied, trying to reassure him, adding that he had just happened to have heard of it since arriving in Naples.

Returning the archbishop's attention to the petition, he asked if the good Catholics of Naples had any problem with its wording.

"Well," the cardinal acknowledged, "things might be going even better if the leaders of our lay organizations were more enthusiastic about it. They can't understand why the petition makes no mention of the need to restore the Bourbon king to power in Naples at the same time as the pope is restored in Rome."[7]

After his discouraging tour through the South, Della Chiesa set out on the final leg of his mission, in central Italy. There, too, the news was not good. Bishops bemoaned the lack of religious spirit in their dioceses and complained that the Vatican was sending out mixed signals about reconciliation with the Italian state. Most depressing of all was the envoy's visit to Ravenna, formerly part of the Papal States and a hotbed of anticlericalism, where even the street names had been changed to eliminate all of the saints and popes and honored instead some of the Church's most notorious enemies.

"Don't expect many people in my diocese to sign the pope's petition," the archbishop told him.

"In a city of twenty thousand people," the archbishop lamented, "we have seventy-three different anticlerical clubs." Rare is the man in Ravenna, he added, who would risk the public humiliation of being seen entering a church.[8]

18

Fears of a European War

WHILE THE POPE, through the endless energy of his new secretary of state, was doing all he could to generate political support from the Italian clergy and laity in the fall of 1887, he knew that if he was to have any hope of regaining even part of the old Papal States, he needed to enlist the help of foreign rulers. After all, this was the way the Church had regained temporal power in 1814 and again in 1849. It wasn't the Italians who had returned Pius VII to power or made Pius IX pope-king again. These were not distant memories and, for some, offered a clear, divine blueprint of what would happen for a third time in the century.

Leo had a two-pronged strategy: exert what direct pressure he could on foreign governments and, at the same time, follow the more indirect route of encouraging Catholics abroad to put pressure on their governments.

On September 15, Rampolla wrote a letter to his nemesis in Vienna, Luigi Galimberti, instructing him to promote popular demonstrations in support of the pope. Following the publication in July of the pope's letter on the need for temporal power, the secretary of state reminded him, the Catholics of both Germany and Belgium had held rallies and other demonstrations on the pope's behalf. Rampolla explained: "It would be in keeping with the Holy Father's desires for the Catholics of the Austro-Hungarian Empire to find a way to make their voices heard in favor of the temporal dominion of the Holy See in consonance with the Catholics of the other States. It does not seem right that a Catholic country like Austria should remain behind Germany, a Protestant country."[1]

In late September, Crispi traveled to Germany and met with Bismarck on October 1. The pope was outraged at the news. Rampolla, never well disposed toward the Germans, tried to use the Crispi-Bismarck meeting to fan the flames of France's resentment against the Italians. The French lent him an eager ear, realizing that in Rampolla they had a strong ally. The French ambassador to the Holy See described the new secretary of state glowingly in a report to Paris: "Hostile to the House of Savoy, opposed to the Triple Alliance, which represents an obstacle to the papacy's claims, he looks upon France with feelings of sympathy, trust, and hope."[2]

On October 7, Rampolla sent a telegram, in code, to the papal nuncio in Paris: "The conversation that has just taken place, not without a certain ostentation, between Signor Crispi and the Prince of Bismarck is a fact worth pondering, for it clearly shows Italy's solidarity with the Austro-German international policies to the detriment principally of France." Rampolla went on to explain how the crafty Bismarck had lured the Italians into his orbit. As long as Bismarck was at war with the Vatican, the Italians had had no cause to worry that the Germans would take the pope's side. But now that Bismarck had made peace with the Holy See, Italian leaders were nervous that a German-Vatican alliance might take shape against them. As a result, Bismarck had been able to get them to agree to an alliance on terms favorable to Germany.

Rampolla told his Paris nuncio that France's current weakness was its own fault, produced by its repudiation of the monarchy, its persecution of the Church within its borders, and its abandonment of its historic role as defender of the pope's claim to Rome. As a result, he argued, France today "finds itself humiliated and exposed to continuing dangers coming from the growing force of its neighboring enemy." Rampolla then gave the nuncio his instructions: "You will not fail to employ all of your intelligence and industry so that, citing Italy's hostile attitude, you ensure that the Roman question is constantly discussed by French public opinion and that the Italian government is never allowed to deprive this question of its eminently international nature." The nuncio was further told to "give the most absolute assurances" to the French government "that the Holy Father will not stop asserting his claim to full and effective independence."[3]

Three days after receiving the telegram, the nuncio replied at length. It is clear, he began, "that the Prince of Bismarck has pulled Italy into his anti-French orbit and that therefore France must now, in the face of its new enemy, Italy, work toward the effective territorial freedom of the Holy Pontiff, in the sense of His Holiness's letter of this past June 15." As for French public opinion, the nuncio explained, there was some good news. "The liberal papers, acting from national malice directed against Italy's recent unification, and the Catholic papers, acting in addition in explicit defense of the Holy See's rights, never stop complaining about the occupation of Rome. As faithful executor, as always, of Your Eminence's orders, I will not fail to keep this sort of agitation in favor of the Holy See alive."

While Rampolla was no doubt encouraged by these opening paragraphs, he could not have been pleased with the rest. The nuncio was dubious about his instructions, believing they were based on wishful thinking rather than a clear understanding of France's situation.

There was little chance, he told Rampolla, that under the current conditions France would champion any drive on the pope's behalf to retake Rome. "I would observe that if this was unlikely in France after 1870, partly due to the more or less openly anti-Christian internal policy that the radical party has imposed on successive governments, and partly due to the fear of offending Germany, it now seems to me rather difficult, and I would say it would even threaten the very existence of France itself." The stakes could scarcely have been higher: "Italy could consider any kind of call or protest by the French Government directed to the Italian Government, to the effect that Rome should be the property of the pope, as grounds for war. France would then be attacked simultaneously by Italy and Germany." Such a war, the French nuncio warned, would quickly lead to "the virtual elimination of France, which on the east would lose additional provinces and on the south would see Italy take back Nice and Savoy."

With the end of the battle against the Church in Germany, the nuncio reported, suspicions were growing that the Vatican was engaged in secret negotiations with Bismarck and Crispi at France's expense. Rumor had it that Bismarck's solution to the Roman question involved returning Rome to the pope and compensating Italy by giving it Nice and Savoy — Italian lands that had been ceded to France just a few decades earlier. Such a dramatic development would crown Bismarck as the master of all Europe, having put an end to the thorny Roman question and won favor among Catholics throughout the continent.

"In the current serious circumstances," the nuncio wrote, "any French cabinet, of whatever stripe, will be reluctant to put itself in a compromising situation with Italy. Indeed, any attempt at all to move it in this direction could be taken as evidence of new machinations of the able Chancellor against France, which he would like to crush in the next war, but which, like the one in 1870, he would prefer started by being attacked first." The picture that the nuncio painted was not pretty: "Given the military and moral preponderance of Protestant Germany, which, after having reduced all of the Catholic nations to impotence, now threatens Europe with a Middle Ages in reverse, I rather doubt that official France has the courage to take an initiative that, humanly speaking, could prove to be fatal."[4]

With tensions growing between France and the countries of the Triple Alliance and talk of war becoming increasingly common in the press, disagreements inside the Vatican were becoming ever more evident. At the center were the two antagonists: Galimberti and Rampolla. Galimberti favored Germany and especially Austria. He believed that reconciliation with Italy was essential and that temporal power was forever lost. By contrast, Rampolla championed France against Austria and Germany and was the principal architect of the pope's rejection of any deal with the Italian state that would abandon his claim to temporal power. Fearful that Galimberti was working against him — and undoubtedly aware that Galimberti, with the pope's approval, was reporting to the pope through messages sent to the Perugians — Rampolla was eager to collect any information that he could use against his rival. French diplomats obliged him with a satisfying staccato of complaints.

On October 19, the Paris nuncio told Rampolla of a recent conversation he had had with Emile Flourens, the French foreign minister. The French government, the nuncio reported, would, despite all the dangers, be willing to initiate a joint action of all the Catholic powers on the pope's behalf "if it did not fear that it would not be listened to in Vienna, where the course of action followed by the pontifical representative there does not converge — in the opinion of Signor Flourens — with that of this nunciature."[5]

Two days later, Flourens summoned a French prelate and told him that he was extremely concerned about Galimberti's attitude, which he said posed "a true international danger."

"Have you not heard it said," Flourens added, "that he favors German interests to the detriment of Catholic interests, for this is what all the reports that I am receiving say."[6]

Shortly after receiving these materials, Rampolla wrote directly to Galimberti. Crispi's recent meeting with Bismarck and the bolstering of the Triple Alliance, the secretary of state told him, along with Crispi's "insolent language" and his scurrilous attacks on the Holy See that had recently appeared in the liberal press, "show clearly that this alliance serves to consolidate Italian actions against the papacy's rights and independence." As a result of the Alliance, he wrote, "the Holy Father's sorry situation is being prolonged, as he is being cruelly abandoned to the mercy of the sects and the revolution." All this had deeply distressed the pope, who now felt "profound disgust," especially at Austria's betrayal of the cause of the Church. Austria, "a Catholic nation, always viewed with particular benevolence by the Holy See," had now allied itself with Italy, the Church's main persecutor. The pope, Rampolla wrote, feared that "rather than work to assist in the restoration of the Holy See's temporal dominion," Austria "would instead work to impede it." In this lamentable situation, he told Galimberti, it was incumbent on him to make known to the Austrian authorities "the disgust and unfavorable impression" that their alliance with Italy had produced in the Vatican.

Finally, Rampolla turned directly to the reports about Galimberti's own behavior. "The Holy Father has been receiving repeated complaints about your attitude from the cabinet in Paris. Reports from Vienna lead them to believe that you have a hostile attitude toward France. Now it is in our interest, and you must realize this, to have good relations with the French Government, which has recently made satisfactory declarations favorable to the temporal dominion of the Holy See, to the point where they say they are disposed to take the initiative for a diplomatic action by the Catholic powers aimed at Italy as long as they can be sure of receiving support. For this and other reasons the Holy Father wants you to improve . . . your personal relations with the French ambassador there and work to remove the sinister prejudices that weigh on Signor Flourens with regard to the hostile sentiments that are being attributed to you." Rampolla ended his letter with a postscript: "Take care not to entrust delicate matters either to the post or to the telegraph service, as the Italian Government is extending its surveillance over us and is watching us from every direction."[7]

Stung, Galimberti hastened to defend himself. Waiting impatiently for the day when, he hoped, he would be called back to Rome for a cardinal's hat and the job that Rampolla now held, he knew he had to be careful.

The accusation that he harbored hostile attitudes toward France and leaned too heavily toward Austria, he wrote to Rampolla, "was hurled at me other times as well, nor is it difficult to trace its origins." Over the past few years, the pope had assigned him various diplomatic tasks that were not to the French government's liking. "The negotiations with Prussia for religious pacification and my trip to Berlin," Galimberti argued, "were viewed negatively in France, which naturally would have preferred that the dispute between the Holy See and the Berlin Government had worsened, rather than be ended." And how, he asked, could he be blamed for Italy's alliance with Austria and Germany when it had originated well before he took up his post in Vienna?[8]

Shortly after this exchange, the pope, still fuming about the lavish reception that the Germans had given Crispi a few weeks earlier, called in Austria's envoy to the Holy See for a dressing-down. "Leo XIII," the envoy recalled in a report of the meeting, "immediately wanted to turn the discussion to Mr. Crispi's visit to Berlin and Italy's alliance with the two empires. The Holy Father told me, in a rather excited tone, that this development had produced a very unfavorable impression on him, but that he was particularly saddened by Austria-Hungary's alliance with the Italian Government, which is now in the hands of the pope's enemies and has but one goal, the struggle against the pope and the Church." Trying to placate the pontiff, the Austrian envoy responded that, far from abandoning the pope, Austria was the best friend he had. It was in the pontiff's interest, he said, to have Italy in the Triple Alliance because it would act as a conservative brake on Italy while helping to ensure peace in Europe.

The pope was not convinced. "If the Powers, especially Austria, had first, before entering into such an alliance with Italy, insisted on measures designed to defend the Church's rights and the safety and independence of the Holy See," Leo XIII told him, "it would be another matter! I would have hoped for at least this much from the Powers, even from Bismarck, from whom I had reason to expect much more."

When Count Kalnóky received his envoy's account, he immediately summoned Galimberti and angrily described what he had learned from Rome. Kalnóky's account of the conversation that followed offers an unusual glimpse into the relationship between Galimberti and the Austrian leadership.

"Monsignor Galimberti," Kalnóky recalled, "told me, in the greatest confidence, that during the summer the Holy Father had been erroneously led to hold out the hope that Prince Bismarck would energetically raise the Roman question with Italy and find a solution. He had been counting on being able to host crowds of pilgrims, on the occasion of his Jubilee, in the papacy's restored temporal dominion." The news that Crispi had traveled to Germany and was being fêted by Bismarck "had produced bitter disillusionment on the part of the pope, who was now venting his spleen against the two central powers."[9]

Leo was not the only leader in Rome who was angry at the Austrians. Crispi was upset as well, albeit for the opposite reason. On September 29, three thousand Austrian demonstrators, led by the bishop of Linz, held a rally culminating in a unanimous vote for a resolution calling for the restoration of the Papal States. This was bad enough, but even worse was that three government representatives had taken part in the rally. Crispi directed his ambassador in Vienna to lodge a complaint but received no satisfactory reply. So on November 23 he again wrote to his ambassador.

"You know as well as I," observed Crispi, "that we could never view the Vatican question, raised anew by Leo XIII's and Rampolla's letters, as an international matter and that Italy would never allow any foreign government to interfere in it. It is an entirely domestic affair." He continued: "The rally at Linz and Kalnóky's silence, together with the Emperor's refusal to return the [Italian king's] visit to Vienna with a visit to Rome, are facts that unfortunately lend themselves to equivocations regarding Austria-Hungary's true sentiments toward us." Given all this, Crispi urged, it was crucial for the Austrian government to take action aimed at "dissipating this ambiguity and demonstrating to Italian public opinion that the Imperial and Royal government does not share our enemies' view on this subject."[10]

Behind the Austrians' action — and their inaction — was their fear of the Vatican's support for France. Such open support would be a disaster on many counts, given how many of the Empire's subjects were Catholic not only in the Austrian heartland, with its overwhelmingly Catholic population, but in many of the more restive regions of the empire, such as the portions of Poland ruled by Austria. While valuing their alliance with Italy, the Austrian leaders were not eager to alienate the Vatican.

This balancing act was on display when Galimberti and Kalnóky met in Vienna on February 16, 1888. The Austrian foreign minister began by congratulating him on the large number of pilgrims who had recently gone to the Vatican for the pope's Jubilee. This display, he said, "revealed to the whole world the Vatican's moral superiority over the Quirinal, which was eclipsed by it." Kalnóky went on to reassure Galimberti on another point: the Austrians would never accept the Italian government's position that the pope's status in Rome was simply a domestic, Italian affair. Clearly, it was a matter to be regulated by international agreement.

The foreign minister then came to the French threat. "The Vatican," Kalnóky said, "is unwise to depend on the support of France, which is opposing Italy only out of bitterness and not out of any devotion to the papal cause." Believing that a war with France was not entirely unlikely, Kalnóky asked Galimberti to caution the pope against supporting a French invasion of Rome. Such an occupation, he warned, "would expose the Holy See to the prospect of a republican form of government, which one day soon might well have a member of the radical party as president."[11]

The death of the German emperor, Wilhelm I, on March 9, 1888, just short of his ninety-first birthday, offered the pope a new chance to drive a wedge between Germany and Italy. On receiving the news, the pope sent Galimberti to Berlin on a special mission, carrying his condolences to the new emperor, Friedrich III. The symbolism of such a visit, Leo believed, could be powerful. Yet arranging for this audience would not be easy, for Friedrich III was known to be in bad health. Rampolla explained what was at stake in the instructions he relayed to Galimberti: "If the emperor has granted an audience to some of the representatives of the other Courts and denies it to the Representative of the Holy See, such a refusal would be too humiliating. If, on the other hand, having denied an audience to the others, he were to concede it to the pontifical representative, this distinction would certainly be most satisfying."

But Galimberti was given a second assignment, as important as the first. He was to use the occasion of the funeral to meet privately with Bismarck and discuss two topics: the situation of the Catholic Church in Germany and the Roman question. Galimberti was to tell Bismarck that his meeting a few months earlier with Crispi had "produced a very painful impression on the Holy Father, all the more so given how well known in Rome are Crispi's character, his revolutionary and sectarian intentions, his attitude toward the Vatican as a former wild Garibaldian, his intimate ties with the radicals, and the profound hatred of the papacy that often leads him to the most undignified acts of violence."[12]

Galimberti arrived in Berlin at midnight on Sunday, March 18, taking up residence at the British Hotel. Two days later, a carriage from the imperial court came to pick him up, carrying him through Berlin's snowy streets — their buildings adorned with black drapes of mourning — to the imperial residence. In the grand room of Charlottenburg Castle, with members of the imperial family in attendance, Galimberti handed the emperor Leo's letter of condolence. The empress, to Galimberti's delight, replied in Italian, asking him to convey their personal thanks to the pope for his kind thoughts. But the papal envoy was shocked to see how ill her husband was. "I fear," Galimberti reported to Rampolla, "that the step from the Charlottenbourg palace to the next Mausoleum will be brief."

Six days later Bismarck received him. "I found the Prince," Galimberti reported, "very tired and very worried. He told me that recent events had made it hard for him to sleep and that he found himself in the sad situation of acting as a nursemaid for the sick." After discussing the Church's situation in Germany, they turned their attention to the Roman question. Galimberti pleaded, on the pope's behalf, for German support.

"Yes," Bismarck responded, "you are right, but you must be patient. Giving Rome back to the Holy See at this time would trigger a revolution in Italy. Such a revolution now would bring with it the fall of the dynasty, and the alliance of a Republican Italy with the French. Such an alliance would end up being useful neither for the Holy See nor for the conservation of order and peace in Europe." As for the pope's displeasure over Germany's alliance with Italy, said Bismarck, he should understand that, given the likely prospect of a French-Russian war against Germany, such a defensive alliance was absolutely necessary.

Should Italy overthrow its monarchy and become a republic, said Bismarck, he would be the first to champion the return of the Papal States, and perhaps too, he added, the restoration of the Kingdom of Naples in the South. But the pope should be patient. "Not only am I not against the temporal dominion of the Holy See," he told Galimberti, "I would not hesitate to take part in its restitution once the victory of conservative forces has assured peace in Europe." And then Bismarck repeated his refrain, *"Il faut savoir attendre"* — be patient.[13]

Patience was certainly needed, since the new German emperor — in agony from the throat cancer that was sapping his life — was in no position to do much of anything, and for another three months Bismarck had to mark time as nursemaid to yet another dying emperor, all the while believing that a new war with France was becoming increasingly likely. But there is reason to think that Rampolla was not entirely displeased that Galimberti had failed to enlist the Germans' help. Aside from drawing satisfaction from his rival's failure, his own view was that success in restoring the pope to power in Rome depended on weaning the Austrians from the Germans and Italians and creating a strategic realignment of the two Catholic powers — France and Austria — with the Vatican against Italy.[14]

On June 19, 1888, just four days after the new German emperor's death and before he could even be buried, Rampolla gave Galimberti new instructions, this time to be carried out in Vienna. The nuncio was to approach the Austrian emperor, as best he could, to ask him to confirm his willingness to provide refuge for the pope. The urgency of the matter, it appears, arose from the dramatic defeat of the Catholic candidates in Rome's municipal elections, which had been held just a few days earlier, and the victory of Crispi's handpicked candidates.

Galimberti was told to inform Franz Josef "that the pope is, more or less directly, being forced by the Italian government and by the radical elements behind it to temporarily leave Rome. Should this happen, it is important to know in advance if the Holy Father can rely on Austrian hospitality and also if he can count on the assistance and cooperation of His Majesty's representative to allow him to leave Italy's borders freely." The pope had an additional request as well. Even if he remained for the time being in Rome, he needed to plan for the eventuality of his own death, for he was an old man. Should "the Sacred College of Cardinals deem it necessary to celebrate the Conclave outside Italy to permit the free and tranquil election of the Holy Pontiff, could this," Galimberti was to ask, "take place in His Majesty's dominions?"[15]

Galimberti succeeded in speaking with Count Kalnóky on July 4. As he had no doubt suspected, the Austrian was not sympathetic. "Count Kalnóky was quite surprised about the matter," Galimberti reported, "and then expressed the opinion that neither he nor the wider diplomatic community gave any credence to the notion that Crispi wants to force the Holy Father to leave Rome." Crispi may have said some radical things when he was a young parliamentary deputy, Kalnóky added, but as prime minister he would act very differently. In any case, said the Austrian leader, Crispi was constrained by the Italian monarchy, by European diplomacy, and by the moderate liberal element in Italy, all of whom opposed the pope's departure from Rome.

Galimberti tried a different tack. We are only talking hypothetically here, he said. Let's not, for the moment, enter into the question of whether the pope will judge it necessary to leave. The question is whether Austria would be willing to take him in if he did.

"Well," asked Kalnóky, "in which of Austria's lands might His Holiness take up residence?"

"Perhaps the city of Trent," Galimberti replied.

"Do you not know, Monsignor, that Trent is a city in which a liberal Italian spirit predominates? The pope would most certainly be uncomfortable there, amid hostile demonstrations, and the incitements coming from the nearby Italian border would certainly not be conducive to his dignity."

The alternative of Salzburg was then raised but dismissed on the grounds that its winters were too cold.

It makes no sense to discuss such details at this point, interjected Kalnóky, since it would be difficult for Austria to consider taking in the pope given current circumstances in Europe. "If it were up to me, or to the Emperor, we wouldn't have to spend a moment to think about it. The Holy Father would always be welcome, and we would be proud to host him and leave it up to him to choose the place where he would most like to live. But," he pointed out, "the Emperor is a constitutional sovereign. I have to answer to the Houses, both of which have to consider both public opinion and the press, which is in the hands of the

Jews and those favorable to the Masons." Yet, despite all these problems, Kalnóky said he would take the question up with the emperor at the first opportunity and get back to him.[16]

True to his word, the Austrian foreign minister met with Franz Josef at the imperial summer residence and on his return to Vienna on Thursday, July 21, summoned the papal nuncio. Galimberti, to his surprise, was told that the emperor had agreed to invite the pope to take up residence anywhere in the Austrian empire that he chose. "The emperor," said Kalnóky, "has asked me to give the Holy Father the most formal assurances on this point." The emperor also promised to allow the Sacred College to hold its next conclave in Austria should it desire.

Although the emperor left the decision to the pope, he was clearly not eager for Leo to take him up on his offer, and Austria's ambassador to Italy was instructed to speak with Crispi. Not surprisingly, Crispi blamed the Vatican for provoking the latest crisis. If the pope would simply stop trying to undermine the Italian state, Crispi said, he would find that he had greater freedom in Italy than anywhere else in the world. Crispi added that he had no intention of forcing the pope to leave Rome; he was all too aware of the difficulties that such a departure would create for his government.[17]

While Leo was putting all the pressure he could on the Austrians, he continued to look with special favor on Europe's other major Catholic power, France, which had the virtue of distrusting the Italian government as much as he did and shared his interest in weakening it.

In mid-July, with the pages of Europe's newspapers filled with threats of the pope's departure from Rome, the papal nuncio to France, Monsignor Luigi Rotelli, met in Paris with René Goblet, the French foreign minister.

Rotelli regaled Goblet with the Vatican's latest litany of woes, listing all of the measures that Crispi's government had recently taken against the Church.

"Yes," Goblet observed, "Monsieur Crispi is extraordinarily fearless. He charges ahead without being afraid of anyone."

"But the European powers should not let themselves be intimidated, much less get bamboozled by the Italian prime minister," objected the nuncio.

"The European powers!" Goblet scoffed. "They're too busy forming an alliance against France to do anything else."

"And all of them," replied Rotelli, "are abandoning the pope. Yet it is in this very isolation of both France and the papacy that we once more see their parallel historical destinies. Doesn't this seem an opportune time, Signor Minister, for the two isolated forces to join together against their common enemies for the well-being of both?"

"But how could republican France do so," asked Goblet, "if Austria itself, an empire that is both Catholic and a monarchy, is allied with Crispi to the detriment of both us and the pope? We French can do no more right now than exercise the greatest caution and reserve to avoid being attacked."

Yes, Rotelli admitted, France was certainly in a difficult situation, but "papal Rome will never give up its historical hopes in its first-born child."

Goblet expressed his pleasure at hearing France's privileged position acknowledged in this way, but he hastened to add that his government could do nothing. He then tried to put the nuncio on the spot.

"The pope's position is very serious, it's true, but who knows whether there isn't some exaggeration in what is being said in the newspapers. Do you really think that the question of the pope's departure from Rome is now being seriously discussed in the Vatican, as the papers say?"

"I know nothing of it," replied the nuncio. "But I think that the latest decision [by the Italian government], saying that the Vatican is on Italian territory, may have revived Pius IX's old project of leaving Rome."

"And where would you think Pope Leo would be able to go? Is it true that he would head for Malta?"

It was the opening that Rotelli was waiting for: "I repeat, I know nothing. But I recall having read in a history of Pius IX that, after 1870, he asked Signor Thiers if he would be able to find exile in France, and that Signor Thiers replied through his ambassador with these precise words: 'Regardless of how disastrous a situation we find ourselves in because of the war and the revolution, we are not yet in such poor shape as to be unable to give refuge to the Pope.'" The nuncio then asked: "If, hypothetically, the Holy Father were to pose the same question today to the French government, could he count on getting the same reply?"

"As this possibility has never been discussed in the cabinet," said Goblet, "I do not believe I am authorized to respond in any way." Instead, he asked a question of his own: "What effect would the Pope's departure produce in Italy?"

"It would be viewed by all Italians — aside from the atheist sectarians and the anarchists — as a true religious and national disaster."

"Well then, why don't the Italians themselves act to ward off such a serious danger?"

"The great majority of Italians," Rotelli replied, "have always done everything that they could to support the Holy See's rights . . . But the Pope's current situation cannot be improved without the joint action of both Catholic and non-Catholic governments."

The papal nuncio concluded by trying a different tack, appealing to France's colonial ambitions.

"One way or another, sooner or later," he told Goblet, "the Holy See will prevail. But what about France? . . . Be warned, two races — the Germans and the Slavs — are now planning how to decide the question of the Orient without France, indeed against France, which is to say without and against the Catholic element, in order to divide European supremacy between themselves. We are always there [in the Orient], France's interests tied always to those of the Church."[18]

Meanwhile, trainloads of pilgrims from across Europe were pouring into Rome to pay homage to the pope and to show their support for his claim to be the one true, divinely appointed ruler of the Holy City. Typical was a gathering of over four thousand northern Italian priests, presided over by the archbishop of Turin, received by Leo on September 27. "None of you, most beloved children," the pope told them, "are unaware of how cunning they are in trying to fool the Italian people regarding the current conditions of the pontificate as they continue to tell the people that the Pontiff has broad and full freedom in Rome and that his authority and his person are respected. But the whole world knows and sees the shameful and intolerable condition to which it has been reduced, at the mercy of the power of others." He went on: "You tirelessly keep repeating that the supreme authority vested in the Pontiff cannot, by its very nature, be subject to any earthly power, and that to be truly free and independent, at least in the current order of Providence, the Pontiff must have real Sovereignty."[19]

Events of the next month did little to reassure the pope, for he faced one of the greatest embarrassments of his papacy. Ever since 1870, when the Italians had taken Rome, no European ruler had set foot there, warned first by Pius IX and then by Leo XIII that visiting the

Italian king in Rome would be tantamount to recognizing his right to rule the Holy City. Time after time Italian prime ministers, working with the Italian court, had tried to get one or another of Europe's rulers to pay such a visit and so provide his stamp of approval, but to no avail. The most that the German emperor Wilhelm I had been willing to do was to visit Milan, thirteen years earlier, following a visit earlier that same year by the Austrian emperor, Franz Josef, to Venice. In each case Victor Emmanuel II had been put in the awkward position of traveling far from his own capital to meet emperors whose capitals he had visited.

The breakthrough for the Italians came when Germany's new twenty-nine-year-old emperor, Wilhelm II, shortly after ascending the throne in June 1888, announced that he wanted to visit his fellow monarch Umberto I in his capital. Angered by the news, the pope again threatened to leave Rome. On July 15, Crispi telegraphed his ambassador in Vienna to report the Vatican's latest efforts: "I have it from an excellent source," Crispi wrote, "that on the 13th of this month Cardinal Rampolla sent a highly confidential note to the papal nuncio [in Vienna], to try to ensure that should Emperor Wilhelm visit our king, the Austro-Hungarian government and the apostolic Imperial Court would use all its influence to see that the visit not occur in Rome. Rampolla has apparently threatened that the Pope would leave the Vatican should Leo XIII's desire not be granted." This threat was duplicitous, Crispi charged, used solely "to frighten Catholic consciences," for the pontiff in fact had no desire to leave. "I hope," Crispi told his ambassador, "that Count Kalnóky and His Majesty the Emperor will not want to lend their support to such a disgraceful maneuver."

That same morning, Crispi sent a similar warning to his ambassador in Berlin. If the Germans paid any heed to the Vatican's pleas and altered the planned visit to Rome, wrote Crispi, not only would it damage their friendship, but it would also lead popular opinion in Italy to shift away from Germany toward France. In such circumstances, Crispi warned, "my authority would be shattered, and I might well be forced to cede my position to men who would not be in favor of the alliance with Germany." Again trying to play the Germans against the French, Crispi urged his ambassador to tell Bismarck that "a large role in Cardinal Rampolla's intrigues is being played by the French ambassador to the Vatican."[20]

At 4:10 P.M. on Thursday, October 11, the twelve-car German imperial train, adorned for the occasion with German and Italian flags, pulled into Rome's central station, a cannon blast announcing the long anticipated arrival. Waiting to receive the emperor were King Umberto, Prime Minister Crispi, and other royal and governmental dignitaries, the men of the royal family wearing full dress uniforms covered with medals. Out stepped the German emperor, dressed in a brilliant red uniform, as a band struck up the Prussian anthem. Embracing, Wilhelm II and Umberto I kissed each other's cheeks four times. To the delight of the cheering crowd, the young emperor then saluted smartly with two fingers to his forehead. Emerging too from the train was a heavy man with a huge bushy mustache, his suit a sign of his diplomatic status. Greeted by Crispi, Herbert von Bismarck, the son of the German chancellor, accompanied the prime minister to his carriage, the first to follow the two carriages bearing the sovereigns and members of their royal families.

In all, twelve horse-drawn carriages, at half-trot, carried the delegation through the streets of Rome, lined by soldiers and cheering and curious citizens, on to the Quirinal Palace. The coach drivers were themselves quite a sight in their red livery, both their wigs and their stockings made of silk. Flowers showered down on them, along with small pieces of paper bearing patriotic inscriptions in both German and Italian. Crispi had ordered triumphal arches built along the route, and a cluster of unsightly buildings facing the Quirinal Palace were torn down before the emperor's arrival.

Once the entourage reached the palace, the emperor and king made their way onto a balcony to salute the crowd while men bearing the crests of all of Italy's major cities lifted them high, standing in a semicircle in the square below. If either monarch noticed that some of the papers raining down on them were red, not white, and bore, not patriotic messages, but Socialist calls for an end to monarchs, they gave no indication. The police meanwhile did their best to chase off the left-wing malefactors who had infiltrated the celebration.[21]

The pope, having lost his battle to keep Wilhelm away from Rome altogether, had wanted at least to keep him from paying his respects to the king before calling at the Vatican, thereby making clear who had the primary claim to rule the Holy City. Yet here, too, he failed. It was all the more galling for the pope to see the emperor received by Umberto in the palace that the Italians had expropriated from his predecessor. But in a nod to Catholic sensibilities, the Germans agreed to devote much of the first full day of the emperor's visit in Rome to the Vatican.

At 10:45 A.M. on Friday, October 12, Wilhelm, along with his brother, Prince Henry, left the Quirinal in a royal carriage bound for the palazzo that housed the Prussian ambassador to the Holy See. The Catholic press would make much of the fact that the German emperor then sent the Italian royal carriage back to the Quirinal and for the rest of the day used his own carriage and horses, brought in for the purpose all the way from Germany. He would not offend the pope by arriving in an Italian carriage.

Greeted by the Prussian ambassador (the heavily Catholic southern German region of Bavaria had its own ambassador to the Vatican), the emperor was ushered into the residence for a lunch in his honor. Sitting on his right was Cardinal Rampolla. Immediately after the meal, the emperor — now wearing his most splendid attire — and his entourage boarded their carriages and made their way to the Vatican.

Leo came out to greet the emperor at the entrance to his quarters. The pope looked tense; he had in fact eaten nothing that day, limiting himself to drinking two eggs and a little glass of marsala wine. The young emperor was no less nervous, dropping the golden cigarette case he had brought as a gift for the pope.

From Vienna, Galimberti had warned the pope that in meeting with the German emperor he should not give in to the temptation to raise the Roman question. But the pope thought this too precious a chance to pass up. As his biographer and confidant, Bishop Soderini, recalled: "Above all, he believed it his duty to take advantage of any occasion to try to regain — even if only in part — his temporal dominion." Forewarned, Bismarck and Crispi hatched a plan to foil the pope. It was arranged that Prince Henry would arrive at the Vatican twenty minutes after the emperor. The pope and Rampolla had planned for both Henry and Herbert Bismarck to be received only after the pontiff had finished his private audience with Wilhelm. But the prince, on his arrival, ordered the papal guard to knock on the pope's door. When the guard hesitated, Bismarck lit into him: "A royal prince of Prussia is not left waiting!" he bellowed. When the guard began to open the door, the pope told him to close it immediately, but Bismarck brusquely pushed it open, making way for Henry. The pontiff's entourage was aghast at the insult, and the pope's wishes for a private conversation with the new emperor were dashed. It is said that later that day the pope, known for never showing his emotions, broke down and cried, less for the missed opportunity to broach the question of Rome than for the offense to his dignity as the pontiff.[22]

Further offenses soon followed, for by 7 P.M. that day the German emperor was the guest at a special court dinner at the Quirinal. That he would proceed almost directly from his audience with Leo to be received by the king in the former papal residence offended all those loyal to the pope. The emperor sat between King Umberto and Queen Margherita, with Prince Henry sitting on the queen's other side.

The toasts that evening had been the object of intense speculation. Would Wilhelm say anything about the king's claim to Rome? Umberto rose first and offered his toast, the message to be sent the world stated clearly: "With profound joy and deep gratitude, here in my Kingdom, here in Italy's capital, I salute Emperor and King Wilhelm II." The German emperor then rose, glass in hand. Following an expression of appreciation for the alliance between the two countries, he said: "Our relations have found the liveliest expression in the wonderful reception that your Majesty's capital has given me."[23]

The proud Leo would never forget his humiliation at the German emperor's hands that day. Any hopes he had nourished that Germany might come to his aid, following the successful negotiations over the end of the *Kulturkampf,* were now gone. One of the casualties of the pope's disillusionment was Galimberti, whose French and philo-French enemies openly gloated. The very month of Wilhelm's visit to Rome, Paris's prestigious journal, *La Nouvelle Revue,* devoted a long, anonymous article to Galimberti, in which he and his friends were charged with being agents in the service of Germany, intent on working from within the Vatican to prepare for "the reign of the Anti-Christ." What had provoked the attack was a newspaper story, widely distributed in Europe just before Wilhelm's Roman visit, claiming that the pope was about to replace Rampolla with Galimberti. The effect of such a move, the French journal charged, would be "to subjugate the Holy See to Germanism, after having Germanized Italy." It would mean, in effect, having "Bismarck installed in the Vatican."[24]

But in the aftermath of the debacle of the German emperor's visit to Rome, there was little reason for the French to worry. Rampolla, ever more insistently championing a French strategy for the Vatican, saw his influence grow with his belief that a European war, and Italy's defeat, was the only way the Holy See would ever get Rome back.[25]

The pope was in no mood now to tolerate any questioning of his rejectionist stance. In March 1889, Bishop Bonomelli of Cremona anonymously published an article urging the pope to make peace with the Italian government as long as the Italians provided him with "a large enough territory so that he could move at his ease, where he would be free, and act as ruler and king." The bishop suggested that the right bank of Rome together with additional land behind the Vatican and a strip reaching to the sea would be sufficient. The pope, incensed, put the work on the Index and forced the bishop to denounce publicly what he had written. Although he felt he had no choice but to obey the pope, Bonomelli was despondent. As he confided in a private letter: "My heart is broken, seeing the sad dispute continue and worsen. I fear for the Church in Italy and I fear for our country. The two extremes are competing with each other to try to push the one and the other toward the abyss."[26]

19

Giordano Bruno's Revenge

ON FEBRUARY 17, 1600, a fifty-one-year-old man, naked except for the gag around his mouth, was brought into Rome's central square of Campo dei Fiori. His captors then tied him to a stake on top of a pile of wood and set it afire. Giordano Bruno, a former friar and one of the better-known philosophers of Europe, saw his flesh erupt in flames before his eyeballs themselves burst from the heat.

The Italians had conquered Rome in 1870, but the completion of the conquest, at least symbolically, came nineteen years later when thousands gathered in the Campo dei Fiori and, to the pope's horror, unveiled a statue honoring Bruno on the spot where Clement VIII had had him burned alive. The devil's own forces, it seemed, had wrested control of the Holy City.

Bruno was an odd choice as a popular hero for the anti-Vatican forces, for he was unknown to all but a few scholars, his works unread and, for the most part, unreadable. He had no popular following of any kind. Yet for the Italian avatars of anticlericalism, Bruno turned out to have much to recommend him, his persecution serving in their eyes as a perfect symbol of the Church's retrograde, repressive nature. His resurrection could serve — or so they hoped — as a way of delegitimating the pope and undermining the Church's power.

Born in the town of Nola, a dozen miles from Naples, his father a soldier, Bruno entered the Dominican order by the time he was seventeen. A bright young man, enamored of theology and philosophy, he quickly made a name for himself as a teacher and writer. But drawn to forbidden authors such as Erasmus, he soon found himself under suspicion of heresy and so in 1576 gave up his Dominican tunic and fled Naples, first for Rome and then to points farther north on the Italian peninsula. By 1579 Bruno had made his way to Geneva, Calvinism's epicenter, and briefly became a Calvinist himself. But he got into arguments with his new coreligionists as well and before long headed west. In 1583 he became attached to the French embassy in London, where his fame was so great that he was invited to frequent the salon of Queen Elizabeth, to whom he dedicated one of his works. Returning to France in 1585, he became embroiled in yet more theological disputes, escaping to Germany and then taking a series of peregrinations through central Europe before moving to Venice in 1591. There he was arrested, charged with heresy, and brought before the Inquisition. He would never again be a free man. Bowing to pressure from the central office of the Roman Inquisition, the Venetians sent Bruno on a boat bound for the Holy City in early 1593.

The trial that followed — many of whose sessions the pope himself attended — lasted through the rest of the decade; it involved a long list of charges, from Bruno's alleged denial of the truth of the biblical story of Christ and Christ's divinity to his opposition to the doctrines of transubstantiation and hell. By late 1599, Bruno was told that he could avoid execution only by renouncing his heretical beliefs and his previous writings. This he refused to do. On February 8, 1600, in the home of the cardinal deacon of the Holy Office of the Inquisition, with the other cardinals of the Holy Office and a large crowd of onlookers present, Bruno's sentence was read. Declared an unrepentant heretic, he was handed over to the civil authorities for execution, all his works consigned to the Index of prohibited books.[1]

The idea of erecting a monument to Bruno on the site of his death originated in 1876 with a group of Roman university students, with strong backing from the Freemasons. Realizing that Bruno was not known to the general population, they organized a flurry of conferences, publications, and speeches to publicize his life. These initial attempts came to nothing, but in the fall of 1884 students at the University of Rome revived the effort and, in March 1885, they sent out an international appeal for funds and support. The list of signatories to the plea was a roll call of Europe's literary and scientific elite, including Victor Hugo in France, Herbert Spencer in England, Ernst Haeckel in

Germany, and Henrik Ibsen in Norway. Italian signatories included Italy's foremost poet, Giosuè Carducci, the famed anthropologist Cesare Lombroso, and many of the national leaders of the left, Crispi included.

The Church soon began its counterattack. In a typical tirade, published as a booklet in 1886, Monsignor Pietro Balan wrote: "To the man who just a few years ago was virtually unknown, to the despised and neglected thinker . . . they now want to build monuments and create eternal fame. Toward this rather peculiar goal, it has been the few, not the many, who have devoted themselves; not the serious scientists, but the youths; not the philosophers, but the politicians; not the Italy of patriotic traditions, but the Italians who follow the new doctrines." What his champions see in him, above all, Monsignor Balan charged, "is hatred of Catholicism, denial of the Christian God, theological impiety . . . apostasy, defection from Christ."

Despite such denunciations, money kept pouring in to the committee. By June 1886, with more than enough funds in hand for the monument, the committee sent a formal request to the city for permission to place the statue in Campo dei Fiori. It was signed not only by the members of the student committee but by many of the Italian members of the honorary committee that had been formed as well, including Crispi and all the other major leaders of the left with the exception of Prime Minister Depretis.[2]

On August 10, 1887, just three days after becoming prime minister, Crispi wrote back to Adriano Lemmi, grand master of the Italian Freemasons, who had written to him on behalf of the organizing committee. Even before receiving Lemmi's request, Crispi explained, he had already spoken to Rome's mayor, saying that the new national government would raise no objection to the erection of a monument to Bruno in the Campo dei Fiori.

The matter was thus left in the hands of the Roman city council, whose approval was needed. But, to the promoters' chagrin, this the council was not willing to give, for it had a solid Catholic majority, and the mayor, Duke Leopold Torlonia, the scion of one of Rome's most prominent noble families, himself had little sympathy for the anticlerical organizers.

But the duke's days as mayor were numbered. On Saturday, December 24, 1887, Torlonia visited Monsignor Lucido Parocchi, the cardinal vicar of Rome, asking him to give his best wishes to the pope on the upcoming celebration of the fiftieth anniversary of his priesthood. For Crispi, it was too much. Long suspicious of Torlonia for his ties to the Church, Crispi told him on December 29 that he was being dismissed. A few days later, Crispi's own choice for mayor, Alessandro Guiccioli, took Torlonia's place.

Enraged, Vatican officials sent a new series of denunciatory circulars to papal nuncios throughout Europe. The major Catholic newspaper in Turin, *L'Unità Cattolica*, in a commentary typical of the Catholic press, called Crispi a new Robespierre.[3]

Guiccioli, a member of the right and an aristocrat, was conservative but not particularly close to the Church. Involved in 1870 in the king's last-minute attempts to strike a deal with Pius IX before invading Rome, Guiccioli had been elected to parliament from a district near Bologna in 1875 and then, defeated in 1882, was subsequently elected to Rome's city council.[4] The Bruno committee lost no time in pressing its case with the new mayor, meeting with him in mid-January 1888. Guiccioli at first tried to stall, arguing that tensions with the Church were then too great to consider putting the matter to a city council vote. In response, the committee announced a strike of Rome's university students, their example quickly followed at the University of Naples.

The Vatican meanwhile began to step up its counterattack. A mass meeting commemorating Bruno's martyrdom, held on Sunday, February 26, in the grand hall of Rome's Collegio Romano — which until 1870 had housed the prestigious Jesuit academy — triggered a Vatican protest sent to all nuncios a few days later. The participants, the secretary of state's letter began, "were united by a single common goal: that is, to direct that demonstration not only against the papacy in particular, but still more against Christianity in general." The two professors who presided over the event, Rampolla reported, were not only enemies of the pope and of God but also notorious proponents of "materialism and Darwinism." The first to speak, Professor Moleschott of the University of Rome, had proclaimed: "Victor Emmanuel, putting an end to papal dominion, . . . has liberated [Italians'] moral sense and love of country from the papal police's chains and bullets, and championed free inquiry and continuous progress instead of a pretended infallibility which not even those who proclaim it actually believe in."

The professor's remarks had been greeted by cries of "Death to the priests!" and "Down with the Vatican!"

Rampolla charged that the sacrilegious rally had in effect been sponsored by the government, for the minister of education had approved the use of the hall, and among those present were various senators, deputies, members of the government, and military officers. The government, Rampolla told the nuncios, had put its weight behind "a function — that of the apotheosis of the unbelief of Bruno — which has stirred up hatred against Catholics and against the state religion." No sooner had the packed hall emptied than the streets filled with anticlerical demonstrations. Many of the Brunonians regrouped at the Campo dei Fiori, where a senator, according to Rampolla, "inveighed against the priests and against the crime committed by the Vatican against Bruno's life, the stain from which could never be removed no matter how much water was used." Several hundred demonstrators had made their way to the Campidoglio, the site of the city government, where, breaking through the police lines, they unleashed "whistles, shouts, and threats against the municipal authorities."

The message that the nuncios were to communicate to the governments they served was simple: "the impossibility of two diametrically opposed powers in perpetual struggle coexisting in Rome." The attempt to erect a monument to Bruno in the capital of Christianity meant only one thing, Rampolla concluded. "The goal of the revolution that has installed itself in Rome is that of dechristianizing Italy and, if possible — after destroying temporal power — destroying the spiritual authority itself of the Head of the Church."[5]

On March 14, at his weekly meeting with Emile Flourens, the papal nuncio in Paris shared Rampolla's circular with the French foreign minister and found a sympathetic response. "Signor Flourens told me that his Government, notwithstanding the difficulty of the times and of local circumstances, wanted to inform us, in an official way, of its desire to draw ever closer to the Holy See." The French foreign minister, the nuncio recounted, "complained about the political isolation imposed on France as far as the Roman Question is concerned and expressed the desire that at least Austria, as a Catholic Power, would support, or at least not get in the way of, France's efforts on behalf of the papacy."[6]

While the Vatican was seething, enthusiasm for the Bruno statue kept growing among Italy's anticlerics; meetings and demonstrations honoring the martyr spread quickly through the peninsula. In mid-April Rampolla received a long, anguished letter from the archbishop of Spoleto, a small city in southern Umbria not far from Rome and until 1860 part of the Papal States. On Easter Sunday, with the cathedral full, the archbishop had given a rousing sermon — if he did say so himself — in which, as he described it, he had contrasted "the divine greatness of the Church, which has for its glory the resurrected Jesus Christ, and the great liars who are the leaders of the sects." Believing that the recent encomiums to the defrocked friar required a firm reply, the archbishop had denounced Bruno and all those who would glorify his memory. Outraged by the attack, the town's anticlerics decided that the best response to the archbishop was to sponsor ceremonies of their own.

The archbishop, learning of their plan, had six hundred copies of a booklet of articles on Bruno from the Vatican's *L'Osservatore Romano* circulated to the clergy and to the most influential of the laity. He also wrote to the mayor, urging him "not to allow any public locality to be used for this orgy." He then called a meeting of all of Spoleto's parish priests to plot their strategy and wrote to the prefect, in nearby Perugia, asking him to outlaw any public procession by the Bruno organizers, noting that the government had forbidden the Church to hold religious processions in the city streets. "I am ready to publish, to preach, to do everything I can to defend God's honor," the archbishop told Rampolla. "But I seek Your Most Reverend Eminence's counsel and the Holy Father's blessing. Would it not be possible for Your Reverend Eminence to use diplomatic means to prevent these most poisonous insults to God, to the Holy Father, and to the Episcopate?"[7]

The archbishop reported the details of the anticlerics' plans as they became known. That national champion of anticlericalism, Giovanni Bovio, famed Neapolitan philosopher and among the most eloquent orators in parliament, would come to Spoleto for the event. A thousand people had signed the manifesto calling for the demonstration. The archbishop was nervous: "The local authorities are weak. They however have promised that my own person and my residence will be protected. But can they be trusted? God let it be so!"

The dreaded day finally arrived. At 3:30 P.M. the procession began, a brass band at its head, followed by groups of veterans, members of the town's target shooting club, students, and representatives from various town councils, workers' societies, and other clubs in the region. At 4:15 P.M. they reached the theater. As they entered the building, banners and flags hung everywhere, but what most caught people's attention was a statue of Bruno, made especially for the occasion, dramatically lit thanks to the remarkable recent invention of electric light.

The head of the organizing committee, a lawyer, spoke first. With a booming voice he told the crowd — the theater, which could hold 1,200, was full — that their new freedom was worth nothing if they did not liberate themselves from the chains of "prejudice and dogma." The clericals, he said, ask if we seek to undermine every principle of religion. "My answer is yes, when religion wishes to put dogma above the nation and the Syllabus in the place of freedom of conscience."

Bovio then strode to the podium. His appearance was described in a sympathetic newspaper the following year: "A severe, dark figure, with bushy eyebrows and mustache the color of ebony, with long goatee, hair standing straight up, flashing eyes, he had the air of a philosopher."[8] From a modest family near Naples, Bovio had begun writing books of philosophy as a young man just after the Kingdom of Naples fell and Italy was unified. By 1876 he was elected to parliament, where he sat in the seats of the extreme left. No member of parliament had been more strident in denouncing the law of guarantees and opposing any privileges for the Church.

"Bruno approached the stake as a moth goes to the light," he told the crowd. "The secret of Bruno's popularity lies truly in this, that the people . . . have understood that his sacrifice was a mysterious and execrable crime for which the Church must settle its account with history." Bovio eventually stepped away from the podium and walked to the front of the stage: "I will only add a few more words, because I know that too much heat, too much crowd, and too much philosopher don't go well together." The crowd laughed. Turning to the illuminated statue, he voiced the hope that the day would soon come when such a monument would arise in the center of Rome.

After the meeting, a celebratory dinner was held at the banquet room of the Lucini Hotel. Bovio, the guest of honor, was surrounded by the mayor of Spoleto, the chief judge of the town court, the vice prefect, and several members of parliament. A representative from nearby Perugia rose to speak, thanking Spoleto for having honored Bruno so magnificently. "It is hard to believe," he added, "that Bruno's enemies have dared to revile him in a region that bears such grave and painful memories of its time under ecclesiastical rule." The festivities concluded with a final toast offered by Ettore Ferrari, the forty-three-year-old sculptor whose own statue of Bruno would soon be installed in the Campo dei Fiori. "Let us not forget," he said mischievously, "that the person who has caused us to gather here was the Monsignor Archbishop with his vituperations. Let us not be ungrateful. So I propose that we drink to the health of the Monsignor. Moreover, the Monsignor has a boss, and so I propose that we also drink to the health of Signor Pecci!"[9]

Ferrari, the favorite sculptor of Italy's anticlerics, firmly believed in the union of art and politics. That same month — June 1888 — he was elected to the Rome city council as part of the attack on the Catholic forces that had been blocking the monument in the Holy City. The municipal elections had come in the wake of a 36–29 vote of the city council on May 11, refusing to give the Bruno committee permission to place its monument in Campo dei Fiori. Twenty-eight of the members on the city council had been elected with the support of the Roman Union, a vehicle for the election of pro-Vatican councilors. Incensed, Crispi vowed to replace them with his own allies. When elections were held in June for nineteen of the seats, Crispi inflicted a bitter defeat on the Catholics. The authorization of the Bruno monument now only awaited a new vote, which came later that year.[10]

On the evening of the election, as the extent of the liberal victory began to be known, crowds of anticlerics took to the streets to celebrate, shouting "Long live Rome the untouchable!" "Long live Crispi!" "Death to the priests!" "Death to the butchers of the Inquisition!" As they passed the offices of the anticlerical paper *Don Chisciotte,* they shouted out with delight, for hanging from the window was a bedsheet on which a priest's crumpled hat was drawn with the legend: "Giordano Bruno has cremated the Roman Union." By now more than three thousand demonstrators — mostly young men — had gathered in front of city hall, and the crowd grew ever more excited: "Down with the little Pope!" "To the gallows with the Most Holy Father!" "Priests in the gutter!" "Long live the martyrs of the Inquisition!" "Down with the black geese!" The jubilant demonstrators made their way to the Campo dei Fiori, calling for the construction of the Bruno monument. But when they began to shout "To the Vatican!" police trumpets sounded and policemen descended on the crowd to prevent its crossing the river. Each night for the next week similar demonstrations erupted, not only in Rome, but elsewhere in Italy.[11]

In the spring of 1889, with permissions in place and Ferrari hard at work on the statue, the student organizing committee sent out an announcement inviting groups to send their representatives: "Victorious in the struggle, battling for over ten years against clerical intolerance, the Statue of the Great Man of Nola will finally arise in the very place of his execution, on June 9, 1889." Noting how apt a way it was to celebrate the hundredth anniversary of the French Revolution, the manifesto portrayed the Bruno monument as a "symbol of mutual tolerance in the context of freedom of thought, of religions, of cults."[12]

The delegations began arriving at the Rome train station on Friday, June 7, representing scores of town councils, fifty different Masonic lodges, numerous student groups, and a kaleidoscope of anticlerical clubs. In all, two thousand organizations sent delegates to be part of the historic rites.

On Sunday morning at nine o'clock the procession set out from the central train station. In the lead was a group waving the banner of the Association of Former Prisoners of the Pontifical Government, along with a phalanx of red-shirted, white-haired men, Garibaldi's aging irregulars. Also near the front strode the mayor of Nola, Bruno's birthplace. Twenty bands marched along playing music, Garibaldi's hymn and "La Marseillaise" being especially popular. The rector of the University of Rome marched, as did many of the faculty. The banners of hundreds of anticlerical, socialist, anarchist, and republican groups were held aloft. But the organizers kept a firm grip on the crowd. Cries of "Long live Bruno!" were encouraged, but the more inflammatory anticlerical chants were silenced.

Although ten thousand people marched, only those bearing tickets issued by the committee were allowed into the Campo dei Fiori. The site of Rome's most famous daily market, it was usually filled with stalls of all sorts, selling everything from old books and paintings to fruits and vegetables. The day offered an unexpected windfall for the poor people with apartments overlooking the square, who rented them out to Rome's wealthy. Not a few members of the royal court were glimpsed at these windows, although none was willing to be seen on the reviewing stand below, which had been occupied since eight o'clock that morning by a variety of officeholders, including 119 members of the House of Deputies and 16 senators.

Once the marchers had made their way into the square, the time for the unveiling was finally at hand. In front of the statue, at center stage, sat Senator Moleschott as well as other members of the organizing committee, along with the mayors of Rome and Nola and the sculptor, Ettore Ferrari. When the sheets were removed from the bronze statue, the crowd broke into applause. Bruno was wearing his Dominican frock, looking down in contemplation, a sad expression on his face. Three scenes were sculpted along the sides of the base of the statue: Bruno lecturing in 1584 to a group of students at Oxford; Bruno appearing before the judges of the Inquisition, flanked by guards; and Bruno aflame at the stake. The front panel bore the main inscription, written by Giovanni Bovio himself. It read:

> To Bruno
> The Century That He Divined
> Here Where He Was Burned at the Stake[13]

The first to speak was the head of the student organizing committee, who formally presented the statue to the mayor. Guiccioli, accepting the monument, dubbed it a symbol of "the triumph of freedom of conscience." The mayor of Nola then spoke briefly, thanking the people of Rome for their tribute "to this martyr of tyranny."

It was now Bovio's turn. It was a historic day, he intoned, struggling to be heard by the enormous crowd. "September 20 is less painful for the Papacy than June 9, for while the first was a conclusion, today is a beginning. Then Italy entered Rome, the final step of its journey. Today Rome inaugurates the religion of reason." The old religion of the Church, he said, had no place in the modern world. "Just as in 313 in Milan, the date when the Christian religion was mandated, by imperial decree, so today on June 9 in Rome, the date of the religion of reason is established, by the agreement of free peoples."

When the speeches were over, representatives of hundreds of organizations formed a line so that they could each lay a wreath at the monument. Among the most elaborate was one whose ribbon read simply: "The Anticlerical Women of Rome."

The Vatican meanwhile was effectively in a state of siege. The previous evening, a sixteen-car train filled with Italian troops arrived in Rome to offer additional protection. Soldiers and police in great number were placed at all the street corners in the vicinity of the Vatican. The Sant'Angelo bridge was crawling with soldiers. Along with numerous uniformed police were many, ever watchful officers in civilian clothes. In the end, order was maintained.[14]

But the Vatican was not letting this symbolic assault pass without a fight. In the days leading up to the ceremonies, bishops throughout Italy and beyond were mobilized to show their support. A typical petition came from Ferrara, sent to the pope on the very day of the rites, and titled "An Act of Reparation for the Scandal that on Pentecost of 1889 dishonors and outrages Catholic Rome." In the honoring of Bruno, it read, "we see the spirit of disbelief that is opposed to the spirit of faith, the spirit of apostasy opposed to the spirit of religion, the spirit of revolt that is opposed to the spirit of obedience, the spirit of pride, of avarice, sensuality, of the most unbridled egoism, which is at war with the spirit of humility, poverty, purity, and every holy sentiment."[15]

Feeling physically under attack, the pope asked various ambassadors to be with him on June 9. The previous Sunday the French ambassador, Lefevre de Béhaine, known for his personal devotion to the pontiff, met with Leo and assured him that he would delay his planned departure from Rome in order to be at his side. Béhaine, good to his word, went to see the pope on the ninth, finding him "in very good health, although very sad." Soon the Austrian ambassador was led in, followed by the Belgian ambassador. The scene recalled nothing so much as the day nineteen years earlier when the Italian army broke through Rome's wall and the besieged Pius IX sought comfort from the assembled foreign ambassadors.[16]

Rampolla drafted a long letter to the nuncios, which he sent two days after the unveiling. They were to give the details of the latest outrage against the Holy See to the governments where they served. The glorification of Bruno — "a man lacking any scientific or literary merit, famous only for his apostasy, for the monstrosity and notoriety of his errors" — had but one goal, Rampolla told them, the destruction of the Catholic religion and the papacy. The Italian House of Deputies, Rampolla reported, had participated in the ceremonies and, although

Crispi had taken care to stay at a distance, he was the true mastermind of the whole affair. World leaders could no longer have any doubt that the pope's position in Rome had become "truly humiliating and intolerable."[17]

The cardinal secretary of state had already prepared the ground. On the day before the inauguration, he had sent a coded telegram to a number of his envoys, including Galimberti in Vienna and his nuncio in Paris, telling them to help drum up protests.[18]

Among those quickly responding was the papal nuncio in Munich, who, at a hastily arranged meeting on June 15, had presented Rampolla's June 11 letter to the Bavarian foreign minister, Baron Crailsheim.

"You know, Monsignor," said the baron, "that the Holy Father's cause is very dear to us. I can add that we were unhappy about the celebrations in Rome for Giordano Bruno." At this point, the nuncio no doubt had a good idea of what was to follow: "However we cannot do anything practical in favor of the Holy See. If the Bavarian government issued a protest against what was going on in Rome, the Italian government — which is very sensitive and possessive on this point — would create difficulties for us."

The nuncio pointed out that as a Protestant, the baron might not fully appreciate the enormity of the offense done to the dignity of the holy pontiff. But he got nowhere. Maddeningly, the foreign minister told him to look on the bright side. "After all," he said, "public order was not disturbed. You have to admit this represents progress compared to what happened the night when the body of His Holiness Pius IX was taken to San Lorenzo."[19]

Galimberti, in Vienna, feared that Rampolla would exploit the Catholics' anger over the ceremonies to build support for his plan to return the pope to power in Rome by destroying the Italian state. He wrote directly to the pope, again going around the secretary of state with the help of the pope's personal secretary. Written on the very day of the Bruno celebration, it told the pope that he faced a crucial choice. "There are two systems, or two programs. One of these takes as its supposition the need for the dissolution or dismemberment of what is now Italy. The other prefers the existence of a sensible, moderate Italy, which, in its own self-interest, recognizes the rights of the Holy See." The first school, Galimberti explained, "holds that Italian unity is incompatible with the real independence of the Holy See." The second, which, he pointed out, the German government supported, "believes the coexistence of the one with the other is possible." Using a somewhat ambiguous passive voice to avoid a direct attack on Rampolla, Galimberti added: "It is supposed that the influence that is currently dominant in the Vatican favors the first hypothesis." [20]

Rampolla's telegram of June 8 found a far more enthusiastic reception in Paris, where the papal nuncio immediately called in the archbishops of Paris, Lyon, and Bordeaux to tell them that it would be a great consolation to the Holy Father if they would send him a message of protest in their own names and in that of their archdioceses. This they did by telegram on the tenth. On the morning of the ninth, while the ceremonies for Bruno were still under way in Rome, the Paris nuncio met with the three main conservative leaders in France, a duke, a baron, and a count. Before he could speak, they told him that they had received "personal instructions" from Rampolla on the matter and had already sent telegrams of protest to the Vatican.

The nuncio called in all of the bishops then in Paris to urge them to organize protests in their dioceses, but he was worried that he was missing those outside the capital. He wrote to the secretary of state, proposing that to remedy this problem he send a circular letter to all of France's bishops.

Rampolla took this proposal to Leo, but the pontiff rejected it. The nuncios were to help prompt mass protests among Europe's Catholics, but it was important that they be viewed as spontaneous expressions of popular outrage, not as part of a campaign orchestrated by the Vatican. [21]

Meanwhile, from Spain, Portugal, Belgium, and elsewhere, reports of Catholic protests poured in to the Vatican. A lone discordant note came from The Hague; the nuncio to the Netherlands wrote, sheepishly, that although he and his assistant had worked for over two hours, they had been unable to decipher Rampolla's coded telegram of June 8. [22]

Finally, on the last day of the month, in an allocution to an assembly of cardinals, Leo spoke out publicly. His situation, he told them, had become intolerable; the hatred aimed at the Vicar of Christ was growing ever more dangerous. The Church's enemies, now in control in Rome, had sought to replace the pope with the champion of what they called the principle of freedom of thought, "but which is nothing other than the negation of God, of his Christ, of the morality embodied in the Gospels, and of all those religious principles on which civil society is based." The whole Catholic world, the pope lamented, was now forced to witness "the most profound humiliation of its Spiritual Head, and of its See, reinforced by the monument glorifying apostasy and impiety." Indeed, he warned, "Our own person is in danger."[23]

The Jesuits of *Civiltà Cattolica* saw the signs of God's wrath everywhere, publishing a long list of natural disasters that had swept Italy since the plans for Bruno's glorification had begun. "Has Bruno, beyond being what he was, become an evil omen, what in Naples they would call someone who gives the evil eye? One thing is indisputable: from the day that they began work on his monument, disasters of every kind — including floods, avalanches, hurricanes and the like — have brought desolation to the lands of many provinces."[24]

It was time for the pope to reconsider his decision to stay in Rome. Perhaps the moment had come when, like Noah, he should sail away, only to return when God's enemies were vanquished.

20

The Pope's Secret Plan

*F*ROM PRACTICALLY HIS FIRST DAYS on St. Peter's throne, Leo XIII turned time and again to the cardinals of the Curia to advise him on whether he should flee Rome, just as, year after year, he had his secretary of state put out feelers to various European governments to see which ones would agree to host him. Not surprisingly, the failure of his halting reconciliation efforts in the spring of 1887, and a series of events over the next two years culminating in the unveiling of the Bruno monument, led to yet another round of frenetic planning. But this time, many believed, the pope's threat to leave Rome was all too real.

By late 1888, continued tensions in Europe had led to widespread expectations of war, including fears by Germany and Austria of a French-Russian attack on their borders. The continuing agitation in France, linked to the possibility of a monarchist revolt led by Boulanger against the republican government, further fueled fears that war was near. On December 6, Galimberti expressed his own worries: "The international situation grows ever more serious and threatening. It would take only a puff of air to blow open the gates of the temple of Mars, which have only recently been closed."[1]

In response to the war fever, that same month Leo summoned two different groups of cardinals — including many of the major figures in the Church — to examine the question of leaving Rome once more. Again, they recommended against immediate flight but advised that if Italy were drawn into a European war — a prospect they viewed as both likely and imminent — he should leave at once. Yet they continued to worry that Italy's clergy might abandon him if he were to go.[2]

The cardinals warned that foreign governments could not be trusted. Should he flee, Leo risked finding himself even worse off. As one put it, "One could argue with certainty that the Holy Father, having taken refuge in a foreign state, far from finding that he had support for reclaiming his various rights there, would not even have the ability to communicate, nor still less that freedom of speech that is left to him in Rome."[3]

Despite these dire predictions, the pope's fears of an imminent war and his sense of being under attack in Italy led him to make more detailed preparations for leaving Rome than he ever had before. Letters were prepared for all the cardinals who served as prefects of the Sacred Congregations that formed the central structure of the Holy See, telling them how to get ready for the pope's flight. Secrecy was tight. "It is the Holy Father's wish," Rampolla's cover letter informed them, "that while you will carefully follow those measures that are specified there and take them at the opportune time, you will guard these sheets with the greatest care so that they do not end up in any other hands and you will observe the greatest secrecy about them, for they are not to be communicated to anyone without prior pontifical authorization, under pain of major excommunication." It was not every day that a pope threatened the cardinals of the Curia with excommunication.

Should the pope leave Rome, the cardinals were told, each of them was to join the pontiff "as soon as the place of the new pontifical residence is known, and without any need for further invitation." They were to bring only those officials and aides whose presence was deemed indispensable for the proper functioning of their department.[4]

Leo had another worry. "In case the Holy Father comes to be prevented by force from any communication with the Church, or is shut up in prison, or even deported," the papal instructions specified, "a special Congregation is to be established composed of no fewer than five cardinals." This body would act on the pope's behalf until he was again free. "Should the Holy Father be taken elsewhere by violence," Rampolla told them, "the cardinals resident in the Curia will decide . . . whether it is better to follow the Holy Pontiff to the place of his deportation, or remain in Rome, or rather go to another country which is safer and freer. In any case, they will take care to always remain together and, so far as possible, close to the Holy Father."[5]

If Leo was afflicted by anxieties about leaving Rome, Crispi was afflicted by an obsession of his own, seeing signs everywhere of a French-Vatican plot aimed at Italy. Crispi's wild accusations contributed mightily to the crisis atmosphere, unsettling not only Rome and Italy but the European powers as well. At one point in 1888, the Italian prime minister urged the British government to send a naval fleet to the Mediterranean to foil what he claimed was a plan by the French navy to launch an attack on Genoa. When the British sent their ships, at great expense, only to find that the report was based on nothing more than an unconfirmed rumor from a Vatican informant, they were not pleased. Although they appreciated Crispi's pro-British bent, they had long viewed him as a hothead, and now they secretly hoped he would be replaced before more damage was done. Nor does it appear that the leaders of Germany or Austria had much respect for him, although they were certainly pleased by his strong support of the Triple Alliance and his antipathy toward France. The previous fall Galimberti, in one of the letters he sent directly to the pope, reported: "Crispi is held in low esteem as both a politician and a diplomat. They laugh constantly at him in Berlin and Vienna."[6]

Papal flight, in Crispi's estimation, was a crucial part of the larger French designs for war secretly backed by the Vatican. In June 1889, just a few days after the Bruno dedication, Crispi wrote himself a note about the suspicious activities of France's ambassador to the Vatican, Béhaine. After a flurry of meetings with Cardinal Rampolla and two additional meetings with the pope, the French ambassador, Crispi wrote, had hastened off to Paris. Something big was afoot. He was sure of it.

A few days later, he sent an urgent telegram to his ambassador in the French capital. "In Paris," Crispi told him, "they are now in the midst of negotiating a pact between the Holy See and the Government of the [French] Republic in which, under certain conditions, France promises to bring back temporal power."[7]

On June 15, with Béhaine still in Paris, his chargé d'affaires, Monbel, had the honor of a private audience with the pope. Monbel's report to Paris reveals how misplaced were Crispi's fears. "The pope has no illusion about the help that can come to him from foreign governments," Monbel wrote. "Austria is tied to Germany and to Italy. Spain is absorbed by domestic matters. For its part, France, threatened by two enemies at the same time, can do no more than make token protests on behalf of the Holy See. The pope is therefore isolated, but he is nonetheless resolved to resist and to do everything he can."

Their conversation then turned to the question of the pope's abandonment of Rome. It was Monbel who brought the subject up, referring to news accounts about the archbishop of Barcelona's recent offer of refuge for the pontiff. "The Holy Father," the French envoy wrote, "assures me that it is not his intention to leave Rome at the present, and that he learned of the offer of a residence in Barcelona only from the newspapers."

"But, if the necessity of departure arises," Leo hastened to add, "I believe I will have an embarrassment of choices. Spain would certainly receive me with enthusiasm. Austria, for its part, has offered me hospitality, as have Switzerland and Belgium. And who knows?" he said. "Perhaps France, in the midst of all this solicitude, would not think it beneath itself to give me shelter there."

Revealingly, in reporting this pointed question, Monbel recalled: "I was unable to respond positively."[8]

Throughout the summer, rumors of the pope's imminent departure spread rapidly, with the Catholic press using the threat to push its own intransigent message. *Civiltà Cattolica* went so far as to attribute the recent uncertainty in Rome's stock exchange to "the fear that the Holy Father has already decided, in the extraordinary meeting of the cardinals in the Vatican, to leave Rome." These suspicions were heightened by the outpouring of new offers by various cities and archbishops to welcome the pope: from Malta to Barcelona, Grenada, Seville, and Majorca in Spain to Auch in southwest France.[9]

Monbel's reports to Paris in early July reveal that the French too were increasingly worried that the pope was about to leave. "I have been convinced," Monbel wrote on July 6, "by the conversations that I have had in recent days with various people of the real importance that must be attributed to the rumors of the pope's departure." He explained: "The likelihood of a European war — which is viewed at St. Peter's as very great and would pit the French against the Italians — along with the recent language of the Italian prime minister, who is doing his best to portray the Vatican as continually conspiring with France against Italy, has led to extreme anxiety." In order to prepare for such an eventuality, Monbel wrote, the Holy See was working feverishly to find the pope a place of refuge. "I have every reason to believe," he added, "that the Sovereign Pontiff's preferences are directed toward Spain."[10]

Monbel followed this brief message with a much longer letter the following day, marked "Confidential. On the Pope's departure." It heralded a new stage in the discussion of the pope's plans.

When he had first heard of the pope's secret meeting with the cardinals the previous week, Monbel wrote, he thought that the threats of leaving had been made simply "to give more weight to the Holy Father's complaints, and to excite the interest of the Catholic world in the papacy's situation." This had been the previous pattern. So often had the Vatican brandished such threats that people had become inured to them. But, Monbel reported, things had taken an unexpected turn. "The language that Cardinal Rampolla has used with me, in two consecutive audiences, allows no doubt that this issue of the departure from Rome — so often dropped and then taken up again — has today assumed great seriousness."

"The pope has been forced into the most painful of situations," Rampolla had told him. "After the Giordano Bruno demonstrations, the most slanderous and hurtful words possible for the Holy Father have suddenly been coming from as high up as the Senate gallery, portraying the pope as a personal enemy of Italy, conspiring against it with France. They are duplicitously interpreting each of his acts in a way designed to excite the Italians' hatred."

"The cardinal," Monbel recounted, "finished, in a bout of melancholy, by leaving me to understand that, in his opinion, the struggle between the monarchy and the papacy was uneven, and that the papacy would, over time, lose what prestige remained to it if it agreed to continue to suffer the humiliations that it had come to be subjected to." From Rampolla's perspective, Monbel concluded, "departure had been imposed on them for more than one reason, including the good of the Church, the most important consideration after that of the personal security of Leo XIII himself."

The French envoy had himself now become convinced that it would be best for the pope to flee. "Necessity," he wrote, "does not allow the pope any other choice than what his secretary of state has in mind. Under the current circumstances, Spain alone can offer the head of Catholicism a safe shelter, for it is assumed that Spain will remain neutral in the European conflict and that its climate, better than others, is most agreeable given the Holy Father's age and health."

Monbel's efforts to determine how far the Vatican's discussions with Spain had gone led him to the Spanish chargé d'affaires, who claimed to know nothing of any negotiations. But he did not allay the French envoy's suspicions, for he found out that the Spanish ambassador to the Holy See had recently been recalled to Madrid for confidential discussions with his government. And, in response to Monbel's queries, the chargé d'affaires admitted that Cardinal Rampolla had, not long before, asked him which of the Spanish crown's palaces would be most suitable for a papal residence.[11]

Alarmed, but also excited, Monbel sought out friendly cardinals to help him piece together what was going on. He first spoke to Cardinal Placido Schiaffino, a fifty-nine-year-old Benedictine monk who, although Monbel did not know it, had served with one of the pope's secret groups of advisers on the question of leaving Rome. Schiaffino, Monbel wrote, saw things the same way Rampolla did. The situation was unstable. The pope's life was in danger, and members of the Sacred College could not walk down Rome's streets without being insulted and threatened. "His Eminence," Monbel reported, "gave me the impression that he believed that war would break out soon, at the latest by October." Little time was left for the pope to make his escape.

Of the cardinals Monbel spoke to, none was more influential than Lucido Parocchi. Cardinal vicar of Rome since 1884 — a post he would hold for fifteen years — Parocchi was trusted by Leo, who had also appointed him to the prestigious position that he himself had occupied before becoming pontiff: chamberlain of the Sacred College of Cardinals.

Cardinal Parocchi, it turned out, was not only urging the pope to depart but was also making clear his displeasure that the pope had so often threatened to leave without ever following through.

"There are things that one does and of which one does not speak," the cardinal vicar told the French envoy. "The pope has, besides, many reasons for leaving Rome." Cast as Italy's enemy, in league with a hostile foreign power, Leo was already a prisoner. True, the pope's departure would, at least in the short run, be disastrous for Italy. But, Parocchi insisted, the Church's cause must come first:

"I myself, although born in Italy, and although I love my country and my language a great deal, can't understand how one could sacrifice the Church's least interest to it. There are questions that are more important than Italy, just as there are nations that are much more important [here Monbel noted parenthetically: "alluding to France"] which the Church should prefer over it. Consequently I don't understand how any hesitation is possible."[12]

Crispi, meanwhile, was doing all he could to convince his allies of the pope's plan to launch a war on Italy. The pope's idea, Crispi charged, was to take refuge abroad, hoping to return behind a triumphant French army. Some of Crispi's spies in the Vatican offered him grist for his mill. Béhaine, they claimed, had written from Paris on July 8, urging the pope to act immediately. "If the Holy See can do nothing more than talk," Béhaine was said to have warned him, "France cannot act." To which, in this account, the Vatican responded by telegram: "Act quickly, because all is ready."[13]

On July 11 Crispi told Domenico Farini, the president of the Italian Senate, he was certain that war with France would begin before fall. When Farini reported this to Umberto, the king initially dismissed the alleged plot as a product of Crispi's all-too-fertile imagination. But on the thirteenth Crispi himself went to see Umberto, a meeting he described telegraphically in his diary entry for that day: "I am with the King at 10 o'clock. I inform him of the possibility of an attack. The necessity for defensive measures. He must see the minister of War, Bertolé, and a special council must be formed." The king, still skeptical but now uncertain, agreed to Crispi's request to establish a special four-member war council, presided over by the king himself and including Crispi and the minister of war.

On the sixteenth Crispi met with the Italian ambassador to London, whom he had recalled to Rome for urgent consultations. Crispi described the meeting in his diary: "I inform him that in France they are ready for war, and their intention would appear to be to attack us by sea. The plan is a bold one, I might also say a foolhardy one, but as the information came to me from a perfectly trustworthy source, we must believe the report, and prepare to defend ourselves." Crispi told the ambassador to find out what the British government was prepared to do. "Should we be defeated," Crispi pointed out, "England would lose a faithful ally on the seas."

Two days later Crispi again went to see the king. "I give him the latest news from the Vatican," Crispi wrote, "which causes him much surprise." That same day, the prime minister sent a dramatic telegram to the Italian ambassador in Paris: "I have received news from the border that French troops are massing there with hostile intent. That, combined with pressures coming from the French embassy to the Vatican, is aimed at forcing the pope to abandon Rome." Crispi added, by way of reproach: "I am amazed at Your Excellency's silence."[14]

That evening, after midnight, Crispi telegraphed his ambassadors in Berlin, Vienna, and London to tell them that war was at hand: "The redoubled weaponry on the French border and the news that comes from Paris confirm that we are close to war . . . The pope's departure from Rome, on the advice of the government of the [French] Republic, seems to have been decided upon." By getting the pope to leave Italy, he charged, "France is trying to manufacture a pretext for a conflict that, in our view, would lead to war." The ambassadors were to speak of the threat with the German, Austrian, and British foreign ministers.

Yet Crispi failed to get the other governments to support his campaign. Typical was the reaction reported in a telegram that Costantino Nigra, the Italian ambassador to Vienna, sent on July 18. The ambassador had hurriedly arranged a meeting with Kalnóky and had read him Crispi's telegram. "He has asked me to tell you," wrote Nigra, "that he does not believe that France has the least intention of making war on Italy at this time, nor that the pope intends to leave Rome any time soon . . . Nor does Kalnóky believe in any conspiracy between France and the pope on this subject."[15]

Nigra's response angered Crispi, who summoned him immediately to Rome. Crispi described their meeting: "I acquaint him with the news we have from France and with what we know about the Vatican. I point out that the pressure brought to bear by M. de Monbel [to get the pope to leave Rome] is meant seriously, and he has failed so far simply owing to the pope's indecision." Crispi went on to attribute the Austrian government's refusal to see the danger to the incompetence of their ambassador to the Holy See. But Nigra was unmoved, insisting that any plans for papal departure could not be concealed from Kalnóky.

Crispi would have none of it. "Be that as it may," he said, "we must know what Austria would do in case we are attacked by France. She would be in duty bound to defend us." Should Austria and Germany come to Italy's aid, Crispi added, "the joint action of the three fleets would overpower France, and if, as is probable, England should join us, we might be sure of victory."[16]

By this time, the French envoy to the Holy See was having second thoughts about his earlier report that the pope was about to leave Rome. "It would seem," he wrote to the French foreign minister, "just as I had initially believed, that the Holy See has raised this burning question both to rekindle Catholics' sentiments for the Head of the Church and to slow the hostile acts that the Italian government and a part of the Italian nation have shown themselves so willingly to aim at the papacy." What prompted Monbel's turnabout was a recent meeting with Rampolla, who had told him that the decision to abandon Rome was being put off.

Monbel added that Italy's leaders, despite their feigned nonchalance, were terrified by the thought that the pope might go, believing that neither the government nor the monarchy itself would last long with the pope outside Italy. He explained:

> The pope in Rome offers the surest guarantee for the Government, both in resisting the invasions of socialism and republican propaganda, and in preventing the formation of a dangerous opposition in the country and in parliament. With the pope here — which is to say with an enemy in the Capital always ready to undermine the legitimacy of the institutions and to ally itself with adversaries from within as from without — no opposition is possible. The simple words "temporal power" are enough to rally men of different opinions around the Government. In the midst of this terror a prime minister can do what he wants, go where he wants, without any pressure, assured of the nation's prior approval. In a word, if Italy did not have the pope, and a *hostile* pope, it would have to invent him.[17]

In France, meanwhile, the press was becoming ever more antagonistic to the Italian government. On July 15 the prestigious — and secular — *Revue des Deux-Mondes* warned that Crispi's recklessness risked disastrous consequences for Italy: "No country would go to war to put Rome back under ecclesiastical domination," the journal observed. "But any country that ends up in a war with Italy will be forced to play the pontifical card against it . . . For Italy, a major war would quite simply mean ruination . . . Bankruptcy, poverty, revolution, may not be the only price of its defeat. It would put something else at risk: its capital."[18]

On July 21 Crispi invited an old friend, Cardinal Gustav von Hohenlohe, to his home. Hohenlohe, from an aristocratic German family, had been made a cardinal at the age of forty-four in 1866, a choice that Pius IX came to regret. A champion of the forces against infallibility at the First Vatican Council, Hohenlohe was nominated by Bismarck as Berlin's first nuncio to the Holy See in 1872, only to suffer the humiliation of having the pope reject his candidacy. Long a proponent of reconciliation, he also, as a good German, strongly supported the Triple Alliance. One of the intransigents' most illustrious enemies, he lived in fear of assassination and had, a few months before his meeting with Crispi, asked for Italian police protection. As a result, he traveled with a secret police agent as his bodyguard. Whether there was any basis for his fears is not clear, but there had been a series of suspicious deaths and murders of high-ranking liberal priests over the past years, including one of his own assistants.[19]

"There is talk of the pope's departure," Crispi told Hohenlohe, "and a certain party is seeking to persuade him to quit the Vatican." He then asked the cardinal to carry a message to the pope:

"I wish to recommend — and this I beg Your Eminence to repeat to the pope — that he be careful not to trigger hostilities, and that he remember what Pius IX's appeal to foreign arms cost him. Not only would religion suffer through such an act, but so would the man himself who is the sovereign prince of that religion."

According to the account that Crispi recorded that day in his diary, Hohenlohe listened carefully, "frequently manifesting his approval of what I was saying by a nod or exclamation." The cardinal then replied:

"I do not often go to the Vatican, but I will go now, and do what you have asked of me. The pope will not leave, but one cannot always be sure of him. He likes the world to be talking about him, and is subject to fits of nervous excitement which not infrequently lead to imprudent decisions."

But, as it turned out, Leo refused to see the cardinal, an affront to Hohenlohe's dignity that was compounded by Rampolla's suggestion that the cardinal speak with him instead. "It seems that they are afraid of me. I don't know why!" he later told Crispi. Rather than talk to Rampolla, Hohenlohe decided to send the pope a letter, which, it seems, simply angered Leo even more.[20]

While Crispi kept warning his Triple Alliance partners of the imminent threat of war, Europe's leaders kept urging him to calm down.[21]

But Crispi was undeterred, using *La Riforma*, the newspaper that had become his unofficial mouthpiece, to keep sounding the alarm. On July 21 *La Riforma* once again warned that the pope's secret plans for departure could only be understood as part of a plot aimed at the restoration of temporal power through foreign invasion. Should Leo put this plan into effect, the paper predicted, it would produce a schism in the Church in Italy, for not only would virtually all lay Italians turn against the pope, but many of the clergy would as well.

Monbel, who reported all this to Paris, added, "The goal that Monsieur Crispi's paper is pursuing is clear, passing Leo XIII off as an enemy of his own country, and arousing, so to speak, in advance the revolt of Italian Catholics and clergy against the Vatican's declared intention of abandoning Rome." The semiofficial paper, Monbel concluded, was certainly not expressing itself in this way out of any concern for the Vatican. Rather, in discouraging the pope from fleeing, the newspaper's fulminations revealed Crispi's strong belief that "Leo XIII's continued residence in Rome is indispensable for the Italian government's security."[22]

Angry that the Germans were not taking his warnings seriously, Crispi wrote to his ambassador in Berlin. The ambassador had earned Crispi's scorn by suggesting that because those in power in France were anticlerics, they would never champion the Vatican's cause against Italy. "Let me observe," Crispi wrote, "that the pope, in France, is, independently of religion, a political force that is used against us. On November 28, 1848, General Cavaignac ordered the expedition to Rome to restore Pius IX, and in that France succeeded. Today they want to repeat the same thing, dragging Leo XIII abroad with the promise of having him return as pope-king. I have positive information to this effect."[23]

Still no one would heed Crispi's warnings. On July 28, 1889, in the latest in what was becoming a monotonous chorus, Italy's ambassador to Vienna telegraphed Crispi on his recent conversation with Kalnóky: "He has authorized me to confirm that all of his information, coming from the best sources, exclude the possibility of France's launching a war on Italy, as well as the possibility of the pope's leaving in case of war.[24]

While not convincing any of the European powers, Crispi's accusations were beginning to rattle the Italian royal court and the military.

By late July their anxiety was evident in the pages of *Fanfulla*, the newspaper most closely identified with the court and the upper echelon of the armed forces. Examining the prospect that France might convince the pope to leave Rome in order "to create the grounds for a war based on the revolt of international Catholic sentiment," the paper fretted: "With the pope outside Rome, public opinion in the Catholic countries would quickly turn against us. Our relations with Austria and its freedom of action in our favor would be impeded, and Spain, His Holiness's likely refuge, would quickly be led into the French orbit." The fact that France's government was dominated by men who were firmly secular might at first sight make this prospect seem unlikely. But, the paper warned, so great were France's internal problems that it was now "plausible that France might really be interested in aiding the intransigents to overcome the pope's resistance."[25]

On July 30, in the wake of the flood of articles appearing in newspapers from Venice to Naples predicting the pope's imminent flight and trumpeting the critical role being played by France, Cardinal Rampolla sought out the French chargé d'affaires to the Holy See. While assuring Monbel that the newspaper stories of the pope's purported decision to leave were filled with "lies and calumnies," he did not deny it was a possibility. On the contrary, he dwelled on the warm welcome the pope would receive were he to go to Spain.

That the French were far from being part of a secret agreement with the Vatican was again clear from Monbel's closing words in his report of this conversation to Paris: "On the actual state of the question, there is no doubt that the greatest reserve is being observed in the Vatican, and that the project, if project there is, has not yet taken any definitive form. In their conversations, the cardinals always admit the possibility of a departure, but there is a notable difference of opinion among them regarding the time when it should occur."[26]

If Crispi was using fears of the pope's flight to drum up political support inside Italy and abroad, Leo and his secretary of state were no less busy doing the same. By this time, Europe's papers were so filled with stories of the pope's likely move to Spain that the Spanish government itself began worriedly asking for the latest news from the Vatican so that it could better divine the pope's intentions. The Spaniards' belief that the pope might be planning a move to their soil got further support when Rampolla called in the Spanish ambassador to the Holy

See and asked him to reaffirm Spain's earlier invitation. Rampolla sought and received similar assurances from the Portuguese ambassador.[27]

In a conversation with Monbel in early August, Rampolla put the French on notice that departure might come quickly, telling the French envoy that "public opinion has just about accepted the need for departure, and even for a departure to come soon. Moreover, Spain is the destination practically imposed by its location and climate, and by its inhabitants' wishes." The Vatican had taken the offensive. "For the first time in many years," Rampolla noted with satisfaction, "Italy has been stopped in its tracks and has had to retreat as a result of the Holy Father's action." The French should be very pleased, he added, for it was not France but the Holy See itself that was now "most responsible for holding the Triple Alliance in check."[28]

In the wake of the dedication of the Bruno monument, with the anticlerical diatribes growing ever louder on the streets, in club meetings, and in the pages of the press, the intransigents were increasingly pressuring the pope to go. In mid-August a new anticlerical paper, *Cronaca Nera*, appeared, with a new series of attacks on Rome's most prominent cardinals. Using apostate priests to write their stories, the inaugural issue took special aim at the cardinal vicar of Rome, Lucido Parocchi. Enraged, Parocchi was ready to pack his bags. "We will certainly be forced to leave Rome," he told one colleague.

A few days after hearing of this episode, Monbel had a long conversation with Monsignor Pujol, Superior of Saint-Louis, France's church in Rome. Pujol too was furious about the newspaper attacks on the high clergy, which he believed the government was behind. He reported that in a recent conversation with Parocchi, the cardinal vicar had told him that it would take just one more unpleasant incident to trigger a move. "Ah," Parocchi had exclaimed, "if only Leo XIII would be so great as to decide to leave Rome!"[29]

Amid these threats of war, of papal flight, and the possibility that Italy's unification could itself be undone, the embattled prime minister decided he needed to relax. Finding himself in Naples, he decided to take his daughter out for an afternoon ride. It was Friday, September 13. As Crispi and his daughter admired the view from their open carriage, a thin young man, shabbily dressed all in gray, appeared out of nowhere running alongside their carriage. He jumped onto the sideboard, and, holding on to the door with his left hand, pulled a large rock out of his right pocket and hurled it with all his strength at the prime minister's face. A middle-aged priest, Don Vito Massari, having stopped by the side of the road to watch Crispi pass, witnessed the attack. Shouting "Stop Crispi's assassin!" he ran toward the carriage just as the attacker began to pull a second large rock from his pocket. Blood poured down Crispi's face where the first rock had hit him; his daughter wailed in horror. Hearing the shouts, a young man passing by also began running toward the site and, arriving first at the scene, collared the would-be assassin before he could hurl his second missile. Blood flowed from the jagged wound on Crispi's face and, more worryingly, oozed from his left ear. The semiconscious Crispi was rushed away. The doctors at first feared a cranial lesion, and with it an uncertain prognosis, but they soon discovered that Crispi was not seriously hurt. Apart from a few stitches needed to close the wound and the discomfort caused by the facial bruising, the prime minister was in good shape and as feisty as ever.

Over the next days, the Catholic press told of the heroic priest who had saved the prime minister's life. The liberal press, for its part, made no mention of him.

In the weeks that followed, try as they might, police investigators could not get the would-be assassin, an impoverished twenty-one-year-old enamored of republican ideals and no friend of the Church, to name any accomplices. The Church papers argued that Crispi — the old revolutionary — had reaped what he had sown. The liberal press charged that it was the Church that was to blame for the near-tragedy, its ceaseless vilification of the prime minister having spread the hatred that had, as filtered through the mind of a disturbed young man, come close to ending the prime minister's life. Characteristically, Crispi himself suspected that the young man had not acted alone but was part of a French plot against him.[30]

It had been almost three decades since the Kingdom of Italy was founded, and almost two since Rome had become its capital. Yet the battle raged on. The Church continued to warn all the faithful that the Italian state was illegitimate, its founding a sacrilege, its leaders doing the work of the devil, its capital an affront to God. Throughout Europe, many wondered whether Italy could last much longer.

Epilogue:
Italy and the Pope

*S*EPTEMBER 20, 1870, marked a historic turning point both for the Roman Catholic Church and for Italy — and, one could say, for the whole Western world as well: on that date the Middle Ages was finally laid to rest. Europe's last theocratic government was ended and with it a model of government based on a mixture of Church law and civil law, of discrimination against those practicing minority religions, of a Church monopoly over education and social services, and the use of police powers to enforce religious observance. In the short run, all this proved traumatic for the Holy See, but from our vantage point today it was, of course, inevitable and, ultimately, liberating for the Church itself.[1]

The pope never did abandon Rome. Yet the last years of the nineteenth century saw little reduction of the tensions between church and state, with periodic flare-ups producing new rounds of denunciations, charges, and fears on both sides. Italy remained perilously weak, its legitimacy undercut by the pope and the Church.

While Leo XIII's earlier hopes of making peace with the Italian state waned and ecclesiastical proponents of reconciliation were silenced, the pope was well aware of the need for a more positive program to adapt the Church to the times and to win greater popular support. Toward this end, in May 1891 he released the historic encyclical *Rerum novarum,* castigating the excesses of capitalism while warning of the evils of socialism. By speaking out forcefully in favor of workers' rights, the pope helped change the Church's image as the handmaiden of the elites.

To mark this new initiative, the encyclical was followed by an endless stream of working-class pilgrims to the Vatican, including, in September of that year, over 20,000 French workers. The scene on September 21, when the French pilgrims crowded into St. Peter's to hear the pope say a special mass for them, was described by a Roman newspaper close to the government: "This old man lifts the chalice with his trembling arm; his court, in resplendent dress, kneels around him in front of the altar; this extraordinary crowd bends their knees or bows their head in the immense temple, where only a sweet music, steeped in mysticism, is heard. It all made for an imposing, truly unique scene."[2]

The coincidence of the massive presence of the French pilgrims with the celebration of the twenty-first anniversary of the taking of Rome was not lost on the Italians. The moderate *Fanfulla* complained: "These so-called pilgrims have come to our capital for the sole purpose of protesting Italy's taking of Rome." Crispi's paper, *La Riforma,* kept tensions high: "The gunpowder is all ready. It will take but a spark for it to explode.[3]

The match was lit on the morning of October 2, when pilgrims from a French Catholic youth group visited the Pantheon, which held Italy's most sacred patriotic shrine, the tomb of Victor Emmanuel. Beside the tomb was a register in which guests signed their name. One of the young Catholics, an eighteen-year-old seminarian, wrote in large letters next to his signature, "Vive le Pape!" Two of his comrades followed his example, scrawling "Long live the Pope!" next to their names.

Word of the affront soon spread through the streets, the sacrilege growing ever more outrageous in the retelling: French pilgrims had defiled the monument to the father of the nation. Crowds of outraged Italian patriots descended on the Pantheon; then groups broke off, rushing through the city's streets, waving Italian flags, and shouting "Long live the King!," "Down with the French Pilgrims!," "Down with the Vatican!" Pilgrims peacefully walking by were chased and harassed. That evening angry patriots made their way to the imposing French embassy, at the Farnese Palace, again waving flags, holding burning torches, and shouting "Down with the Pope!" "Down with the French!" Dispersed by a large contingent of police and soldiers, they surged into the nearby Campo dei Fiori, where they cheered the statue of Giordano Bruno. Similar demonstrations began the following evening in Turin and other Italian cities. In Bari and Palermo, the authorities succeeded in stopping the demonstrators as they marched on the local French consulates. Meanwhile, the young man who triggered the outbreak with his scribbling in the Pantheon guestbook was arrested, jailed, then released on October 10. He was escorted to the French border and received by his countrymen as a Catholic hero.[4]

These old battles continued, but forces of change began to appear, forces that would eventually encourage the Church to come to terms with the Italian state. The end of the century, and the years that followed, saw the dramatic growth of the socialist movement in Italy, viewed by both Italian and Church leaders as a mortal threat. With the expansion of suffrage, those in power grew ever more frustrated with the *non expedit* that kept Catholics from voting. In 1894, just returned to the prime ministership after a two-year absence, Crispi tried once again to initiate secret negotiations with the Vatican aimed at forming a coalition directed against the growing ranks of the extreme left, relying this time on Monsignor Isidoro Carini, the son of an old friend.

Yet these efforts would come to nothing, partially because Crispi was constrained by those around him from making any territorial concessions to the pope — if in fact he was ever inclined to do so himself, which is doubtful — and because the pope, surrounded by intransigents, was in no mood to entirely renounce his claims to temporal power. In January 1895, any chance for these secret negotiations ended when the healthy fifty-one-year-old Monsignor Carini suddenly became ill and died. Rumors that he had been poisoned by intransigents in the Vatican quickly spread. Cardinal Hohenlohe, another proponent of reconciliation who had long feared such a fate for himself, had no doubts: "They've poisoned him, because he was inconvenient for certain people." He added: "In Rome, you risk being poisoned every half hour." Monsignor Carini's family asked for an autopsy. Their request was denied.[5]

Crispi's new government, facing spreading peasant revolts in Sicily, responded by sending troops to the island and proclaiming martial law. The rapid expansion and increased militancy of socialist organizations throughout northern Italy were, likewise, dealt with by the introduction of new repressive laws. Socialists, anarchists, disgruntled peasants, and government corruption scandals all left the Italian leadership battered. With the enthusiasms of national unification a distant memory for most, Italian nationalists feared for the future of their country.

Some sense of this mood can be gleaned from the diary of one of the most acute chroniclers of Italy's fin de siècle, Domenico Farini, president of the Italian Senate and confidant of the king.

Eager to generate greater popular support for the state and its institutions, Farini and like-minded patriots saw the upcoming twenty-fifth anniversary of the taking of Rome as an opportunity that they could not afford to pass up. But they had to contend with other conservatives in parliament, who feared that any festivities marking September 20 would anger the pope.

In a March 1894 diary entry, following a parliament vote against the initial plans for the anniversary celebrations, Farini expressed his dismay. The vote had confirmed his worst suspicions. "The Italians," he wrote, "are tired of Rome and of unification. The papal partisans are overjoyed. There is really no longer any room in this city for anyone other than the pope. The Romans who were with us as long as they had, or hoped to get, certain benefits are now increasingly turning away. Here either the reds or the blacks will prevail."[6]

The following February, the plan to create a committee of luminaries to serve as honorary sponsors of the twenty-fifth anniversary celebrations was put off. Members of parliament had nixed it, as one explained, "in order not to offend the Vatican." Farini was incensed: "Strange confession . . . They think that they can befriend the Vatican by repudiating the celebration of September 20. It would take a lot more! They would have to restore all that September 20 took from them. And even that would not be enough! They would then also want what was taken in 1860. Because the government of the priests does not die, it does not give an inch, it does not give up."

A week later, Farini was accosted by a group of senators who were angry because a government minister had signed on as an official sponsor of the anniversary ceremonies.

"Why make that poor old man in the Vatican unhappy?" one of the senators asked.

"In order not to offend him," replied Farini, "the Senate and the king would have to leave Rome."

Farini was convinced that the Italian state was in serious trouble. Moderates and conservatives were so afraid of the socialist threat, he thought, that they could no longer resist the temptation to seek the pope's support, at whatever cost. "We are," he wrote, "on an extremely dangerous slope. To protect itself, society feels the need for religion, for the clergy, for the pope. The State is forced to invoke it, while the pope cannot recognize — and will never resign himself to — the Italian state in the form in which it now exists. And so the conservatives will abandon the Italian state."[7]

Despite the conservatives' misgivings, plans for the twenty-fifth anniversary commemoration went ahead, strongly supported by Prime Minister Crispi. The highlight of the ceremonies in Rome took place on September 20, when a huge equestrian statue of Garibaldi was unveiled at the top of the Gianiculum hill. The symbolism was not lost on the Vatican. It was Garibaldi who had branded the papacy a cancerous growth on Italian society and argued that Rome's priests could be put to more productive use by being sent to drain the nearby marshes. This same Garibaldi, much larger than life, now had his head turned left, looking out toward the Vatican, while his horse advanced toward the center of the city.

Nor did the speech that Crispi gave in front of the statue that day help calm Italian souls. Noting that the statue was erected in the midst of the battlefield where, in 1849, Garibaldi had led the defense of the Roman republic against the French army, Crispi denounced the French "invader" for having "taken on the barbarous mission of restoring the priestly tyranny." He then went on to lecture the Church on its proper mission: "If Christianity, following the teachings of Paul and John, was able, without the aid of worldly arms, to conquer the world, it is difficult to understand why the Vatican must still aspire to civil rule in order to carry out its spiritual activities." Crispi then set out to explain the Vatican's true motivations, as he saw them: "It is not for the protection nor for the prestige of religion that our adversaries invoke the Holy See's restoration of temporal power, but for human reasons: their lust for a kingdom, their earthly greed."[8]

The king, Umberto I, found his prime minister's remarks vulgar and offensive and unnecessarily provocative, but he was not especially surprised. As he confided to one of his retinue: "Crispi is a pig, but a necessary pig."[9] Yet Crispi's fabled indispensability was about to desert him. A few months later, after the disastrous defeat of Italian troops at Adua, in Ethiopia, violent popular protests forced his resignation. Nor would the king last much longer himself, the end of his reign brought by an anarchist's bullet in July 1900. He was fifty-six years old.

Leo XIII, aged ninety, had by then occupied St. Peter's chair for twenty-two years, during which time he had never set foot outside the precincts of the Vatican. In his last years, weakened by age and embittered by a life lived under siege, he had given up on his earlier dream of reconciliation with the Italian state. In the winter of 1901–2, sensing that death was near, he dictated what came to be known as his "political last testament," ordering that it be read at the conclave following his death. In it he denounced the conditions in which the pope found himself, "robbed of his civil sovereignty, and therefore of his independence and freedom, and reduced to living under hostile domination." The pope reaffirmed the impossibility of two sovereigns living in Rome and expressed his belief that God would ultimately bring an end to the unholy revolt against His kingdom. In his final remarks, Leo fondly recalled the "pontiffs best known for their wisdom and holiness, who in defense of their independence and their civil principality did not hesitate to use, with great vigor, both spiritual and material arms."[10]

Leo died in 1903. Rampolla, believed by many to be his logical successor, saw his ambitions crushed by the Austrians — who had long resented his French sympathies — an Austrian cardinal casting his country's veto before he could get the votes needed for election.[11] And so Leo was succeeded by Pius X, a man who, in his gregarious personality, peasant family background, and disdain for international diplomacy, could hardly have been more unlike his predecessor. Yet Pius X continued the Church's battle against modern times and refused to recognize the Italian state. It was only on his death and with the papacy of Benedict XV in 1914 that a new attitude began to take hold in the Vatican. It had been over half a century since the Kingdom of Italy was founded, and it was by then impossible to believe that the Papal States could ever be brought back.

By the time the First World War was over, it was clear to virtually everyone in the Vatican that the growing socialist movement presented a much greater threat than any posed by the moderate forces that controlled the Italian government. And so, in 1919, Benedict XV agreed to the creation of a Catholic political party, a move that his predecessors had so long resisted. The Italian Popular Party was formed, led by a priest, Luigi Sturzo, but not directly dependent on the Vatican or the Church hierarchy. With the approach of the first elections in which the new party would appear, in November of that year, the pope finally lifted the *non expedit*, which for so many decades had prohibited Catholics from voting or serving in parliament.

In fact, the Catholic party did very well, receiving 21 percent of the vote, coming in second only to the Socialist Party, which received 32 percent. For the "liberals" who had controlled the Italian government for decades, the only way to form a cabinet that excluded the socialists was by relying on the deputies of the Popular Party. This they did. Yet the new government faced ever more militant trade unions and peasant leagues on its left and, on its right, the spread of fascist violence. Led by Benito Mussolini, the fascists won the favor of the police and military, who turned a blind eye to the attacks mounted by their squads of thugs. Amid all the violence, the state itself began to totter. In October 1922, in a grand theatrical gesture, Mussolini led his fascist acolytes on a March on Rome, where a craven Victor Emmanuel III, Umberto's diminutive son, hastily named him the new prime minister.

Mussolini acted quickly to consolidate his power and by the mid-1920s had abolished all political organizations other than his own. In this he was helped by the Vatican, which decided that its best bet was to pull the plug on its own Catholic party and support Mussolini's more effective efforts to rid Italian society of the scourge of socialism. For his part, the Duce saw the tremendous benefit to be had — both domestically and internationally — by becoming the first Italian leader to make peace with the Church. And so, on February 11, 1929, Mussolini himself, alongside the Vatican's secretary of state, Pietro Gasparri, signed the Lateran Pacts, ending the hostility that had existed between church and state since the Kingdom of Italy was proclaimed in 1861. The Vatican agreed to recognize the legitimacy of the Italian state and of its capital in Rome. In exchange, the pope was given a large payment for the loss of the Papal States and a concordat regulating relations between the Catholic Church and Italy. The Vatican was deemed to have the rights of a sovereign state, to be called Vatican City. The Catholic religion became Italy's sole official religion. Catholic religious instruction was made obligatory in the public schools, and Catholic religious imagery was returned to schoolrooms and public offices throughout the country.

On July 25, 1929, after celebrating mass in St. Peter's, Pope Pius XI led a joyful procession through the great doors of the basilica and into the public square, where he pronounced his blessings to the multitudes. For the first time in almost fifty-nine years a pope had left the walls of the Vatican.

The following year, in deference to the Vatican, the fascist state abolished September 20 as a national holiday. The origins of modern Italy in the battle against the political power of the papacy had now become a part of history that Italians were encouraged to forget.

Fascism's fall a decade and a half later left Mussolini's deal with the Vatican intact, with the Lateran Pacts enshrined in the new, postwar Italian constitution. But the Savoyard monarchy was not so lucky. Angered by the king's support for fascism and his cowardly behavior during the war, the Italian people voted to replace the monarchy with a republic. Although it had taken longer than Pius IX had imagined, his prediction had finally come true: Rome had room for but a single sovereign.

One consequence of this burying of the hatchet was that Italy became a country rather unlike others, a country unable to celebrate its own birth, a country whose founding fathers had become an embarrassment.

Not a year now goes by without a torrent of new books bemoaning the Italians' lack of national spirit and the weakness of their allegiance to the Italian state. The role played by the Vatican's decades-long refusal to recognize the state's legitimacy is hard to ignore here. Yet Italy today is a country where placards marking historic battles for national unification — at least those in its capital and in the rest of what were once the Papal States — must carefully avoid mentioning against whom those battles were actually fought. Teaching schoolchildren the views of the greatest hero of national unification, Giuseppe Garibaldi, has now become unthinkable. Celebrating the date when the capital was finally captured from the hands of the principal foe of national unification is considered unseemly, the name of the enemy itself unmentionable.

September 20, 2002, passed in Rome with little public notice. The annual mass held by the Catholic faithful, mourning the anniversary of the day when Rome was taken from the pontiff, received, as usual, no more than a paragraph in the papers the next day. On the front page of Rome's daily newspaper on September 21, the only story related to church and state was a piece written by Monsignor Manlio Asta defending the placement of the crucifix in public classrooms on the grounds that the cross was a universal symbol of European civilization.[12]

But two months later, Romans witnessed a dramatic scene. A black

Mercedes convertible pulled up to the Montecitorio Palace, the home of Italy's House of Deputies. The car bore a distinctive license plate: VATICAN CITY 1. Gingerly, but without assistance, the elderly, ailing passenger, dressed in his white robes and white skullcap, emerged from the back. There to receive him were the presidents of the House and the Senate. As John Paul II made his way into the great hemisphere of the parliamentary hall, an enthusiastic burst of applause erupted from the assembled dignitaries, a rare joint session of the House and Senate, with Prime Minister Silvio Berlusconi and the members of his cabinet present. The pontiff spoke for forty-six minutes, urging the Italian state to more fully embrace Catholic values. When he finished, the members of parliament and cabinet ministers rushed to greet him, some getting down on their knees before him, others kissing his hand. For the first time since Pius IX lost the Holy City, the distinctive papal white and yellow flag flew proudly over the center of power in Rome.

Far from sacred today, by contrast, are the heroes of Italian unification, their motives questioned, their honesty impugned, and their project of national unification itself viewed negatively by the growing chorus of voices emboldened by the current atmosphere to express sentiments that in an earlier period would have targeted them for public scorn.

In 1999 the archbishop of Bologna, Cardinal Giacomo Biffi, one of the Italian Church's best-known figures, published a small book on the Risorgimento. There he quoted Feodor Dostoyevsky as asking, in 1877, apropos of Cavour's success in unifying Italy: "And so just what did Count Cavour accomplish? A little second-rate kingdom, of no international importance, without ambitions, made bourgeois." Biffi went on to assert that the Risorgimento had in fact undermined Italy's stature: "Just at the moment when — with an 'Italian' government, an 'Italian' parliament, and an 'Italian' army — we were welcomed among the peoples as an autonomous, identifiable subject, it would seem that we no longer had anything to say to anyone." In the old days, when Italians had been divided into different states, "they continued to teach something to everyone." By contrast, "once they had achieved the hoped-for unity and political independence, they tried only to imitate a bit of everyone, especially the French and the English, up to the present day, when they have resigned themselves to being a cultural colony of the United States."

The big mistake, both of the Risorgimento's leaders and of liberals more generally, in Cardinal Biffi's estimation, was their failure to recognize Catholicism as the cornerstone of Italian national identity. Trying to establish a nation based on other principles — the principles of the Risorgimento — could only lead to disaster.[13]

Today there is little doubt in Rome who is the most powerful leader. One man alone is the object of great reverence, one man alone is seen as embodying society's deepest aspirations, a man whose every act is the object of adulatory front-page coverage in the press, even of the left. And were Garibaldi somehow to come to life and climb down from his horse on top of the Gianiculum, he would be better advised to keep his thoughts on the Vatican to himself. From the perspective of Italians of the twenty-first century, the hero of Italian unification, the Hero of Two Worlds, is looking more and more like an embarrassing crackpot.

Acknowledgments
Notes
References Cited
Illustration Sources
Index

Acknowledgments

THANKS ARE DUE, first of all, to Wendy Strothman and Eric Chinski, who both believed in this book from the beginning and who made me feel welcome at Houghton Mifflin. Eric's keen editorial eye and literary sensibility have resulted in a better book. Thanks, too, to Janet Silver at Houghton Mifflin for her strong support and for her help in crafting the final version of the book.

Authors whose books are based primarily on archival materials depend on the goodwill and aid of those who run and control the archives. This book is no exception. It has been made possible by help from archivists at the Vatican (particularly at the Archivio Segreto Vaticano and the Archivio della Congregrazione per gli Affari Ecclesiastici Straordinari), at the Archivio di Stato di Roma, and at the archives of the Ministère des Affaires Etrangères in Paris. I would like to thank in particular the director (Giuseppe Talamo), the curator (Marco Pizzo), and the archivist (Fabrizio Alberti) of the archives of the Istituto per la Storia del Risorgimento Italiano in Rome for their help. Thanks too to Carmelo Catania for assisting me with the photographing of images at that archive. At the archive of the Museo Civico del Risorgimento, Bologna, I would like to thank the directors, Mirtide Gavelli and Otello Sangiorgi.

Valuable advice along the way was offered by Giuseppe Pizzorusso and Matteo Sanfilippo, who also read a much longer, early version of the manuscript and provided helpful comments. John A. Davis and Scott Lerner are also to be thanked for their comments on that draft,

ACKNOWLEDGMENTS

as are Paolo Zaninoni, my multitalented editor at Rizzoli, and Gian-vittorio Signorotto. Thanks to Michael Putnam for his help on my schoolboy Latin.

At Brown, I was greatly aided by my excellent research assistants, Simone Poliandri and Vika Zafrin. Erick Castellanos, Chiara Sartori, Jenny Asarnow, Kathy Grimaldi, Shirley Gordon, and Matilde Andrade also provided valuable assistance at Brown, and thanks are due to Laura Scotto and Vittoria Serafini for their work with archival material in Rome.

For their help in the final production process at Houghton Mifflin, I'd like to thank Meg Lemke, for her careful work in coordinating the publication process, and Luise Erdmann, whom I was fortunate to have as manuscript editor. Finally, my appreciation, as always, for all the support provided by my literary agent, Ted Chichak.

Notes

Abbreviations used for archival sources

ASV: Archivio Segreto Vaticano
  SS: Segreteria di Stato
  EM: Epoca Moderna
AAEESS: Archivio Storico, Sacra Congregazione degli Affari Ecclesiastici
  Straordinari
  SE: Stati Ecclesiastici
ASR: Archivio di Stato di Roma
  Questura di Roma
  Prefettura di Roma
  Tribunale Civile e Correzzionale
MAE: Archives, Ministère des Affaires Etrangères, Paris
  CP: Correspondance Politique
  MAES: MAE, Saint Siège
  MAEI: MAE, Italie

Abbreviation used for published documents

DDI: *Documenti diplomatici italiani*, from series 1, vol. 13 (1870), to series 2, vol. 22 (1889). Ministero degli Affari Esteri (1960–1997). Roma: Libreria di Stato.

Complete citations for nineteenth-century newspaper articles may be found in the endnotes. All other published works cited in the endnotes may be found in References Cited.

Prologue

1. *Falti nuovi*, p. 36.

Introduction: *Italy's Birth and Near Demise*

1. According to one estimate, only 2 percent of the population had played any role in bringing about Italian unification (Mazzonis 2003, p. 140).
2. This portrait of Bismarck is based largely on Pflanze (1990). The quotation is also from Pflanze (1990:46).

1. *Destroying the Papal States*

1. Aubert 1990b, p. 147.
2. Blakiston 1962, n. 292, Odo Russell to Earl R., 16 February 1864. Russell occupied a peculiar position because Britain had no official ambassador to the Holy See, so

technically Russell had no diplomatic status in Rome. Yet despite this, and despite his known sympathy for the Italian liberals, he met regularly with Antonelli and often with the pope himself (d'Ideville 1875, p. 43).

3. Cadorna 1898, pp. 9–10. The move of the capital to Florence came at no small cost, outraging especially the citizens of Turin, where fifty-two died in protests.

4. Mack Smith 1989, pp. 21–22.

5. Tivaroni 1897, p. 285; Mundt's comments are quoted in Negro 1977, p. 161; Pirri 1958, pp. 102–3; Coppa 1990, p. 188.

6. Blakiston 1962, n. 303, O.R. to Earl R., 14 November 1864.

7. Lawlessness and disorders of various kinds were rampant in the South in these years, the flames fanned by partisans of the old Bourbon dynasty and opponents of the new Italian state. Branding the problem one simply of brigandage, the government declared martial law and sent in large numbers of troops from the North to restore order.

8. Blakiston 1962, n. 305, O.R. to Earl R., 22 November 1864. On receiving Russell's report, the London foreign office decided that the British prime minister, Lord Palmerston, should read it himself. The note that he penciled in the margin shows that he shared Antonelli's and Prince Altomonte's interpretation of the French emperor's motives. "It has been evident for a long time," Palmerston wrote, "that the object of the Emperor as regards Italy is not its unity but its division into separate states."

9. Blakiston 1962, n. 310, O.R. to Earl R., 17 January 1865.

10. Blakiston 1962, n. 335, O.R. to Earl of C., 22 January 1866. The pope's remarks here are a paraphrase.

11. Blakiston 1962, n. 329, O.R. to Earl of C., 3 July 1866.

12. Blakiston 1962, n. 330, O.R. to the Earl of Clarendon, 10 July 1866.

13. Blakiston 1962, n. 353, O.R. to Lord Stanley, 27 July 1866; n. 354, O.R. to Lord S., 23 August 1866; n. 357, O.R. to Lord S., 4 December 1866; n. 359, O.R. to Lord S., 15 December 1866.

14. Viallet 1991, pp. 336–37; Mack Smith 1956, pp. 158–61.

15. Mack Smith 1956, pp. 164–65.

16. Blakiston 1962, n. 349, O.R. to Lord S., 16 January 1868; n. 383, O.R. to Lord S., 26 March 1868.

2. The Pope Becomes Infallible

1. Quoted in Martina 1986, p. 329.

2. Martina 1986, p. 331: Pius IX letter to Franz Josef 19 February 1864.

3. Aubert 1990a.

4. This is my translation of the Italian text.

5. On the ties of the Jesuits to the aristocracy, see Aubert 1972, p. 8.

6. Blakiston 1962, n. 310, Odo Russell to Earl R., Rome, 17 January 1865. Russell wrote of his meeting with Antonelli: "I am assured that he opposed its publication, but was overruled by the Pope, Mérode, and the Jesuits, who are now all powerful in Rome."

7. Blakiston 1962, n. 309, Russell to Earl R., Rome, 17 January 1865.

8. Blakiston 1962, n. 337 and n. 336, Russell to Earl of C., Rome 26 March and 8 February 1866.

9. The English text of the 1868 call for the Council, with its Manichean language of the "vast evils" of modern times, can be found in Butler 1962, p. 69.

10. Quoted in Aubert 1990b, p. 492, Freppel to Larange, June 15, 1869.

11. These letters are found in Hennesey 1963, pp. 82, 175.

12. Quoted in Aubert 1990b, p. 487, Janus, *Der Papst und das Konzil*, Leipzig 1869, p. ix. On Döllinger, see Gadille 1968. On the origins of Quirinus, see Quirinus 1870.

13. Aubert 1990b, p. 492.

14. Opponents of infallibility, on the other hand, charged that the great overrepresentation of the Italians among those with voting rights at the Council was, in effect, disenfranchising the mass of Catholics elsewhere. While the German diocese of Breslau had but a single bishop for its 1.7 million Catholics, what was left of the Papal States, with only 700,000 inhabitants, was represented by 62 bishops. While Germany's 12 million Catholics had just 14 bishops, Naples and Sicily together had 62. As the Council was called to order, almost all of the Austrian, German, and Hungarian bishops stood against papal infallibility, as did many of the French. Yet there were many more Italian bishops than all of them put together (Martina 1995, p. 283; Quirinus 1870, pp. 140–41).

15. Aubert 1990b, p. 497; Martina 1986, p. 166; Hennesey 1963, pp. 36–37.

16. Gregorovius 1907, pp. 345, 347.

17. Blakiston 1962, n. 446, Russell to the Earl of C., Rome, 15 February 1870.

18. Blakiston 1962, n. 454, Earl of C. to O. R., 1 March 1870.

19. Gregorovius 1907, p. 366.

20. The English translation is mine. The Italian original reads: *Quando Eva morse, e morder fece il pomo, Gesù per salvar l'uom, si fece uomo; Mà il Vicario di Cristo, il Nono Pio Per render schiavo l'uom, si vuol far Dio.* From *Pasquino*, cited by Gregorovius 1969, p. 359, in his diary on March 27, 1860.

21. Martina 1990a, pp. 173, 175.

22. Martina 1990a, pp. 205–7, 555–57. The text of the conversation between Guidi and the pope comes from the account provided by Vincenzo Tizzani, who spoke with Cardinal Guidi immediately after the encounter.

23. Antonelli, who had no strong theological feelings on the question of infallibility — or on much else, for that matter — shared the minority's fears. In a June 3, 1870, letter, an influential French bishop reported that Antonelli, despairing of the diplomatic damage that the impending pronouncement of infallibility would wreak, had said, "The Pope has already brought the Papal States to ruin, and now he wants to ruin the Church as well" (Martina 1990a, p. 210).

24. Even in this much milder form, the proposal continued to stir strong opposition among the bishops. As a result, when the infallibility doctrine was first put to a vote, on July 13, 1870, the pope was doubly displeased. Not only was the version being voted on much weaker than he wanted, but a substantial number of bishops still refused to support it. With many bishops absenting themselves from St. Peter's rather than be forced either to break openly with the pope or to vote for a proposition they opposed, the infallibility doctrine obtained only 451 votes in favor, 62 in favor with reservations *(placet juxta modum)*, and 88 against. It took courage for those 88 bishops to cast their votes against the wishes of the pope who had appointed virtually all of them. Curiously, among those who stayed away from the proceedings was Cardinal Antonelli himself (Martina 1990a, p. 212). Martina notes that roughly half

of those voting in favor with reservations *(placet juxta modum)* did so because they thought the proposition was too weak. But he estimates that between the other half who voted *placet juxta modum,* due to opposition to declaring papal infallibility at all, and those who voted against and those who absented themselves out of opposition to the doctrine, at least a quarter of the episcopate were against even this mild form of papal infallibility.

25. Pflanze 1990, pp. 181–82.
26. DDI, series 1, vol. 13, n. 197, 212. Emerico Tkalac al Ministro degli Esteri Visconti Venosta, Roma, 18 and 19 luglio, 1870.
27. Gadille 1968, pp. 87, 161; Otmar 1972, p. 297; Blakiston 1962, n. 535, Odo Russell to Earl G., Rome, 18 July 1870. Even before the first session of the Council, European governments were expressing alarm about the implications of a pronouncement of papal infallibility. In April 1869, for example, Bavaria's foreign minister expressed these concerns in a dispatch to Bavarian ambassadors abroad: "It is unlikely that the Council will occupy itself solely with doctrines of pure theology. The only dogmatic thesis that Rome would wish to be proclaimed at the Council is the papal infallibility. It is evident that this pretension raised to a dogma would pass beyond the purely spiritual domain, and would become a question eminently political, raising the power of the Pope, even on the temporal side, above all princes and peoples of Christendom. This doctrine is therefore of a nature to arouse the attention of all Governments with Catholic subjects" (Butler 1962, p. 77). Within months of the proclamation of papal infallibility, too, Döllinger would be excommunicated, and a splinter group of Old Catholics would form in Germany (Gallon 1971).

3. The Last Days of Papal Rome

1. DDI, series 1, vol. 13, n. 350, Il conte Kulczycki al Segretario Generale degli Affari Esteri Blanc, Terni, 1 agosto 1870.
2. DDI, series 1, vol. 13, n. 341, Il conte Kulczycki al Segretario Generale degli Affari Esteri Blanc, Terni, 30 luglio 1870.
3. Rothan 1885, vol. 2, p. 67.
4. Wetzel 2001, pp. 20–23.
5. English-language accounts of the Franco-Prussian War include Howard (1961) and Wawro (2003).
6. Duggan 2000, pp. 380–82.
7. Howard 1961, pp. 64–65.
8. Duggan 2000, pp. 383–85.
9. DDI, series 1, vol. 13, n. 212, Tkalac to Visconti Venosta, 19 luglio 1870.
10. DDI, series 1, vol. 13, n. 357, Il conte Kulczycki al Segretario Generale degli Affari Esteri Blanc, Terni, 2 agosto 1870.
11. *L'Osservatore Romano,* 1 agosto 1870, p. 1; 2 agosto 1870, p. 3.
12. Mack Smith 1994b, pp. 204–11.
13. Cadorna 1889, pp. 28, 35.
14. With the Holy See no longer protected by French troops, some in the Vatican turned to the Prussians, praying that they would take the place of their defeated foe. Rumors of promises by King Wilhelm to come to the pope's aid soon began to circulate in the Holy City. On August 16, the British envoy in Rome commented: "It is remarkable to hear how confidently support is expected to come to the papacy

from the Protestant Powers, whose Catholic populations are supposed to be sufficiently powerful to exact for it from their governments more or less active protection against its enemies." (Halperin 1939, pp. 32–33.)

Two days later Count Kulczycki reported that the Jesuits, aware that the days of papal control of Rome were dwindling, were urging the pope to flee. He could either escape to Malta or to Germany, confident that he would soon be returned to power behind the Prussian army. The Jesuits, in the meantime, were frantically arranging fictitious sales of their considerable property holdings in Rome to cooperative nonclericals, certain that one of the first acts of the Italian government once its soldiers arrived would be to expropriate their property and send the Company of Jesus packing. As it turned out, their fears were fully justified. (DDI, series 1, vol. 13, n. 528, Il conte Kulczycki al Segretario Generale degli Affari Esteri Blanc, Terni, 18 agosto 1870.)

15. Martina 1972, p. 91.
16. "Ultime notizie," *L'Osservatore Romano,* 17 agosto 1870, p. 3.
17. DDI, series 1, vol. 13, n. 540, Il conte Kulczycki al Segretario Generale degli Affari Esteri Blanc, Terni, 20 agosto 1870. The count added that he could guarantee the accuracy of this account, as it came directly to him from someone in His Holiness's entourage.
18. Boiardi 1989, p. 3.
19. De Leonardis 1980, pp. 192–93, based on the British diplomatic correspondence.
20. ASV, SS, EM, a. 1870, r. 165, fasc. 2, f. 14v.
21. *L'Osservatore Romano,* 20 agosto 1870, p. 2, quoting "La questione di Roma," in *L'Opinione.* The Church newspaper was also reporting that England would not allow the Italians to cross over the border into Roman lands ("Ultime notizie," *L'Osservatore Romano,* 29 agosto 1870, p. 3).
22. "Ultime notizie," *L'Osservatore Romano,* 22 agosto 1870, p. 3; ASV, SS, EM, a. 1870, r. 165, fasc. 2, ff. 17v-18v.
23. ASV, SS, EM, a. 1870, r. 165, fasc. 1, ff. 95v, 103v-106r.
24. Lanza 1938, n. 1864, Rapporto 25 agosto 1870.
25. Tivaroni 1897, pp. 303–5.
26. Rosi 1937, pp. 580–81.
27. Aliberti 1989, pp. 411–28; Chabod 1951, pp. 564–68.
28. DDI, series 1, vol. 13, n. 580, Il Ministro degli Esteri, Visconti Venosta, ai Rappresentanti Diplomatici all'Estero, 29 agosto 1870; DDI, series 1, vol. 13, n. 581. Ministro Degli Esteri, Visconti Venosta, al Ministro a Parigi, Nigra, 29 agosto 1870.
29. Lanza 1938, n. 1865, Colucci a Lanza, Caserta, 31 Agosto 1870.
30. *L'Osservatore Romano,* 31 agosto 1870, p. 3.
31. DDI, series 1, vol. 13, n. 661, Il conte Kulczycki al Segretario Generale degli Affari Esteri, Blanc, 5 settembre 1870.
32. Tavallini 1887, vol. 2, pp. 40–41.
33. DDI, series 1, vol. 13, n. 681, Ministro Degli Esteri, Visconti Venosta, ai Rappresentanti Diplomatici Al'Estero, 7 settembre 1870.
34. DDI, series 1, vol. 13, n. 677, Ministro Degli Esteri, Visconti Venosta, al Ministro a Parigi, Nigra, 7 settembre 1870.
35. Lanza 1938, n. 1919, Lanza a Ponza di San Martino, 8 settembre 1870.
36. Pirri 1951, n. 113, Vittorio Emanuele II a Pio IX, Firenze, 8 settembre 1870, with an-

nex of the same date from the Presidenza del Consiglio dei Ministri. It is worth noting that in the king's offer, the Leonine city was defined as including the Vatican palaces, the Castel Sant'Angelo, and the neighborhood between the Vatican and the Tiber, all of which were surrounded by the wall built by Pope Leo IV in the ninth century.

37. DDI, series 1, vol. 13, n. 712, Il conte Kulczycki al Segretario Generale degli Affari Esteri, Blanc, 8 settembre 1870.

38. Ugolini 1989, p. 450.

39. Pirri 1951, n. 115, Relazione del Card. Antonelli dell'incontro col Conte Ponza di San Martino, 9 settembre 1870. Ponza's own report on his meeting to Lanza is much less detailed; it paints a picture of a secretary of state who, while not ceding an inch, was a sufficient realist to see the futility of papal resistance.

40. Lanza 1938, n. 1931, Ponza di San Martino a Lanza.

41. Reproduced in Cadorna 1889, p. 120.

42. Reproduced in Bardi 1970, p. 32.

43. Pirri 1951, n. 114, Pio IX al Re Vittorio Emanuele II, 11 settembre 1870.

4. Conquering the Holy City

1. ASV, SS, EM, a. 1870, r. 165, fasc. 2, ff. 43 v-44v, undated but 11 settembre 1870.

2. ASV, SS, EM, a. 1870, r. 165, fasc. 2, ff. 44v-r, 12 settembre 1870, nunzio apostolico, Vienna, to Antonelli. Beust himself wrote a long letter to Cav. Palombo, in Rome, on September 13, setting out much the same reasoning for Austria's decision. See ASV, SS, EM, a. 1870, r. 165, fasc. 2, ff. 50v-55v. Palombo was serving as Antonelli's unofficial representative in making the Holy See's case to the Austrian government. Although Beust apparently did not tell the Austrian nuncio, he had, on September 13, sent a long letter to Visconti, in Florence, calling on the Italian government, in marching into the papal state, to show the greatest regard for the pope and do nothing to increase the anxiety already being felt in the Catholic world about the fate of the Holy See. In Bardi 1970, pp. 164–65.

3. The various quotes are from citations in Martina 1990a, pp. 234–38. Martina (1995, p. 311) credits this account of the pope's remarks to Ponza and believes Ponza left them out of his report due to his fear that they would displease Lanza.

4. These three documents are reproduced in Cadorna 1889, pp. 152–54.

5. Lanza 1938, n. 1995, Rapporto, 17 Settembre 1870.

6. These two documents are reproduced in Cadorna 1889, pp. 167 and 172–73. While Cardorna here appeared to define the boundaries of the Leonine city as extending all the way up the Gianiculum hill to the Porta San Pancrazio, the boundaries of what was generally viewed as the Leonine city — identified as the area within the ninth-century wall — were less extended.

7. This account is taken from the testimony at Pius IX's beatification proceedings: Pirri 1951, n. 116, Dal Processo Romano di beatificazione di Pio IX.

8. Discussed in two dispatches of Count Kulczycki: DDI, series 1, vol. 13, n. 721 (8 settembre 1870) and n. 739 (10 settembre 1870). The day before the Italian attack, Pius issued new instructions. "Now that a great sacrilege is about to be committed," he wrote to General Kanzler on September 19, "and the greatest injustice, as the troops of a Catholic king, without any provocation, indeed without even the fig leaf

of any pretext, have besieged the Capital of the Catholic world, I want first of all to thank you, Signor General, and all of your troops." He then gave his final orders. The goal of the defense "must only consist in an act of protest against the violence, and nothing more; that is, talks for a surrender should be undertaken as soon as the breach [in the walls] has been made." Pius continued: "At a time in which all of Europe deplores the large number of victims of a war taking place between two great nations [France and Prussia], it should never be said that the Vicar of Jesus Christ, however unjustly attacked, agreed to a large loss of life. Our Cause is that of God, and We put Our defense entirely in his hands." These instructions represented a slight, but important, change from those he had given the generals earlier. The pope had first told his generals to initiate talks for surrender "at the first sounds of cannon fire." Now he was telling them instead to keep fighting until the Italian army had breached the city's walls. The change was made against the advice of Antonelli, who feared that the pope would be blamed for needless bloodshed. Pius IX had been convinced to amend his orders at the last minute by Kanzler, who had come to see him earlier on the nineteenth and begged him to allow his soldiers to fight. Since these feelings meshed with the pope's own wish to make clear to the world that the Holy City was being taken by violence, he went along. As a result, scores of Italian and papal soldiers would die, and scores of others would carry wounds for life (Pirri 1951, n. 117, Pio IX al Generale Kanzler, Pro-Ministro delle Armi, 19 settembre 1870. On the change in orders, see Martina 1990a, pp. 239–43).

9. The text of the proclamation was published in *L'Osservatore Romano*, 13 settembre 1870, p. 1.

10. Stock 1945, pp. 354–56, D. M. Armstrong to Hamilton Fish United States consulate, Rome, 23 September 1870.

11. Tivaroni 1897, pp. 251–53; Cadorna 1889, p. 56; Halperin 1939, p. 60. Bixio died three years later, having left the navy to seek his fortune as captain of a commercial vessel. He contracted cholera while bound for southeast Asia.

12. "Cronaca cittadina," *L'Osservatore Romano*, 17 ottobre 1870, p. 2 (this was the first issue of the paper after the taking of Rome).

13. Quoted from the *Tribuno*, in Bartoccini 1985, p. 418.

14. Martina 1990a, pp. 243–45; Pirri 1951, n. 116, Dal Processo Romano di beatificazione di Pio IX; Cadorna 1889, pp. 191–202.

5. The Leonine City

1. Martina 1972, p. 99.

2. DDI, series 2, vol. 1, n. 41, Il Ministro a Vienna, Minghetti, a Lord Acton, Vienna, 23 settembre 1870.

3. Cadorna 1889, pp. 216–18.

4. Lanza 1938, n. 2022, Lanza a Cadorna, 22 settembre 1870.

5. Talamo 1979, p. 2–12; Gallon 1971, p. 87.

6. Idem.

7. Cadorna 1889, p. 158, Lanza to Cadorna, 1 ottobre 1870. DDI, series 2, vol. 1, n. 153, Blanc to Visconti, 2 ottobre 1870.

8. Cadorna 1889, pp. 266–69. In all of the Roman territories that day, about 80 percent of those registered voted. Unlike the electoral system in place for parliament, in the

plebiscites the rules specified that all adults had the right to vote, regardless of their literacy or wealth. It was regarded as so obvious that women were excluded from this right that no mention was made of it in the regulations (Pavone 1957, pp. 336–44).

9. *Civiltà Cattolica*, 1871, I, pp. 220–21.

10. DDI, series 2, vol. 1, n. 158, Blanc to Visconti, 2 ottobre 1870.

11. DDI, series 2, vol. 1, n. 207, Blanc to Visconti, 7 ottobre 1870.

12. ASV, SS, EM, a.1870, r.165, fasc.2, f. 71v.

13. DDI, series 2, vol. 1, n. 251, Blanc to Visconti, 12 ottobre 1870.

14. Pavone 1958, pp. 346–48. See also Visconti's letter to Minghetti, then Italian ambassador in Vienna; DDI, series 2, vol. 1, n. 164, 3 ottobre 1870. La Marmora's reputation was not helped by his having been been the general in charge of the Italian forces at the biggest military debacle of the Risorgimento, the battle of Custoza (Tivaroni 1897, 302.).

15. Lanza 1938, n. 2072, Lanza a La Marmora, 13 ottobre 1870.

16. Lanza 1938, n. 2095, La Marmora a Lanza, 19 ottobre 1870.

17. Sella quoted in Fiorentino 1996, p. 45. See also Quazza 1999, v. 3, p. 230. DDI, series 2, vol. 1, n. 371, Visconti al fratello Giovanni, 25 ottobre 1870.

18. Gregorovius 1907, pp. 388, 390; diary entries for October 30 and November 27, 1870.

19. ASV, SS, EM, a. 1870, r. 165, fasc. 4, ff. 17v-r.

20. ASV, SS, EM, a. 1870, r. 165, fasc. 4, f. 73v.

21. ASV, SS, EM, a. 1870, r. 165, fasc. 2, ff. 56v-57r.

22. ASV, SS, EM, a. 1870, r. 165, fasc. 2, ff. 69v-r, 1 ottobre 1870. The pope's complaint about his lack of freedom to use the mails and telegraph prompted the Italian foreign minister to send a circular to all his ambassadors on October 11. Nothing could be further from the truth, Visconti argued; the Vatican had been allowed unfettered access to post and wire service. Antonelli had turned down the government's offer to establish a separate Vatican post and telegraph service, with direct access to the foreign postal services guaranteed, an offer that Visconti reiterated. (DDI, series 2, vol. 1, n. 237, Il Ministro degli Esteri, Visconti Venosta, ai Rappresentanti Diplomatici all'Estero, 11 ottobre 1870.)

To give the Italian ambassadors more ammunition in lobbying foreign governments, the following week Visconti sent them a new circular, arguing that the pope's continued exercise of temporal power, which he described as "the last debris remaining of the institutions of the Middle Ages," had no place in the modern world. "Political sovereignty that does not rest on popular consent," wrote Visconti, "can no longer exist." (DDI, series 2, vol. 1, n. 282, Il Ministro degli Esteri, Visconti Venosta, ai Rappresentanti Diplomatici all'Estero, 18 ottobre 1870.)

23. DDI, series 2, vol. 1, n. 321, Il Ministro degli Esteri, Visconti Venosta, ai Rappresentanti Diplomatici all'Estero, 22 ottobre 1870.

24. Quoted in *L'Osservatore Romano*, 19 ottobre 1870, p. 1. The meeting was held on October 11.

25. ASV, SS, EM, a. 1870, r. 165, fasc. 4, ff. 50 v-53v. The nuncio's report is dated 20 ottobre 1870, and the archbishop's letter to the Prussian king dated 7 ottobre 1870.

26. ASV, SS, EM, a. 1870, r. 165, fasc. 3, ff. 35v-r.

27. ASV, SS, EM, a. 1870, r. 165, fasc. 3, ff. 38v- 39r, 31 ottobre 1870.

28. ASV, SS, EM, a. 1870, r. 165, fasc. 1, 103v-106r, 110v-112r, Tours, 27 ottobre 1870.

29. "Ultime notizie," *L'Osservatore Romano,* 25 ottobre 1870, p. 3; "Rivista dei giornali," *L'Osservatore Romano,* 26 ottobre 1870, p. 2.

30. ASV, SS, EM, a. 1870, r. 165, fasc. 1, ff. 130v-135r, Tours, 10 novembre 1870.

31. ASV, SS, EM, a. 1870, r. 165, fasc. 1, ff. 139v-143r, 12 novembre 1870.

32. The nuncio's telegram (ASV, SS, EM, a. 1870, r. 165, fasc. 2, f. 156v, 17 novembre 1870) reporting this conversation was followed by a longer report (ASV, SS, EM, a. 1870, r. 165, fasc. 2, ff. 163v-164v, 18 novembre 1870).

33. ASV, SS, EM, a. 1870, r. 165, fasc. 4, ff. 11v-112r, 19 novembre 1870.

6. The Reluctant King

1. My description in these opening paragraphs is based largely on Dalla Torre 1972 and Mack Smith 1989. The Venetian appearance is described by Grimaldi 1970, p. 111.

2. Mazzonis 2003, pp. 111–18, 146.

3. Mack Smith 1989, p. 23.

4. Quoted in Mack Smith 1989, pp. 42–43.

5. Quoted in Mack Smith 1989, p. 7.

6. Chabod 1997, pp. 199–203.

7. Negro 1977, p. 10; Bartoccini 1985, p. 416; Russo 1989, p. 25.

8. Quoted in Halperin 1939, p. 136.

9. Typical was the experience of Italy's ambassador to Bavaria. On September 29, the Bavarian foreign minister advised him that, if the pope was not to flee Rome, it was advisable for Italy not to rush into moving its capital. "Italy has already taken Rome, national sentiment has been satisfied," the Bavarian foreign minister said. "It should view the moving of the capital as a secondary question." Cadorna 1889, pp. 366–67.

10. DDI, series 2, vol. 1, n. 338, Il Ministro degli Esteri, Visconti Venosta, al Ministro a Vienna, Minghetti, 23 ottobre [1870].

11. Lanza 1938, n. 2110, Lanza a La Marmora, 27 ottobre 1870.

12. Lanza 1938, n. 2117, Lanza a La Marmora, 31 ottobre 1870.

13. Lanza 1938, n. 2119, La Marmora a Lanza, 2 novembre 1870.

14. Lanza 1938, n. 2121, La Marmora a Lanza, 5 novembre 1870.

15. Pelczar 1911, vol. 3, p. 4.

16. Ghisalberti 1978, pp. 180–82.

17. Pesce 1970, pp. 279–90.

18. Quoted in Fiorentino 1996, p. 111. Also see Gregorovius's entry for December 31: Gregorovius 1907, p. 393.

19. Curiously, before learning of the king's plan, Pius IX had himself told a group of his advisers: "If I were King Victor Emmanuel, I would choose this occasion to come to Rome, because it would give me a plausible humanitarian pretext and so I could avoid political demonstrations, compromises, and unpleasantness" (Ghisalberti 1978, pp. 188–89).

20. Ballerini, Raffaele "Le due capitali in Roma: L'8 dicembre 1881," *Civiltà Cattolica* 1881, IV, p. 651.

21. Dalla Torre 1972, pp. 161–62; Ghisalberti 1978, pp. 192–94.

22. Rothan 1885, vol. 2, entry dated 6 janvier 1871, pp. 178–79; Pelczar 1911, vol. 3, p. 8.
23. Quoted in Halperin 1939, p. 145.
24. Visconti himself, the envoy reported, "recognized that the very existence of Italy would be compromised if, by the force of events, following the complete transfer, they had to abandon Rome."
25. Correspondence found in Rothan 1885, pp. 388–98.
26. DDI, series 2, vol. 2, n. 484, Il Ministro a Vienna, Minghetti, al Ministro degli Esteri, Visconti Venosta, 5 giugno 1871.
27. Gregorovius 1907, pp. 404–5.
28. Halperin 1939, p. 208; Mazzonis 2003, pp. 147–48.
29. Martina 2000, p. 1064; Bartoccini 1985, p. 482.

7. Pius IX in Exile Again?

1. In Halperin 1939, pp. 101–2.
2. Chadwick 1998, p. 366, discusses this point. Much of the concern of the high French clergy, and French government, about a rapprochement between the Vatican and the Italian state stemmed from this fear. In a January 1871 letter, for example, Charles Lavigerie, the archbishop of Algiers, wrote to a colleague: "The pope will not leave Rome. This is a great misfortune, because it is already leading to compromises, which will end up wounding . . . many Catholics." He warned, "What is certain is that Italy is openly showing its intention of employing the central government of the Church as an extension of its influence in the world." Here the cardinal mentioned in particular a presumed Italian plan to use the Catholic missions in the Orient to replace France's influence there. Four years later, Lavigerie — who went on to become an influential cardinal — was still fearful, as can be seen in a letter he wrote to the French minister of Cults: "The head of the Church, deprived of his temporal power and political independence that his sovereignty assured him, is, from now on, in effect, in the hands of the Italian government" (Aubert 1972, pp. 25–26).
3. The text of the law of guarantees is found in AAEESS, Italia, pos. 973–74, fasc. 319, ff. 19r-21r.
4. DDI, series 2, vol. 2, n. 444, Il Ministro degli Esteri, Visconti Venosta, ai Rappresentanti Diplomatici all'Estero, 20 maggio 1871.
5. English translation taken from www.papalencyclicals.net. The Italian version is published in *Civiltà Cattolica*, 1871, II, pp. 719–29, Ministro degli Esteri Visconti Venosta al Ministro a Berlino, de Launay, 7 marzo 1871.
6. DDI series 2, vol. 2, n. 230, Il Ministro degli Esteri, Visconti Venosta, al Ministro a Berlino, de Launay, Firenze, 7 marzo 1871.
7. Martina 2003, pp. 19–20, 73.
8. Aubert 1990a, pp. 443–44.
9. Acton 1870, p. 97.
10. Gregorovius 1907, p. 396, entry for March 5, 1871.
11. Theiner was an unusual character. A member of the Oratorian order and a German cobbler's son, he had a scholarly reputation throughout Europe for his work on Church history. In 1855, Pius IX named him prefect of the Vatican Secret Archives. Theiner's appointment was controversial; just three years earlier he had published a book on Clement XIV, praising the pope who had disbanded the Jesuits. This

stance, along with a more general reputation for free thinking, had earned him the enmity of the Jesuits, a feeling he heartily reciprocated. When Fiorentini came to see him that November day, Theiner had even more reason to resent the order. A few months earlier the pope had urgently summoned him and, quaking with anger, ordered him to hand over the keys to the Vatican archives at once. At this, the sixty-six-year-old monk began to sob uncontrollably, finally gaining enough composure to ask the pope why he was so enraged. You have been giving secrets of the Vatican archives to my enemies at the council, the pope told him, and I will not have it. Despite Theiner's protestations of innocence, he was dismissed. The special door that gave the monk direct access to the archives from his apartment in the Vatican was bricked up so that there was no chance he could sneak in again. In Theiner's view, it was the Jesuits who had poisoned the pope's mind against him (Martina 1986, pp. 629–36; Hill 2000, pp. 209–10, 240–41; Chadwick 1978, pp. 51–76).

12. Lanza 1938, n. 2180, Fiorentini a Lanza, 21 novembre 1870.

13. Lanza 1938, n. 2229, Fiorentini a Lanza, 17 dicembre 1870.

14. Matteo Liberatore, "L'Unità italiana e l'intervento straniero," *Civiltà Cattolica* 1871, II, pp. 145–56. Many in the Vatican saw no reason why it should not happen again this time. Even before Rome was taken, some were advising the pope to follow the strategy he had successfully used back then. In late 1866, Odo Russell reported that "the Jesuit party" was urging the pope "to fly from the Vatican and seek a safe asylum abroad, from whence he would call upon the Catholic Powers to protect the Holy Church against the Revolution and go to war with Italy" (Blakiston 1962, n. 357, Odo Russell to Lord S., 4 December 1866).

15. DDI, series 1, vol. 13, n. 341, Il Conte Kulczycki al Segretario Generale agli Esteri, Blanc, 30 luglio 1870; n. 528, Il Conte Kulczycki al Segretario Generale agli Esteri, Blanc, 18 agosto 1870.

16. Lanza 1938, n. 1901, Cornacchi a Lanza, 6 settembre 1870.

17. Lanza 1938, n. 1929, Maurizio a Lanza, Genova, 9 settembre 1870. With the approach of the Italian army, Antonelli began a flurry of correspondence with his nuncios, urging them to explore the attitudes of the various foreign powers. Would they provide a refuge for the elderly pontiff? On August 22, 1870, the papal nuncio in Vienna reported Austria's decision to offer the Holy Father asylum in "an Italian city of the Empire: either Trent, or Gorizia, or Zara, or some other city in Dalmatia." These lands, populated by ethnic Italians, lay in the area in the northeast of Italy, then part of the Austro-Hungarian Empire. Two days later the nuncio reported that the Austrians were prepared to send transport ships to carry off the pope and all those in his entourage (ASV, SS, EM, a. 1870, r. 165, fasc. 2, ff. 17v, 22v; 22, 24 agosto 1870).

18. Arnim quote in Halperin 1939, pp. 59–60. A report received by Visconti four days after the taking of Rome added to the government's anxieties. Albert Blanc, secretary general of Foreign Affairs, telegraphed him with the news that, while Antonelli was urging the pope to stay in Rome, various influential cardinals were pleading with him to go (DDI, series 2, vol. 1, n. 42, 24 settembre 1870).

19. Martina 1990a, pp. 248–49.

20. These quotations and those that follow from the cardinals responding to the pope's request are found in AAEESS, SE, pos. 968, fasc. 318, ff. 38r ff: "1870, c. eventuale partenza del Sommo Pontefice Pio IX da Roma."

21. Emphasis in the original letter.

22. E.g., Cadorna 1889, pp. 369–70, Il Ministro del Re a Londra al Ministro degli Affari Esteri, 27 settembre 1870.

23. DDI, series 2, vol. 1, n. 99, Ministro degli Affari Esteri, Visconti Venosta, al Ministro a Berlino, de Launay, 28 settembre 1870; n. 100, Ministro degli Affari Esteri, Visconti Venosta, al Ministro a Vienna, Minghetti, 28 settembre 1870.

24. DDI, series 2, vol. 1, n. 114, Il Segretario Generale agli Esteri, Blanc, al Ministro degli Esteri, Visconti Venosta, 28 settembre 1870.

25. DDI, series 2, vol. 1, n. 109, Il Segretario Generale agli Esteri, Blanc, al Ministro degli Esteri, Visconti Venosta, 28 settembre 1870.

26. DDI, series 2, vol. 1, n. 113, Il Generale Masi al Presidente del Consiglio e Ministro dell'Interno, Lanza, 27–28 settembre 1870.

27. DDI, series 2, vol. 1, n. 125, Il Ministro a Vienna, Minghetti, al Ministro degli Esteri, Visconti Venosta, 29 settembre 1870.

28. The British documents are quoted in Wallace 1948, pp. 131–32. On Arnim, see Bagdasarian 1976, pp. 146–47.

29. DDI, series 2, vol. 1, n. 138, Il Segretario Generale agli Esteri, Blanc, al Ministro degli Esteri, Visconti Venosta, 30 settembre 1870; Wallace 1948, p. 131.

30. ASV, SS, EM, a.1870, r. 165, fasc.1, ff. 28v-29r, Archevêche de Tours, 30 settembre 1870; f. 30v., Antonelli, 8 ottobre 1870.

31. Halperin 1939, pp. 77–78; Wallace 1948, pp. 135–36.

32. Found in Halperin 1939, p. 89, his English translation: Favre to Lefebvre de Béhaine, March 26, 1871.

33. Rothan 1885, pp. 355–58, Dépêche de M. Favre à M. Rothan. 16 mars 1871.

34. Found in Halperin 1939, p. 89, his translation: Favre to Choiseul, April 20, 1871.

35. DDI, series 2, vol. 2, n. 377, Visconti al Ministro a Versailles, Nigra, 19 aprile 1871.

36. Halperin 1939, p. 156, Kálnoky to Beust, June 20, 1871 (translation by Halperin).

37. DDI, series 2, vol. 2, n. 498, Conte Kulczycki a Lanza, 11 giugno 1871; n. 554, Conte Kulczycki a Lanza, 23 giugno 1871.

38. DDI, series 2, vol. 2, n. 574, Principe E. Ruspoli al Ministro degli Esteri, Visconti Venosta, 29 giugno 1871.

8. The Papal Martyr

1. Martina 1971, pp. 316–17.

2. Quoted in Bartoccini 1985, p. 436.

3. Thiers's enthusiasm for papal temporal power had little to do with religious commitment. Rather, he saw the unification of Italy as a threat to France. In a speech to the French legislature in 1865, for example, he had said: "As for me, I have always been convinced that Italian unity was a political idea that, sooner or later, would end up being very unfortunate for France" (d'Ideville 1875, p. 379).

4. Quoted in Halperin 1939, p. 189.

5. Quoted in Lecanuet 1931, p. 144. On Favre's attitude toward temporal power, see Guiral 1972, pp. 349–50.

6. Quoted in Halperin 1939, p. 198; and Camiani 1976, p. 731, from De Franciscis 1872, vol. 1, p. 46.

7. DDI, series 2, vol. 2, n. 428, Diomede Pantaleoni al Ministro degli Esteri, Visconti Venosta, 10 maggio 1871.

8. Halperin 1939, pp. 202–7.

9. Lecanuet 1931, pp. 149–51. Aubert, France's foremost historian of the Church in this period, argues that the main effect of all the French Catholic agitation on behalf of the pope in these years was to turn the Italian government away from France and into the arms of Germany (Aubert 1972, pp. 22–23).

10. Halperin 1939, pp. 231–34.

11. DDI, series 2, vol. 3, n. 210, L'incaricato d'affari a Parigi, Ressmann, al Ministro degli Esteri, Visconti Venosta, 10 novembre 1871.

12. Despite all the assurances they were getting. Among others, they included the French foreign minister's assurances to the Italian ambassador, Costantino Nigra, at the beginning of December 1870, that, for the moment at least, the danger that the pope would leave had lessened. A few days later, Adolphe Thiers himself assured Nigra that the pope was getting no encouragement from the French to leave Rome (DDI, series 2, vol. 3, n. 240, 243, Il Ministro a Parigi, Nigra, al Ministro degli Esteri, Visconti Venosta, 2 dicembre 1871, 6 dicembre 1871. DDI, series 2, vol. 3, n. 245, Il Conte Kulczycki al Segretario Generale degli Affari Esteri, Artom, 5 dicembre 1871).

13. In Halperin 1939, p. 235.

14. Among the discussions of the *Orénoque* episode, see Lecanuet 1931a, pp. 165–68; Hanotaux 1925, pp. 226–27; Graham 1952, pp. 28–29; Halperin 1939, pp. 267–68.

15. DDI, series 2, vol. 4, n. 296, Il Ministro degli Esteri Visconti Venosta, al Ministro a Parigi, Nigra, 16 gennaio 1873.

16. DDI, series 2, vol. 5, n. 220, Il Ministro degli Esteri Visconti Venosta, al Ministro a Parigi, Nigra, 15 gennaio 1874. Lecanuet 1931a, pp. 177–78.

17. Pelczar 1911, v. 3, pp. 8–9.

18. Raffaele Ballerini, "Il nodo romano," *Civiltà Cattolica* 1871, I, pp. 30–31.

19. The story of the straw is told by Salvemini, cited by Valenti 1977, p. 14n13; Launay 1997, p. 14.

20. Quoted in Pelczar 1911, p. 54, and translated back from his Italian into English.

21. Pirri 1951, part 2, n. 139, Pio IX a Sua Maestà il Re Vittorio Emanuele, 21 agosto 1871.

22. De Franciscis 1872, v. 3, Discorso CCCIII ai Capi degli Ordini Religiosi, 15 dicembre 1873; Discorso CCCVII. Alla Deputazione Belga, 25 dicembre 1873. Pursuing the same theme in an address in December 1872, the pope called attention to a rash of catastrophic fires and volcanos from Asia to America, claiming that they were clear signs of God's wrath at what had happened on September 20, 1870 (Camiani 1976, p. 708).

23. Cited in Gullo 1971, p. 128. *Civiltà Cattolica*, in late 1871 and again the following year, put the matter this way: "Is it possible that God would allow His Church to define the necessity for the pope to have temporal power in such a solemn way when He actually desired such power to permanently or even for a long time to cease to exist? . . . To intend the abolition of temporal power, and at the same time have the infallible organ of Christian belief declare that such power is necessary to the regular workings of the Church . . . What reason could God have to do such a thing?" (Matteo Liberatore, "Gli intendimenti divini sopra il potere temporale del papa nel tempo presente," *Civiltà Cattolica* 1871, IV, pp. 641–58).

24. Gregorovius 1907, p. 437. But Pius did have various diversions to cheer him up. He delighted in receiving groups of small schoolchildren and was especially tickled, according to Perodi's unconfirmed report (1980, pp. 148–49), to hear them sing a song that their Catholic school teachers taught them for such visits:

La bandiera tricolore	The tricolored flag
Sempre è stata la più brutta	Has always been the ugliest
La vogliamo stracciar tutta	We want to tear it to pieces
Calpestrarla con i pié.	Trample it under our feet.

9. Anticlericalism in Rome

1. Quoted in Chabod 1951, pp. 232–33, the last of which dates from 1875.
2. Quotes from Garibaldi 1874, pp. 55, 195, 231, 298.
3. Quotes from Garibaldi 1874, pp. 35, 110, 156.
4. Verucci 1996, pp. 296–97, 301–2. See Verucci 1996 more generally for this history of anticlericalism. The deputy's remarks are taken from *Atti Ufficiali della Camera*, p. 366, 24 gennaio 1871. On July 6, 1871, at the pope's request, the cardinal vicar of Rome issued a prohibition, forbidding Catholics from reading any of a list of eleven newspapers, including *La Capitale*, on the grounds that reading them risked undermining their faith (Martina 1971, p. 356).
5. Scholars have uncovered over 215 documents of Leo XIII containing condemnations of the Freemasons (Isastia 1989, p. 51).
6. ASR, Questura di Roma, b.1, f.9 (1870), Frascati, n. 44, 116, 134. Similar cases saw a conflict over priests refusing to baptize a child with the name Vittorio — the name of the Italian king — or accompanying a funeral procession in which someone was carrying an Italian flag (Gallon 1971, p. 92). Such incidents were innumerable.
7. ASR, Questura di Roma, b.1, f.9 (1870), Roma — Presidenza del Rione III Colonna, Li 6 dicembre 1870, Oggetto: Progetto di dimostrazione politica.
8. ASR, Questura di Roma, b. 1, f. 9 (1870), Presidenza del Rione Borgo — Roma. Protocollo N. 42, Roma li 6 dicembre 1870, Al Ill.mo Signore Questore di Roma.
9. ASR, Questura di Roma, b. 1, f. 9 (1870), N. 1894 Gab.to, Sig. Procuratore Generale del Re. Roma, Roma 9 dicembre 1870. On the part of the anticlerics, all of the arrested men were from Rome, three in their early twenties and one thirty-seven. They were charged with promoting disorders and inflicting bodily injury on others, although it was difficult to prove given the chaos. The three papal defenders arrested were even younger, and also from Rome, ranging from eighteen to twenty-two.
10. ASR, Questura di Roma b. 1 f. 9, Presidenza del Rione Borgo, Roma li 11 dicembre 1870, Roma Protocollo N. 338, Oggetto: Assembramenti in Piazza di San Pietro della sera delli 11 dicembre; ASR, Questura di Roma, b. 1, f. 9, Presidenza del Rione Borgo, Protocollo N. 55, Roma li 12 dicembre 1870. For the Vatican view of the derogatory use of the term *caccialepri*, see "I caccialepri," *L'Osservatore Romano*, 25 ottobre 1870, p. 1.
11. Matteo Liberatore, "I disordini di Roma nella mattina del 10 marzo," *Civiltà Cattolica* 1871, II, pp. 39–51.
12. DDI, series 2, vol. 2, n. 276, Il Ministro degli Esteri, Visconti Venosta, ai Rappresentanti Diplomatici all'Estero, Circolare 91, Firenze, 19 marzo 1871.
13. *Civiltà Cattolica* 1871, II, Cronaca contemporanea, pp. 365–68. A year later, anticlerics got to stage their largest and most intricate series of funeral observances on the occasion of the death of Giuseppe Mazzini. An ambitious attempt to embalm his body for permanent display — against his wishes — ended in putrefying failure.

Luzzatto (2001) tells the story of the "mummy of the Republic" with great verve and insight.

14. Verucci 1996, pp. 138–39.

15. Halperin 1939, pp. 291–2. The Jesuit's remarks are quoted in Martina 1973, p. 249.

16. Fiorentino 1996, p. 250; Perodi 1980, p. 154.

17. Pelczar 1911, v. 3, pp. 26–27.

18. *L'Unità Cattolica,* 28 settembre 1876, quoted in Mellano 1982, p. 39.

19. Quoted in Halperin 1939, p. 408. For Depretis's family background and his earlier years, see Talamo 1970.

20. Just a few days before his death, Antonelli told a colleague: "I see that my days are growing ever shorter. The only thing that I am sorry about is that I am leaving this poor old pope alone, and God only knows where these insatiable wolves of the revolution will drag him next."

21. Negro 1977, p. 162; Coppa 1990, 179; Martina 1990a, pp. 297–98. The woman lost her case, although many believed she deserved to win. For more on the case, see Pirri 1958, pp. 105–17. Coppa (1990, p. 181) disputes the claim that Antonelli had acquired a fortune through illicit means while secretary of state and also disputes the claim that he left little to the Church in his will.

22. Jemolo 1965, pp. 40–41.

23. Halperin 1939, p. 424.

24. Mancini's circular is reproduced in De Franciscis 1872, p. 695: Circolare del M. Mancini sull'Allocuzione Pontificia del 12 marzo 1877, Roma, 17 marzo 1877.

25. The Senate vote was 92 in favor, 105 against. In reporting this result to Paris, the French ambassador to the Holy See explained what had happened: "Monsieur Mancini's efforts have failed despite the extreme confidence that he seemed to have in his success. No other Minister spoke out in favor of his project. His colleagues left him to carry all the weight and responsibility in the debate." Had just a handful of votes gone the other way, the results would have been disastrous. "The Senate in its wisdom and by its firmness in this circumstance has rendered a great service to Italy. It recognized the danger of taking the path of religious persecution that inevitably leads to civil strife." The French ambassador also reported that the new Vatican secretary of state, Cardinal Giovanni Simeoni, had been using the proposed clerical abuses bill to rally support for foreign intervention. When the ambassador suggested that the pope would be wise to face reality and give up the idea that he would ever regain Rome, Simeoni had a ready reply. The pope's dreams of a return of papal rule were far from naïve. Was it not true, he asked, that when the French had demanded Nice and Savoy from Victor Emmanuel as the price for its support against the Austrians in 1859, the king had immediately handed over these two lands, which until then were seen as absolutely central to the Savoyard Kingdom? Was it so unrealistic, then, to think that, given sufficient diplomatic pressure, the Italian government would conclude that giving Rome back to the pope was the wiser course? (MAES, CP, Rome, vol. 1061, ff. 360r-363v).

10. Two Deaths

1. Pirri 1951, part 2, n. 190c. Notizie sull'ultima malattia del Re.

2. Bishop Marinelli's account is found in AAEESS, Italia, pos. 631, fasc. 402, Docu-

menti relative alla morte e funerali di Vittorio Emanuele. Relazione di Monsig. Marinelli sulla sua visita al Quirinale. Vaticano 12 Gennaio 1878.

3. AAEESS, Italia, pos. 631, fasc. 402, Documenti relativi alla morte e funerali di Vittorio Emanuele, n. 3. Dichiarazione di Mons. Vicegerente sul permesso da Lui dato di amministrare a Vittorio Emanuele gli ultimi Ssmi sacramenti — 14 Gennaio 1878.

4. AAEESS, Italia, pos. 631, fasc. 402, Documenti relativi alla morte e funerali di Vittorio Emanuele, n. 4. Relazione dettagliata del Parroco de' SS. Vincenzo ed Anastasio dell'amministrazione del Ssmo Viatico al Re Vittorio Emanuele e della di lui morte — 13 Gennaio 1878.

5. MAES, CP, Rome, vol. 1063, f. 24r, Ambassade de France près de Saint Siège DP no. 4 à M. Waddington, le 9 Janvier 1878, Mort de S. M. le Roi Victor Emmanuel.

6. *Civiltà Cattolica* 1878, I, Cronaca contemporanea, p. 250.

7. Quotations found in Martina 1990b, pp. 855–57.

8. Pirri 1951, part 2, n. 190b, Dichiarazioni ufficiose diramate dall'Agenzia Stefani.

9. Quazza 1999, n. 3891, Sella a Clotilde Sella, Roma, 16 gennaio 1878.

10. Pasztor 1968, p. 197.

11. Pirri 1951, part 2, n. 187.

12. Martina 1990a, pp. 516–517.

13. AAEESS, Italia, pos. 631, fasc. 402, pp. 17–18, Documenti relativi alla morte e funerali di Vittorio Emanuele, n. 5. Circolari Segrete ai Vescovi del Regno in ordine ai funerali pel defunto Re, Roma dalla Segreteria di Stato, Li 10 Gennaio 1878; and Roma, 12 Gennaio 1878.

14. *Civiltà Cattolica* 1878, I, Cronaca contemporanea, p. 376.

15. *Civiltà Cattolica* 1878, II, Cronaca contemporanea, pp. 104–5. The French ambassador to Italy reported on January 19, 1878, that the pope did allow bishops to perform funeral services in the lands that the Vatican considered to be legitimately ruled by the Savoyards, which included both Piedmont and Lombardy. MAES, CP, Rome, vol. 1063, f. 45r, AF SS DP no.7, à M. Waddington, MAE, le 19 janvier 1878.

16. *Civiltà Cattolica* 1878, I, Cronaca contemporanea, pp. 364–79; Martina 1990a, pp. 518–19. Duggan 2000, pp. 452–53.

17. The French ambassador to the Holy See, who was close to Pius in his last year, observed that the older he got, the more mystical he became. As he despaired of gaining help from the mighty of this world, he became ever more convinced that God would intervene directly to ensure the Church's triumph. (MAES, CP, Rome, vol. 1061, ff. 17r-23r, Ambassade de France, M. le Duc Decazes près le St. Siège, Ministre des Affaires Etrangères, le 10 janvier 1877; ff. 69r-70v, 9 février 1877.)

18. Matteo Liberatore, "La conclusione dell'Enciclica di Leone XIII," *Civiltà Cattolica* 1878, III, p. 11; Ignesti 1988, pp. 81–82.

19. Pelczar 1911, v. 3, p. 391; Manfroni 1920, p. 331; Soderini 1934, p. 3; ASR, Questura di Roma, b. 15, f. 104, 7/2/78 ore 13, Crispi a Comm. Bolis; MAES, CP, Rome, vol. 1063, f. 104r; Pflanze 1990, p. 410.

20. *Civiltà Cattolica* 1878, I, pp. 599–603; ASR Questura b. 15 (1878), Ufficio di Pubblica Sicurezza del Rione Borgo, n. 31, Affollamento in San Pietro per la morte del Papa; "I Romani ai piedi di Pio IX," *L'Osservatore Romano*, 11 febbraio 1878, p. 1.

21. Manfroni 1920 , p. 338.

22. "Ultime notizie," *L'Osservatore Romano*, 15 febbraio 1878, p. 3.

23. MAEI, CP, Rome, vol. 51, ff. 167r, 169r.

24. ASR, Questura di Roma, b. 15, f. 104, fasc. Disposizioni ministeriali preliminari sui servii per la morte del Papa, 4 sett. 1871; MAEI, CP, Rome, v. 51, f. 165, 11 février 1878, n. 11778/3743; Manfroni 1920, pp. 334–42; "La tumulazione di Pio IX," *L'Osservatore Romano*, 14 febbraio 1878, p. 1.

25. For example — and this is one of a huge number — in giving the chronology of major events in the pope's life, *L'Osservatore Romano*'s entry for September 20, 1870, reads: "Rome taken and imprisonment of Pius IX," while its last entry was "February 7, 1878, Pius IX dies in Rome in the Vatican palace where he had been a prisoner since September 20, 1870" ("I fasti cronologici di Pio IX," *L'Osservatore Romano*, 15 febbraio 1878, p. 1).

26. Halperin 1939, p. 471; Chadwick 1997, pp. 365–66; Aubert 1990b, pp. 755–56; Candeloro 1953, p. 157.

11. Picking a New Pope

1. DDI, series 2, vol. 2, n. 484, Il Ministro a Vienna, Minghetti, al Ministro degli Esteri, Visconti Venosta, 5 giugno 1871.

2. DDI, series 2, vol. 3, n. 22, Il Ministro degli Esteri, Visconti Venosta, al Ministro a Parigi, Nigra, 16 luglio 1871.

3. Rothan 1885, vol. 2, p. 391.

4. Soderini 1934, p. 91.

5. DDI, series 2, vol. 3, n. 376, Il Ministro a Lisbona, Oldoini, al Ministro degli Esteri, Visconti Venosta, 28 febbraio 1872; n. 551, Visconti a Nigra, 10 giugno 1872.

6. DDI, series 2, vol. 3, n. 513, Il Ministro degli Esteri, Visconti Venosta, al Ministro a Lisbona, Oldoini, "Mémoire confidentiel," Roma, 10 maggio 1872.

7. DDI, series 2, vol. 3, n. 537, Il Ministro degli Esteri, Visconti Venosta, al Ministro a Berlino, de Launay, 29 maggio 1872.

8. In fact, unbeknownst to the Italian government, the French were then engaged in secret discussions with both the Austrians and the Portuguese, aimed at pushing the idea of a non-Italian pope. They had no luck, for both the Austrians and Portuguese suspected that the French wanted to elect a French pope who would serve French interests (Engel-Janosi 1954, p. 361).

9. DDI, series 2, vol. 4, n. 493, Il Ministro a Vienna, di Robilant, al Ministro degli Esteri, Visconti Venosta, 13 maggio 1873; n. 503, Il Ministro degli Esteri, Visconti Venosta, al Ministro a Vienna, di Robilant, 20 maggio 1873.

10. DDI, series 2, vol. 5, n. 70, Il Ministro a Vienna, di Robilant, al Ministro degli Esteri, Visconti Venosta, Vienna, 5 settembre 1873.

11. DDI, series 2, vol. 6, n. 228, Il Ministro degli Esteri, Visconti Venosta, al Ministro a Parigi, Nigra, 6 giugno 1875.

12. As it happened, Visconti needn't have worried, for Patrizi died before the end of the year.

13. DDI, series 2, vol. 6, n. 558, Il Ministro degli Esteri, Visconti Venosta, al Ministro a Lisbona, Oldoini, 19 gennaio 1876.

14. DDI, series 2, vol. 7, n. 303, Il Segretario Generale all'Interno, LaCava, al Ministro degli Esteri, Melegari, 5 agosto 1876; n. 316, Il Ministro degli Esteri, Melegari, all'Incaricato d'Affari a Parigi, Ressman, 10 agosto 1876.

15. DDI, series 2, vol. 7, n. 424, L'Incaricato d'affari a Parigi, Ressman, al Ministro degli Esteri, Melegari, 16 settembre 1876.

16. DDI, series 2, vol. 7, n. 452, L'ambasciatore a Londra, Menabrea, al Ministro degli Esteri, Melegari, 4 ottobre 1876.

17. MAES, CP, vol. 1061, ff. 239r-242v, Baude à M. le Duc Decazes, Ministère des Affaires Étrangères, 3 avril 1877. These two quotes are paraphrases.

18. Aubert 1990a, pp. 61–62.

19. Ballerini, Raffaele, "Una nuova confessione del liberalismo," *Civiltà Cattolica* 1878, I, pp. 149–60.

20. Reproduced in *Civiltà Cattolica* 1878, I, p. 611, Cronaca contemporanea.

21. MAES, CP, tome 1063, ff. 115r-120v, 9 février 1878.

22. Gregorovius 1907, p. 354, entry for February 6, 1870.

23. MAES, CP, tome 1063, ff. 18r-20r, 8 janvier 1878; Conclave: Opinion du Cardinal Manning.

24. The following day, February 8, France's ambassador to the Holy See offered this description of the debate and vote of the previous day, based on his own informants. Early in the evening he wrote: "The faction that wants to move the conclave out of Rome is stronger than one would have thought. One can only hope that wisdom will prevail and that this new cause for incalculable difficulties for the Church in Europe and in our country will be avoided." A few hours later that same evening, he reported worrisome new developments. "Although Cardinal Simeoni has practically refused to speak, invoking the rigor of the oath he has taken, I was able to learn that the 38 cardinals who met today in a consistory that lasted six hours were unable to reach agreement on the place where the conclave should be held. The majority, contrary to the impression that I was able to get yesterday from my conversation with the Cardinal Chamberlain, seem to prefer to leave Rome. The question will be taken up again tomorrow." The ambassador added that he hoped that the French cardinals would arrive in time to act as a moderating influence on their Italian colleagues (MAEI, CP, v. 51, f. 149r, 7 février 1878; MAES, tome 1063, f. 109r-109v, 8 février 1878; MAES, tome 1063, 110r-110v, 8 février 1878).

25. MAES, CP, tome 1063, ff. 111r-112r, 9 février 1878.

26. Soderini 1934, pp. 10–17.

27. MAES, CP, tome 1063, f. 108r, 8 février 1878; ff. 137r-143r, Annexe à la minute du D. P. no. 8 du 10 février 1878.

28. Soderini 1934, pp. 92–93; Lecanuet 1910, p. 2. It does not appear that the French government had ever in fact supported Cardinal Riario-Sforza, but in any case the archbishop of Naples was no longer in the running, having died five months earlier.

29. O'Reilly 1887, pp. 299–308.

30. "If the heads of the French clergy take no account of all that the government has done and push things to an extreme, our situation in the future will become extremely delicate with respect to the Italian government and public opinion in Italy" (MAES, CP, tome 1063, ff. 152r-153v, Noailles à Ministère des Affaires Etrangères, 16 février 1878).

31. MAEI, CP, v. 51, ff. 178r-178v, Noailles à Ministère des Affaires Etrangères, 17 février 1878; MAES, CP, vol. 1063, ff. 156r-156v, Waddington à Baude, 17 février 1878 ; ff. 154r-154v, Baude à Ministère des Affaires Etrangères, 17 février 1878 ; ff. 155r-155v, Baude à Ministère des Affaires Etrangères, 17 février 1878, ff. 155r-155v.

32. Soderini 1934, pp. 82, 88.

33. Aubert 1990a, pp. 63–64, intro. As the conclave began, Europe's leaders rummaged through their records to learn what they could about the cardinals. The Italian government had compiled a complete file on each of them a few years earlier which they now dusted off. In addition to giving basic background information, it offered brief evaluations of each one. They were on the whole less than kind. Among some of the more prominent cardinals we find such characterizations as these: Costantino Patrizi, dean of the Sacred College: "Most humble servant of Pius IX, his confessor and the recipient of the Pope's last wishes. As pompous as the Pope, but short on intelligence and subject to the Jesuitical influence of his relatives." Carlo Sacconi, protégé of Antonelli and former papal nuncio to Paris: "Old diplomat. A man who is closed, ignorant, and miserly." Of the intransigent faction's leading candidate for the papacy, Luigi Bilio: "He has an extremely high opinion of himself and has opinions of the greatest violence and ferocity against liberal ideas." Of Cardinal Lucien Bonaparte, a cousin of Emperor Napoleon III, still in his forties, the comment consisted of three words only: "ascetic and lunatic." As for Rome's current cardinal vicar, Raffaele Monaco la Valletta, the report described him as "one of Pius IX's favorites, who distracts him by regaling him with humorous stories sprinkled with jokes. Sworn enemy of national unity. Man of superficial erudition, of which he makes ostentatious display." Nor was the portrait of the man who would soon become pope especially flattering. Cardinal Gioacchino Pecci, born on March 2, 1810, and currently the archbishop of Perugia: "Bends to every wind. He was liberal, then reactionary, and now seeks to muddle through while doing himself the least harm possible" (ASR, Questura di Roma, b. 15, n. 13, 1878, I Cardinali italiani relativamente al Conclave).

34. Halperin 1961, p. 106.

35. Soderini 1934, pp. 33–66.

36. I follow Aubert's (1990a, p. 64) account. Soderini 1934, p. 19, gives a slightly different count for the first vote. On the vestments, see Soderini 1934, p. 102.

37. O'Reilly 1887, pp. 312–13.

38. Waddington 1905, p. 146. Perodi 1980, pp. 327–28.

39. Aubert 1990a, pp. 68–73; Schmandt 1961, p. 19.

40. Mellano 1982, pp. 72, 87; Schmandt 1961, p. 33; Launay 1997, pp. 20–21.

41. Manfroni 1920, p. 350.

42. MAEI, CP, vol. 51, ff. 202r-204r, Noailles à Waddington, 23 février 1878; Lecanuet 1910, p. 6. «Cet italien encore plus diplomate que prêtre . . . me semble du meilleur augure; . . . s'il ne meurt pas trop tôt, nous pourrons espérer un mariage de raison avec l'église . . . C'est un opportuniste sacré» (Trincia 2001, p. 12).

43. Copious evidence can be found in ASR, Questura di Roma, b. 15.

44. Spadolini 1991, p. 152; Manfroni 1920, p. 358; ASR, Questura di Roma, b. 16, fasc. febbraio 1878, Dimostrazioni contro la legge delle Guarentigie.

45. Based on the account published in L'Italie (28 février 1878), found as annexe à la Dépêche de Rome D. P. n. 18, MAES, tome 1063, ff. 195r-197r, 28 février 1878.

46. Manfroni 1920, pp. 360–65.

47. ASR, Questura di Roma, b. 15, n. 1355, Dimostrazione sul Corso, 4 marzo 1878; MAEI, CP, v. 51, ff. 230r-232r, Noailles à Waddington, 5 mars 1878, Démonstrations à l'occasion du couronnement de Léon XIII; Civiltà Cattolica 1878, I, pp. 747–48,

Cronaca Contemporanea; *Civiltà Cattolica* 1878, II, pp. 95–97, Cronaca Contemporanea.

12. Keeping the Bishops in Line

1. MAES, v. 1063, ff. 187r-190r, Baude à Waddington, 25 février 1878.
2. Manfroni 1920, p. 375.
3. MAES, v. 1063, ff. 259r-262v, 9 avril 1878, Croy à Waddington, Lettre pastorale sur le Pouvoir temporel.
4. *Civiltà Cattolica*, 1878, II, pp. 465–66, Rivista della stampa italiana; *Civiltà Cattolica*, 1878, III, p. 220, Cronaca Contemporanea; emphasis in original.
5. This is certainly the sense in MAES, v. 1063, ff. 272r-275v, 19 avril 1878, Croy à Waddington, "Pèlerinages. Mode de réception adopté par Léon XIII."
6. In late April 1878, the French ambassador to the Holy See informed Paris that the secretary of state had denied these stories of plans to summer at Castel Gandolfo. Leo XIII, the French envoy added, was reported to have said, "I was placed here as a sentry and I do not have the right to abandon my post." MAES, CP, v. 1063, ff. 299r-301r, 28 avril 1878, Croy à Waddington, Villégiature du Pape.
7. Mazzonis 2003, pp. 148–51.
8. Drake 1980, p. xviii; Casalegno 2001, p. 12.
9. Carocci 1956, p. 193; Duggan 2000, pp. 450–51; Mack Smith 1994a, p. 71; Pelczar 1911, p. 389.
10. His aide, Paolo Paulucci (1986, p. 32), reports this in his memoirs. See also Mack Smith 1994a, p. 72.
11. Guiccioli 1936, pp. 182, 190; Casalegno 2001, p. 75; Pinto 2002, p. 12.
12. MAES, CP, v. 1065, ff. 235r-237r, n. 35 à M. Waddington, Nouvelles diverses, 29 avril 1879; Farini 1961, p. 676. Paolucci 1986, p. 27. Paolucci, though, notes that Umberto was close to Monsignor Anzino and turned to him not only for his blessings but also for political advice.
13. AAEESS, Italia, pos. 631, fasc. 402, ff. 27–28, Documenti relativi al primo viaggio del Re Umberto per le provincie del Regno. Num 7.
14. Soderini 1934, pp. 121–22; "Lettera della Santità di Nostro Signore Leone XIII a Sua Eminenza Reverendissima Il Signor Cardinale Lorenzo Nina, Segretario di Stato," *Civiltà Cattolica* 1878, IV, pp. 128–34; Liberatore, Matteo, "Sgomento della Rivoluzione italiana prodotto dalla lettera di Papa Leone XIII, *Civiltà Cattolica* 1878, IV, pp. 135–44; Mellano 1982, p. 84.
15. AAEESS, Italia, pos. 267, fasc. 67, ff. 4r-5v, 20 agosto 1878.
16. AAEESS, Italia, pos. 267, fasc. 67, ff. 8r-14v, 20 agosto 1878.
17. AAEESS, Italia, pos. 267, fasc. 67, ff. 16r-24r, Rapporto della adunanza di 22 ago. 1878.
18. AAEESS, Italia, pos. 267, fasc. 67, ff. 36r-37v, Progetto d'istruzioni da comunicarsi agli Ordinari delle Provincie usurpate in occasione della visita del Re. 23 agosto 1878
19. AAEESS, Italia, pos. 267, fasc. 67, ff. 44r-47v, Venezia, 29 agosto 1878.
20. AAEESS, Italia, pos. 267, fasc. 67, ff. 48r-49v, Monsig. Vescovo di Brescia, 30 agosto 1878.
21. AAEESS, Italia, pos. 267, fasc. 67, ff. 50r-50v, Emo Sig. Card.e de Marchesi di Canossa Vescovo di Verona, 30 agosto 1878.
22. AAEESS, Italia, pos. 267, fasc. 67, ff. 73r-74v, 1 settembre 1878.

23. AAEESS, Italia, pos. 267, fasc. 67, ff. 76r-77r, 28 agosto 1878.

24. AAEESS, Italia, pos. 267, fasc. 67, ff. 79r-80r, Brescia, 2 settembre 1878.

25. AAEESS, Italia, pos. 267, fasc. 67, ff. 81r-82v, Vescovato di Piacenza, 1 settembre 1878; ff. 83r-83v, 5 settembre 1878.

26. AAEESS, Italia, pos. 267, fasc. 68, ff. 8r-12r, Catania, 9 settembre 1878.

27. AAEESS, Italia, pos. 267, fasc. 68, ff. 14r-18r, all'Arcivescovo di Catania, 18 settembre 1878.

28. Luciani 1997, p. 176.

29. Masini 1989, p. 30.

30. *Civiltà Cattolica* 1878, IV, pp. 620–22; emphasis in original.

31. AAEESS, Italia, pos. 271, fasc. 70, ff. 4r-5r, Sul contegno che la S.Sede debba prendere in occasione dell'attentato al Re Umberto I, compiutosi a Napoli il 17 novembre 1878, Istruzione al Card. Vicario circa il canto del "Te Deum" nella suddetta occasione.

32. AAEESS, Italia, pos. 271, fasc. 70, ff. 6r-7r, Arcivescovado di Napoli, Napoli, 18 novembre 1878; ff. 12r-13r, 20 novembre 1878; ff. 20r-21r, Segretario di Stato, 22 novembre 1878.

33. Grimaldi 1970, pp. 152–53.

34. Candeloro 1953, pp. 137–38.

35. The correspondence, from the AAEESS, is dated October 19 and 26, 1878, with a subsequent reply by the archbishop on November 4, 1878, and is reproduced in Mellano 1982, pp. 147–51.

36. Leo XIII's opposition to a Catholic political party identified with the right would shortly extend to France as well. In 1885 he would call a halt to a project led by Albert de Mun to form a French Catholic party (Launay 1997, p. 44).

37. The story of this struggle is told in Ignesti 1988; De Rosa 1970, pp. 131–33; and Fonzi 1990, pp. 277–79. Also see Campello's (1910, p. 142) first-person account.

38. Zocchi 1881; *Civiltà Cattolica* 1881, I, pp. 7, 9; emphasis in original.

13. The Pope's Body

1. ASR, Tribunale Civile e Correzionale, processi penali, b. 3849, fasc. 23135, Trasporto della salma di Pio IX, 12 Luglio 1881; "Il testamento di Pio IX," *L'Osservatore Romano,* 16 febbraio 1881, p. 1; Pelczar 1911, v. 3, p. 401.

2. Halperin 1939, p. 404; "L' 'Ostentazione insolente' di Satana e i prossimi trionfi di Gesù in Roma," *L'Unità Cattolica,* 20 giugno, 1889, p. 581.

3. ASR, Prefettura di Roma, Gabinetto, b. 212, Trasporto della salma di Pio IX, 23 Giugno 1881 Vespignani a Gravina; 28 Giugno 1881, Gravina a Tonelli e Vespignani; 5 luglio 1881, Vespignani a Gravina; 10 luglio 1881, Gravina a Vespignani.

4. ASV, SS, EM, a. 1882, r. 241, fasc. 3, ff. 22v-23r, 15 luglio 1881, Dichiarazione relativa al permesso domandato ed ottenuto dal Questore di Roma per l'accompagnamento della salma di Pio IX nella notte del 13 Luglio.

5. ASV, SS, EM, a. 1880, r. 241, fasc. 4, ff. 67v-68v, Appunti per la Inchiesta ordinata dal Ministro dell'Interno al Comm.re Astengo sui fatti avvenuti in Roma la notte del 13 Luglio 1881, Interrogatorio del Questore Bacco. It is unclear how this handwritten copy came into the Vatican archives. ASR, Prefettura di Roma, Gabinetto, b. 212, Bacco al Prefetto, 11 luglio 1881.

6. ASR, Prefettura di Roma, Gabinetto, b. 212, Prefetto al Questore, 12 luglio 1881;

Telegramma, Bacco al Prefetto 12 luglio 1881, ore 14,10; Prefetto al Signor Comandante la Divisione Militare di Roma, 12 luglio 1881; Sindaco di Roma al Prefetto di Roma, 12 luglio 1881.

7. Giovanni Cornoldi, "La notte del 13 luglio in Roma," *Civiltà Cattolica* 1881, III, pp. 258–59; *Civiltà Cattolica* 1881, III, pp. 374–75, Cronaca Contemporanea. The *Civiltà Cattolica* itself, realizing that its estimate was likely to be disbelieved, made its case this way: "And so that no one thinks that we are exaggerating, just listen to what *la Libertà*, a Judaic paper and so above suspicion, had to say: 'To offer a very low estimate, one could say that along the nearby road and in St. Peter's Square there were no fewer than 100,000 people.'"

8. Manfroni 1920, pp. 53–54; *L'Osservatore Romano*, 14 luglio 1881, pp. 1–2.

9. This description is based on a large number of police reports and other documents found in ASR, Prefettura di Roma, Gabinetto, b. 212, Trasporto della salma di Pio IX; and ASV, Segreteria di Stato, a. 1882, r. 241, fasc.4 (salma Pio IX); as well as Guiccioli 1936, p. 304; Manfroni 1920, pp. 48–56; and *Fatti nuovi*, vol. 1; and the above-cited accounts in *Civiltà Cattolica*.

10. Chadwick 1997, pp. 373–79.

11. ASR, Prefettura di Roma, Gabinetto, b. 212, Prefetto al Ministro dell'Interno, Telegramma urgente, 13 luglio 1881, ore 5 ant.

12. Atti Parlamentari, Senato del Regno, Sessione del 1880–81, Tornata del 13 Luglio 1881, Interrogazioni dei Senatori Alfieri e Cambray-Digny al Minstro dell Interno, copy attached to ASV, SS, EM, a. 1880, r. 241, fasc. 4, ff. 108v-113r.

13. ASV, SS, EM, a. 1882, r. 241, fasc. 4, ff. 67v-71v, Appunti per la Inchiesta ordinata dal Ministro dell'Interno al Comm.re Astengo sui fatti avenuti in Roma la notte del 13 Luglio 1881, Interrogatorio del Questore Bacco; Ciampani 2000, p. 262. Manfroni, who also took some of the blame, was outraged by what he regarded as the whitewash of the affair and the failure of those higher up to take the responsibility he thought they bore for the disaster (1920, pp. 57–58).

14. He first telegraphed his nuncio in Paris with an account of the disorders, instructing him: "See that this is published in the Catholic newspapers, and send this telegram in code to the offices of Vienna, Madrid, Lisbon, and Munich, for it is not prudent to telegraph them directly from Rome" (ASV, SS, EM, a. 1882, r. 241, fasc. 3, f. 10v, 13 luglio 1881).

15. ASV, SS, EM, a. 1882, r. 241, fasc. 3, ff. 13v-16r, prot. 45390, circolare, 15 luglio 1881. Leo XIII's attitude is described by the French ambassador to the Holy See: MAES, v. 1070, ff. 255r-259r, Desprez à Ministère des Affaires Etrangères, 18 Juillet 1881. Catholic newspapers inside Italy were similarly using the funeral debacle to demonstrate that their characterization of the pope as a prisoner of the Vatican was not an exaggeration. As *Veneto Cattolico*, Venice's Catholic paper, put it: "the savage scenes of last night demonstrate to the whole world that where the Revolution has implanted itself by force, the popes are necessarily condemned to perpetual imprisonment" (quoted in "Stampa italiana," *L'Osservatore Romano*, 16 luglio 1881, p. 2).

16. DDI, series 2, vol. 14, n. 102, Il Ministro degli Esteri, Mancini, agli Ambasciatori a Berlino, de Launay, a Londra, Menabrea, a Pietroburgo, Nigra, a Vienna, di Robilant, ai Ministri a Bruxelles, Fe' d'Ostiani, a l'Aja, Bertinatti, a Lisbona, Oldoini, a Madrid, Greppi, e agli Incaricati d'Affari a Parigi, Marochetti, e a Berna, Riva, 15 luglio 1881.

17. ASV, SS, EM, a. 1882, r. 241, fasc. 3, ff. 143v-144r, Nunzio Vienna a Jacobini, 21 luglio 1881.

18. MAES, v. 1070, ff. 292r-293v, 23 Juillet 1881, Ministère des Affaires Etrangères à Desprez.

19. DDI, series 2, v. 14, n. 112, L'Ambasciatore a Berlino, de Launay, al Ministero degli Esteri, Mancini, 24 luglio 1881. Throughout Europe, bishops were sending denunciatory letters to the priests in their dioceses to read to their congregations, aimed against the Italian government. In one case, the primate of Spain, Cardinal Moreno, after recounting what happened to the funeral procession, concluded: "This is the reason that the Church so insistently calls for temporal power for the Holy See, now more necessary than ever for the free exercise of spiritual power . . . In Rome there cannot be any sovereign other than the pope . . . The Papal States belong to the Catholic world" (dated 16 July 1881, reproduced in "Il trasporto della salma di Pio IX, l'episcopato cattolico," *L'Osservatore Romano*, 31 luglio 1881, p. 2).

20. ASV, SS, EM, a. 1882, r. 241, fasc. 2, ff. 117v-121v, circolare ai nunzi, 27 luglio 1881.

21. "Conseguenze," *L'Osservatore Romano*, 4 agosto 1881, p. 2.

22. Manfroni 1920, vol. 2, pp. 58–59.

23. MAEI, v. 64, ff. 201r-202r, Noailles à M. St. Hilaire, Ministère des Affaires Etrangères, 3 août 1881; DDI, series 2, v. 14, n. 134, L'ambasciatore a Vienna, di Robilant, al Ministro degli Esteri, Mancini, 4 agosto 1881.

24. Isastia 1989, pp. 37–52; Chadwick 1997, p. 377; Della Peruta 1989, pp. 104–9.

25. Perodi 1980, p. 431.

26. Fonzi 1977, pp. 60–61.

27. For a selection of Alberto Mario's anticlerical writings, see Mario 1867, 1964.

28. ASV, SS, EM, 1882, r. 241, fasc. 3, ff. 176v-176r, Comizio tenuto nel Politeama Romano il 7 agosto 1881, allegato alla Circolare ai Nunzii, 8 agosto 1881; MAES, v. 1071, ff. 43r-45r, de Bâcourt à M. Barthélemy St. Hilaire, Ministère des Affaires etrangères, 8 août 1881. On the confiscation of *L'Osservatore Romano*, see "Il sequestro dell'Osservatore Romano," *L'Osservatore Romano*, 10 agosto 1881, p. 1; on the other newspaper confiscations, see Talamo 1979, p. 83. The Vatican lost no time in bringing these new outrages to the world's attention. The day after the Politeama meeting, Cardinal Jacobini sent a circular to all the nuncios with a detailed account attached. The calls for the end of the law of guarantees and, indeed, for the seizure of the Vatican, the secretary of state reported, had been met by the feeblest of government reactions. They had only stopped the meeting after it was largely completed, and they had only confiscated the Roman newspapers that reported the speeches after most of the copies had been sold. The Holy Father had been declared a liar, he had been repeatedly referred to as "Signor Pecci" and called an enemy of the people. "Thus is the dignity and security of the Pontiff protected in Rome." The nuncios were instructed to bring the matter to the attention of the governments at which they were stationed in order to make clear "the Holy Father's true condition and how well founded his apprehensions are." The nuncios were also told to give the material to the Catholic press in each country (ASV, SS, EM, 1882, r. 241, fasc. 3, ff. 176v-176r, Circolare ai Nunzii, 8 agosto 1881; f. 178v, Jacobini al nunzio, Parigi, 8 agosto 1881). Mancini, knowing just what use the Vatican would want to make of the Politeama events, sent a telegram on the evening of the eighth to all the Italian ambassadors in Europe. He wrote, he explained, to correct erroneous accounts of what had tran-

spired. Various violent speeches against the law of guarantees had been made, but when a motion was read that not only called for the abolition of the guarantees but advocated the occupation of the Apostolic palaces, "an officer of public safety, following instructions given him by his superiors, immediately dissolved the assembly without having to resort to force. The city remained entirely calm." The lesson to be drawn from the events was clear: "The government has thus demonstrated that it is fully committed to reconciling its scrupulous respect for the freedom of assembly with the absolute protection for the freedom and the guarantees of the Sovereign Pontiff. Newspapers using the occasion of the meeting to publish articles offensive to the pope were immediately seized and brought before the court for action" (DDI, series 2, v. 14, n. 141, 8 agosto 1881).

14. Rumors of a French Conspiracy

1. Cornold, Giovanni, "La notte del 13 luglio in Roma," *Civiltà Cattolica* 1881, III, pp. 264–65.
2. This quotation is from correspondence cited in Chadwick 1997, pp. 374–79.
3. Ciampani 2000, pp. 264–66.
4. ASV, SS, EM, a. 1882, r.241, fasc. 3, ff. 162v-163r, nunzio Vienna a Jacobini, 29 luglio 1881.
5. *Civiltà Cattolica*, 1881, III, Cronaca contemporanea, pp. 624–26; "Via da Roma!," *L'Osservatore Romano*, 20 luglio 1881, p. 2.
6. MAES, CP, vol. 1071, St. Hilaire à M. de Bâcourt, chargé d'affaires de France, Saint Siège, 14 août 1881.
7. Chadwick 1997, p. 380; Duggan 2000, pp. 502–3; Giordano 1994, p. 38. The text of the first Triple Alliance agreements can be found in Anchieri 1959. For a discussion of some of the reasons that Bismarck decided to back a treaty with Italy at this time, see Pflanze 1990, p. 93.
8. MAEI, CP, vol. 64, ff. 254r-255v, Noailles à M. St. Hilaire, 15 août 1881.
9. ASR, Questura, b. 16, fasc. 106, 26 agosto 1881, Notizie sul Vaticano. Pilgrimages to Rome had of course a very long history, but with the pronouncement of papal infallibility, the taking of Rome, and the centrality of the image of the prisoner of the Vatican, the nature of these pilgrimages changed from one that focused on visiting the major churches to the desire to see the pope himself. At the same time, the advent of the train and other improvements in transportation made such trips much easier and less expensive (Papenheim 2001, pp. 141–42).
10. MAEI, CP, vol. 65, ff. 43r-46r, Reverseaux à M. St. Hilaire, 17 octobre 1881.
11. These deliberations are discussed in Ciampani 2000, pp. 212–16.
12. MAEI, CP, vol. 65, ff. 211r-214r, Audience du roi, à M. le Président du Conseil, 27 novembre 1881.
13. MAEI, CP, vol. 65, ff. 322r-322v, Reverseaux à M. Gambetta, Ministère des Affaires Etrangères (telegram), 26 décembre 1881; ff. 323r-327r, Reverseaux à M. Gambetta, Ministère des Affaires Etrangères, 26 décembre 1881; ff. 328r-329r, Tamburini à M. de Reverseaux, Livourne, 22 décembre 1881.
14. DDI, series 2, vol. 14, n. 348, L'Incaricato d'affari a Berlino, Tugini, al Ministro degli Esteri, Mancini, 3 dicembre 1881. Diplomatic relations between Germany and the Vatican would, in fact, be reestablished in April 1882 (Aubert 1972, p. 37).

15. MAES, CP, vol. 1071, ff. 340r-345v, Desprez à M. Gambetta, Discours du Pape aux Cardinaux, ca. 26 décembre 1881.

16. Matteo Liberatore, "La condizione del pontefice in forza dell'occupazione di Roma," *Civiltà Cattolica* 1882, I, pp. 257–68.

15. Preparing for Exile

1. Ciampani 2000, pp. 298–300; Ticchi 2001, pp. 367–72.

2. Not long after the secretary of state assured the other cardinals of Franz Josef's renewed invitation for the pope to take up residence on Austrian soil, the Austrian foreign minister, Kalnóky, pleaded with the Italian ambassador to Austria, Di Robilant, for Italy to do everything possible to keep the pope from wanting to go. In his report to the Italian foreign minister, Di Robilant recounted that, out of the blue, the Austrian had raised his concerns about the danger that the Holy Father might soon decide to leave Rome. Trying to calm his fears, Di Robilant told him that there was little prospect of such a move, reminding him of words attributed to Pius IX: "You don't change an old horse's stable." He added that even if the pope wanted to go, "it could hardly be clearer that no State seeks the honor of hosting the Holy Father . . . beginning with Austria!" Kalnóky, the Italian ambassador reported, agreed, "but nonetheless wanted once again to say that despite everything, the possibility in question could not be excluded and that the Italian Government ought not to lose sight of this." Di Robilant, on reflection, agreed: "There is no doubt," he wrote to the Italian minister for foreign affairs, "that the Holy Father's departure from Rome would produce a shock in the Catholic world that at the very least would create considerable embarrassment for the Italian Government, a result that might turn out to be decisive in the Pontiff's decision" (DDI, series 2, vol. 17–18, n. 159, L'ambiasciatore a Vienna, Di Robilant, al Ministro degli Esteri, Mancini, 8 aprile 1884).

3. They were, in order, Monaco La Valletta, Simeoni, Ludovico Jacobini, Nina, Parocchi, and Laurenzi.

4. AAEESS, SE, pos. 1060, fasc. 341, ff. 1r-13r, Motu proprio del S. P. Leone XIII, del 25 agosto 1884. The individual letters to the cardinals are to be found in the following pages, "Persone presso cui sono custodite le disposizioni pontificie riguardo al futuro Conclave ed al caso di impedita comunicazione dei fedeli col Capo della Chiesa," ff. 38r-54r. The instructions on the protection and care of the Vatican palaces, "Leo XIII Al Marchese *Urbano Sacchetti* Foriere maggiore dei sacri Palazzi Apostolici," are found at ff. 67r-73r.

5. AAEESS, SE, pos. 1070, fasc. 343, ff. 6r-10v, Relazione sull'attuale condizione a cui sono ridotti la Santa Sede e il Sommo Pontefice in Roma.

6. AAEESS, SE, pos. 1070, fasc. 343, ff. 13r-34v, Osservazioni in proposito fatte da un Cardinale.

7. AAEESS, SE, pos. 1070, fasc. 344, ff. 37r-86v, per incarico della Commissione, Parere del Rev. P. Graniello sull'allontanamento del Papa da Roma in caso di guerra, 1887.

8. The Graniello report was discussed at a series of meetings: AAEESS, SE, pos. 1070, fasc. 344, ff. 9r-12r Seduta del 14 febbraio 1887; ff. 12r-22r, 18 febbraio 1887; ff. 22r-26r, Seduta del 23 febbraio 1887; ff. 27r-29v, Seduta del 26 febbraio 1887; ff. 30v-33r, Seduta del 12 marzo 1887; ff. 35r-36r, Seduta del 12 marzo 1887.

16. Hopes Dashed

1. Trincia 2001, p. 48.
2. Procacci 1929, pp. 8–9. Trincia 2001, pp. 51, 47.
3. Jemolo 1965, pp. 72–74; Fonzi 1990, p. 285; Procacci 1929, p. 31.
4. Fonzi 1990, pp. 171–72. Back in 1882, Depretis, the prime minister, had secretly floated the idea of offering the pope a strip of land that ran from the Vatican all the way to the sea; there the Holy See would enjoy a certain degree of immunity while the territory would technically remain under Italian sovereignty. But, with the Vatican's anger over Pius IX's chaotic funeral procession still fresh, discussions got nowhere (Marongiu Bonaiuti 1971, p. 81).
5. Manfroni 1920, p. 156.
6. Procacci 1929, pp. 59–60.
7. Procacci 1929, pp. 46–47.
8. "Un dubbio ragionevole," *L'Osservatore Romano*, 19 maggio 1887, p. 1.
9. Procacci 1929, pp. 64–66. The text of the allocution is found in *L'Osservatore Romano*, 26 maggio 1887, p. 1. The reaction is found in "L'Allocuzione pontificia," *L'Osservatore Romano*, 28 maggio 1887, p. 1, with further commentary about the need for the return of temporal power, and Rome, to the pope three days later (31 May 1887, p. 1).
10. Procacci 1929, pp. 72–77.
11. Procacci 1929, pp. 85–86.
12. Duggan 2000, pp. 584–85.
13. *L'Osservatore Romano*, 5 giugno 1887, p. 1.
14. Procacci 1929, pp. 88–92. Yet it is worth noting that, in his memoirs, Manfroni (1920, vol. 2, p. 157) insists that he had heard from a reliable Vatican informant — who had himself seen the draft — that the pope had read Tosti's work before publication and had approved of it.
15. Procacci 1929, pp. 67–68.
16. Trincia 2001, p. 84.
17. Trincia 2001, pp. 50, 86.
18. Trincia 2001, pp. 79–80.
19. Procacci 1929, p. 43; Candeloro 1953, p. 209.
20. An authorized (hagiographic) biography of Rampolla was written by Monsignor G. Pietro Sinopoli di Giunta (1923). On Rampolla, see also Aubert 1990a, pp. 91–92.
21. In April 1887, he confided in the Prussian ambassador to the Holy See, "I would never accept a politically dominating secretary of state, as Consalvi was for Pius VII or as Cardinal Antonelli was for Pius IX. I myself am my own Prime Minister and I seek a secretary of state who attends to routine business, the formalities, and daily matters" (Trincia 2001, p. 25).
22. Trincia 2001, p. 90.
23. Trincia 2001, p. 35.
24. Valenti 1977, p. 38.
25. Duggan 2000, pp. 586–87; Jemolo 1965, pp. 76–77; Adorni 1999.
26. Mola has written a biography of Lemmi and a history of the Freemasons in Italy (1985, 2001). On the Freemasons and Lemmi in this period, see also Lyttleton 1983.

27. Grande Oriente della Massoneria in Italia e nelle colonie italiane, circolare n. 30, 20 gennaio 1882, found in AAEESS, SE, pos. 389, fasc. 132, ff. 33v-34r.

28. Mola 1985, pp. 205–6, Lemmi a Crispi, 6 novembre 1887.

29. De Rosa 1970, p. 140; Procacci 1929, pp. 118–23; Fonzi 1962, p. 190. So worried were the French that Leo XIII might be negotiating secretly with the Italians that months later, in mid-August, long after the Vatican had publicly abandoned the reconciliation efforts, the French foreign minister continued to press the papal nuncio in Paris for assurances that the matter was dead. Rampolla, informed of the French worry, told the nuncio: "Nothing has happened in the Holy See's policies that could justify the fears being expressed with such insistence" (Rampolla's letter of 22 agosto 1887 is reproduced in Mori 1974, p. 37).

30. Cornély 1888, pp. 27–29.

31. *L'Osservatore Romano* (27 luglio 1887, p. 1) was explicit about the intended audience: "The Pope's letter . . . is not only directed to Cardinal Rampolla, the primary person responsible for executing the pontifical plans, it is directed to all honest Italians." See also the comments of Jemolo 1965, p. 78.

32. "Lettera di S. S. Papa Leone XIII al Cardinale Mariano Rampolla suo segretario di stato," *L'Osservatore Romano*, 26 luglio 1887, pp. 1–2.

33. AAEESS, SE, pos. 1075, fasc. 346, ff. 6r-7v, Card. Mariano Rampolla al nunzio apostolico di Vienna, 17 luglio 1887. At the same time Rampolla sent a long letter to all the nuncios with a similar message: ignore any newspaper reports to the contrary; the pope must regain temporal power. The full text is reproduced in Sinopoli di Giunta 1923, pp. 181–86. Tosti himself was finally forced to write a full apology for his booklet, which was published in *L'Osservatore Romano* on July 28 (p. 3). The Vatican paper charged that publication of the work had hurt the pope deeply.

17. The Bishops' Lament

1. AAEESS, SE, pos. 1075, fasc. 346, ff. 18r-38v, Relazione di Mons. Della Chiesa sulla missione compiuta.

2. Santangelo 1976, p. 207; Moscati 1964, pp. 110, 145–46.

3. The description of Crispi is by the French journalist Jacques Saint-Cère, quoted in Duggan 2000, p. 567.

4. Duggan 2002, p. 476.

5. AAEESS, SE, pos. 1075, fasc. 346, ff. 40r-40v, Rampolla all'Arcivescovo di Palermo, 9 agosto 1887; ff. 42r-43r, Arcivescovo di Palermo a Rampolla, 21 agosto 1887.

6. AAEESS, SE, pos. 1075, fasc. 347, ff. 6r-8r, Istruzioni ai Vescovi d'Italia, n.d.

7. This is a paraphrase of the conversation described by the papal envoy.

8. The report of the papal envoy's visits is found in AAEESS, SE, pos. 1075, fasc. 347, ff. 10r-51v. These last quotations are paraphrases, drawn from this report.

18. Fears of a European War

1. AAEESS, SE, pos. 1075, fasc. 346, ff. 60r-61r, Rampolla al Nunzio Apostolico, Vienna, 15 settembre 1887.

2. Trincia 2001, p. 90.

3. AAEESS, SE, pos. 1075, fasc. 346, ff. 92r-93r, Rampolla al Nunzio Apostolico, Parigi, 7 ottobre 1887.

4. AAEESS, SE, pos. 1075, fasc. 346, ff. 94r-95v, Nunzio Apostolico, Parigi, a Rampolla, 10 ottobre 1887.

5. AAEESS, SE, pos. 1075, fasc. 346, ff. 98r-101v, Nunzio Apostolico, Parigi, a Rampolla, 19 ottobre 1887.

6. AAEESS, SE, pos. 1075, fasc. 347, ff. 63r-65v, Paris, 18 octobre 1887.

7. AAEESS, SE, pos. 1075, fasc. 347, ff. 57r-59r, Rampolla a Galimberti, 1 novembre 1887.

8. AAEESS, SE, pos. 1075, fasc. 347, ff. 60r-61v, Galimberti a Rampolla, n.d. (early November 1887).

9. Procacci 1929, pp. 40–42.

10. DDI, series 2, vol. 21, n. 231, L'incaricato d'Affari a Vienna, Avarna, al Presidente del Consiglio e Ministro degli Esteri ad Interim, Crispi, 16 ottobre 1887; n. 336, Il Presidente del Consiglio e Ministro degli Esteri ad Interim, Crispi, all'ambasciatore a Vienna, Nigra, 23 novembre 1887.

11. AAEESS, SE, pos. 1075, fasc. 347, ff. 70r-71r, Galimberti a Rampolla, 17 febbraio, 1888. Three months earlier, in his direct report to the pope, Galimberti had notified him that the leaders of both Germany and Austria believed that war was imminent and would begin no later than the spring of 1888 (Galimberti a Leone XIII, 18 novembre 1887, document 9 in Trincia 2001, p. 156).

Later the same month, a major Austrian newspaper published an article claiming that the recent secret treaty between Austria and Italy included a clause ensuring that "the question of [the pope's] temporal dominion had been buried." Leo asked his secretary of state to demand clarification. Kalnóky, in Vienna, denied the report, blaming it on French intrigue. (AAEESS, SE, pos. 1091, fasc. 358, ff. 10r-13v, Galimberti a Rampolla, 27 febbraio 1888; ff. 18r-20r, Lettre confidentielle, Comunicata al Segretario di Stato dal Conte Paar Ambasciatore Austro-Ungarico per incarico del Cte. Kalnoky, 1 mars 1888.)

12. Crispolti and Aureli 1912, pp. 419–25, Rampolla to Galimberti, 14 marzo 1888. In January 1888, the German government had signed a supplementary military defense pact with the Italians aimed specifically against France, which was further angering both the French and the Vatican at the time (Giordano 1994, p. 84). The renewal of the Triple Alliance had been signed in February of the previous year (for text, see Anchieri 1959).

13. AAEESS, SE, pos. 1083, fasc. 355, ff. 48r-55v, Galimberti a Rampolla, Berlino, 26 marzo 1888.

14. Trincia 2001, p. 122. On Bismarck's belief that war was likely, see Pflanze 1990b, pp. 309–12.

15. AAEESS, SE, pos. 1091, fasc. 358, ff. 26r-28v, Rampolla a Galimberti, 19 giugno 1888.

16. AAEESS, SE, pos. 1091, fasc. 358, ff.31r-34r, Galimberti a Rampolla, 10 luglio 1888.

17. AAEESS, SE, pos. 1091, fasc. 358, ff. 37r-40r, Galimberti a Rampolla, 21 luglio 1888.

18. AAEESS, SE, pos. 1083, fasc. 355, ff. 98r-101r, Rotelli a Rampolla, 12 luglio 1888. The French government's response should also be seen in light of the Boulanger crisis then in course, with many predicting that civil war could break out at any time between the monarchist and clerical forces supporting General Boulanger arrayed against the republican government and its supporters (Langer 1956, pp. 461–63).

19. Civiltà Cattolica, 1888, IV, pp. 226–27, Cronaca contemporanea.

20. DDI, series 2, vol. 22, n. 153, Il Presidente del Consiglio e Ministro degli Esteri ad In-

terim, Crispi, all'Ambasciatore a Vienna, Nigra, 15 luglio 1888; n. 154, Il Presidente del Consiglio e Ministro degli Esteri ad Interim, Crispi, all'Ambasciatore a Berlino, De Launay, 15 luglio 1888.

21. "L'arrivo in Roma e ricevimento al Quirinale di Guglielmo II," *Unità Cattolica*, 13 ottobre 1888, pp. 957–59; *Civiltà Cattolica* 1888, IV, pp. 367–68, Cronaca contemporanea.

22. Soderini 1933, p. 399; Crispolti and Aureli 1912, pp. 265–71; *Civiltà Cattolica* 1888 IV, pp. 488–89, Cronaca contemporanea.

23. "I brindisi di Re Umberto e di Guglielmo II," *L'Unità Cattolica*, 14 ottobre 1888, p. 963.

24. Quoted in Trincia 2001, pp. 128–29,

25. "Rampolla," the Austrian ambassador to the Holy See wrote Kalnóky in January, 1888, "prophesizes a storm, and in particular a storm that destroys the Kingdom of Italy and the Triple Alliance." Quoted in Trincia 2001, p. 132.

26. Letter to Bonghi, in Maturi 1942, vol. 1, p. xxix.

19. Giordano Bruno's Revenge

1. Foa 1998; Parinetto 1999; Ricci 2000.

2. Manzi 1963; Comitato Universitario 1889.

3. "Either we can no longer make any sense of anything," the author of a typical letter in the Catholic press argued, "or the punishment inflicted on Torlonia is in open contradiction with both the law and good sense." The writer cited the text of an article of the law of guarantees: "The Italian government renders the Holy Pontiff, in the territory of the Kingdom, sovereign honors, and accords him the high honors that Catholic Sovereigns assign him." It follows, the writer concluded, "that Torlonia acted in full conformity with the laws." The *Unità Cattolica* pieces cited here are from "La storia della visita del duca Torlonia al Cardinale Parocchi," 5 gennaio 1888, pp. 13–15; "Il sindaco di Roma fulminato," 12 gennaio 1888, pp. 33–34; and "Le destituzioni in odio al Papa e parallelo tra Robespierre e Crispi," 20 gennaio 1888, p. 61. A discussion of the political context of the incident can be found in Ciampini 2000, pp. 449–54; and Bartoccini 1985, pp. 726–27. For Rampolla, Torlonia's firing simply made clear to the world what he had long known, that the new prime minister was but an old anticlerical revolutionary disguised in the clothes of the establishment. In late July 1888, writing to Galimberti, the secretary of state laid out these views. "The official war on the papacy in Italy and especially in Rome is now not only openly declared, but being pushed on with increasing speed." While the government was trying to maintain a public appearance of moderation, wrote Rampolla, it had in reality adopted a revolutionary program. "The prime minister, a product of the revolution, accustomed to conspiracies and notoriously involved in the network of sects, maintains direct relationships and friendships with the most subversive and dissolute elements of society while distinguishing himself by his implacable hatred of the Head of the Church and by the audacity of his perverse designs" (AAEESS, SE, pos. 1091, fasc. 358, ff. 43r-48r, Rampolla a Galimberti, 31 luglio 1888). For an account of the discussion of the Catholic council members that lay behind the visit, see Campello (1910, p. 149).

4. Ugolini 1989.

5. ASV, SS, EM, a. 1889, r. 241, fasc. 3, ff. 13v-15v, circolare, 4 marzo 1888.

6. AAEESS, SE, pos. 1075, fasc. 347, ff. 72r-73r, nunzio, Paris, a Rampolla, 18 marzo 1888.

7. ASV, SS, EM, a. 1889, r. 241, fasc. 3, ff. 27v-29r, Arcivescovo di Spoleto a Rampolla, 16 aprile 1888.

8. ASV, SS, EM, a. 1889, r. 241, fasc. 3, *Il Diritto*, supplemento straordinario al n. 160, Roma, 9 giugno 1889, p. 4.

9. This account is based on "Spoleto a Giordano Bruno," *La Nuova Umbria*, 3 giugno 1888, which was sent by the archbishop of Spoleto to Rampolla along with one of his reports and can be found in ASV, SS, EM, a. 1889, r. 241, fasc. 3, following f. 43.

10. Jemolo 1965, p. 81; Bartoccini 1985, p. 630; Duggan 2000, pp. 657–58; Ciampani 2000, p. 456; Ticchi 2001.

11. AAEESS, SE, pos. 1075, fasc. 347, ff. 88r-92r, Relazione; *Civiltà Cattolica* 1888, III, pp. 106–9, Cronaca contemporanea.

12. Comitato Universitario 1889.

13. "A Bruno, il secolo da lui divinato, qui dove il rogo arse."

14. Among the sources used in this account of events on June 9, 1889, are AAEESS, SE, pos. 1107, fasc. 361, ff. 86r-90v, Relazione dell'accaduto in Roma all'inaugurazione del monumento a Giordano Bruno; Manzi 1963; MAEI, vol. 87, ff. 274r-276v, Mariani à Ministère des Affaires Etrangères, Paris, 10 juin 1889; *Il Diritto*, supplemento straordinario al n. 160, Roma, 9 giugno 1889; "La cronaca per le feste di Giordano Bruno," *L'Osservatore Romano*, 11 giugno 1889, pp. 2–3.

15. ASV, SS, EM, a. 1889, r. 241, fasc. 1, f. 180v, Atto di protesta, Ferrara.

16. MAES, CP, vol. 1096, ff. 9r-9v, Béhaine à Ministère des Affaires Etrangères, Paris, 2 juin 1889; f. 15r, Béhaine à Ministère des Affaires Etrangères, Paris, 5 juin 1889; f. 21r, Béhaine à Ministère des Affaires Etrangères, Paris, 9 juin 1889.

17. ASV, SS, EM, a. 1889, r. 241, fasc. 3, ff. 146v-146r, 11 giugno 1889, Circolare.

18. ASV, SS, EM, a. 1889, r. 241, fasc. 3, f. 118v, 8 giugno 1889.

19. ASV, SS, EM, a. 1889, r. 241, fasc. 4, ff. 93v-95r, nunzio Bavaria a Rampolla, 16 giugno 1889.

20. "Considerzioni sull'alleanza fra Germania ed Italia," Vienna 9 giugno 1889, attached to Galimberti a Boccali, 9 giugno 1889; documents 43–44, Trincia 2001, pp. 203–9.

21. ASV, SS, EM, a. 1889, r. 241, fasc. 4, ff. 101v-102v, nunzio Parigi a Rampolla, 18 giugno 1889; f. 103v, Rampolla al nunzio, Parigi, 22 giugno 1889.

22. ASV, SS, EM, a. 1889, r. 241, fasc. 4, ff. 129v-130v, nunzio Aja a Rampolla, 15 giugno 1889.

23. AAEESS, SE, pos. 1107, fasc. 361, ff. 91r-93r, Allocuzione del S. P. Leone XIII tenuta nel Concistoro del 30 giugno 1889. The full Italian text was also published in *L'Osservatore Romano*, 3 luglio 1889, p. 1.

24. *Civiltà Cattolica*, 1889, II, p. 744, Cronaca contemporanea.

20. *The Pope's Secret Plan*

1. Rampolla a Galimberti, 1 dicembre 1888, document 37 in Trincia 2001, pp. 196–97; Galimberti a Rampolla, 6 dicembre 1888, document 39, in Trincia 2001, pp. 198–99.

2. The report read in part: "and in the Prelature itself the damage caused by modern tendencies is great. Liberal ideas have for many years now been cleverly introduced;

because they have not been fought clearly or vigorously, they have entered many minds and are becoming ever more influential. Even among the bishops many are attracted to these new developments."

3. AAEESS, SE, pos. 1093, fasc. 359, ff. 2r-26v, Verbali e appunti di alcune Sedute tenutesi dalla Commissione speciale nei giorni 6, 9, 16, 23, e 30 dicembre 1888, scritti dal Card. Pallotti.

4. AAEESS, SE, pos. 1108, fasc. 362, Roma 1889; Carte relative ai diversi provvedimenti da prendersi nel caso di forzato allontanamento di S. P. Leone XIII da Roma, in vista della condizione politica dell'Italia, contraria alla Santa Sede; Istruzione pei Cardinali Prefetti delle S. Congregazioni e pei Capi degli altri Dicasteri ecclesiastici della Romana Curia.

5. Istruzioni pel sacro Collegio. The pope also made provisions for a conclave to be held should he die while in exile in a secret *motu proprio* he signed on May 30, 1889 (Disposizioni relative al futuro Conclave, Leo PP. XIII, Motu proprio, 30 maggio 1889), followed by further instructions for cardinals heading congregations, specifying how their offices should be run in Rome after the departure of the pope and all the cardinals (Istruzioni per le Segreterie delle SS. Congregazioni ed altri Uffici ecclesiastici della Romana Curia).

6. Mack Smith 1989, pp. 90–91; Galimberti a Leone XIII, 18 novembre 1887: documento n. 9, Trincia 2001, p. 156.

7. DDI, series 2, vol. 22, n. 603, Appunto del Presidente del Consiglio e Ministro degli Esteri ad Interim, Crispi, 15 giugno 1889; n. 608, Crispi all'Ambasciatore a Parigi, Menabrea, 19 giugno 1889; n. 609, Crispi a Menabrea, 19 giugno 1889.

8. MAES, CP, vol. 1096, ff. 97r-100v, Monbel à M. Spuller, 25 juin 1889.

9. *Civiltà Cattolica*, 1889, II, pp. 235–36, Cronaca Contemporanea; Ticchi 2001, p. 394.

10. MAES, CP, vol. 1096, ff. 148r-148v, Monbel à Spuller, 6 juillet 1889.

11. MAES, CP, vol. 1096, ff. 149r-153r, Monbel à Spuller, 7 juillet 1889; ff. 167r-168v, Monbel à Spuller, 10 juillet 1889.

12. MAES, CP, vol. 1096, ff. 154r-157r, Monbel à Spuller, 8 juillet 1889.

13. Reported in Duggan 2000, p. 678.

14. Duggan 2000, p. 679.

15. DDI, series 2, vol. 22, n. 633, Crispi agli ambasciatori a Berlino, De Launay, e a Vienna, Nigra, e all'incaricato d'affari a Londra, Catalani, 18 luglio 1889; n. 634, Nigra a Crispi, 18 luglio 1889.

16. Crispi 1912b, pp. 393–99.

17. MAES, CP, vol. 1096, ff. 189r-193r, Monbel à Spuller, 18 juillet 1889, Départ du Pape. The stress is in the original text.

18. All these quotations come from Raffaele Ballerini, "Nell'anniversario della breccia della Porta Pia," *Civiltà Cattolica* 1889, III, pp. 641–54.

19. Duggan 2000, p. 680; Hill 2000, pp. 199–200.

20. Crispi 1912b, 400–4; Duggan 2000, p. 680.

21. DDI, series 2, vol. 22, n. 636, L'Incaricato d'affari a Londra, Catalani a . . . Crispi, 21 luglio 1889; n. 641, L'ambasciatore a Berlino, De Launay, a . . . Crispi, 21 luglio 1889.

22. MAES, CP, vol. 1096, ff. 220r-221v, Monbel à Spuller, 23 juillet 1889.

23. DDI, series 2, vol. 22, n. 651, De Launay a Crispi, 25 luglio 1889; n. 652, Crispi a De Launay, 25 luglio 1889.

24. DDI, series 2, vol. 22, n. 656, L'ambasciatore a Vienna, Nigra, a Crispi, 28 luglio 1889; MAES, CP, vol. 1096, ff. 241r-242r, Monbel à Spuller, 26 juillet 1889.

25. MAES, CP, vol. 1096, ff. 245r-250r, Monbel à Spuller, 28 juillet 1889.

26. MAES, CP, vol. 1096, ff. 275r-278r, Monbel à Spuller, 31 juillet 1889.

27. Ticchi 2001, p. 395.

28. MAES, CP, vol. 1097, ff. 32r-36v, Monbel à Spuller, 10 août 1889. Meanwhile, *L'Osservatore Romano* ("Sulla partenza del Papa," 1 agosto 1889, p. 1) was reporting that "the possibility that the Pope will abandon Rome is at the top of all of the [government's] other worries." It went on to say: "a huge number of foreign newspapers, and certainly not clerical or even favorably disposed to the Church, have been forced to admit that the moment may well arise when the behavior and the very position of the Italian government is such as not to permit the Pope to remain in Rome."

Near the end of the month, Rampolla wrote a rather stern letter to Galimberti in Vienna, saying that the pope was very upset at credible reports he had been receiving that Germany, acting on behalf of Italy, was doing everything possible to convince the Spanish throne not to allow the pope to escape there, and had also succeeded in getting the Spanish government to prevent numerous public demonstrations of Spain's Catholic population aimed at begging the pope to take refuge there. Two weeks later Galimberti wrote back, saying that Rampolla's allegations were groundless, although admitting that the Germans were not eager to see the pope leave Rome (Rampolla a Galimberti, 26 agosto 1889; Galimberti a Rampolla, 10 settembre 1889, Trincia 2001, documents 45, 47, pp. 209–10, 214–15).

29. MAES, CP, vol. 1097, ff. 83r-87v, Monbel à Spuller, 23 août 1889. To another colleague Parocchi later said: "I am the only official link between the Holy See and Italy, for I have administrative functions in Rome recognized by the government, and yet they allow me to be publicly insulted. What would the Sovereign Pontiff do in a similar case if it happened that his Representative abroad was the object of such attacks in the country where he served? He would immediately be recalled, and relations would be broken. We will be forced to arrive at the same solution here, because my situation vis-à-vis official Rome is comparable to that of a papal nuncio in another country" (MAES, CP, vol. 1097, ff. 55r-58v, Monbel à Spuller, 18 août 1889).

30. Duggan 2000, pp. 693–94. The Catholic press also found a way of highlighting the fact that Emilio Caporali, the twenty-one-year-old man who tried to kill Crispi, came from the southern Italian district represented by Giovanni Bovio, the featured speaker at the recent events commemorating Bruno. A bricklayer studying to become an architect, Caporali had become enamored with republicanism, although no evidence was ever found linking him to any republican organization. For examples of the Catholic press coverage of the assassination attempt, see "Il prete nell'attentato contro F. Crispi," *L'Unità Cattolica*, 17 settembre 1889, pp. 869–71; and "I complici di Emilio Caporali," *L'Unità Cattolica*, 18 settembre 1889, p. 873.

Epilogue: Italy and the Pope

1. Aubert 1972, p. 6; Martina 1971, pp. 343–44, 371.

2. Taken from *La Tribuna*, quoted in Lecanuet 1910, p. 475.

3. Ibid., p. 476.

4. Billot 1905, pp. 368–77.

5. Duggan 2000, pp. 799–802. Soderini (1933, vol. 2, p. 127), Leo XIII's official biographer, who knew him well, writes that while he had no illusions of being able to reclaim all of the Papal States, the granting of "only the Leonine city, with or without a strip of land to the sea, did not seem sufficient to him."

6. Farini 1961, p. 437, 7 marzo 1894.

7. Farini 1961, pp. 626–27, 3 febbraio 1895; p. 635, 10 febbraio 1895.

8. Crispi 1895.

9. Farini 1961, pp. 765–66, 10 settembre 1895; pp. 775–76, 20 settembre 1895; Mack Smith 1989, p. 115.

10. Martina 1986; Martina 2000, p. 1092. According to Martina, there is no evidence that Leo XIII's letter to the cardinals was ever actually read at the conclave. Martina speculates that Rampolla may have thought better of it.

11. Valenti 1977, p. 41n97.

12. Monsignor Manlio Asta, "Non tagliare le radici più profonde," *Il Messaggero,* 21 settembre 2002, pp. 1, 5.

13. Biffi 1999, pp. 17, 23–26, 44, 60. Some Catholic historians have joined in this recent execration of the Risorgimento (e.g., Pellicari 2000).

References Cited

Acton, J. 1870. "The Vatican Council." *North British Review* 53, pp. 95–120.

Adorni, Daniela. 1999. *Francesco Crispi: Un progetto di governo.* Florence: Olschki.

Aliberti, Giovanni. 1989. "Emilio Visconti Venosta." Pp. 409–33 in *Il Parlamento Italiano*, vol. 4. Milan: Nuova CEI.

Anchieri, Ettore. 1959. *La Diplomazia contemporanea. Raccolta di documenti diplomatici (1815–1956).* Padua: Milano.

Aubert, Roger. 1972. "L'Église face au problème de Rome." Pp. 3–32 in *La fine del potere temporale e il ricongiungimento di Roma all'Italia.* Rome: Istituto per la Storia del Risorgimento Italiano.

Aubert, Roger. 1990a. *Il Pontificato di Pio IX*, vol. 1, trans. and ed. by Giacomo Martina. Milan: Edizioni Paoline.

Aubert, Roger. 1990b. *Il Pontificato di Pio IX*, vol. 2, trans. and ed. by Giacomo Martina. Milan: Edizioni Paoline.

Bagdasarian, Nicholas Der. 1976. *The Austro-German Rapprochement, 1870–1879: From the Battle of Sedan to the Dual Alliance.* London: Associated University Presses.

Bardi, Paolo. 1970. *Roma piemontese (1870–1876).* Rome: Bardi.

Bartoccini, Fiorella. 1985. *Roma nell'Ottocento. Il tramonto della "Città Santa," Nascita di una Capitale.* Bologna: Cappelli.

Biffi, Giacomo. 1999. *Risorgimento: stato laico e identità nazionale.* Casale Monferrato (Alessandria): Piemme.

Billot, A. (former ambassador). 1905. *La France et l'Italie. Histoire des années troublées 1881–1899*, 2 vols. Paris: Plon-Nourrit et cie.

Blakiston, Noel, ed. 1962. *The Roman Question: Extracts from the Dispatches of Odo Russell from Rome, 1858–1870.* London: Chapman & Hall.

Boiardi, Franco. 1989. "Cronologia storico-parlamentare 1870–1874." Pp. 3–18 in *Il Parlamento italiano*, vol. 3. Milan: Nuova CEI.

Butler, Edward C. 1962. *The Vatican Council, 1869–1870, based on Bishop Ullathorne's Letters.* London: Collins and Harvill.

Cadorna, Raffaele. 1889. *La liberazione di Roma nell'anno 1870 ed il plebiscito.* Rome: Roux.

Cadorna, Raffaele. 1898. *La liberazione di Roma nell'anno 1870 ed il plebiscito.* Turin: Roux Trassati e C° editori.

Camaiani, Pier Giorgio. 1976. "Castighi e trionfo della chiesa. Mentalità e polemiche dei cattolici temporalisti nell'età di Pio IX." *Rivista storica italiana* 88:708–44.

Campello Della Spina, Paolo. 1910. *Ricordi di 50 anni dal 1840 al 1890.* Rome: Loescher.

Candeloro, Giorgio. 1953. *Il movimento cattolico in Italia.* Rome: Edizioni Rinascita.

Carocci, Giampiero. 1956. *Agostino Depretis e la politica interna italiana dal 1876 al 1887.* Turin: Einaudi.

Casalegno, Carlo. 2001. *La regina Margherita.* Bologna: Il Mulino.

Chabod, Federico. 1951. *Storia della politica estera italiana dal 1870 al 1896,* vol. 1. Bari: Laterza.

Chabod, Federico. 1997. *Storia Della Politica Estera Italiana. Dal 1870 al 1896.* Bari: Editori Laterza.

Chadwick, Owen. 1978. *Catholicism and History: The Opening of the Vatican Archives.* Cambridge: Cambridge University Press.

Chadwick, Owen. 1997. "The British Ambassador and the funeral of Pope Pius IX," pp. 365–80 in Nigel Aston, ed., *Religious Change in Europe, 1650–1914: Essays for John McManners.* New York: Oxford University Press.

Chadwick, Owen. 1998. *A History of the Popes 1830–1914.* Oxford: Clarendon.

Ciampani, Andrea. 2000. *Cattolici e liberali durante la trasformazione dei partiti. La "questione di Roma" tra politica nazionale e progetti vaticani (1876–1883).* Rome: Archivio Guido Izzi.

Comitato Universitario per il Monumento a Giordano Bruno. 1889. *Roma. Ricordo del IX Giugno MDCCCLXXXIX.* Rome.

Coppa, Frank J. 1990. *Cardinal Giacomo Antonelli and Papal Politics in European Affairs.* Albany: SUNY Press.

Cornély, Jules. 1888. *Rome et le Jubilé de Léon XIII: notes d'un pèlerin.* Paris: Société Générale de Librairie Catholique.

Crispi, Francesco. 1895. *A Giuseppe Garibaldi.* Discorso tenuto in Roma il 20 Settembre 1870, MCRR 333, 12 (21), pp. 1- 8.

Crispi, Francesco. 1912a. *Carteggi politici inediti di Francesco Crispi (1860–1900),* ed. by T. Palamenghi-Crispi. Rome: L'universelle imprimerie polyglotte.

Crispi, Francesco. 1912b. *The Memoirs of Francesco Crispi,* vol. 2, *The Triple Alliance,* trans. Mary Prichard-Agnetti, from the documents collected and edited by Thomas Palamenghi-Crispi. New York: Hodder & Stoughton.

Crispolti, Crispolto and G. Aureli. 1912. *La politica di Leone XIII da Luigi Galimberti a Mariano Rampolla*. Rome: Bontempelli-Invernizzi.

Dalla Torre, Paolo. 1972. *Pio IX e Vittorio Emanuele II dal loro conteggio privato negli anni del dilaceramento (1865–1878)*. Rome: Istituto di Studi Romani.

De Franciscis, Pasquale. 1872. *Discorsi del sommo pontefice Pio IX pronunziati in Vaticano ai fedeli di Roma e dell'orbe dal principio della sua prigonia fino al presente*. vol. 3. Rome: G. Aurelj.

De Leonardis, Massimo. 1980. *L'Inghilterra e la Questione romana, 1859–1870*. Milan: Vita e Pensiero.

De Rosa, Gabriele. 1970. *Il movimento cattolico in Italia. Dalla restaurazione all'età giolittiana*. Bari: Laterza.

Della Peruta, Franco. 1989. "Petroni e Mazzini." Pp. 101–20 in *Giuseppe Petroni dallo Stato Pontificio all'Italia unita*, ed. by Romano Ugolini and Vincenzo Pirro. Terni: Edizioni Scientifiche Italiane.

Drake, Richard. 1980. *Byzantium for Rome: The Politics of Nostalgia in Umbertian Italy, 1878–1900*. Chapel Hill: University of North Carolina Press.

Duggan, Christopher. 2000. *Creare la nazione: Vita di Francesco Crispi*. Rome: Laterza.

Duggan, Christopher. 2002. *Francesco Crispi 1818–1901: From Nation to Nationalism*. Oxford: Oxford University Press.

Engel-Janosi, Friedrick. 1954. "Aspects politiques du Conclave de Léon XIII." *Rassegna storica del Risorgimento* 41:360–65.

Farini, Domenico. 1961. *Diario di fine secolo*, ed. by Emilia Morelli, 2 vols. vol. 1: 1891–95. Rome: Bardi.

Fatti (I) della nuova Roma contro alla salma di Pio IX e l'omaggio delle nazioni a Leone XIII. Memorie storico-politiche di un Professore romano. 1885. 2 vols. (721 pp. and 1120 pp.). Ratisbona: Federico Pustet.

Fiorentino, Carlo Maria. 1996. *Chiesa e Stato a Roma negli anni della Destra storica 1870–1876. Il trasferimento della capitale e la soppressione delle Corporazioni religiose*. Rome: Istituto per la Storia del Risorgimento Italiano.

Foa, Anna. 1998. *Giordano Bruno*. Bologna: Il Mulino.

Fonzi, Fausto. 1962. "Documenti sul conciliatorismo e sulle trattative segrete fra governi italiani e S. Sede dal 1886 al 1897." Pp. 167–242 in R. Aubert, A. M. Ghisalberti, and E. Passerini d'Entrèves, eds., *Chiesa e stato nell'Ottocento*, vol. 1. Padua: Editrice Antenore.

Fonzi, Fausto. 1977. *I cattolici e la società italiana dopo l'Unità*. 3rd ed. Rome: Studium.

Fonzi, Fausto. 1990. "La Chiesa e lo stato italiano." Pp. 273–335 in Elio Guerriero and Annibale Zambarbieri, eds., *La Chiesa e la società industriale (1878–1922)*. Milan: Edizioni Paoline.

Gadille, Jacques. 1968. *Albert du Boÿs. Ses "Souvenirs du Concile du Vati-*

can, *1869–1870.*" *L'intervention du gouvernement impérial à Vatican I.* Louvain: Publications Universitaires de Louvain.

Gallon, Feliciano. 1971. "La stampa romana e la vita religiosa." Pp. 47–94 in Paul G. Droulers and P. Tufari, eds., *La vita religiosa a Roma intorno al 1870.* Rome: Università Gregoriana.

Garibaldi, Giuseppe. 1874. *I mille.* Turin: Cailla e Bertolero.

Ghisalberti, Alberto. 1978. "Vittorio Emanuele a Roma." Pp. 179–96 in Alberto Ghisalberti, *Uomini e cose del Risorgimento e dopo.* Catania: Bonanno.

Giordano, Giancarlo. 1994. *Storia della politica internazionale 1870–1992.* Milan: Angeli.

Graham, Robert A. (S.J.). 1952. *The Rise of the Double Diplomatic Corps in Rome.* The Hague: Nijhoff.

Gregorovius, Ferdinand. 1907. *The Roman Journals of Ferdinand Gregorovius, 1852–1874.* London: G. Bell & Sons.

Gregorovius, Ferdinando. 1969. *Diari romani 1852–1874.* Rome.

Grimaldi, Ugoberto A. 1970. *Il re "buono."* Milan: Feltrinelli.

Guiccioli, Alessandro. 1936. "Diario del 1881 (II)." *La Nuova antologia,* 1 agosto 1936, fasc. 1545, pp. 302–28.

Guiral, Pierre. 1972. "Francia." Pp. 341–59 in *La fine del potere temporale e il ricongiungimento di Roma all'Italia.* Rome: Istituto per la Storia del Risorgimento Italiano.

Gullo, Francesco. 1971. "Fatti, idee e sentimenti negli scritti di alcuni predicatori dell'epoca." Pp. 111–35 in Paul G. Droulers and P. Tufari, eds., *La vita religiosa a Roma intorno al 1870.* Rome: Università Gregoriana.

Halperin, Samuel William. 1939. *Italy and the Vatican at War, a study of their relations from the outbreak of the Franco-Prussian War to the death of Pius IX.* Chicago: University of Chicago Press.

Halperin, Samuel William. 1961. "Leo XIII and the Roman Question." Pp. 99–124 in Edward T. Gargan, ed., *Leo XIII and the Modern World.* New York: Sheed and Ward.

Hanotaux, Gabriel. 1925. *Le Gouverment de M. Thiers 1870–1873,* vol. 2. Paris: Plon.

Hennesey, James (S. J.). 1963. *The First Council of the Vatican: The American Experience.* New York: Herder and Herder.

Hill, Roland. 2000. *Lord Acton.* New Haven: Yale University Press.

Howard, Michael. 1961. *The Franco-Prussian War. The German Invasion of France, 1870–1871.* London: Methuen.

Ideville, Henri Amédée Le Lorgne, comte d'. 1875. *Journal d'un diplomate en Italie; notes intimes pour servir à l'histoire du second empire. Turin, 1859–1862.* Paris: Hachette et cie.

Ignesti, Giuseppe. 1988. *Il tentativo conciliatorista del 1878–1879: le reunioni romane di Casa Campello.* Rome: Editrice A. V. E.

Isastia, Anna Maria. 1989. "Anticlericalismo e massoneria in Giuseppe Petroni." Pp. 35–59 in Romano Ugolini and Vincenzo Pirro, eds., *Giuseppe Petroni dallo Stato Pontificio all'Italia unita*. Terni: Edizioni Scientifiche Italiane.

Jemolo, Carlo Arturo. 1965. *Chiesa e Stato in Italia, Dalla Unificazione a Giovanni XXIII*. Turin: Einaudi.

Langer, William L. 1956. *European Alliances and Allignments 1871–1890*. 2nd ed. New York: Alfred A. Knopf.

Lanza, Giovanni. 1938. *Le carte di Giovanni Lanza*, 11 vols. ed. by C. M. De Vecchi di Val Cismon. Turin: Regia Deputazione Subalpina di Storia Patria. vol. 6 (1870 sett-dic.).

Launay, Marcel. 1997. *La papauté à l'aube du XXe siècle: Léon XIII et Pie IX (1878–1914)*. Paris: Cerf.

Lecanuet, Edouard (padre). 1910. *L'Eglise de France sous la Troisième République, vol. 2, Pontificat de Léon XIII*. Paris: J. de Gigord.

Lecanuet, Edouard (padre). 1931. *Les dernières années du pontificat de Pie IX (1870–1878)*. Paris: Alcan.

Luciani, Francesco. 1997. "La 'Monarchia popolare'. Immagini del re e nazionalizzazione delle masse negli anni della Sinistra al potere (1876–1891)." Pp. 141–88 in Filippo Mazzonis, ed., *La Monarchia nella storia dell'Italia unita. Problematiche ed esemplificazioni*. Rome: Bulzoni Editore.

Luzzatto, Sergio. 2001. *La mummia della Repubblica*. Milan: Rizzoli.

Lyttleton, Adrian. 1983. "An old Church and a new state: Italian anti-clericalism (1876–1915)." *European Studies Review* 13: 225–48.

Mack Smith, Denis. 1956. *Garibaldi*. New York: Knopf.

Mack Smith, Denis. 1989. *Italy and Its Monarchy*. New Haven: Yale University Press.

Mack Smith, Denis. 1994a. *Italy and Its Monarchy*, 2d ed. New Haven: Yale Unviversity Press.

Mack Smith, Denis. 1994b. *Mazzini*. New Haven: Yale University Press.

Manfroni, Giuseppe. 1920. *Sulla soglia del Vaticano, 1870–1901*, ed. Camillo Manfroni. Vol. 1 (1870–78); vol. 2 (1879–1901). Bologna: Zanichelli.

Manzi, Pietro. 1963. *Cronistoria di un monumento. Giordano Bruno a Roma in Campo de' Fiori*. Nola.

Mario, Alberto. 1867. *La questione religiosa di ieri e di oggi*. Florence: Capponi.

Marongiu Bonaiuti, Cesare. 1971. *Non Expedit: Storia di una politica (1866–1919)*. Milan: A. Giuffrè Editore. Series: Pubblicazioni dell'Istituto di Studi Storico-Politici, Università di Roma — Facoltà di Scienze Politiche, n. 20.

Martina, Giacomo. 1971. "Il discorso di Pio IX al corpo diplomatico la mattina del 20 settembre." *Rivista della Storia della Chiesa in Italia* 25:533–45.

Martina, Giacomo. 1972. *La Fine del Potere Temporale e il Ricongiungimento di Roma all'Italia*. Rome: Istituto per la Storia del Risorgimento Italiano.

Martina, Giacomo. 1973. "La situazione degli istituti religiosi in Italia intorno al

1870." Pp. 194–335 in AA.VV., *Chiesa e religiosità in Italia dopo l'unità (1861–1878)*, vol. 1. Milan: Vita e Pensiero.

Martina S. J., Giacomo. 1986. *Pio IX (1851–1866)*. Rome: Pontificia Università Gregoriana.

Martina S. J., Giacomo. 1990a. *Pio IX (1867–1878)*. Rome: Pontificia Università Gregoriana.

Martina, Giacomo. 1990b. "La morte di Vittorio Emanuele II." Pp. 855–57, Appendice VIII, in: Roger Aubert, *Pontificato di Pio IX*, vol. 2, Milan: Edizioni Paoline.

Martina, Giacomo. 1995. *Storia della Chiesa da Lutero ai nostri giorni, vol. 3: L'età del liberalismo*, rev. ed. Brescia: Morcelliana.

Martina, Giacomo. 2000. "Roma, dal 20 settembre 1870 all'11 febbraio 1929." Pp. 1061–1101 in Luigi Fiorani and Adriano Prosperi, eds., *Roma, la città del papa*. Storia d'Italia, annali 16. Turin: Einaudi.

Martina, Giacomo. 2003. *Storia della Compagnia di Gesù in Italia (1814–1983)*. Brescia: Morcelliana.

Masini, Pier Carlo. 1989. "L'Attentato di Passanante." Pp. 30–31 in *Il Parlamento Italiano*, vol. 5. Milan: Nuova CEI.

Maturi, Walter. 1942. "Prefazione." Pp. i-xxxii in Walter Maturi, ed., *Ruggiero Bonghi, Stato e Chiesa*. vol. 1. Milan: Garzanti.

Mazzonis, Filippo. 2003. *La Monarchia e il Risorgimento*. Bologna: Il Mulino.

Mellano, Maria Franca. 1982. *Cattolici e voto politico in Italia. Il "non expedit" all'inizio del pontificato di Leone XIII*. Casale Monferrato: Marietti.

Mola, Aldo. 1985. *Adriano Lemmi, Gran Maestro della nuova Italia (1885–1896)*. Rome: Erasmo.

Mola, Aldo. 2001. *Storia della Massoneria italiana*. 4th ed. Milan: Bompiani.

Mori, Renato. 1974. *La politica estera di Francesco Crispi (1887–1891)*. Rome: Edizioni di storia e letteratura.

Moscati, Amedeo. 1964. *I ministri del Regno d'Italia*. vol. 4. Naples: Edizione del Comitato Napoletano.

Negro, Silvio. 1977 [1943]. *Seconda Roma, 1850–1870*. Milan: Hoepli.

O'Reilly, Bernard. 1887. *Life of Leo XIII from an Authentic Memoir Furnished by his Order, written with the encouragement, approbation and blessing of His Holiness the Pope*. New York: Webster.

Otmar Frhr. v. Aretin, Karl. 1972. "Germania." Pp. 291–301 in *La fine del potere temporale e il ricongiungimento di Roma all'Italia*. Rome: Istituto per la Storia del Risorgimento Italiano.

Papenheim, Martin. 2001. "Il pontificato di Pio IX e la mobilitazione dei cattolici in Europa." *Rassegna storica del Risorgimento* 88: supplement: 137–46.

Parinetto, Luciano, ed. 1999. *Processo e morte di Giordano Bruno. Saggio introduttivo di LP. Tutti i documenti del processo*. Santarcangelo di Romagna: Rusconi.

Pasztor, Layos, 1968. "La Congregazione degli Affari Ecclesiastici Straodrinari tra il 1814 e il 1850." *Archivium Historiae Pontificiae* 6: 191–318.

Paulucci, Paolo. 1986. *Alla corte di re Umberto. Diario segreto*, ed. by Giorgio Calcagno. Milan: Rusconi.

Pavone, Claudio. 1957/1958. "Alcuni aspetti dei primi mesi di governo italiano a Roma." *Archivio storico italiano* 115: 299–346 and 116: 346–80.

Pelczar, Giuseppe. 1909–11. *Pio IX e il suo pontificato sullo sfondo delle vicende della Chiesa nel secolo XIX*. 3 vols. Turin: Berruti.

Pellicciari, Angela. 2000. *L'altro Risorgimento. Una guerra di religione dimenticata*. Casale Monferrato (Alessandria): Piemme.

Perodi, Emma. 1980 (1896). *Roma Italiana 1870–1895*. Rome: Centro Romano Editoriale.

Pesce, Ugo. 1970. *Come siamo entrati in Roma*. Ricordi di Ugo Pesce. Milan: Palazzi.

Pesci, Ugo. 1907. *I primi anni di Roma capitale (1870–1878)*. 2nd ed. Florence: Bemporad.

Pflanze, Otto. 1990. *Bismarck and the Development of Germany. Volume III: The Period of Fortification, 1880–1898*. Princeton, N.J.: Princeton University Press.

Pinto, Paolo. 2002. *Il Savoia che non voleva essere re*. Casale Monferrato: Piemme.

Pirri, Pietro (S. J.). 1951. *Pio IX e Vittorio Emanuele II dal loro carteggio privato, 5, La questione romana (1864–1870)*. Miscellanea historiae pontificiae, vols. 24 (parte 1), 25 (parte 2). Rome.

Procacci, Virgilio. 1929. *La Questione Romana: le vicende del tentativo di Conciliazione del 1887*. Florence: Vallecchi.

Quazza, Guido, ed. 1999. *Epistolario di Quintino Sella*. Rome: Archivio Guido Izzi.

Quirinus. [J. J. Döllinger]. 1870. *Letters from Rome on the Council*. Reprinted from the *Allgemeine Zeitung*. London: Rivingtons.

Ricci, Saverio. 2000. *Giordano Bruno nell'Europa del Cinquecento*. Rome: Salerno Editrice.

Rosi, M. 1937. "Visconti Venosta, Emilio." Pp. 580–86 in *Dizionario del Risorgimento Nazionale*, vol. 4. Milan: Vallardi.

Rothan, G. 1885. *L'Allemagne et l'Italie 1870–1871*, 2 vols. Paris: Calmann Lévy.

Russo, Maria Teresa Bonadonna. 1989. "Il trasferimento della Capitale a Roma." Pp. 21–28 in *Il parlamento italiano*, vol. 3. Milan: Nuova CEI.

Santangelo, Paolo Ettore. 1976. "Il problema Crispi." Pp. 201–14 in Romain Rainero, ed., *I personaggi della storia del Risorgimento*. Milan: Marzorati.

Schmandt, Raymond H. 1961. "The Life and Work of Leo XIII." Pp. 13–48 in Edward T. Gargan, ed., *Leo XIII and the Modern World*. New York: Sheed and Ward.

Scoppola, Pietro. 1973. "Laicismo e anticlericalismo." Pp. 225–74 in AA.VV., *Chiesa e religiosità in Italia dopo l'Unità (1861–1878)*, vol. 2. Milan: Vita e Pensiero.

Sinopoli di Giunta, (Mons.) G. Pietro. 1923. *Il Cardinale Mariano Rampolla del Tindaro*. Rome: Tip. Poliglotta Vaticana.

Soderini, Eduardo. 1933. *Il Pontificato di Leone XIII, vol. 3, Rapporti con la Germania*. Milan: Mondadori.

Soderini, Eduardo. 1934. *The Pontificate of Leo XIII*, vol. 1. London: Burns Oates & Washbourne.

Soderini, Edoardo. 1894. *Roma ed il Governo (1870–1894)*. Rome: Enrico Filiziani.

Spadolini, Giovanni. 1991. *L'opposizione cattolica da Porta Pia al '98*, 2 vols. Florence: Le Monnier.

Stock, L. F. 1945. *Consular Relations between the United States and the Papal States. Instructions and Dispatches*. Washington, D.C.: American Catholic Historical Association.

Talamo, Giuseppe. 1970. *La formazione politica di Agostino Depretis*. Milan: Giuffrè.

Talamo, Giuseppe. 1979. *Il "Messaggero" e la sua città. Cento anni di storia*. vol. 1 (1878–1918). Florence: Le Monnier.

Tavallini, Enrico. 1887. *La vita e i tempi di Giovanni Lanza*. 2 vols. Turin: Roux.

Ticchi, Jean-Marc (2001). "Ubi Roma, ibi papa: les projets de fuite du pape hors de Rome sous Léon XIII (1878–1895)" *Rassegna Storica del Risorgimento* 88: 357–95.

Tivaroni, Carlo. 1897. *L'Italia degli italiani, vol. 3: 1866–1870*. Turin: Roux Frassati.

Trincia, Luciano. 2001. *Il nucleo tedesco. Vaticano e Triplice Alleanza nei dispacci del nunzio a Vienna Luigi Galimberti 1887–1892*. Brescia: Morcelliana.

Ugolini, Romano. 1989. "Alessandro Guiccioli." Pp. 450–1 in *Il parlamento italiano*, vol. 3. Milan: Nuova CEI.

Valenti, Calogero. 1977. *Crispi e la questione romana (1887–1894)*. Palermo: S. F. Flaccovio.

Verucci, Guido. 1996. *L'Italia laica prima e dopo l'Unità: 1848–1876. Anticlericalismo e ateismo nella società italiana*, 2nd ed. Rome: Laterza.

Viallet, Jean-Pierre. 1991. *L'anticlericalisme en Italie (1867–1915)*. Paris: Université Paris X. 8 vols.

Waddington, Mary King. 1905. *Letters of a Diplomat's Wife, January-May 1880–February-April 1904*. New York: Charles Scribner's Sons.

Wallace, Lillan Parker. 1948. *The Papacy and European Diplomacy, 1869–1878*. Chapel Hill: University of North Carolina Press.

Wawro, Geoffrey. 2003. *The Franco-Prussian War*. Cambridge: Cambridge University Press.

Wetzel, David. 2001. *A Duel of Giants: Bismarck, Napoleon III, and the origins of the Franco-Prussian War*. Madison: University of Wisconsin Press.

Zocchi, Gaetano (S. I.). 1881. *Le due Rome dieci anni dopo la breccia*. Prato: Giachetti.

Illustration Sources

AKG: AKG Images, Ltd.
AMRB: Archivio del Museo del Risorgimento di Bologna
MCRR: Museo Centrale del Risorgimento, Roma
MR: Museo di Roma

Pius IX with court: MCRR C-337. / Cardinal Antonelli: MCRR S-3549. / Garibaldi in red shirt: MCRR S-1419. / Satirical image of Garibaldi: *Il Lampione,* 18 March 1863. Harvard University Library. / Victor Emmanuel II: MCRR Airoldi I-33. / "Rape of the Sabines": MCRR 8A-17. / Papal tiara: MCRR 8A-12. / Pius IX with signature: MCRR S-3368. / "The Sickly Temporal Power": MCRR 8A-15. / Vatican Council and ravens: MCRR 9-45. / Church-state battle: *La Rana,* 1 July 1870. AMRB. / Giovanni Lanza: MCRR S-3253. / Napoleon III: In Archibald Forbes, *Life of Napoleon the Third.* New York: Dodd, Mead and Company, 1897. No source indicated for the photograph. / Giovanni Mazzini: Jessie W. Mario, *Della vita di Giuseppe Mazzini per Jessie W. Mario. Opera illustrata con ritratti e composizioni d'insigni artisti.* Milan: Edoardo Sonzogno Editore, 1886, p. 465. Engraving by Mantegazza. / Ferdinand Gregorovius: MCRR R-644. / Hermann Kanzler: MCRR R-1108. / Porta Pia: Altobelli Gioacchino (Terni 1814–Roma c. 1879), "Porta Pia con i segni del bombardamento delle truppe italiane," 1870. 240 x 192 mm. MR AF-6813. / Ambassadors and Pius IX: MCRR S-3395. / Nino Bixio: Jessie W. Mario, *Della vita di Giuseppe Mazzini per Jessie W. Mario. Opera illustrata con ritratti e composizioni d'insigni artisti.* Milan: Edoardo Sonzogno Editore, 1886, p. 441. Engraving by Barberis. / Harry von Arnim: AKG 1-A29-C1870. / Pope blesses troops: MCRR 9A-205. / Religious image: MCRR 10-2. / Pius IX as prisoner: MCRR 10-52. / "Changes in Residence": *La Rana,* 5 May 1871, p. 71. AMRB. / Umberto holds father's hand: MCRR R-134. / Pantheon: MCRR 10C-33. / Body of Pius IX: Author unknown. "Il cadavere di Pio IX esposto in Vaticano," 1878. 505 x 385 mm. MR GS-650. / King Umberto: MCRR B-323. / Leo XIII: Francesco DeFedericis, "Ritratto di Papa Leone XIII seduto allo scrittoio," 1878. 166 x 202 mm. MR AF-239. / Antagonists embrace: *La Rana,* 22 February 1878, pp. 30–31. AMRB. / "In This World": *La Rana,* 1 March 1878, pp. 34–35. AMRB. / Cardinal Mariano Rampolla: Edoardo Soderini, *Il pontificato di Leone XIII. Vol. II: Rapporti con l'Italia e con la Francia.* Milan: A. Mondadori Editore, 1933. No source indicated for the photograph. / Luigi Galimberti: Edoardo Soderini, *Il pontificato di Leone XIII. Vol. III: Rapporti con la Germania.* Milan: A. Mondadori Editore, 1933. No source indicated for the photograph. / Luigi Tosti: Luigi Tosti, *La conciliazione fra l'Italia ed il papato nelle lettere del P. Luigi Tosti e del Sen. Gabrio Casati, con un saggio su la questione romana negli opuscoli liberali fra il 1859 e il 1870 e note di Ferruccio Quintavalle.* Milan: Casa Editrice L. F. Cogliati, 1907. No source indicated for the photograph. / Giacomo Della Chiesa: Edoardo Soderini, *Il pontificato di Leone XIII. Vol. I: Il conclave. L'Opera di ricostruzione sociale.* Milan: A. Mondadori Editore, 1932. No source indicated for the photograph. / Alberto Mario: Jessie W. Mario, *Della vita di Giuseppe Mazzini per Jessie W. Mario. Opera illustrata con ritratti e composizioni d'insigni artisti.* Milan: Edoardo Sonzogno Editore, 1886, p. 401. Engraving by Barberis. / Giovanni Bovio: MCRR S-1138. / Chancellor Bismarck: AKG 1-B49-A1886. / Francesco Crispi: Edoardo Soderini, *Il pontificato di Leone XIII. Vol. II: Rapporti con l'Italia e con la Francia.* Milan: A. Mondadori Editore, 1932. No source indicated for the photograph. / Wilhelm II: Hermann Schoenfeld, *Bismarck's Speeches and Letters.* New York: D. Appleton and Company, 1905. No source indicated for the photograph. / Bismarck and Wilhelm: AKG 1-B49-F1888-11. / Statue of Giordano Bruno: Artist unknown. "Inaugurazione del monumento dedicato a Giordano Bruno in piazza di Campo dei Fiori," 1889. 865 x 640 mm. MR GS-2320.

Index